The Final Countdown Tribulation Rising Volume 1 The Jewish People & the Antichrist

FIRST PRINTING

Billy Crone

Cover Design:
CHRIS TAYLOR

To my wife, Brandie.

Thank you for being so patient
with a man full of dreams.
You truly are my gift from God.
It is an honor to have you as my wife
and I'm still amazed that you willingly chose
to join me in this challenging yet exhilarating
roller coaster ride called the Christian life.
God has truly done exceedingly abundantly above all
that we could have ever asked or even thought of.
Who ever said that living for the Lord was boring?!
One day our ride together will be over here on earth,
yet it will continue on in eternity forever.
I love you.

Contents

Preface

As I've stated in other books, it wasn't until the catastrophic events of 9/11 that I finally began to teach on Bible prophecy as a Pastor. Even though I knew I was supposed to, and fully trained to do so in seminary, I like many other Pastors, simply procrastinated and rationalized it all away. But after that horrible incident, I immediately began teaching through the Book of Revelation in the adult Sunday school class of the church I was pastoring in at that time in California. Then I even began teaching the very first original prophecy related study for Sunday morning services called, *The Final Countdown*. Surely that was the end of all prophecy studies, right? Hardly! Soon God called us to New York where I taught through that study in an even more in-depth way and for the first time was able to add a handful of video clips as visual evidence. It seemed like the pinnacle of all prophecy studies. What more could there be to preach on, right? Funny! Then the Lord moved us to Las Vegas and after about a year there, members of the congregation asked if I could teach on prophecy since they had never really been taught it, even though the church had been in existence for about 60 years. So, naturally, I began what was to be called *The Final Countdown Ultimate* study. It was 50 weeks of prophecy related events chock full of tons of video evidence expanded in even greater detail than ever before. If ever there was a climax to preaching on prophecy, this was it, right? What more could be shared after 50 weeks? Yet, I found myself within a year or so back in the pulpit preaching a 30-week study called *The Final Countdown Update*. So now we're at 80 weeks of in-depth massive video driven Bible prophecy studies that surely was going to last for a while, right? Wrong. If only you could see the stack and stacks of articles in my office, not to mention the hundreds and hundreds of video clips I have archived, you would come to realize what I have. We are living in the Last Days and prophecy related events are happening at such a rapid pace that it's impossible to keep up with all of them. I literally study, research and catalog every single day and it never ends. Therefore, this study, *The Final Countdown Tribulation Rising* is the latest attempt to equip you, the reader, with the latest and greatest prophecy related events concerning the days we live in. May it bless you as it has blessed me. One last piece of advice; when you are through reading this book will you please READ YOUR BIBLE? I mean that in the nicest possible way. Enjoy and I'm looking forward to seeing you someday!

Billy Crone
Las Vegas, Nevada
2019

Chapter One

The Jewish People & Their Eternal Covenants

Well hey, how many of you have ever had a really bad day, you know what I'm saying? I mean, a really bad one! Okay, well as bad as it was, whatever it was, I bet it wasn't as bad as this one!

"I got a nephew that I think a lot of, and he works for the Shell Oil Company. About four years ago they moved him down to South America and I ain't seen him since.

But he still thinks about me an' Ma Crabapple. Every Christmas he sends us a nice present.

This past Christmas he sent us a live bird. Green bird, 'bout this tall, had a little yella top notch on his head, with some red on it and a hooked beak – sent it to us live from South America.

I'll tell you sumpthin' – that bird was delicious, yes sir.

We had him for Christmas dinner. We fixed him with some dressin' an' cranberry sauce, sweet pertater souffle.

Well, after Christmas, my nephew called. Wanted to know if we got the bird. I said, "We got him." Wanted to know how we liked him. I said, "He was delicious."

He said, "you don't mean you ate that bird!" I said, "Well, a course we did." My nephew got all upset an' just pitched a fit.

He said, "I paid a fortune for that bird!" He said, "That thing's worth a fortune." He said, "That bird could speak two different languages."

I said, "Well – he shoulda said sumpthin'."

Seriously folks, whoever that was, how many of you would say that Nephew, who bought that bird, was having a pretty bad day, you know what I'm saying? I mean, his family ate his gift! Wow! How much money went down the tubes in a frying pan, right? What a waste! I can't think of a better way to describe our world today! The average person today, even the Christian, is wasting their time, money and resources on things that are going to be burned up…talk about a waste! It's all because somebody 'shoulda said sumpthin' in multiple languages. We're living in the Last Days…. stop wasting your life…. get busy living for Jesus and stop wasting your time and resources on things that are going to be burned up…OR…If you're not saved you better get saved now! WHY? Because you're flirting with the worst day ever! And it goes something like this. You're sitting on the couch, goofing off and being lazy watching the game, you know, the American dream, and all of a sudden, your whole family disappears, right there in the living room! You jump up and look out the window and you see cars crashing into each other with no drivers in them. People are coming out of their houses screaming because their loved ones are missing too. Then a pilotless airplane comes careening out of the sky and smashes into your neighborhood and catches the whole block on fire. And just then TV interrupts the game you had on with a special news report declaring that millions of people have vanished all over the planet. And that's when you see your spouse's Bible sitting on the coffee table and it suddenly dawns on you that your family was correct when they kept telling you about the Rapture of the Church. At that moment, to your horror, you realize that you've been left behind and you're about to be catapulted into the 7-year Tribulation that's coming upon the whole world. It's an outpouring of God's wrath on a wicked and rebellious planet. Jesus said in **Matthew 24** that it would be a "time of greater horror than anything the world has ever seen or will ever see again" and that "unless God shortened that time frame, the entire human race would be destroyed!" Praise God, God's not only a God of wrath, He's a God of love as well, and because He loves you and I, He has given us many warning signs to wake us up, so we'd know when the 7-year Tribulation was near, and the Return of Jesus Christ was rapidly approaching. That's why in the past we went through our studies called, The Final Countdown and The Final Countdown Update, 10 signs given by God to wake us up and give our lives to Him before it's too late, if we're not saved, or if we are saved, to get motivated before it's too late, and stop wasting our lives. Even though it's been over 3½ years since we finished that last study, so much has happened since then, and continues to happen every single day...I thought I'd better say sumpthin! So that's what we're going to do. I hope you'll enjoy the next segment called, *The Final Countdown: Tribulation Rising.* And boy, signs of the 7-year Tribulation are definitely rising! It's time to get motivated! There's no time to waste, so let's get started!

The **1st update** on *The Final Countdown: Tribulation Rising* is none other than **The Jewish People & the Antichrist.**

Now, as we saw before, one of the first and foremost important prophetic events on God's end time calendar is concerning the Jewish people. If you want to know how close we are to the end, pay attention to the Jewish people. You might be thinking, "Well why? What's the big deal about the Jewish people? I mean, I get the Antichrist, but what makes the Jewish People so special? Why are they always in the discussion when it comes to end times events?" Well, first of all, you do realize that Jesus was Jewish, don't you? I just thought I'd throw that out there in case you forgot. Our Lord and Savior, Jesus Christ, came from the Jewish people. But beyond that, when you look at the Scriptures, both Old and New Testaments, the Jewish people are key to understanding not only the future, but past, present, and the future, because they're the centerpiece of the Bible. They are the common thread of God fulfilling His promises to redeem mankind, from the beginning of creation, after the fall of mankind, when it got all messed up at the Garden of Eden, to the very end of creation, to the eternal state. But don't take my word for it. Let's listen to God's.

Genesis 3:6-15 "When the woman saw that the fruit of the tree was good for food and pleasing to the eye, and also desirable for gaining wisdom, she took some and ate it. She also gave some to her husband, who was with her, and he ate it. Then the eyes of both of them were opened, and they realized they were naked; so, they sewed fig leaves together and made coverings for themselves.

Then the man and his wife heard the sound of the LORD God as He was walking in the garden in the cool of the day, and they hid from the LORD God among the trees of the garden. But the LORD God called to the man, 'Where are you?' He answered, 'I heard you in the garden, and I was afraid because I was naked; so, I hid.' And He said, 'Who told you that you were naked? Have you eaten from the tree that I commanded you not to eat from?' The man said, 'The woman you put here with me – she gave me some fruit from the tree, and I ate it.' Then the LORD God said to the woman, 'What is this you have done?' The woman said, 'The serpent deceived me, and I ate.' So, the LORD God said to the serpent, 'Because you have done this, cursed are you above all the livestock and all the wild animals! You will crawl on your belly and you will eat dust all the days of your life. And I will put enmity between you and the woman, and between your offspring and hers; he will crush your head, and you will strike his heel."

Now what you have here is the infamous Genesis 3:15 promise. It's also called "The Protoevangelium" or "The First Gospel." It's called that because it's the first time we see God declaring some "good news" to us. Even though mankind blew it in the Garden of Eden, as we just read, and sinned and rebelled against God, since we are created in the image of God, God will one day make provision for us, and redeem us, in other words save us. He'll undo what the devil did, bringing a curse upon us and all of creation. That's what we see in the statement made by God, "One day He (speaking of the Messiah, Jesus) will crush your head, and you will strike his heel." You can survive your heel getting struck, and Jesus did raise again from the grave, but you aren't going to survive getting your head crushed, and that is satan being doomed to the Lake of Fire forever! So, the question is, "How does that "protoevangelium" the "first Gospel" take place? How does God put it into action?" Well, it starts with The Jewish people! That's why they are so important, past, present, and future. Later, God raises up The Jewish People starting with Abraham, to Moses, to King David. Because from their lineage, ultimately would come the fulfillment of the Genesis 3:15 promise, where the Messiah, Jesus, would crush the head of the serpent on the cross. That's why the Bible says this.

1 John 3:8 "The reason the Son of God appeared was to destroy the devil's work."

The reason we have John 3:16 is because of Genesis 3:15. Jesus fulfilled that first promise, "He will crush your head, and you will strike his heel." You thought you had Him on the cross, but He beat you! It's all wrapped together with The Jewish people. BUT, they not only come up in the past, leading up to the cross, the Jewish people are all over the future. Even at the very end of time, God is still dealing with the Jewish people. Let me show you what I mean.

Revelation 21:1-2 "Then I saw a new Heaven and a new earth, for the first Heaven and the first earth had passed away, and there was no longer any sea. I saw the Holy City, the new *Jerusalem*, coming down out of Heaven from God, prepared as a bride beautifully dressed for her husband."

This is at the very end of the Bible, and notice we're talking about, not a new New York City, or a new London, or a new Rio de Janeiro, NO! It's the new *Jerusalem*, the capital of the Jewish People. Why? Because from the beginning to the end the Jewish people are all over the place as the common thread throughout the Bible. And the reason why is because God made covenants with the Jewish people that explain the events of the Old and New Testaments as well as the past, present and future events yet to come. If you don't understand this, you'll not only wrongly apply and misinterpret the Bible for today, but you really mess it up when it comes to properly understanding the future events. Let me show you what I mean. First of all, a covenant is an agreement between two parties. Sometimes they're conditional and sometimes they're unconditional. A conditional covenant is an agreement that is binding on both parties for its fulfillment. Both parties agree to fulfill certain conditions. If either party fails to meet their responsibilities, then the covenant is broken and neither party must fulfill the expectations of the covenant. But an unconditional covenant is an agreement between two parties where only one of the two parties must do something. Nothing is required of the other party. This is what we see with the first Jewish Covenant called The Abrahamic Covenant that was made around 2000 BC. It's an unconditional covenant made by God that required nothing of Abraham. We see this in Genesis 12 & 15.

Genesis 12:1-3 "The LORD had said to Abram, 'Leave your country, your people and your father's household and go to the land I will show you. I will make you into a great nation and I will bless you; I will make your name great, and you will be a blessing. I will bless those who bless you, and whoever curses you I will curse; and all peoples on earth will be blessed through you.'"

And we see its unconditional nature here.

Genesis 15:6, 9-10,12,17-18 "Abram believed the LORD, and He credited it to him as righteousness. So, the LORD said to him, 'Bring me a heifer, a goat and a ram, each three years old, along with a dove and a young pigeon.' Abram brought all these to Him, cut them in two and arranged the halves opposite each other. As the sun was setting, Abram fell into a deep sleep, and a thick and dreadful darkness came over him. When the sun had set, and darkness had fallen, a smoking firepot with a blazing torch appeared and passed between the pieces. On that day the LORD made a covenant with Abram and said, 'To your descendants I give this land, from the river of Egypt to the great river, the Euphrates – the land of the Kenites, Kenizzites, Kadmonites, Hittites, Perizzites, Rephaites, Amorites, Canaanites, Girgashites and Jebusites.'"

Again, if this was a conditional covenant, Abram would not have been sleeping through the contract, he would have been walking through the contract. But as you can see, the promises of the Abrahamic Covenant included a promise of land, a promise of descendants, and a promise of blessing to all the nations. The fulfillment of the covenant fell to God alone. Now, an important element of the Abrahamic Covenant is that it still demands a future fulfillment with the Messiah's coming kingdom rule.

(1) Israel as a nation will possess the totality of the land in the future. Numerous Old Testament passages anticipate the future blessing of Israel and her possession of the land as promised to Abraham. Ezekiel envisions a future day when Israel is restored to the land (Ezekiel 20:33–37, 40–42; 36:1–37:28).

(2) Israel as a nation will be converted, forgiven, and restored (Romans 11:25–27).

(3) Israel will repent and receive the forgiveness of God in the future (Zechariah 12:10–14). The Abrahamic Covenant finds its ultimate fulfillment in connection with the return of the Messiah to rescue and bless His people Israel. It is through the nation Israel that God promised to bless the nations of the world. That ultimate blessing will issue in the forgiveness of sins and Messiah's glorious kingdom reign on earth.[1]

The Mosaic Covenant is a conditional covenant made between God and the nation of Israel at Mount Sinai (Exodus Chapters 19-24). It would set the nation of Israel apart from all other nations as God's chosen people through whom God would sovereignly choose to bless the world with both His written Word and the Living Word, Jesus Christ the Messiah. God reminded the people of their obligation to be obedient to His law (Exodus 19:5), and the people agreed to the covenant when they said, "All that the Lord has spoken we will do!" (Exodus 19:8). It differs significantly from the Abrahamic Covenant and later biblical covenants because it is conditional and the blessings that God promises are directly related to Israel's obedience to the Mosaic Law. If Israel is obedient, then God will bless them, but if they disobey, then God will punish them. The blessings and curses are found in Deuteronomy 28. Israel was to be God's light to the dark world around them. They were to be a separate and called-out nation so that everyone around them would know that they worshiped Yahweh, the covenant-keeping God.

The Mosaic Law was also to be a schoolmaster pointing the way towards the coming of Christ (Galatians 3:24-25). The Mosaic Law would reveal to people their sinfulness and their need for a Savior, and it is the Mosaic Law that Christ Himself said that He did not come to abolish but to fulfill. Also, the sacrificial system of the Mosaic Covenant did not really take away sins (Hebrews 10:1-4); it simply foreshadowed the bearing of sin by Christ, the perfect high priest Who was also the perfect sacrifice (Hebrews 9:11-28). Therefore, the Mosaic Covenant itself, with all its detailed laws, could not save people. It is not that there was any problem with the Law itself, for the Law is perfect and was given by a holy God, but the Law had no power to give people new life, and the people were not able to obey the Law perfectly (Galatians 3:21). This is why the Mosaic Covenant, also referred to as the Old Covenant, (2 Corinthians 3:14; Hebrews 8:6, 13) was replaced by the New Covenant in Christ.[2]

The Davidic Covenant refers to God's promises to David through Nathan the prophet. It is found in 2 Samuel 7 and later summarized in 1 Chronicles 17:11–14 and 2 Chronicles 6:16. This is another unconditional covenant where God promises to David and Israel, that the Messiah (Jesus Christ) would come from the lineage of David and the tribe of Judah and would establish a kingdom that would endure forever. The Davidic Covenant is unconditional because God does not place any conditions of obedience upon its fulfillment. The surety of the promises made rests solely on God's faithfulness and does not depend at all on David or Israel's obedience. First, God reaffirms the promise of the land that He made in the first covenant with Israel (the Abrahamic Covenant). 2 Samuel 7:10, "I will provide a place for my people Israel and will plant them so that they can have a home of their own and no longer be disturbed. Wicked people will not oppress them anymore." God then promises "Your house and your kingdom will endure forever before me; your throne will be established forever" (verse 16). What began as a promise that David's son Solomon would be blessed and build the temple turns into something different—the promise of an everlasting kingdom. Another Son of David would rule forever and build a lasting House. This is a reference to the Messiah, Jesus Christ, called the Son of David in Matthew 21:9.[3]

As you can see, two of the three covenants that God made with Israel, the Jewish people, were unconditional and they still have events that are yet in the future. And I'll add, even the one that was conditional, the Mosaic Covenant, led to the New Covenant, which became unconditional. Meaning that when you get saved through Jesus, who's responsible for keeping that covenant intact? Your works? NO WAY! It's all on Jesus' work on the cross! He does it all for us! It's unconditional! But here's my point. The Jewish people not only became the one's whom God made a covenant with, to bring forth the Messiah, the fulfillment of the Genesis 3:15 promise in the past, but the other covenants, the Abrahamic and Davidic are unconditional and which still have things that have not yet been fulfilled...they are future! They have the promise of possessing the totality of the land in the future and the promise of the Messiah coming from the lineage of David and His glorious kingdom reign on earth, speaking of the Millennial Kingdom. That's all future! So that means, guess what? God isn't done with the Jewish People! He can't be because these unconditional promises haven't been completely fulfilled. And yet we actually have people today, even in the Church, that say God is done with the Jewish people, they have no future and that the Church has basically replaced Israel! It's called Replacement Theology and it's a lie from the pit of hell!

Replacement theology (also known as supersessionism) essentially teaches that the Church has replaced Israel in God's plan. Adherents of replacement theology believe the Jews are no longer God's chosen people, and God does not have specific future plans for the nation of Israel. They would even say that the many promises made to Israel in the Bible are fulfilled in the Church, not in Israel. In essence, the Church totally replaces Israel. In fact, the prophecies in Scripture concerning the blessing and restoration of Israel to the Promised Land are now spiritualized or allegorized into promises of God's blessing for the Church. However, if this were true and Israel has been condemned by God and there is no future for the Jewish nation, then how do we explain the supernatural survival of the Jewish people over the past 2,000 years, despite the many attempts to destroy them? And how do we explain why and how Israel reappeared as a nation in the 20th century after not existing for 1,900 years?[4]

Not to mention, how can we trust in the covenant God made with us? If God can't keep His promises to Israel, the Jewish people, how then do we know He'll keep His promises to us? If their covenants were unconditional and people want to say He's done with them, then how can we be assured of our own unconditional covenant with God, called the New Covenant? Maybe it's not secure. Do you see the problem? But again, if you get this wrong, if you buy into the lie of Replacement Theology, it not only leads to insecurity, but it leads to a misapplication of future events because God is not done with the Jewish people. And you have to understand this to get it right. So where is the Church in all this? Well let's now take a look at how the Church fits in with future Israel.

The view that Israel and the Church are different is clearly taught in the New Testament. Biblically speaking, the Church is distinct from Israel and the terms Church and Israel are never to be confused or used interchangeably. We are taught from Scripture that the Church is an entirely new creation that came into being on the day of Pentecost and will continue until it is taken to heaven at the Rapture (Ephesians 1:9–11; 1 Thessalonians 4:13–17). The Bible teaches that after the Rapture, prior to the 7-year Tribulation, God will restore Israel as the primary focus of His plan. Why? Because He's not through fulfilling His promises that He made to them. During this time when the Church is absent, the world will be judged for rejecting Christ, while Israel is prepared, through the trials of the 7-year tribulation, for the second coming of the Messiah, so that when Christ does return to the earth, at the end of the tribulation, Israel will be ready to receive Him. Then the remnant of Israel who survive the 7-year Tribulation will be saved, and the Lord will establish His kingdom on this earth with Jerusalem as its capital. With Christ reigning as King, Israel will be the leading nation, and representatives from all nations will come to Jerusalem to honor and worship the King—Jesus Christ. The Church will return with Christ (Revelation 19) and will reign with Him for a literal one thousand years (Revelation 20:1–5). The Church has not replaced Israel in God's plan. While God may be focusing His attention primarily on the Church in this dispensation of grace, also known as the Church Age, God has not forgotten Israel and will one day restore Israel and fulfill all His unconditional promises that He made to Abraham and David.[5]

This is why the Bible says that the Church, we Gentiles, non-Jewish people, have been grafted into Israel's promised blessing from God.

Romans 11:11,17-18 "Again I ask: 'Did they stumble so as to fall beyond recovery?' Not at all! Rather, because of their transgression, salvation has come to the Gentiles to make Israel envious. If some of the branches have been broken off, and you, though a wild olive shoot, have been grafted in among the others and now share in the nourishing sap from the olive root, do not boast over those branches. If you do, consider this: You do not support the root, but the root supports you."

In other words, don't get a big head Church. God's not done with Israel. We're grafted into Israel. We're the mysterious Bride of Christ. We the Church are the Bride of God's Son. But the Jewish people are God's wife and they will continue to be His wife in the future. Right now, we're in what's called the Church Age where God is making a Bride for His Son, but when it's time for the Son to go get His Bride He will snatch her up "harpazo" which is what the word Rapture means and take her back to the Father's House.

John 14:1-3 "Do not let your hearts be troubled. Trust in God; trust also in Me. In My Father's house are many rooms; if it were not so, I would have told you. I am going there to prepare a place for you. And if I go and prepare a place for you, I will come back and take you to be with Me that you also may be where I am."

But after that, when we're gone at the Rapture, or what's called the fullness of the Gentiles, God's focus goes back on His wife, the Jewish people because He still has a future for them as well. It's all wrapped up in the covenants! And again, that's good news for us because if God doesn't keep his covenants with the Jewish people, then how do you know He will keep His covenant with us? Including the promise of the future event God made with us called The Rapture, the Blessed Hope! You see, when you understand the unconditional covenants God made with Israel and how the Church properly fits into the overall timeline, even in the future, you see that the future has nothing to do with the Church on the earth! Rather it's all about God fulfilling the unconditional covenants He made with the Jewish People, where He calls back a remnant of the Jewish People and pours out His wrath on the Gentile Nations. It has nothing to do with the Church. And if you don't get this, it will invariably mess up your view on the Rapture as well. For instance, if you think that the Church is in the 7-year Tribulation at any point, mid-way, three-quarters, all the way to the end, then you're preaching a form of Replacement Theology whether you realize it or not! Think about it. If you make the Church the object of focus in the future 7-year Tribulation when it's supposed to be about Israel, you are replacing Israel with the Church which is the definition of Replacement Theology! But the Bible is clear! The 7-year Tribulation has nothing to do with the Church, it's all about the Jewish people!

The **1ˢᵗ way** we know the Church has nothing to do with the 7-year Tribulation is in **The Purpose of the Tribulation**. But don't take my word for it. Let's listen to God's.

Daniel 9:20-27 "While I was speaking and praying, confessing my sin and the sin of my people, Israel, and making my request to the LORD my God for his holy hill – while I was still in prayer, Gabriel, the man I had seen in the earlier vision, came to me in swift flight about the time of the evening sacrifice. He instructed me and said to me, 'Daniel, I have now come to give you insight and understanding. As soon as you began to pray, an answer was given, which I have come to tell you, for you are highly esteemed. Therefore, consider the message and understand the vision: Seventy 'sevens' are decreed for your people and your holy city to finish transgression, to put an end to sin, to atone for wickedness, to bring in everlasting righteousness, to seal up vision and prophecy and to anoint the most holy. Know and understand this: From the issuing of the decree to restore and rebuild Jerusalem until the Anointed One, the ruler, comes, there will be seven 'sevens,' and sixty-two 'sevens.' It will be rebuilt with streets and a trench, but in times of trouble. After the sixty-two 'sevens,' the Anointed One will be cut off and will have nothing. The people of the ruler who will come will destroy the city and the sanctuary. The end will come like a flood: War will continue until the end, and desolations have been decreed. He will confirm a covenant with many for one 'seven.' In the middle of the 'seven' he will put an end to sacrifice and offering. And on a wing of the temple he will set up an abomination that causes desolation, until the end that is decreed is poured out on him.'"

So, here we see why we have a 7-year Tribulation. If you've ever wondered why it's specifically a "7" year Tribulation and not 94 or 135 or even a 2-year Tribulation, here it is. This is where it all began. The 7-year Tribulation is the final "seven" of "seventy sevens" prophecy given to the Jewish man Daniel. And here's the purpose. There will be a "total" of 70 sevens until God basically wraps up history for the Jewish people and fulfills the rest of His promises that He made to them. However, after 69 sevens have passed, after the decree that goes out to restore and rebuild Jerusalem from Daniel's time, the Anointed One or the Messiah will be "cut off." And that just happens to be exactly what we see with Jesus' Triumphal entry into Jerusalem. History records for us that date was 445 B.C. when King Artexerxes issued a decree to rebuild Jerusalem. So, if you take the 69 "sevens" before the Messiah is cut off, and times it by 7, you get a total of 483 years, or 173,880 days according to the Jewish Lunar Calendar. So, what happened 173,880 days after the decree to rebuild Jerusalem? Well again, that's the exact date when Jesus made His Triumphal entry into Jerusalem where He was rejected or cut off from His people! But here's the point. You still have one final week, the 7-year Tribulation, the 70th week, to finish up this prophecy. And if you look at the text, you'll see this final week has nothing to do with the Church.

And the 1st **reason** why is in the **Verbiage**.

- Verse 20 – "my sin and the sin of my people Israel" (Daniel & the people of Israel)
- Verse 20 - "making my request to the LORD my God for his holy hill" (Daniel & Jerusalem)
- Verse 22 – "Daniel, I have now come to give you" (Daniel a Jewish Person)
- Verse 24 – "Seventy 'sevens' are decreed for your people and your holy city" (The Jewish people & Jerusalem)
- Verse 25 – "From the issuing of the decree to restore and rebuild Jerusalem" (Jerusalem)
- Verse 26 – "The people of the ruler who will come will destroy the city and the sanctuary" (Jerusalem)
- Verse 27 – "And on a wing of the temple he will set up an abomination that causes desolation" (Rebuilt Temple in Jerusalem)

So, as you can see in the verbiage, the Church is nowhere in this discussion! It's all about the Jewish people and Jerusalem and their rebuilt Jewish Temple, not the Church. So why are you trying to "squeeze" the Church in here? It has nothing to do with the Church! In fact, the text clearly states that the "seventy sevens" including the final seven, the 7-year Tribulation, are "decreed" for your people, Daniel's people, not the Church!

The **2nd reason** we know the Church has nothing to do with the 7-year Tribulation is the **Timing**.

Now, the approximate date for when Daniel wrote this book containing the 70th week prophecy, which includes the 7-year Tribulation, is between 536-530 B.C. The obvious question is, "Where was the Church when this book and prophecy was written?" Answer: nowhere! Why? Because the Church didn't even come into existence until Acts Chapter 2 which is almost 570 years later!

So how could Daniel be referring to the Church in this passage dealing with the 7-year Tribulation, the final week of Daniel's 70th week prophecy, when the Church wasn't even in existence yet? Answer: He can't! This is also why the Apostle Paul referred to the Church as an O.T. "mystery." These people at that time had no knowledge of it.

Ephesians 3:2-5 "Surely you have heard about the administration of God's grace that was given to me for you, that is, the mystery made known to me by revelation, as I have already written briefly. In reading this, then, you will be able to understand my insight into the mystery of Christ, which was not made known to men in other generations as it has now been revealed by the Spirit to God's holy apostles and prophets. This mystery is, that through the gospel, the Gentiles are heirs together with Israel, members together of one body, and sharers together in the promise in Christ Jesus."

In other words, the Church was a "mystery" to the Old Testament writers, which obviously would include Daniel, right? So again, how in the world could Daniel be referring to the Church in this passage dealing with the 7-year Tribulation, when the Church wasn't even in existence yet and he had no knowledge of it? Answer: He can't! Just as the Church had an abrupt *beginning* after the conclusion of the 69th week, so the Church will have an abrupt *removal,* the Rapture, shortly before the beginning of the 70th week. Makes perfect sense, if you hold to the Pre-Trib position!

The **3rd reason** we know the Church has nothing to do with the 7-year Tribulation is the **Audience**.

Now, we already saw by the context that Daniel Chapter 9 and the 70th week prophecy, the 7-year Tribulation, is clearly dealing with Daniel and the Jewish people, not the Church. Other passages also state that the audience is the Jewish people, not the Church. Let's look at just one of them.

Jeremiah 30:4-7 "These are the words the LORD spoke concerning Israel and Judah: This is what the LORD says: 'Cries of fear are heard – terror, not peace. Ask and see: Can a man bear children? Then why do I see every strong man with his hands on his stomach like a woman in labor, every face turned deathly pale? How awful that day will be! None will be like it. It will be a time of trouble for Jacob, but he will be saved out of it.'"

But notice to "whom" the Lord is speaking about this horrible time frame. It's Israel and Judah, not the Church! That's why God says it's going to be a "time of trouble for Jacob," not a "time of trouble for the Church." The 7-year Tribulation, Daniel's final week of the 70th week prophecy has nothing to do with the Church. It's a time of Jacob's trouble, not the Church's trouble. It's not "Paul's Doom" or "Peter's Demise" or even "Ananias' Agony." No! It's Jacob's trouble, a Jewish name, for a Jewish people, for a Jewish time, not the Church. It is a time when God "refines" Israel, "redeems" Israel, and "fulfills" all His promises that He made to Israel as far back as the time of the Patriarchs and King David. The Bible says right now they are under a "temporary" blindness until the Church Age is over, or what's called the "fullness of the Gentiles." And when that time "comes in" or is "over," the Church is removed via the Rapture and Israel becomes the object of God's focus again. This is what Paul states in the Book of Romans to the Church:

Romans 11:25-27 "I do not want you to be ignorant of this mystery, brothers, so that you may not be conceited: Israel has experienced a hardening in part until the full number of the Gentiles has come in. And so, all Israel will be saved, as it is written: 'The deliverer will come from Zion; He will turn godlessness away from Jacob. And this is My covenant with them when I take away their sins."

So, God is clearly not done with the Jewish people. Right now, they're under a temporary hardness, but when the Church departs at the Rapture, God will once again "deliver" them and fulfill His "covenants" He made with them and the 7-year Tribulation is the very instrument He uses to get the job done, to restore Israel! It has nothing to do with the Church! So again, this is why the Jewish people are so important. This is why they are the common thread throughout the Bible, past, present, and future. And if you don't get this, you're going to get everything wrong including the future event we call the Blessed Hope, the Rapture!

"God began the nation of Israel with Abraham in Genesis 12. He began the Church on the day of Pentecost in Acts 2. So, if Israel and the Church had a separate beginning, then why couldn't they have a separate conclusion?

The Scripture tells us that God has a very definite plan for Israel and He has a very definite plan for the Church. We are not Israel. We are not the new Israel. We do not receive the promises of Israel. They are still for Israel. If you have the Church receiving all the promises for Israel, then God is a liar, because God made promises to Israel which He is not keeping. And so there must be a distinction.

Who has God destined for His judgment in the 7-year Tribulation? Israel and the Gentile nations. God has not destined the Church for wrath. There is no point in the Church going through the 7-year Tribulation. All the wrath that God's judgment could pile on us has already been piled on whom? Christ at the cross. To say that we go through the 7-year Tribulation is to depreciate the work of Christ on the cross and to assume that there needs to be more wrath that we must take ourselves. That's blasphemy.

God does not will our destruction, as the Church, but our deliverance. He doesn't make us the subjects of His wrath. He has no point in putting us under punitive action and then sudden destruction. He cherishes no angry purposes toward His Church. We are His beloved bride.

Remember the story of the Old Testament where Israel is seen to be the wife of Jehovah, right? The whole book of Hosea, the whole thing is devoted to a historical allegory of the relationship between God and Israel. Israel is seen as God's wife. What kind of wife? Adulteress, untrue, a harlot. And the promise is that the harlot would be restored in the kingdom.

Now watch. Israel is a wife, but a harlot. The Church though is a bride and a virgin. Those are not the same. You got it? They cannot be the same. The Church is a chaste virgin. That's the mystery. That's the new thing. The new thing is the Church presented to Christ sanctified without spot, without blemish, clean and pure.

That can't be Israel. Israel is still an adulteress wife, fooling around with other gods, committing spiritual adultery and doesn't get restored yet until the time comes for the trouble in the 7-year Tribulation. Don't confuse the chaste virgin presented to Christ with Israel, an adulteress, wretched harlot unfaithful to God. The one He whips into believing is Israel.

That's why when I think about the future, as a Christian, I think about the fact that Jesus is coming for me and that's why I'm not looking for the 7-year Tribulation and I'm not looking for the antichrist. I'm looking for Jesus Christ. He is coming to get me, and we want to be ready when He gets here. I hope you're ready."[6]

I hope you're a Bride not a Wife. Oh, the Wife, will eventually be saved, Israel, God's not done with the Jewish people, but they have to go through a time of whipping first, the 7-year tribulation. You don't want to do that. You want to become a Bride right now! And that's precisely why, out of love, God has given us this update on *The Final Countdown: Tribulation Rising* concerning the Jewish People & the Antichrist to show us that the Tribulation is near and the 2nd Coming of Jesus Christ is rapidly approaching. And that's why Jesus Himself said...

Luke 21:28 "When these things begin to take place, stand up and lift up your heads, because your redemption is drawing near."

People of God, like it or not, we are headed for *The Final Countdown*. The signs of the 7-year Tribulation are Rising! Wake up! If you're a Christian here today and you're not doing anything for the Lord, shame on you! Get busy doing something for Jesus now! Stop wasting your life! We need you! Don't sit on the sidelines! Get on the front line and help us! Let's get busy working together doing something splendid for Jesus with what time is left and get busy saving souls! Amen? But, if you're reading this today and you're not a Christian, then I beg you, please, heed these signs, heed these warnings, give your life to Jesus now, become a Bride before it's too late. Because when the Rapture occurs, the whipping begins, the 7-year Tribulation, and you don't want to be here for that.

I Corinthians 15:52: "In a moment, in the twinkling of an eye, at the last trump: for the trumpet shall sound, and the dead shall be raised incorruptible and we shall be changed."

"As many people are standing in the street a bright light suddenly appears in the sky. They have to shield their eyes because this is a light that they have never seen before. They know something is terribly wrong as the sirens start going off telling them some kind of an emergency is taking place. They don't know what to do or where to go for protection.

Suddenly, as they are trying to break through the barriers that the police put up to hold the people back, bright lights start to ascend into the sky. First just a few, then thousands of these lights rise to Heaven. All going towards the blinding light in the sky. People are screaming, automobile alarms are going off. Everyone is in a panic. They can't understand what is going on.

Suddenly everything is calm. The lights have stopped going to the sky. The light in the sky is gone. But when they look around, they find that many of the people that had been there previously have now disappeared. Now they are really in a panic. Where did these people go? A truck without a driver has just crashed into another parked car. Millions Vanish!!! The weary cry Rapture! Experts purport Gamma Ray Burst! Now begins the Great Tribulation."

Revelation 12:12: "Woe to those who dwell upon the earth! For the Devil has come down to you having great wrath, because he knows he has only a short time!"

"They are running but don't know where to run to. They are so scared. The News comes on: "Breaking News! Planetary Pole Shift! Planet X spawns global havoc! Geomagnetic storm!" They try to explain away what just has happened, but it doesn't calm the crowds.

The skies turn dark and a storm starts to take place. A tornado, larger than ever seen before is coming down on the city. That one tornado turns into two. They are so strong that the planes in the airport are being taken up into the air just to be brought down to crash into the earth. But now which planes are empty and which ones have passengers in them. They are all crashing onto the ground.

As the planes are being sucked up the two tornadoes have now split up into many. Tearing up the cities, taking cars, trucks, and people in the air. Again, people are running in a panic, but they have nowhere to run. Everything is destroyed."

Revelation 16:18: "And then there was a great earthquake such as there had never been since man was on the earth."

"The earthquake tears through the city causing the buildings to fall, pipelines to break and they start fires all through the city. There is no way to escape the wrath that has come upon the earth. The bridges are collapsing, thousands are dying from the buildings being destroyed on top of them or many falling into the water as the bridges cave in on top of them. There is no way to get away from all this death and destruction. The whole city seems to be caving into the giant hole caused by the earthquake and the shaking doesn't stop."

Revelation 8:7: "And there followed hail and fire mixed with blood."

"Hailstones as big as a car are now falling to the earth. There is nowhere to run. As the earthquake causes the earth to crash into the ocean the waves get bigger and the people are now trying to get to higher ground to try to survive the water, but then meteors start falling from the sky. What wasn't destroyed by the earthquakes is now blowing up from the meteors. There is nowhere to hide. The destruction from one meteor causes the earth to explode in what resembles the bombs that hit Japan years before."

Revelation 8:8: "Something like a great mountain burning with fire was thrown into the sea."

"As it hits the ocean, the water starts to recede from the beaches. A wave taller than the highest skyscraper is heading towards the city. There is nowhere to run, nowhere to hide to get away from all this destruction. The ocean is now covering the entire city.

Revelation 16:8: The sun was given power to scorch people with fire."

"Now the sun is burning everything that is left. Everything is on fire. The earth by now is totally destroyed by fire and everyone that is left alive is destroyed with it."

BE READY!!!

Chapter Two

The Jewish People & Their
Past Prophecies

In the previous chapter we answered the big question that many people seem to be asking, "What's up with the Jewish People? What's the big deal about them? Why are they always in the discussion when it comes to end times events?" Well again, as we saw, first of all, Jesus was Jewish, if that helps answer the question, and it does, because it shows us that in the past, God was fulfilling His promises made to Adam and Eve, in the Garden of Eden with the Genesis 3:15 promise, through the Jewish People, to undo the damage the devil had done. That one day, the Messiah, Jesus, who did come through the Jewish people, would crush the head of the serpent, satan, which He did on the cross and then He rose again from the grave! We also saw the future promises God made with the Jewish people in the unconditional covenants He made with them which means He's not done with them yet! The Bible says God still has future promises to fulfill with the Jewish people, like them possessing all the land He gave them, as well as Jesus Christ literally ruling and reigning in Jerusalem and all over the planet in the Millennial Kingdom. Obviously, that hasn't happened yet, so that means God is not done with the Jewish people! And as we saw, that also means that the Church has not replaced Israel, like the lie of Replacement Theology would have you and I to believe, which includes putting us in the 7-year Tribulation. This is a time all about Israel and not about the Church! This is good news for us because if God can't keep His unconditional covenants He made with the Jewish people then how do we know He'll keep His unconditional promise with us in the New Covenant? Praise God He's a covenant-keeping God! But this is why the Jewish people are one of the most important prophetic events on God's end time calendar. This is why they are mentioned all over the Bible, past, present, and future! And this this is also why we find so many prophecies about them! In fact, speaking of prophecies, before we get to the future ones, that's in the next chapter, Lord willing, showing us, we're living in the Last Days, let's take a look at a few of the past prophecies concerning the Jewish people and see if God gets them right, and what we can learn from them today. But first let's read what God has to say.

Deuteronomy 28:62-64 "You who were as numerous as the stars in the sky will be left but few in number, because you did not obey the LORD your God. Just as it pleased the LORD to make you prosper and increase in number, so it will please Him to ruin and destroy you. You will be uprooted from the land you are entering to possess. Then the LORD will scatter you among all nations, from one end of the earth to the other. There you will worship other gods – gods of wood and stone, which neither you nor your fathers have known."

1) **Dispersion** – The Jews were warned repeatedly that they would be dispersed worldwide if they were not faithful to the conditional Mosaic covenant with God. Moses said, "The Lord will scatter you among all peoples, from one end of the earth to the other..." (Deuteronomy 28:64; Leviticus 26:33).

Jeremy Gimpel: *"We know that if the Jewish people don't live a Godly life in the land of Israel, they were promised to be scattered to the four corners of the earth."*

Ken Spiro, Historian: *"Which is guaranteed to be an extinction of many people. Scattered around the world, they are going to be gone."*

Jeremy Gimpel: *"The last thing you would want to do to an eternal people is scatter them across the world with no common culture, no common language, no internet, no form of communication, how will the Jewish people stay Jewish? How will they stay eternal if they are scattered around the world? Yet that is exactly what happened."*

Rabbi Berel Wein: *"We remained the people, not only just the faith and religion, but a family."*

Deuteronomy 4:27: God will scatter you among the people and you will be left few in numbers.

Jeremy Gimpel: *The most recent census number of the Chinese people is 1.3 billion, plus or minus 12 million. 12 million, that is the entire number of all of the Jewish people worldwide. We're a statistical error when just counting the people in China, that's how small we are."*

Yep, just what God says, you will have a huge population, but one day the prophecies say you will be dispersed around the world and specifically left few in number and that certainly has come to pass. Now that's just the first one. There are several past prophecies concerning the Jewish people, obviously God gets them all right.

2) **Persecution** – The Lord also warned the Jews that they would be persecuted wherever they went. Again, the words of Moses tell us…

Deuteronomy 28:65: "And among those nations you shall find no rest, and there shall be no resting place for the sole of your foot; but there the Lord will give you a trembling heart, failing of eyes, and despair of soul."

Rabbi Berel Wein: *"The fact that we are scattered and small, and we have been subject to the greatest hatred in human history."*

Jeremy Gimpel: *"The Torah tells us the atrocities and the curses that would come upon the Jewish people throughout the exile."*

Leviticus 26:3; And you, I will scatter among the nations, I will unsheathe the sword after you."

Jeremy Gimpel: *"And no one has suffered as we have suffered, no one has been as persecuted."*

Rabbi Berel Wein: *"Anti-Semitism, the oldest universal irrational intent of hatred in the world, the crusades, the inquisition, Muslim oppression, nation after nation, religion after religion, (Arab TV "We will treat the Jews as our enemies even if they return Palestine to us. As Muslims, our blood vengeance against them will only subside with their annihilation, Allah willing")"*

Ari Abramowitz: *"And the persecution we face has always transcended all logic and rational thoughts. When we were poor and destitute in the ghetto, we were hated for being parasites, when wealthy we were hated for being money grubbing. One thing that we could always rely on was that there would always be a reason, a pretext, to hate us."*

If you have ever done any studies of the Holocaust, that was the worst persecution of any people on the planet.

3) **Desolation** – God promised that after their dispersion, their land would become "desolate" and their cities would become "waste", but Moses put it even more graphically when he said...

Deuteronomy 29:22-23: "The foreigner who comes from a distant land...will say, 'All its land is brimstone and salt, a burning waste, unsown and unproductive, and no grass grows in it."

Rabbi Yom Tov Glazer: *"The Torah tells us that if the Jews don't do their charge, they will be sent out of the land and while they are away the land will become desolate. The land in the late 1800's was barren, full of rocks, it couldn't produce anything there."*

Jon Voight: *"Mark Twain came here in 1850. He talks about all these places he tried to pay respects to. He was saddened by the fact that it was desolation. Nothing grew here.*

Leviticus 26:32 "I will lay waste the land, so that your enemies who live there will be appalled."

And that is exactly what happened. We will get into that in future chapters. But we saw that come to pass as well. How is God's track record so far? God never gets it wrong. Past, present and future, He is very consistent.

4) **Preservation** – But God in His marvelous grace promised He would preserve the Jews as a separate people during their worldwide wanderings. (Isaiah 66:22; Jeremiah 30:11; 31:35-37). Isaiah adds that the Lord could no more forget Israel than a mother could forget her nursing child (Isaiah 49:15). He then adds that God cannot forget Israel because He has them tattooed on the palms of His hands! (Isaiah 49:16).

Jeremy Gimpel: *The first promise to Israel was made to Abraham. An eternal covenant"*

Genesis 17:7: "And I will establish a covenant between me and you and between your offspring after you, throughout their generation as an everlasting covenant."

Jeremy Gimpel: *"The Jewish people are the only ancient people alive today. The Assyrians, Babylonians, Jebusites, the Canaanites, all of them are gone."*

Rabbi Berel Wein: *"The one nation that has survived such scattering and then remained the nation, they became a symbol and eventually any trace of the original was gone."*

Jeremy Gimpel: *"We the eternal people stand alive today."*

Why? Because God's not done with them. We read this in the last chapter. I don't mean to belabor this point but if you don't understand this, you mess up all the interpretation of the scripture past, present, and future. The Jewish people need to be saved just like everybody else through Jesus Christ. But God is not done with them because of the unconditional promises that he made through Abraham and David. That's why they are still around today. The importance of that is the fulfillment of these prophecies.

5) **Fulfillment** – God has fulfilled all four of these prophecies during the past 2,000 years. In 70 A.D. the Romans destroyed the city of Jerusalem and took the Jewish nation into captivity, desolating the land and scattering the Jewish people across the face of the earth. As prophesied, everywhere they went they were persecuted, with their persecution culminating in the Nazi Holocaust of World War II. But God also preserved the Jews, and the fulfillment of this prophecy has been one of the most remarkable miracles of history. No other people have ever been so dispersed and yet been able to retain their identity as a nation.[1]

Jeremy Gimpel: *"Why are the Jewish people in Israel today? Is it random, is it coincidence, or is it destiny? What is happening in Israel today is the culmination of Jewish history. For almost 2000 years the Jewish people have been living on faith, faith in prophecies given thousands of years ago. Promises that seem irrational, promises that seem almost impossible. Promises that depend on the one before and if one isn't true then none of them are true. We were given these* *visions and promises thousands of years ago for our time, for our generation. Every single promise has come to pass."*

That tells us that God is a covenant keeping God. When God makes a promise what does He do? He keeps it. This is why the Jewish people are still around today. This is why we are seeing them in the news every day. This is why everybody wants to make peace in the Middle East which involves the Jewish people, little bitty tiny Israel. God's not done with them due to the unconditional covenants He made with them as we saw last time! But here's my point. If God got the past prophecies right about the Jewish People right down to a tee, then what do you think is going to happen to the future ones He made? He's going to get those right too! He's God. He never gets anything wrong! He's the same yesterday, today, and forever! And remember this is good news for us because if God keeps His unconditional promises to the Jewish people then that means we can also trust Him with our unconditional New Covenant in Jesus. But this is also a major mega sign we're living in the Last Days! This is why the Jewish people are all over the news today! It shows us that God is getting ready to deal with them again! They are the object of focus in the 7-year Tribulation. Which means, the Rapture could happen at any moment because we, the Bride, are out of here before any of that begins! Now that's the good news. The bad news is, there's a problem. We the Bride, even though we're not going into the 7-year Tribulation, we're wasting away our opportunity, we're squandering away our chance to do something splendid for Jesus, with what time we have left! We're losing our rewards because we're distracted! And that's the last thing you want to do! Because if there's one message loud and clear for us today in these past prophecies of the Jewish People it's that when God says to do something, you better what? You better do it! And when He warns about not doing something, you better what? You better take heed to that warning, right? He's serious about it! And it's the same thing with the Church. Now, we're not Israel and we don't replace Israel, and no we don't go into the 7-year Tribulation, but there's still a lesson for us to learn here as well in these past prophecies with the Jewish People! It's wrapped around God's consistent character! God told us to do something as well and He also warned us of what not to do prior to the Rapture, right? Let me share that with you.

Matthew 28:19-20 "Therefore go and make disciples of all nations, baptizing them in the name of the Father and of the Son and of the Holy Spirit, and teaching them to obey everything I have commanded you. And surely, I am with you always, to the very end of the age."

James 5:1-3,5,7-9 "Now listen you rich people, weep and wail because of the misery that is coming upon you. Your wealth has rotted, and moths have eaten your clothes. Your gold and silver are corroded. Their corrosion will testify against you and eat your flesh like fire. You have hoarded wealth in the last days. You have lived on earth in luxury and self-indulgence. You have fattened yourselves in the day of slaughter. Be patient, then, brothers, until the Lord's coming. See how the farmer waits for the land to yield its valuable crop and how patient he is for the autumn and spring rains. You too, be patient and stand firm, because the Lord's coming is near. Don't grumble against each other, brothers, or you will be judged. The Judge is standing at the door!"

So, Jesus tells us to do something today just like the Jewish People in the past and He also warns us of not doing something today, just like the Jewish people of the past, very consistent! God tells us, the Church, in this time frame, the Church Age, to get busy sharing the Gospel and stop living a life of self-indulgent luxury while we await the Rapture, the Blessed Hope, right? So surely that's what we're doing! I mean we just saw God's with us wherever we go, even to the end of the age, the Church Age, which means He's watching us, He's seeing everything we're doing, He is the Judge at the door! We also see He has a consistent character, He's the same yesterday, today, and forever! Yesterday with the Jewish people, or today with the church, God is consistent forever! We may not have the same plan, but we serve the same God! And so, if He tells us or the Jewish people to do something, He's expects it to be done, right? He's not blowing hot air! And if He warns us or the Jewish people of bad behavior, then we better take heed and listen up, right? So, we're doing what He said to do, we're taking heed to His warning, right? Wrong! We the Church are being just as obedient as the Jewish people and we've even turned the rescue mission into a pleasure cruise, like these people! And we don't think we're going to be judged???

"SPV "Rosa Mary" 44' North 127" West Pacific Ocean. A sailor is pulling on a rope onboard the ship when there is an explosion. He yells....NO! as bodies and barrels are flying through the sky. The radio operator is calling Mayday, Mayday, Mayday, trying to call for help. 'This is the Rosa Mary and an explosion has taken out our starboard aft and we have a fire onboard. We only have minutes here, over.' The reply is, 'Roger, Rosa Mary, this is the coast guard.

All our vessels in this area of 44' North 127" West are to report and prepare immediate assistance, over'. PV Corpus Christi reports, 'we are in the area 43'

North 128' West Pacific Ocean, we will be there in seven minutes, over.' The captain on board another ship asks the pilot what is going on.

He is told the Corpus Christi has just reported that they have a crew of 7 with 24 life boats ready. The captain replies that he wants the coordinates of the Rosa Mary immediately and a status report of the Corpus Christi. 'You have 5 minutes.' 'Yes Sir!' He replies. During the time that all this is transpiring, another officer on the ship is coming down the hallway to a dinner party that is going on. He is stopped by a man standing in the shadows.

"Mr. McMillin, this is quite a night for your first tour of duty." "Who are you?" Mr. McMillin asks. The man answers, "Choices, Jack, you are about to enter the valley of decision." McMillin answers, "I'm sorry..." The man interrupts him, "Let me ask you a question, what takes precedence, the vessels facilities or its overall purpose?" He answers, "I believe the purpose of this vessel is quite clear sir."

"Precisely, a purpose should be quite clear. Jack, we are heading into dangerous territory, no way around that. However, inside this vessel is a comfortable place to be. And therein lies your choice. Would you go or are you also content to merely study about going?" McMillin answers, "Sir I do have to go. I have to serve the party. It's about to start." "Jack, the party is almost over."

On the bridge the captain is talking to a crew member. He tells him to run to the party that is going on, to warn the people there. "The captain has ordered everyone to immediately report to Officer Burlow on the second level deck for emergency rescue operations. Officer Burlow has the lifeboats ready and we are ready to deploy. Everyone, follow me!"

Another officer in a white suit says, "Emergency operation, this man is dripping on my floor. My good man, Officer Brock, let me assure you of one thing, there will be no rescue operation." Officer Brock replies, "But sir..." The officer then says, "Think, do you know who takes this ship out in this kind of weather? Those who wish to remain unnoticed. So if some group of drug runners run afoul, I would even laugh to risk life and limb to save them."

"But sir. This boat after all..." Officer Brock tries to tell him. The officer in the white suite interrupts again, "I know perfectly well the purpose of this vessel, do you wish to have us all killed?" "N, no, sir" Again the officer in the white suit

interrupts, *"the purpose of a boat like this is to protect us from the outside, is this not clear to you Officer Brock?"*

"Well, maybe," he answers. *While this conversation is going on, McMillin is listening and thinking about what he should do. Officer Brock turns to walk out of the room and says as he is leaving, "Well maybe not sir." McMillin turns to exit the room after Officer Brock. The officer in the white suit calls to him, "Seaman McMillin, is that you I see joining the wise men?" He turns and walks out the door.*

The officer in the white suit turns to the rest of the people in the room and says "Everybody, 1:45 sharp, church." Officer Brock is now on the deck. He calls out, "Nobody is here yet. They are ready to release the life boats to go rescue the people on the Rosa Mary but only 4 people come down the stairs to help. He is asked where they are, where are the rest of them to come help?" He replies, "I don't know."

Officer Burlow says, "No, No, No, this is only a handful of people. You don't understand, I just raised all these 24 lifeboats, everything we've got and you have brought 6 people? You are aware that it takes 6 people to launch one of these boats. You're telling me we are about to launch 3 lifeboats to rescue 76 people? Have you lost your mind?"

He replies, "No sir!" 'Those people will have only managed to survive with our help, and you have only brought me a half dozen people. What is going on up there?"

Back at the party a couple of men are sitting on the couch discussing the design of the new rack and how they are pulled up from the stern. "You want to be 12 ft of the sea and you are pulling someone up from the stern, you can't even reach them. Trust me I went over this thing for 3 weeks with Burlow, I memorized the manual. You better catch up on some of your homework. Man, have you ever been on a lifeboat?" "Aren't you glad you aren't out in that weather tonight. I've got to go to church."

As the Rosa Mary is going down, a mother is watching her daughter in the water trying to stay afloat. She is calling for her mother. Her mother is unable to get to her. The little cries "MOMMY, MOMMY!" The radio officer is telling someone that the Rosa Mary was on its way to Vancouver. "They filed a manifest crew of 12 and 64 passengers. Can you please report the status of the operation?"

"Three lifeboats have been dropped and are operational, over." "Sir, this is US Coast Guard James Meyer, you and your crew are under orders to deploy all available life boats and crew immediately. Do you comprehend the situation you are in? You are their only chance." The response is silence. They have the boat to beat all boats, 64 crew, 24 rescue boats, and they launch three.

Back in the water the little girl keeps calling, "MOMMY WHERE ARE YOU?!" As she slowly vanishes under the water, the mother is pulled back from the edge of the lifeboat as she sees her daughter go under for the last time. Meanwhile the party continues in the upper deck.

Welcome to the American Church, 95% of the people who claim to be Christians today have never once gone on a rescue mission. Never once led one soul to Jesus Christ. But do you know what, they are excited about the economy, so they can continue to enjoy their self-indulgence. Get busy sharing the Gospel and stop living a life of self-indulgent luxury while we await the Rapture. What have we done Church? We turned the rescue mission into a pleasure cruise, and we don't think the judge is at the door, just like with the Jewish people? Oh, we won't be judged for salvation, praise God that's been taken care of by the cross of Christ! But we will be judged at the Bema Judgement Seat for rewards and that will determine whether or not you have anything to show for your so-called appreciation for the cross of Christ.

1 Corinthians 3:12-16 "If any man builds on this foundation using gold, silver, costly stones, wood, hay or straw, his work will be shown for what it is, because the Day will bring it to light. It will be revealed with fire, and the fire will test the quality of each man's work. If what he has built survives, he will receive his reward. If it is burned up, he will suffer loss; he himself will be saved, but only as one escaping through the flames."

Don't you know that you yourselves are God's temple and that God's Spirit lives in you? In other words, He's watching the whole thing! This is why, out of love, God has given us this update on *The Final Countdown: Tribulation Rising* concerning the *Jewish People & the Antichrist*. It's not for your entertainment, it's to show us that the 7-year Tribulation is near, and the Return of Jesus Christ is rapidly approaching. This is why Jesus Himself said…

Luke 21:28 "When these things begin to take place, stand up and lift up your heads, because your redemption is drawing near."

He's trying to get it through our heads that whether we like it or not, we are headed for The Final Countdown. The signs of the 7-year Tribulation are Rising all around us! It's time to wake up! And so, the point is this. If you're reading this today and you're not a Christian, then I beg you, please, heed these signs, heed these warnings, give your life to Jesus now! You don't want to be here when God pours out His Judgment. It's the worst time in the history of mankind, so horrible that unless God shortened the timeframe the entire human race would be destroyed! Get saved NOW! If you're reading this today and you are a Christian, then stop turning the rescue mission into a pleasure cruise! This is no time to be living a life of luxury and self-indulgence! The judge is at the door! Get busy being a faithful bride and patiently share the Gospel with as many as you can because the Lord's coming is near! That's the point…. Amen?

Chapter Three

The Jewish People & Their Return to the Land

Now let's take a look at the future prophecies concerning the Jewish People and see just how close we're getting to the Last Days.

The **1st End Time Prophecy** concerning the Jewish people letting us know we're living in the Last Days is that **Israel Would Return to The Land.**

You see, the Old Testament prophets repeatedly promised that one day God would regather the Jews back into their land, no matter how far they got scattered on the planet. But don't take my word for it. Let's listen to God's.

Isaiah 11:11-12 "In that day the Lord will reach out His hand a second time to reclaim the remnant that is left of His people from Assyria, from Lower Egypt, from Upper Egypt, from Cush, from Elam, from Babylonia, from Hamath and from the islands of the sea. He will raise a banner for the nations and gather the exiles of Israel; He will assemble the scattered people of Judah from the four quarters of the earth."

So here we see God clearly declaring that one day, against all odds, no matter what it looks like, no matter how long it's been, He would one day regather the Jewish people back into the land He gave them. Why? They were so obedient and wonderful? NO! Because of His great Name and the unconditional covenant, He made with them concerning the land.

Ezekiel 36:22,23,24,28 "Therefore say to the house of Israel, 'This is what the Sovereign LORD says: It is not for your sake, O house of Israel, that I am going to do these things, but for the sake of My Holy Name, which you have profaned among the nations where you have gone…then the nations will know that I am the LORD…For I will take you out of the nations; I will gather you from all the countries and bring you back into your own land. You will live in the land I gave your forefathers; you will be my people, and I will be your God.'"

Jeremiah 16:14-15 "'However, the days are coming,' declares the LORD, 'when men will no longer say, 'As surely as the LORD lives, who brought the Israelites up out of Egypt,' but they will say, 'As surely as the LORD lives, Who brought the Israelites up out of the land of the north and out of all the countries where He had banished them.' For I will restore them to the land I gave their forefathers.'"

So here we see God clearly saying He will bring the Jewish people back to the land, so the world will know that He is not just real, but that He's a Holy and Righteous God who keeps His promises. And here's the point. This incredible gathering of the Jews from the four corners of the earth has occurred in our lifetime. Which means, we're living in the Last Days! In fact, God ALSO predicted the exact order in which the Jewish people would return to the land in the Last Days!

Isaiah 43:5-6 "Do not be afraid, for I am with you; I will bring your children from the east and gather you from the west. I will say to the north, 'Give them up!' and to the south, 'Do not hold them back.' Bring my sons from afar and my daughters from the ends of the earth."

Since the destruction of the Jewish Temple in 70 A.D., the Jewish people have been scattered all over the earth. But during the past century alone, millions of Jews have returned to Israel, fulfilling this very prophecy. In fact, just like the Bible said, they not only came specifically from the east, the west, the north and the south, but they came in that exact order! First from the East, in the early 1900's, when many of the Jews living in the Middle East moved to Israel. Then from the West, during mid-1900's, hundreds of thousands of Jews living in the West (Europe and the United States) began moving to Israel. In 1900 there were only 40,000 Jews in all of Israel. But by the end of World War II that number had ballooned to over 600,000! Then from the North, during the 1980's & early 90's, Russia finally began to allow hundreds of thousands of Jews to return to Israel. In the past, Russia held the world's largest Jewish population, but they were unable to return to the land because they were being held captive in the Soviet Union. The Russians hated the Jews, they blamed them for all their nation's problems. But God said the Jews would come from the North and it just so happens Russia is the uttermost part of the north. So, when God says, "I will say to the north, 'Give them up!'" guess what? Not even Russia can stop it! And sure enough, in fulfillment of this prophecy, the Russian empire began to crumble, and Gorbachev suddenly opened the door for the Jewish people to flood back into Israel. In fact, in just two years, almost 400,000 Russian Jews arrived in Israel, averaging over 16,600 per month, and for many years during this period, Russia had a higher rate of immigration to Israel than any other country on the planet.

The Jewish people did all this knowing these sobering facts…

- They would have to abandon all valuables.
- They would face the necessity of learning Hebrew.
- They would have to live in minimal housing.
- They would face military service.
- They would find a non-existent job market.
- They would have to pay some of the highest taxes in the world. They would face the constant threat of terrorism and war.[1]

They were fully aware of these stark realities because all of them had relatives living in Israel. Yet, despite all these hardships, they came. Why? Because God had placed in their hearts to return home. Why? Because we're living in the Last Days! And next from the South, Israel struck a deal with Ethiopia's communist government. And on the weekend of May 25, 1991, 14,500 Ethiopian Jews were airlifted to Israel. It was called "Operation Solomon" and it dealt with the largest Jewish population to the south of Jerusalem made up of the Black Ethiopian Jews. No one knows for sure the origin of these Jews. The most common speculation is that they resulted from a union between King Solomon and the Queen of Sheba (2 Chronicles 9). But we know for sure they did exist because in the Book of Acts, Chapter 8, it contains the story of an Ethiopian Jew who came to Jerusalem to observe the feasts and who converted to Christianity on his way back home to Africa by Philip the Evangelist.

But in the late 1980s the Jews of Ethiopia began to feel a tug on their hearts to return to the Jewish homeland just like the Jews did in the North in Russia. So, they started migrating by the thousands and camped out around the international airport there, demanding transportation to Israel. Well, the government adamantly refused to let them leave. But what did God say? "I will say to the north, 'Give them up!' and to the south, 'Do not hold them back,'" and so in fulfillment of this prophecy…. In 1991, the Ethiopian government began to crumble in the midst of a civil war, and the United States and Israel intervened, providing bribes to military leaders which caused the government to relent and provide a 48-hour window for the refugees to depart. The resulting airlift was amazing. In just under 36 hours, 14,500 Ethiopian Jews — nearly the entire Jewish population — was flown to Tel Aviv in 40 flights involving 35 aircraft. At one point there were 28 planes in the air at one time. And a world record was set when one Boeing 747, designed to carry about 350 people, was loaded up with 1,086 passengers. This was possible because all the seats had been stripped out of the plane, the Ethiopians weighed very little, and they had no luggage. When that particular plane reached Tel Aviv, there was a total of 1,088 on board because two babies had been born en route!

As one guy said, "When I read about that development in the newspapers at the time, I immediately thought of a prophecy in Jeremiah 31:8…which reads…

Jeremiah 31:8 "Behold, I am bringing them from the north country, and I will gather them from the remote parts of the earth, among them the blind and the lame, the woman with child and she who is in labor with child, together; a great company, they will return here."

And today, over 6 million Jews — as many as were killed in the Holocaust — have been gathered back to their homeland, and they are still coming, returning to Israel every single year from all over the world. First from the East, West, North, and South. Just like the Bible said they would! When? In the last days! It's time we wake up folks! This is all a major prophecy sign, as this man shares.

Jeremy Gimpel *"The Ingathering of the exiles is the most prophesized event in the Bible, it is mentioned over 40 times, unprecedented in history. Never before has a nation been scattered across the world then scattered back to its ancient* *homeland and yet every single prophet mentioned this miraculous feat that has happened."*

Jeremiah 31:7: "I will bring them from the land of the North and gather them from the ends of the earth. Among them will be the blind and the lame, the pregnant and the birthing together, a great congregation will return."

"We hereby proclaim the establishment of the Jewish state in the land of Israel to be known as the state of Israel."

Jon Voight: *"And now they have been returned to the land and the land is still carrying the names of the great history of this people. It's unbelievable."*

Jeremy Gimpel: *"Today in Israel you see universalism. Jews from Ethiopia, Africa, Asia, North America, South America, Russia, the entire world has now returned to the land of Israel."[2]*

And remember this is good news for us because if God does keep His unconditional promise to the Jewish people to return to the land then that means we can also trust Him with our unconditional New Covenant in Jesus to take us to Heaven. This is also a major mega sign we're living in the Last Days! Now with all that said, there's a problem. Even though God shares all these amazing prophecies about the Jewish People in advance, so we would be encouraged in our promises with Him, and also know we're living in the Last Days, there are people, even in the Church, who have either, as we saw before, bought into the lie of Replacement Theology, and/or who don't even read the Bible let alone study Bible Prophecy or who aren't even Christians in the first place. So, they flat out don't even care what God says about His eternal covenant with the Jewish people which includes the promise to return to the land in the Last Days. But this lack of Biblical knowledge and false teaching has led to another problem. People not only don't catch the significance of the Jewish people returning to the land, but they now say they have no right to the land! What?! And this attitude is basically called, "Anti-Zionism." That the Jews have no right to go back to Zion, or the land God promised to them. It's crazy because we already saw the Abrahamic Covenant which promised it, and which was later reiterated in the Davidic Covenant, both of which are unconditional by the way. But even beyond that, it's like, what Bible are you reading? Because if there's one thing that's clear in the Scripture it's that God created the earth and all the things in it, (Colossians 1) and that He also owns all of it

Psalm 24:1 "The earth is the LORD's, and everything in it, the world, and all who live in it."

Therefore, God has the right to give it to whoever He wants! And that's why He says He not only gave this specific section of the land to the Jewish People, but He gave it to them forever!

Genesis 17:7-8 "I will establish My covenant as an everlasting covenant between Me and you and your descendants after you for the generations to come, to be your God and the God of your descendants after you. The whole land of Canaan, where you are now an alien, I will give as an everlasting possession to you and your descendants after you; and I will be their God."

Psalm 105:6-11 "O descendants of Abraham His servant, O sons of Jacob, His chosen ones. He is the LORD our God; His judgments are in all the earth. He remembers His covenant forever, the word He commanded, for a thousand generations, the covenant He made with Abraham, the oath He swore to Isaac. He confirmed it to Jacob as a decree, to Israel as an everlasting covenant: 'To you I will give the land of Canaan as the portion you will inherit."

Ezekiel 37:25 "They will live in the land I gave to My servant Jacob, the land where your fathers lived. They and their children and their children's children will live there forever, and David My servant will be their prince forever."

Romans 11:28,29 "But as far as election is concerned, they (the Jewish People) are loved on account of the patriarchs, for God's gifts and His call are irrevocable."

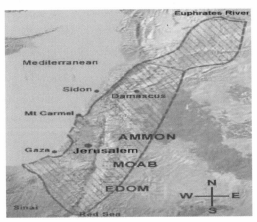

In other words, they're going to get the land! In fact, here's what that irrevocable promise of land for the Jewish people looked like. Hence, what we know as "The Promised Land." This is the general area.

"In fact, there are over 130 verses in the Bible that reiterate the truth that the land of Israel had been divinely given to the Jewish people." Yet, you have the false teaching of Replacement Theology saying things like this!

A widely distributed Christian magazine published an article concerning Israel and the following are quotes from that article:

- *"It is a mistake for Christians to exalt Israelis to the position of being 'God's chosen people.'"*
- *"The progressive revelation of Scripture makes it clear that, today, God has only one people, and it is the Church."*
- *"We must not apply Old Testament prophecies to the State of Israel when Jesus, Peter and Paul have radically redirected our thinking concerning the covenants of promise. They are now directed to the Church."*
- *"The Israeli claim to Palestine as a Jewish State by divine right is incorrect, and their continued enforcement of this claim by military oppression is unjust."*

As one guys says, *"These statements are typical of what is taught in "Replacement Theology" that teaches the Church has replaced Israel. How is this substitution possible?"*[3]

I agree, especially if you read the Bible, which is what we Christians are supposed to base truth on! But speaking of Palestine, this is an argument that comes up with the Non-Christian over the land that was given to the Jewish people. They say, "It belongs to the Palestinians and that the Jewish people are illegally occupying their land." Really? First of all, did you know there is not now and never has been a country called Palestine? It's a regional name, not the name of a country. It's like saying the states on the East Coast of the U.S. are New England. It's a regional name, not the name of a country. We also call the states in the Middle of the U.S. the Bible Belt. That's not the name of a country. I grew up in Kansas. I didn't put down as my country of origin The Bible Belt. And so, it is with Palestine. It's not a country but a region. There's no country for the Jewish people to "illegally occupy." Furthermore, the name for the "region" Palestine came as a result of a later renaming of the land by the Romans of Judea that belonged to the Jews.

We often hear these historic claims about the Palestinians.

Mahmoud Al-Habbash, Minister of Religious Affairs, Palestinian Authority: *"The Palestinians have been on this land for 5000 years."*

What's fact and what's fiction?

"The early versions of the word Palestine, Peleset, Palashtu, Palaistine, refer to a small region on the Mediterranean coast of Egypt and to the Philistines, a great Greek people, like many others, the Hitites, Canaanites, Amorites, Nubtans, and the Jebusites, have vanished over time and have no connection to today's Palestinians. The word Palestine was first formally used by the Roman Emperor Hadrian.

During his rule Hadrian massacred the rebellious Jewish population in the kingdom of Judea and sent most of the remaining Jewish population into exile. Hadrian was determined to obliterate thousands of years of Jewish presence in the land that is documented in expansive archeological findings that we use today. So, he decided to rename of the Province of Judea, and Syria, Palaestina after the vanished nemesis of the ancient Jews, the Philistines."[4]

And again, note the Philistines are no longer in existence from which we get the name Palestine, which means, there is no such thing as a Palestinian people, historically speaking, right? The term "Palestine" was just a renaming, out of spite, of Judea that belonged to the Jewish People, but there are no "true" Palestinians! So, the question is, "Who are the people in that land who are "claiming" to be Palestinians that no longer exist? Well, they're Arabs who are descendants of Ishmael who were not promised the land!

Genesis 17:18,21 "And Abraham said to God, 'If only Ishmael might live under your blessing!' Then God said… 'My covenant I will establish with Isaac.'"

So, no, no matter what they want to say in the media, the Arabs who call themselves Palestinians, are descendants of Ishmael, who have no part in the Abrahamic Land Covenant. I didn't say that. God did! Only descendants of Isaac who gave birth to Jacob, whose name was later changed to "Israel" who gave birth to the 12 Tribes, which is where we get the accurate name for an actual country of an actual people called ISRAEL! But then you'll have people say, "Well, the Jewish People are being greedy with the land. They need to share!" Really? Well, first of all, It's their land! I mean, if you have a home, would it be right for people to force you to share your home with people who have no right to your home, and you don't even know? And not just total strangers but to people who want to kill you on top of that and take over your home! And yet that's exactly what Israel has repeatedly done!

David Brog, Executive Director, Maccabee Task Force: *"If Israel just allowed the Palestinians to have a state of their own, there would be peace in the Middle East. Right? That's what you hear from the U.N. Ambassadors, diplomats, and most college professors. But what if I told you that Israel has already offered the Palestinians a state of their own. And not just once but on five separate occasions.*

Don't believe me? Let's review the record. After the breakup of the Ottoman Empire in 1914, following WWI, Britain took control of most of the Middle East, including the area that constitutes modern Israel.

Seventeen years later in 1936 the Arabs rebelled against the British, and against the Jewish neighbors. The British formed a task force, the Peel Commission, to study the cause of the rebellion.

The commission concluded that the reason for the violence was that two peoples, Jews and Arabs, wanted to govern the same land. The answer, the Peel Commission concluded, would be to create two independent states. One for the Jews and one for the Arabs, a two-state solution. The suggested split was heavily in favor of the Arabs.

Britain offered them 80% of the disputed territory. The Jews the remaining 20%. Yet despite the tiny size of their proposed state the Jews voted to accept this offer. The Arabs rejected it and resumed their violent rebellion. That was rejection #1. Ten years later in 1947, the British asked the United Nations to find a new solution to the continuing tensions. Like the Peel Commission, the U.N. decided that the best way to resolve the conflict was to divide the land. In November 1947 the U.N. voted to recreate two states, again the Jews accepted the offer and again the Arabs rejected it. Only this time by launching an all-out war. Rejection #2.

Jordan, Egypt, Iraq, Lebanon and Syria joined the conflict, but they failed. Israel won the war and got on with the business of building a new nation. Most of the land set aside by the U.N. for an Arab state, the West Bank and East Jerusalem became occupied territory. Occupied not by Israel but by Jordan.

Twenty years later in 1967, the Arabs, led this time by Egypt, and joined by Syria and Jordan, once again sought to destroy the Jewish state. The 1967 conflict, known as the 6-Day war, ended in a stunning victory for Israel. Jerusalem and the West Bank, as well as the area known as the Gaza strip, fell into Israel's hands. The government split over what to do with this new territory. Half wanted to turn the West Bank back to Jordan and Gaza to Egypt in exchange for peace.

The other half wanted to give it to the region's Arabs who had begun referring to themselves as the Palestinians in the hope that they might build their own state there. Neither initiative got very far. A few months later the Arab League had met in Sudan and issued it's infamous '3-nos', no peace with Israel, no recognition of Israel and no negotiations with Israel. Again, the two-state solution was dismissed by the Arabs, making this rejection #3.

In 2000, Israeli Prime Minister Ehud Barak, met at Camp David with Palestinian Liberation Organization chairman Yasser Arafat to conclude a new two-state plan. Barak offered the Palestinian state all of Gaza and 94% of the West Bank with East Jerusalem as its capital. But the Palestinian leader rejected the offer. In the words of the U.S. President Bill Clinton, 'Arafat was here 14 days and said 'no' to everything.' Instead the Palestinians launched a bloody wave of suicide bombings that killed over 1000 Israeli's and maimed thousands more on buses, in wedding halls, and in Pizza Parlors. Rejection #4.

In 2008, Israel tried yet again. Prime Minister Ehud Olmert went even farther than Ehud Barak had, expanding the peace offer to include additional land to sweeten the deal. Like his predecessor the new Palestinian Leader Mahmoud Abbas turned the deal down. Rejection #5.

In between these last two Israeli offers Israel unilaterally left Gaza giving the Palestinians complete control there. Instead of them developing this territory for the good of its citizens the Palestinians turned Gaza into a terrorist base from which they fired thousands of rockets into Israel. Each time Israel has agreed to a Palestinian state, the Palestinians have rejected the offer, often violent."[5]

And yet, Israel is the bad guy who won't share their home with people who have no right to it and who want to kill them! As one diplomat was quoted as saying in The Jerusalem Post, *"The Arabs never miss an opportunity to miss an opportunity!"*[6]

But even then, people will still say that the Jewish people just have way too much land and they need to give up even more land for all these Palestinian refugees. REALLY? First of all, again, there are no such people as the Palestinian people. They're called that now, but historically they don't exist and they're Arab descendants of Ishmael, who have no right to the land. These refugees are political pawns in the hand of the Muslim nations who created them in the first place! They are only using them as tools to try to dupe the world into getting Israel out of the land. The Muslim nations, in the past, told the Arabs living in that area to leave their homes and let them, the Muslims, destroy Israel, and then, when they were done destroying the Jewish people, they could go back to their homes and even retake the Jewish homes. Great deal, right? Well, the problem was, they lost! They are NOT going to defeat Israel! So now, these Arabs who got duped by the Muslim nations into leaving their homes, have been purposely left wandering around. They are now who we call the Palestinian refugees! Yet, the Muslims say the Jewish People need to give up their land to make room for these refugees that they created, when the whole time, the Muslim nations have plenty of room to take care of their own!

"Now in terms of Israel giving up land, they gave back the Sinai and the Gaza Strip. How much does Israel actually have in comparison to the other countries in the region? I'd like for you to see Israel in comparison to the other countries.

What we are going to do is compare members of the Arab League, not counting the PLO and we are going to add Iran, Afghanistan, and Pakistan to this mix, and we are going to compare those countries with Israel. The following maps are to scale: First we are going to start in Northwest Africa, Morocco, Western Sahara and Mauritania, Algeria and Tunisia, Libya and Sudan, Djibouti, Somalia and Comoros, these are all Arab League Nations, also included are Egypt, Syria, Lebanon, and Jordan and further East Iraq, Kuwait, Bahrain, Qatar, United Arab Emirates, Saudi Arabia, Yemen, Oman and then finally Iran, Afghanistan, and Pakistan.

And now Israel, a tiny little piece of land in the middle of all these Arab Nations. I get the same response every time I show this map. Silence……. People do not understand just how small Israel is. Sometimes Israel is compared to the state of New Jersey. I compare it more to Lake Michigan.

The whole country of Israel can fit into Lake Michigan. Yet the world says they have too much land. The total land mass of all the Arab League states is 464 times greater than that of Israel's. So, I ask the question, is there no room for a Jewish state? The world's answer is no, or we'll determine how large or we'll carve it up."[7]

But you might want to read God's warning about those who would do that!

Joel 3:1-2 "In those days and at that time, when I restore the fortunes of Judah and Jerusalem, I will gather all nations and bring them down to the Valley of Jehoshaphat. There I will enter into judgment against them concerning My inheritance, My people Israel, for they scattered My people among the nations and divided up My land."

You know, the very thing we see in the news, every single day, that everybody, including our own President, wants to do! Folks, we're living in the Last Days and it's time to get motivated! And this is why, out of love, God has given us this update on *The Final Countdown: Tribulation Rising* concerning the Jewish People & the Antichrist to show us that the 7-year Tribulation is near, and the Return of Jesus Christ is rapidly approaching. That's why Jesus Himself said…

Luke 21:28 "When these things begin to take place, stand up and lift up your heads, because your redemption is drawing near."

People of God, like it or not, we are headed for The Final Countdown. The signs of the 7-year Tribulation are Rising all around us! It's time to wake up! And so, the point is this. If you're reading this today and you're not a Christian, then I beg you, please, heed these signs, heed these warnings, give your life to Jesus now! You don't want to be here when God pours out His Judgment upon the nations. It's the worst time in the history of mankind, so horrible that unless God shortened the timeframe the entire human race would be destroyed! The only way to escape is through Jesus! Take the way out now before it's too late. Get saved today! BUT, if you're reading this today and you are a Christian, then would you please stop goofing off like this guy?!!!

An erupting volcano is a serious hazard, but it's reasonable to assume these guys only want to know if said hazard is literal.

Hawaii's Kilauea volcano has destroyed 36 structures, including 26 homes, since it first began releasing lava on May 3, 2018, according to NBC News, which provides these details:

If Hawaii's Kilauea volcano blows its top in the coming days or weeks, as experts fear, it could hurl ash and boulders the size of refrigerators miles into the air, shutting down airline traffic and endangering lives in all directions, scientists say. "If it goes up, it will come down," said Charles Mandeville, volcano hazards coordinator for the U.S. Geological Survey. "You don't want to be underneath anything that weighs 10 tons when it's coming out at 120 mph."

And yet, here we see - courtesy Getty Images and photographer Mario Tama - a man holding his finish as a plume of ash rises into the air behind him.[8]

When I first saw this, I thought it was a joke, but it's an actual photo of a guy in front of Hawaii's Kilauea volcano erupting recently, and this guy's actually golfing with his back to it like it's no big deal! And yet, how many Christians are acting like this spiritually! The planet is getting ready to blow, God's giving us all these signs, and we're walking around goofing off playing golf or whatever when the whole time God says get busy sharing the Gospel! What are you doing? We're on a rescue mission not a pleasure cruise! It's not about you, it's about reaching the lost. So, let's heed these signs ourselves and get busy doing something splendid for Jesus like sharing the Gospel. Not golfing in front of a volcano! Amen?

Chapter Four

The Jewish People & Their Rebirth as a Nation

In the last chapter we took a look at the first of the future prophecies concerning the Jewish People. He lets us know we're living in the Last Days by **Israel Returning to The Land**.

We saw that just like God prophesied that the Jewish People, against all odds, would not only return to the land, but they did it in the exact order God said they would! First from the east, the west, the north and the south, in that exact order! Then we dealt with those people who, along with the lie of Replacement Theology in the Church, say Israel has no right to the land, which is also called Anti-Zionism. That is crazy because if there's one thing that's clear in the Bible it's that God made an unconditional eternal covenant with the Jewish People which included the land with Abraham and reiterated with David and we saw that the land went to the descendants of Isaac not Ishmael, which means the Arabs, who today call themselves the Palestinians, have no right to the land! It's God's Land & He gave it to the Jewish People. Which is why He said divide it at your own peril! Lord willing, we'll get to that, even more so, in a future chapter. All these events surrounding Israel returning to the land is a major mega sign that we're living in the Last Days! But that's not all.

The **2ⁿᵈ End Time Prophecy** concerning **The Jewish People** letting us know we're living in the Last Days is that **Israel Would Become a Nation Again**.

But don't take my word for it. Let's listen to God's.

Isaiah 11:10-12 "In that day the Root of Jesse will stand as a banner for the peoples; the nations will rally to Him, and His place of rest will be glorious. In that day the Lord will reach out His hand a second time to reclaim the remnant that is left of His people from Assyria, from Lower Egypt, from Upper Egypt, from Cush, from Elam, from Babylonia, from Hamath, and from the islands of the sea. He will raise a banner for the nations and gather the exiles of Israel; He will assemble the scattered people of Judah from the four quarters of the earth."

So here we see God clearly declaring that one day, against all odds, no matter what it looks like, no matter how long it's been, He would not only one day regather the Jewish people back into the land, as we saw last time, but He'd also what? He would "raise a banner for them" or in other words, make them a nation again. The Hebrew word for "banner" there is "nace" which literally means, "a flag." And that's why some translations literally say. "He will raise a flag among the nations for Israel to rally around" i.e. He would make them a nation again. Why? Because they're so obedient and wonderful? NO! But because of the unconditional covenants He made with them. God's not done with the Jewish people including them operating as a nation on the world scene. And it's too bad we don't see any signs of that happening now, are you kidding me?

Ever since 721 BC approximately 14 different peoples have possessed the land of Israel. Yet as we saw, the Bible specifically said that the nation of Israel would one day be reborn. One day they would regain their independence. Can you guess what happened on May 14, 1948? That's right! After waiting centuries and centuries, the people who were scattered all over the world, not only returned to the land, but they also became a nation again! From out of nowhere and against all odds, Israel was reborn. In fact, here's the actual U.S. News Clip of that time frame declaring the news of Israel becoming a nation again!

BIG STORY! Universal Newsreel, Voice: Ed Herlihy Edited by: Ed Bartsch
The newsreel opens with hundreds of Jews on a ship moving towards Israel in 1948 as The Nation of Israel is born under Prime Minister David Ben Gurion.

"October 1947, two shiploads of Jewish refugees from Europe attempt to land in Palestine only to be turned away by the British and sent to internment on Cyprus. The British mandate in Palestine was about to end however and the U.N. was debating the partition of Palestine, between the Jews and the Arabs as a solution to the turmoil in that country.

In May of 1948 a new Jewish state, Israel, was born in a bath of blood. Jewish troops routed Arab forces from the city of Haifa in the first of a series of battles that were to reverberate through the years. In the year of independence, fighting was fierce in the Negev desert area. Here the Israeli troops routed the Arabs and took dozens of prisoners.

Meanwhile on May 14, 1948 the new government headed by David Ben Gurion is installed in Tel Aviv. Thus, for the first time since the Roman legion destroyed Jerusalem in the year 70 AD, the Jewish people have a nation of their own. United Nations teams accompany Israeli soldiers under the white flag to retrieve bodies of soldiers killed in the continuing strikes with Arab troops.

The U.N. was able to affect some easy pacts calling for a truce, but skirmishes continued to break out. Doctor Heim Viessman joined Premier Ben Gurion in the government. The Jewish patriot became president as Israel went before the United Nations to seek a place in that world body. The Middle Eastern Arabic nations were in violent opposition and when Israel was voted a membership they walked out in a body and for the rest of the day their seats remained empty, but they returned the next morning to no further incident.

Thus, history was made as the Jewish state of Israel was born, conceived in strife and weaned in violence. Israel has flourished to become a constructive voice in world affairs where their flag became a symbol of hope in a troubled world."[1]

And notice, of all things for them to mention on the actual news footage of the event, that it was a flag that was raised as a symbol of hope in a troubled world…

That's exactly what the Bible said would happen nearly 2,700 years ago, as a sign you're living in the Last Days! And it happened in our lifetime! Which is why one guy said...

"This is the cornerstone prophetic event of our age. It is an event that prophetic scholars have pointed to for 400 years amid much scoffing and ridicule by those who did not believe that Israel would ever exist again as a nation."[2]

Ah ha, ha, ha! God's done with the Jewish people! They're never coming back! The Church has replaced them! No, He's not! When God says something's going to happen, including the Jewish People coming back to the land again and becoming a nation again, it's going to happen, and nothing can stop it, including your scoffing! The Jewish People became a nation exactly as God said they would! Now here's my point. There are those who do get excited about this event, and rightly so, because it is a huge prophetic event, a cornerstone event, but sometimes they make a fatal error. They say something like, "Yeah! The Jewish people are back in the land again and they even became a nation again,

"What happened to Dedication" and Purim?

which means they'll be celebrating the Jewish Feasts again and that's exciting for us because we all know the Rapture has to happen on the Jewish Feast of Trumpets!" Really? Can we examine that for a minute? This is my concern with that.

First of all, how many of you have heard that theory? That the Rapture is going to happen on the Feast of Trumpets which is also called Rosh Hashanah or "Head of the Year," the Jewish New Year. It's very popular today, especially every September when that event typically occurs. But for those of you who aren't familiar with it, let me give you a breakdown of it. There are seven Jewish festivals or feasts outlined in the Bible. These include Passover, Unleavened Bread, First-Fruits, Weeks, Trumpets, Atonement, and Tabernacles. While they are mentioned throughout the Scripture, we find instructions for all seven laid out in **Leviticus 23**. The Book of Leviticus contains God's instructions to His chosen nation, Israel, on how they were to worship Him. It contains detailed instructions about the duties of the priests as well as instructions on observing and obeying God's Law and the sacrificial system. God designated these seven specific feasts that Israel was to celebrate each year. However, Christians are no longer under any obligation to observe any of the Old Testament feasts. *Really?*

Colossians 2:16 "Therefore do not let anyone judge you by what you eat or drink, or with regard to a religious festival, a New Moon celebration or a Sabbath day."

Nonetheless, here's what some Christians say we need to know about these Jewish Feasts.

1. The Feast of Passover was fulfilled by the death of the Messiah.
2. The Feast of Unleavened Bread was fulfilled by the righteous character and sinlessness of the Messiah's blood-offering upon His death.
3. The Feast of First-Fruits was fulfilled by the Resurrection of the Messiah.
4. The Feast of Weeks was fulfilled by Pentecost or the birth of the Church.
5. The Feast of Trumpets will be fulfilled by the Rapture of the Church.
6. The Day of Atonement will be fulfilled by the Great Tribulation with Israel's national salvation at the end of that period.
7. The Feast of Tabernacles will be fulfilled by the establishment of the Messianic Kingdom.[3]

So that's the basic belief and I'm not saying there's some truth to that, but here's my concern with it. First, we know when the Feast of Trumpets takes place every year, and so if you say the Rapture has to take place on The Feast of Trumpets, then isn't this a form of date-setting? The Bible says the Rapture is an imminent event, which means it can happen at "any moment," hence "imminent" nobody knows when it's going to happen! So, if you say the Rapture happens on this Feast then isn't this predicting a date for the Rapture, which is a violation of the Scripture? But then they'll say, "Oh no, wait a minute. The Feast of Trumpets changes each year, so we don't really know the exact time." OK…can we examine that too? Yes, you are correct, it changes each year. For instance, this is from Judaism 101, from their website and the dates of the Feast of Trumpets.

According to them, Rosh Hashanah will occur on the following days of the secular calendar:

- Jewish Year 5777: sunset October 2, 2016 - nightfall October 4, 2016
- Jewish Year 5778: sunset September 20, 2017 - nightfall September 22, 2017
- Jewish Year 5779: sunset September 9, 2018 - nightfall September 11, 2018
- Jewish Year 5780: sunset September 29, 2019 - nightfall October 1, 2019
- Jewish Year 5781: sunset September 18, 2020 - nightfall September 20, 2020[4]

So, I'll give that you, the Feast of Trumpets could happen the first part of September or even up to the first part of October, depending on the year, so there's about a month variance on the date, I'll give you that. But my problem is, while yes, the date changes for each year, my problem is this still narrows down the Rapture to a one-month time period! So, does that mean I get to goof off for 11 months and not worry about the Rapture because it can only happen during the first part of September to the first of October, somewhere in-between there depending on the year? Or conversely, does this also mean I can't get excited about the Rapture for 11 months of the year, November through August, because it'll never happen according to those dates, due to that's not when the Feast occurs? Stop and think about it! It destroys Imminency! Not to mention, as we just saw, I can go to a website and look at the exact date of when it's going to occur on the Jewish Calendar every single year, so how is that not date-setting? This is why every September for the last several years, people are getting all wigged out about the Rapture and then all bummed out when it doesn't happen! And it won't happen as long as you keep setting a date. The lost are watching all this saying, "You Christians are a bunch of date-setting wackos crying wolf with the Rapture every single September and nothing ever happens! Why should I listen to you?" It's a bad witness! Now, could the Rapture occur on the Feast of Trumpets? Of course, it could! But not because of a Jewish Feast, but because

Study this ?!

it's an imminent event! It could happen on any day including that day! So, I'll give you that. But the problem is when you get overly dogmatic about it and thus box the Rapture in, which is a form of date-setting, and at the same time you destroy immanency and ruin your witness to the lost!

Secondly, as we saw, the focus of the Jewish Feasts is for Israel, not the Church. And so, if you take the focus of these Feasts from Israel and replace it with the Church, then isn't that a form of Replacement Theology again? Stop and think about it. I'm not saying the Rapture couldn't happen on the Feast of Trumpets, and maybe there is some symbolism going on there. I'm just saying be careful in being so overly dogmatic about it because you'll destroy imminency and encourage Replacement Theology, whether you realize it or not! To me, the greater point of Israel becoming a nation again is not about the Feasts or whether or not we the Church celebrate them or even what's going to happen next September or the first part of October and get excited about that. No! Rather, the point is, it means we are living in the Last Days and since the Rapture is imminent, I can get excited today! I don't need the month of September or a Jewish Feast to get me exited once a year or one month out of the year. I can get excited about the Rapture every day! Don't take the news of Israel becoming a nation again in the wrong way and rob yourself or other people of the blessings of imminency. And certainly, don't let it become a bad witness! It's a sign we're living in the Last Days and it's time to get motivated and a time to get excited now!

The **3rd End Time Prophecy** concerning the Jewish people letting us know we're living in the Last Days is that **Israel Would Be Brought Forth In One Day**.

Isaiah 66:8 "Who has ever seen or heard of anything as strange as this? Has a nation ever been born in a single day? Has a country ever come forth in a mere moment? But by the time Jerusalem's birth pains begin, the baby will be born; the nation will come forth."

Now, for those of you who may not know, on May 14, 1948, at precisely 4 pm, the members of the People's Council signed the proclamation and the declaration was made that, "The State of Israel is established. This meeting is ended." Israel not only became a nation again, but it was brought forth as a nation, literally in one day. Just like the Bible said would happen when you're living in the Last Days!

In fact, the Jewish Agency Chairman David Ben-Gurion, who later became Israel's first Premier, proclaimed that the State was to be Israel with these words, "We hereby proclaim the establishment of the Jewish state to be called Israel." Hence establishing the first Jewish state in nearly 2,000 years all in one day. This, of course, prompted applause and tears from the crowd and the Jewish People began to dance in the streets, but not for long. Gun shots already started to erupt and Arab nations surrounding Israel launched an all-out assault against them that very evening and it has never stopped even to this day. Just turn on your news! Now as bad as that was, you've got to understand the pressure David Ben-Gurion was under in making this announcement for Israel to become a nation in one day to appreciate the miracle it truly was, as this transcript shows...

"This year we celebrate 70 years of the re-establishment of our beloved country, Israel. For the first time in 2000 years, a Jew can be born in the land of Israel, live a full life, and die in the land of Israel. Free, never knowing the exile.

This year we celebrate 1948, one thousand, nine hundred and forty-eight years ago the Roman Empire destroyed our lives. They burned and demolished our temple and exiled the Jews from Jerusalem all while gloating their vicious imperial conquest in victory. The Jews rebelled and fought valiantly for their freedom.

The rebellion was crushed, and the Jewish people found themselves homeless. Helpless and lost for centuries upon centuries. The long and bitter Jewish exile reached the darkest time in human history. As we celebrate 70 years we must remember where we were only 74 years ago.

Ezekiel 37: "And I saw a great open space with dry bones. Can these bones live? Only you know."

After the U.N. voted in favor of the Partition Plan on May 14, 1948 the V of ER, the British Mandate, was due to expire. The year was fraught with countless dangers, escalating violence across the land of Israel combined with threats of annihilation from every border and country.

American President Harry Truman, in a power play against Russia, began to pressure the U.N. to reject the Partition Plan and snuff out Israel's hope for independence. The Generals of the Hegana and Hamas stood together opposing

Ben Gurion's plan to declare a state. On May 13ᵗʰ, the eve of the Declaration of Independence, General George Marshall, then Secretary of State of the United States sent Ben Gurion a brutal ultimatum demanding the postponement of the Declaration of Independence.

Marshall, together with the Secretary of Defense, James Forrestal, imposed a military embargo. They threatened that Ben Gurion's Declaration of Independence would trigger a regional war that would doom the Jewish people to a second Holocaust in less than 10 years. And the United States would not provide any assistance to the Jews.

Intel arrived that Britain had supplied arms to Egypt, Jordan, and Iraq, preparing them for the attack. The force of the Hagana numbered only 300. They had almost no equipment, no uniforms, only half the men in each unit had guns. All the freedom fighters of Israel, the Hagana, Etzel together numbered only a few thousand.

On the eve of the Declaration, Israel's army was ill-equipped, unorganized, with no tanks, no real Air Force and no battle plan against five professional armies trained and funded by the British. How could the Jews defend themselves?

Standing alone against Israel's top military and political ranks, betrayed, isolated, and threatened by the international community including the United States, with Arab armies invading from every front it was now or maybe never. Under extraordinary pressure a self-proclaimed secular Zionist, Ben Gurion was overcome, possessed, with a courageous spirit of biblical proportion.

David Ben Gurion: *"In Israel, to be a realist you have to believe in miracles."*

He gives his speech and just like that, 2000 years of exile came to an end. One thousand, nine hundred and forty-eight years ago Jerusalem was destroyed. We are celebrating the most legendary comeback story in human history. Can these bones live? Son of man, these bones are the whole house of Israel. They say our bones are dried up and our hope is gone. Thus, saith the Lord, I'm going to open your graves and lift you out of your graves my people and bring you to the land of Israel."[5]

Why? Because God's a miracle-working God and He's not done with the Jewish People. When He says they're going to become a nation again in one day that's exactly how it's going to happen no matter who's against it! But once again, we have a problem. There are those who do get excited about this event, and rightly so, but they too make a fatal error. They say something like, "Yeah! The Jewish People are back in the land again and they even became a nation again in one day. And speaking of this day, since we know the exact day, they became a nation again, this means that this generation will not pass away until the Rapture occurs! It's just around the corner! How many of you have heard that? Yeah, it's pretty popular out there too, but let's take a look at that as well. Here's the problem. They misquote the words of Jesus in Matthew 24 concerning the future events in the 7-year Tribulation.

Matthew 24:34 "I tell you the truth, this generation will certainly not pass away until all these things have happened."

Now, what is "all these things?" In the context it's clearly the 7-year Tribulation. And what they say is we just need to calculate then, when the Jewish People became a nation, 1948, and then add how long a generation is to that date and voila! We have the beginning of the 7-year Tribulation, which means the Rapture happens just prior to that! It's time to get excited! Well, I agree, it's time to get excited that Israel became a nation, again, even in one day, but not for those reasons you propose. First of all, this is where the games begin because people who believe in this don't even agree on how long a generation is! Some say it's 37, no it's 40, no maybe 50, or no maybe 70 or how about 80 and on and on it goes! And each try to pull out a verse to try to prove their point. But what they don't realize is that this generational guessing-game was popularized by the false teaching date-setting cult Jehovah's Witnesses! This is partly why they predicted so many false dates for the end of the world! Like 1914, 1925, 1951, 1975, 2000 and on and on it goes! A lot of it came from a wrong application of this verse! They even have six different and contradictory ideas of "who" this "generation" is. Is it the "ungodly," the "anointed," the "contemporary," or maybe even a "mixture of both?"[6]

It's all wrong because that's not what Jesus was saying in that verse! The context of **Matthew 24** is talking to the Jewish People not the Church, number one, and two, it's talking about a future event, the 7-year Tribulation! Context, context, context! The generation He's talking about is the future Jewish people who would be in the future 7-year Tribulation, not the Church, when these things, the 7-year Tribulation, take place, that generation of Jewish people in the 7-year Tribulation, will certainly not pass away until all these things (the 7-year

Tribulation) have happened. Why? Because God's not done with the Jewish People! They don't get destroyed in the 7-year Tribulation! The 7-year Tribulation is the instrument God uses, to "refine," "redeem," "save," and "restore" a remnant of Israel, fulfilling His promises way back to the time of Abraham and King David, again, back to the unconditional covenants! That's what Daniel's 70th week prophecy, the 7-year Tribulation, is all about! That's why, as we saw before, Paul says right now the Jewish People are under a "temporary" "blindness" or "hardness" until the Church Age is over, or what's called the "fullness of the Gentiles." But, when that time "comes in" or is "over," the Church is removed via the Rapture, then Israel, the wife, becomes the object of God's focus again and the 7-year Tribulation begins, that's the 70th week prophecy! That's the future time and future people Jesus is talking about and to whom He gives this future promise of preservation to! He's reiterating the unconditional covenants! To me, the greater point of Israel becoming a nation again, even in one day, is not about predicting a date for the Rapture or even the start of the 7-year Tribulation and then getting excited about that, NO! Rather, the point is, it means we are living in the Last Days and since the Rapture is imminent, I can get excited about it RIGHT NOW! I don't need a generational calculation to get me excited over, however long it ends up being on whoever's calculation, based on whatever math or verse you want to dig up! I can get excited about the Rapture now because it can happen now! Don't take the news of Israel becoming a nation again, even in one day, in the wrong way! Otherwise you'll rob yourself of the blessings of Imminency, again!

The **4th End Time Prophecy** concerning the Jewish people letting us know we're living in the Last Days is that **Israel Would Be A United Nation Again.**

Ezekiel 37:21-22 "And give them this message from the Sovereign LORD: I will gather the people of Israel from among the nations. I will bring them home to their own land from the places where they have been scattered. I will unify them into one nation in the land. One king will rule them all; no longer will they be divided into two nations."

Now for those of you who may not know, in about 930 BC, the Jewish people became a divided nation. The Northern 10 tribes were called Israel, and the Southern 2 tribes were called Judah. And God repeatedly sent prophets **to** both of them to get them to return back to Him, to repent, but to no avail. To Israel the Northern Tribes, God sent Elijah with the words like.

1 Kings 18:21 "How long will you waver between two opinions? If the LORD is God, follow Him; but if Baal is God, follow him.' But the people said nothing."

So, God kept the prophets coming with Elisha, Amos, Hosea, Jonah, Nahum, Daniel, and Obadiah, but the people didn't respond so God sent them off into exile in the Assyrian Captivity in 722 BC. Then to the Southern Tribes in Judah (Judah & Benjamin), God sent Joel, Isaiah, Micah, Habakkuk, Jeremiah, and even Ezekiel, but they wouldn't listen either! So, God sent them into exile with the Babylonian Exile in 586 BC. In fact, in Micah, the last book of the Old Testament, God ends with these words of warning...

Malachi 4:5-6 "See, I will send you the prophet Elijah before that great and dreadful day of the Lord comes. He will turn the hearts of the fathers to their children, and the hearts of the children to their fathers; or else I will come and strike the land with a curse."

This was spoken about 430 BC and led to what was called the 400 years of Silence where God did not speak again to the Jewish people and basically closed up the Old Testament until John the Baptist shows up on the scene, ending the silence, as the forerunner to Jesus, preparing the people's hearts for the Messiah, thus fulfilling Micah's prophecy. Even though the Jewish people had periods of independence, they were still divided as a nation, until now! When the Jewish people regained independence in 1948, for the first time in 2,900 years, Israel was again united as a single nation, not two. Just like the Bible said would happen, when you're living in the Last Days! In fact, speaking of reuniting all the tribes of Israel, just recently the first batch of the members of a "lost tribe" of Israel arrived back in the Land![7]

They're called the Bnei (children) Menashe who are descendants of the tribe of Menashe (or Manasseh), and they are one of the Ten Lost Tribes of Israel which were exiled by the Assyrian empire some 2,700 years ago. They just came back from northeastern India from the state of Manipur, after receiving permission from the Israeli government to make Aliyah (or immigration). Thousands are already back in Israel with many thousands more to come and their Jewish brothers and sisters from the other tribes said, "Your arrival is part of the miracle, the miracle of Israel's return to its Land." Here's one news report:

CBN.COM Reports: *"For nearly 2700 years, a tribe called the Bnei Menashe inside India have kept their Jewish roots. Many believe they are the Lost Tribes* *of Israel. Now they are returning to their ancient homeland. As Chris Mitchell explains this return is also seen as Biblical Prophecy."*

Chris Mitchell: *"Brother found brother, family members of all ages recently reunited with family members at the Ben Gurion Airport. They are part of the Lost Tribe of Manasseh, called in Hebrew, Bnei Menashe, returning from India back to Israel. The term goes back to ancient times when 10 of Israel's 12 tribes were banished from the land. Michael Freund, from Shavel Israel has worked for years to bring about this moment. He believes that the Bnei Menashe return fulfills Biblical Prophecy."*

Michael Freund, Founder, Shavel Israel: *"We are watching as prophecy comes to life before our eyes. God remembers his promises to His people Israel. God is faithful. He is gathering His children in from all over the earth."*

Chris Mitchell: *"The Assyrian empire exiled the tribe almost 300 years ago. Although they settled in Northeast India, tribe members kept their Jewish roots for more than 2000 years."*

Zvi Hauteh, Bnei Menashe Coordinator: *"After two thousand seven hundred years of exile, Bnei Menashe is coming back. One of the Lost Tribes, Bnei Menashe has come back."*

Chris Mitchell: *"They are the latest Jews that the prophets foretold thousands of years ago, the ingathering of the exiles."*

David Parsons, ICEJ Media Director: *"We believe it is the hand of God. The Lord said He scattered the Jewish people, but He would never leave them scattered among the nations. He would always come and find them even if they were scattered to the ends of the earth and He said I am going to bring your sons from the East, in the Book of Isaiah. And these are certainly Jewish people, an ancient Israelite tribe that are coming home from the East."*

Michael Fruend: *"It's something that their ancestors dreamed about for two thousand seven hundred years and despite being cut off from the rest of the people of Israel for so long, the Bnei Menashe never forgot who they are. They never forgot where they came from. And they never forgot where they dreamed of one day returning. And now, thank God, they are back home."*

Chris Mitchell: *"Their arrival was tearful and emotional."*

One Bnei Menashe member: *"I feel like I'm home."*

Ephraim: Bnei Menashe member: *"I am extremely, it's unexplainable, deep in my heart I feel like crying."*

Michael Fruend: *"The prophet Isaiah says, 'fear not for I am with you' God says. 'From the east I will bring your descendants.' These are the descendants of Israel and they are coming back from the East. It's as if the headline of today was written by Isaiah the prophet."*

Chris Mitchell: *"The flight from India to Israel lasted only 7 hours but the arrival of the Bnei Menashe has been a journey that took nearly 3000 years in the making."*

Michael Freund: *"I think what is happening here today is nothing less than a miracle of Biblical and historic proportions."*[8]

Why? Because God's not done with the Jewish People! And isn't it interesting how even the non-Christian secular Jewish people recognize the prophetic importance of their becoming a united nation again, even with their Lost Tribes returning to them...just like God said He would. But for most of us we have no clue about the importance of what's going on here let alone how it proves just how close we really are to the end of times! Israel not only became a nation again, and not only in one day, but for the first time nearly 3,000 years, Israel is now a single united nation with all the tribes returning back to the land under one banner! That's exactly what the Bible said would happen when you're living in the Last Days! And yet, what's our attitude? We're either in one spectrum or the other! Either we've got our excitement in the wrong place because we've placed it in a Jewish Feast for a false teaching surrounding a date setting technique, which destroys imminency or encourages Replacement Theology or we could just flat out give a rip! "How's the economy doing? Who's going to win the playoffs? Hey, when does football start? Are we really going to listen to this every single week? I didn't come for this." And yet, Israel becoming a nation again, even in one day, as a single united nation, is one of the biggest watershed prophetic moments in history. As the gentlemen stated, *"This is the cornerstone prophetic event of our age."* Why? Because without these events taking place none of these future events could take place!

Until Israel becomes a Nation again….

- There can be No Peace Treaty with the Antichrist (Daniel 9)
- No Beginning of the 7-year Tribulation (Revelation 6)
- No 144,000 male Jewish Witnesses (Revelation 7&14)
- No Two Jewish Witnesses (Revelation 11)
- No Rebuilt Jewish Temple (Revelation 11)
- No Abomination of Desolation (Matthew 24)
- No Persecution by the Antichrist of 2/3rds Jews die (Zechariah 13)
- No Sovereign protection by Michael Archangel for Jews (Revelation 12)
- No Global Catastrophic Events (Revelation 6-19)
- No Second Coming of Jesus (Revelation 19)
- No Judging of the Antichrist & False Prophet (Revelation 19)
- No Separation of Sheep and Goats (Matthew 25)
- No Binding of Satan (Revelation 20)
- No Millennial Reign (Revelation 20)
- No Abrahamic & Davidic Covenants Upheld (Genesis 12&2 Samuel 7)
- No Judging of Satan (Revelation 20)
- No New Heavens & New Earth (Revelation 21)
- No Eternal State (Revelation 21)

But here's the point…. ALL THESE EVENTS can NOW TAKE PLACE since Israel has BECOME a NATION again!

That's what makes it so important and why you can get excited now about the Rapture because all those events happen after the Rapture takes place! It tells us the Rapture is getting close! I don't need a Jewish Feast for that. I don't need some generational calculation theory. I just need to know Israel is a nation again, in one day, and united, with the tribes coming back. WHOO HOO! I don't know the day nor the hour, but that's what tells me it's getting close! And this is why, out of love, God has given us this update on *The Final Countdown: Tribulation Rising* concerning the *Jewish People & the Antichrist* to show us that the 7-year Tribulation is near, and the Return of Jesus Christ is rapidly approaching. And that's why Jesus Himself said…

Luke 21:28 "When these things begin to take place, stand up and lift up your heads, because your redemption is drawing near."

Like it or not, we are headed for *The Final Countdown*. The signs of the 7-year Tribulation are rising all around us! It's time to WAKE UP! And so, the point is this. If you're reading this today and you're not a Christian, then I beg you, please, heed these signs, heed these warnings, give your life to Jesus now! You don't want to be here when God pours out His Judgment upon the nations. It's the worst time in the history of mankind, so horrible that unless God shortened the timeframe the entire human race would be destroyed! The only way to escape is through Jesus! Take the way out now before it's too late. Get saved today! BUT…if you're reading this today and you are a Christian, then it's high time we stop goofing off and being so disinterested and distracted and get busy working together sharing the Gospel with as many as we can! Let's leave here being that faithful excited Bride of Christ longing for His return occupying our minds until He comes! Amen?

Chapter Five

The Jewish People &Their Capitol, Currency, & Language

We've already seen the **first four** future prophecies concerning the Jewish People, letting us know we're living in the Last Days, was that **Israel would return to the land, Israel would become a nation again**, Israel would become **a nation again in one day,** and Israel would become a **United Nation again!**

Even the so-called lost tribes, as we saw, aren't lost anymore. Even they are coming back to the land. And all these events have taken place in our lifetime showing us we're living in the Last Days! For the first time in nearly 3,000 years, Israel is a single united nation with all the tribes coming back to the land under one banner! Why? Because God is getting ready to deal with His Wife again, Israel, which means, the Church, the Bride of Christ, could leave here at any moment at the Rapture! That's our action point with this prophetic information! But that's not all.

The **5th End Time Prophecy** concerning **The Jewish People** letting us know we're living in the Last Days is that **Israel would recapture Jerusalem again.**

This is important because from God's viewpoint, Jerusalem is basically the center of the earth! I mean, think about it! This is where the line of the Messiah started! King David ruled from there. This is where Jesus (the actual Messiah) died on a cross. This is where the End Times culminate with the Battle of Armageddon outside of Jerusalem. This is where Jesus returns at His 2nd Coming, and this is where Jesus reigns after His 2nd Coming. It's all in Jerusalem! But the problem is, when the Jewish people came back to the land again and even became a nation again, they didn't control Jerusalem, until now! Exactly like the Bible said they would, one day they would take it back! But don't take my word for it. Let's listen to God's.

Zechariah 8:4-8 "This is what the LORD Almighty says: 'Once again men and women of ripe old age will sit in the streets of Jerusalem, each with cane in hand because of his age. The city streets will be filled with boys and girls playing there.' This is what the LORD Almighty says: 'It may seem marvelous to the remnant of this people at that time, but will it seem marvelous to Me?' declares the LORD Almighty. This is what the LORD Almighty says: 'I will save My people from the countries of the east and the west. I will bring them back to live in Jerusalem; they will be My people, and I will be faithful and righteous to them as their God."

So here we see clearly that in the Last Days that God will not only bring the Jewish People back into the land again, but they will specifically be living in Jerusalem, dancing, singing, playing, living to a ripe old age. But again, the problem was when they first came back to the land, they didn't control Jerusalem. In fact, the Jewish People had not been in control of Jerusalem even before 70 A.D. when their Temple was destroyed by the Romans and they were dispersed. And even when they came back to the land it was still under foreign control. For instance, the West Bank and eastern Jerusalem was at that time in Jordanian hands and they were not only violating agreements they made with the Jews, but they were even denying them access to their holiest places in eastern Jerusalem, and on top of that they were desecrating and destroying many of those holy sites. Then the Gaza Strip was under Egyptian control, with harsh military rule being imposed on the local residents. The Golan Heights were regularly being used to shell Israeli communities far below, and it belonged to Syria. And then on top of that, the Arab world, who had no right to the land, being descendants of Ishmael, not Isaac, like the Jewish People, they continued to refuse Israel the right to even exist.

Around this time the (PLO) or the Palestinian Liberation Organization, which supported war against Israel, was established with the goal of obliterating Israel. Egypt's President at that time, Gamal Abdel Nasser, demanded that the UN peacekeeping forces in the area be removed. And shamefully, without even consulting Israel, the UN complied, which left no buffer between the Arab armies and Israel. Then Egypt blocked Israel's shipping lanes in the Red Sea, which was their only maritime access to the trade routes with Asia and Africa. Even the U.S. spoke out at that time about breaking the blockade, but we didn't act. At that point, France got in on the action, who was Israel's principal arms supplier at the time, they announced a ban on the sale of weapons for Israel. And furthermore, just 22 years after the holocaust, the Egyptian and Syrian leaders repeatedly declared that war was coming and that their objective was to totally wipe Israel off the map. They wanted an extermination of Jews, and still do to this day, which is well-documented fact and Lord willing we'll get into that in another study. But here's my point. When you put all this together, you begin to see that the Jewish People were just fighting to stay alive in the land, let alone thinking about ever getting Jerusalem again! But all that changed in June of 1967 and the Six Day war. War broke out, and out of survival, the Jewish People fought back, and against all odds, they totally annihilated the Arab armies coming against them! Jewish commandos advanced to the southern end of the old walled city of Jerusalem and under heavy fire they broke into the city through the Lion's Gate. And for the first time in nearly 2,500 years, the Jewish People were in control of Jerusalem, just like God said would happen in the Last Days! In fact, here's a transcript of some original video footage of that event.

The 700 Club reports: "June 7th, just 2 days after the war, Israel had already pushed deep into Egypt, had pushed Jordan out of much of the West Bank and pummeled Syria with artillery fire. On the Sinai Peninsula, Israel surrounded the Egyptian army and the rout of Egypt was well under way. In fact, Egypt's retreat was so chaotic that Israel's advance was slowed by all the Egyptian vehicles.

The same day, Israel's navy reached Sharm El Sheikh to reopen the strategic Straits of Tiran. On the West Bank, Israel's military victories forced Jordan to declare a cease fire and withdraw completely from the Biblical lands of Judea and Samaria. Israel now had control of cities rooted in Jewish history, such as Hebron, Jericho, and Bethlehem. Now on day 3, Israel's leaders were poised to do the unthinkable.

To recapture Jerusalem and bring the city back under Jewish control after nearly 2500 years. One day earlier, Israel's 55th Paratrooper Brigade had fought its way to the walls of Jerusalem's old city. Now at sunrise of June 7th, Israel's military command ordered the paratroopers to take the city. They advanced through the Lions Gate and experienced house to house combat along the way.

*That morning, soldiers reached the Western Wall of the Temple Mount, the
holiest place in Judaism. In nearly 20 years of Jordanian rule, no Jew had been
allowed in the area. Military leaders, Moshe Dayan and Yitzhak Rabin arrived at
the wall where many of the paratroopers wept for their fallen comrades. Rabbi
Goren blew the shofar and Israel reclaimed its heritage in the ancient city. It was
one of the most joyful moments in Jewish history.*

*General Moshe Dayan later ruled that Muslims could keep control of the Temple
Mount, the site of the Al-Aqsa mosque and the Dome of the Rock. His decision
angered many Jews who had been denied access to their Holy places for so
long.*"[1]

Which just so happens to be a problem we're still dealing with today. But
as you can see, against all odds, and with virtually no support from other
countries, Israel once again occupied Jerusalem. So, you might be thinking,
"Okay so what? So, they're in Jerusalem. What's the big deal? What's that got to
do with me today?" Well, believe it or not, the Jews being in Jerusalem, has
everything to do with your future! Let's look at the Biblical importance of
Jerusalem and why it's such a watershed prophetic event.

- The first mention of Jerusalem in the Bible is found in (Genesis 14:18) where
  we are told that Abraham paid tithes to the King of Salem, Melchizedek.
  Salem is the root word of the city's later name, Jerusalem.
- Later, we are told that Abraham went to Mt. Moriah, just north of ancient
  Jerusalem, to offer his son, Isaac, as a sacrifice (Genesis 22:2). That mountain
  was later incorporated into the city of Jerusalem during the time of Solomon,
  becoming the Temple Mount.
- The first mention of the city by the name of Jerusalem is found in Joshua
  10:1 where a coalition of kings came against Joshua and were defeated.
- Two centuries later David conquered it and made it the capital of the Jewish
  nation. (2 Samuel 5)
- After he conquered it, Jerusalem was often referred to as "the city of
  David" (2 Samuel 5).
- This occurred 1,000 years before the birth of Jesus — or some 3,000 years
  from where we stand now in human history.
- On September 25th, 1995, the government of Israel celebrated the 3,000th
  anniversary of the conquest of the city of Jerusalem by King David.

- This is why no other city on the face of the earth as important as the city of Jerusalem. All the other great cities of the earth — New York, London, Moscow, Paris, and even Rome — pale by comparison.
- What other city can claim to be "the city of God" or "the city of the Great King"? (Psalm 48).
- God loves Jerusalem, has desired the mountain of Zion "for His abode" and that He intends to "dwell there forever." (Psalms 68 & Psalm 132)
- Jerusalem is identified as "the center of the nations" (Ezekiel 5) and as "the center of the world." (Ezekiel 38)
- Jerusalem is where the Son of God shed His precious blood.
- It is where Jesus ascended into Heaven.
- And it is where He prophesied about the future of Jerusalem. Pointing at Jerusalem and its temple: "As for these things which you are looking at, the days will come in which there will not be left one stone upon another which will not be torn down" (Luke 21:6).
- This prophecy was fulfilled later when the Romans, under Titus, completely destroyed the city, including the Temple.
- Later, in the same discourse, Jesus stated that "Jerusalem will be trampled underfoot by the Gentiles until the times of the Gentiles be fulfilled" (Luke 21:24).
- The Romans were followed by the Byzantines, and they were succeeded, in order, by the Muslims, the Crusaders, the Mamelukes, the Turks, the British, and the Jordanians.
- Just as Jesus prophesied, the city suffered under a long period of Gentile control until June 7, 1967 when — for the first time in 1,897 years — the Jews regained sovereignty over the city. It was on that day that Rabbi Shlomo Goren went to the Western Wall and cried out: "I proclaim to you the beginning of the Messianic Age."
- In other words, now the future events concerning Jerusalem can take place!
- Jerusalem will be the scene of history's last battle when satan rallies the nations at the end of the Millennium and leads them in revolt against the Lord.
- Jerusalem is where Jesus will return to be crowned King of Kings.
- When Jesus returns, He is going to reign over all the world for a thousand years, and His reign of peace, righteousness and justice will be based in Jerusalem: (Isaiah 2)
- Jerusalem will be the political, economic and religious center of the world. (Micah 4).

- The city will be very different from the one we know today. A great worldwide earthquake will occur when Jesus returns that will radically change the earth's topography, including that of Jerusalem (Isaiah 40).
- The Bible indicates that Jerusalem will be greatly expanded in area and will be lifted up higher, perhaps becoming the highest point on the earth (Zechariah 14).
- The city will be considerably enlarged and greatly beautified, and the most magnificent temple in history will be built in the midst of it under the personal supervision of the Messiah. (Ezekiel 40-48).
- Jerusalem in those days will be as glorious as "a crown of beauty in the hand of the Lord" "a praise in the earth" and for the first time in its long bloody history, it will be a refuge of peace (Isaiah 62, Joel 3, Zephaniah 3)
- It will be the greatest wonder on the earth. It will house the Prince of Peace and will contain His temple. It will serve once more as the home of God's spectacular Shekinah glory. But that glory will not be contained within the Holy of Holies. Incredibly, Isaiah says that the Shekinah will hover over the whole city of Jerusalem as a cloud by day and a fire by night, providing a canopy to protect the city from heat and rain (Isaiah 4).
- Zechariah says the nations of the world will send delegations to Jerusalem each year and Ezekiel says that the name of the city will be changed to "The Lord is there."
- Then at the end of the Millennium, after the earth has been renovated by fire, the new Jerusalem will be lowered down to the new earth, and the Redeemed, in their new glorified bodies, will live in this new city in the presence of Almighty God, who will come down from Heaven to live forever with His children (Revelation 21).
- It will be a 1,500-mile cube with 12 foundations made of precious stones — each one named for one of the 12 apostles. Likewise, there will be 12 pearly gates, one named for each tribe of Israel. The walls will be made of jasper. The city itself will be pure gold, like clear glass.
- And it has been calculated that the space available for each person will be, assuming at least 50% of the area would be used for common purposes (streets, parks, recreation centers, etc.) and assuming that 20 billion people have been saved in the course of human history, that each person would have a cube with 75 acres on each surface! Much more than we have now.
- But the best part of this city will not be its beauty or its spaciousness, it will be the personal presence of our Lord Jesus and Almighty God, the Father. Revelation 22 says we will eternally serve God in this city and that we

will "see His face," meaning we will have an intimate, personal fellowship with our Creator eternally, which should cause us to stand in awe.

- And that's why we should pray for the peace of Jerusalem (Psalm 122:6), ✶ because in doing so we are really praying for the return of the Lord, because Jerusalem will never experience true peace until the Prince of Peace returns.[2]

Let alone all those events we just saw concerning Jerusalem in the future. This is why it's a big deal that the Jewish People have recaptured Jerusalem. None of the future events can take place until the Jewish people once again are in complete control. And guess what? They are now! Which means all of these events have been given a green light, by God, to go ahead once the Rapture happens. And that can happen at any moment! It's all part of His way of saying, you're living in the Last Days!

The **6th End Time Prophecy** concerning **The Jewish People,** letting us know we're living in the Last Days, is that **Israel's currency would become the Shekel.**

Ezekiel 45:12,13,16 "The standard unit for weight will be the silver shekel. This is the tax you must give to the prince. All the people of Israel must join the prince in bringing their offerings."

Here we see how the Bible clearly predicted that in future temple sacrifices, the people of Israel would not just be paying their taxes, but specifically paying them in what? In shekels, right? But the problem is that Israel's currency wasn't the shekel, but the British pound. That is, until 1980,

when it just so happened it was changed to the shekel. They use it to this very day. The Israeli pound was the currency of the State of Israel from June 1952 until February 23, 1980, when it was replaced with the shekel on February 24, 1980. So after nearly 2,000 years, the shekel has been reinstated as the common currency in Israel again, just like the Bible said would happen in the Last Days! It's not just being used again as their common currency, but it's being used again for sanctuary Temple purposes just like Ezekiel prophesied. In fact, they just produced a new silver half-shekel for

Temple purposes with our President's head on it! This is wild! I bought the actual coin. Here's a close-up shot of the coin.

They did that in honor of President Trump's general support of Israel and for his recent recognizing of Jerusalem as the capital of Israel. In fact, this coin was purchased from the Mikdash (Temple) Educational Center in Israel. The Temple Movement and Jewish Sanhedrin issues this Half-Shekel Coin with the profile of Trump and Cyrus. The Torah mandates every Jewish male must donate to the Temple, this coin having the weight of 9.5 grams in real silver. On the face of the coin is a picture of the Temple with the inscription "Half Shekel." On the other side is the figure of US President Donald Trump, alongside Cyrus, King of Persia, who made the building of the Second Temple possible. The producers of the coin say that it is in high demand and Prof. Hillel Weiss, Chairman of the organization, says that the motivation to embed the image of the President of the United States on the coin is gratitude for his support of Israel and especially for the recognition of our sovereignty over Jerusalem.

"This is a historic act for which the Jewish people are grateful," says Weiss, who believes that the declaration sets off a process which allows the Temple to be rebuilt."

"The Trump Declaration must continue, with a declaration of the role of the Jews, in establishing the Temple in its place. Only then will President Trump's international ambitions come true in the Middle East."

"Trump's political agenda can only succeed if it is focused on building the Third Temple on the place that God chose: the Temple Mount. He must not advance any two-state solution, or this will lead to his downfall.

Trumps goals will come to fruition only if they're geared towards rebuilding the Jewish Temple." "This coin shows that President Trump is a positive part of the Temple process reminding us of what the Jews need to do."[3]

WOW! So once again, a warning against dividing the land and the question is, "Is Trump really going to a part of building The Third Jewish Temple?" I don't know. But what we do know is that temple will be the actual Temple that the antichrist goes into to declare himself to be god.

2 Thessalonians 2:3-4 "Don't let anyone deceive you in any way, for that day will not come until the rebellion occurs and the man of lawlessness is revealed, the man doomed to destruction. He will oppose and will exalt himself over everything that is called God or is worshiped, so that he sets himself up in God's temple, proclaiming himself to be God."

Halfway into the 7-year Tribulation, the antichrist will go up into this rebuilt Jewish Temple and declare himself to be God! They go on about the silver half-shekel:

"Anyone who owns this coin is showing that he agrees with our gratitude for what Trump has done and the reminder that Jerusalem is the place of the Jewish Temple...and what still needs to be done." I.E. to build it.

And of course, when I bought the coin my wife was faithful enough to point out how I just helped financially to build the Temple for the Antichrist! Which is apparently why I should have read the fine print. They go on to say...

"This coin is intended to help in preparations for the Temple and anyone can take part in that at any time. Proceeds from the sale of the coin will be used in reenactments of Temple services as well as in other educational and practical endeavors that help prepare for the Third Temple. Should the need arise, the proceeds will be used for the actual building of the Temple."

In other words, my wife was right! Go figure! But apparently, I'm not the only one doing what it takes to get the temple ready for the antichrist, making coins or whatever. So are the Jewish People in general. They are itching to build that Third Temple now! Here's just one of many commercials they keep pumping out to encourage the people to build that Temple now!

"An old Rabbi sits down on the park bench. He is holding a black book. He sits silently for a few minutes then he opens the book. It is the Torah. He reads a while then looks over at some boys that are playing ball a few yards from his park bench.

He then turns to his other side and sees young people sitting in the grass with musical instruments playing and singing. A little way from there is another group of young men talking and laughing. Suddenly the boys stop playing ball and look across the city. Pointing at something that is going on. Then the music stops. They too are looking at something that is happening. They are also pointing to show the others they need to look also.

They jump up and run over to where the other boys are to get a better look. As they pass by the guys talking, they tap them on the shoulder to show them what is going on. They also run over to get a better look. The old man keeps reading as a crowd starts to gather looking at what is going on in the city. When he finally looks up, he sees they are all standing in front of him. Looking at him.

One holds out his hand to help the old man stand up. They lead him over to see what they have been looking at. He gets a big smile on his face as he sees it. It is the new Third Temple. It is being built on the Temple Mount. It is a beautiful sight."

This is the generation. The children are ready.
The Temple Institute Productions.[4]

And again, this coin, the silver half shekel that was just minted, is for, *"Practicing procedures for the sacrificial rituals, preparing spiritually, ritually, and educationally for the Temple services, and for building the Temple."* And, *"It is our prayer that this coin will be used in a new era in the land of Israel, when the Temple will be rebuilt."*

Folks, we better wake up! We are living in the Last Days and it's time to get motivated! The Shekel is back on the scene after nearly 2,000 years and it's not only being used as common currency, but for the Jewish Temple. Exactly like God said would happen in the Last Days!

The **7th End Time Prophecy** concerning **The Jewish People** letting us know we're living in the Last Days is that **Israel's language would become Hebrew again.**

Zephaniah 3:9 "For then I will restore to the peoples a pure language, that they all may call on the name of the Lord, to serve Him with one accord."

So here we see that in the Last Days God clearly said He would even restore the original Hebrew language for the people to speak with, serve Him with, and be unified in. Can anybody guess what has happened right before our eyes? The Hebrew language has literally been revived from the dead and is now the official language of the state. It didn't used to be this way. When the Jews were scattered worldwide in the first century, they ceased speaking the Hebrew language. The Jews who settled in Europe developed a language called Yiddish (a combination of Hebrew and German). The Jews in the Mediterranean area mixed Hebrew with Spanish to produce a language called Ladino. Still other Jews spoke Arabic, Spanish and even Russian—but not Hebrew. Hebrew became confined to the synagogues where it was used for the Torah readings and by the beginning of the 20th Century, most Jews could not understand the Torah readings. It was like going to a Catholic mass when they read it in Latin. But all this was to change miraculously, just like the prophet Zephaniah prophesied, that a time would come when the Hebrew language would be revived from the dead and Israel would once again speak it. The significance is, this is the only example in world history where an ancient language was revived as the spoken language of a modern nation. It's been called, "A unique historical phenomenon." The man God used to revive the Hebrew language from the dead was a guy named Eliezer Ben Yehuda (1858-1922).

As a teenager, he got involved in what was called, "The Jewish Enlightenment Movement" and fell in love with the Hebrew language as a living language. And he said, "This love for Hebrew was a great and all-consuming fire that the torrent of life could not extinguish." So, he began going about encouraging the Jewish People to relearn Hebrew. And believe it or not, he faced major opposition from his own people.

It was the attitude at that time that the Hebrew language was not to be used for everyday conversation, it was considered holy, and even if you wanted to, there wasn't sufficient words to carry on a modern-day conversation. In fact, they even made statements like this, "Hebrew's time has passed, and it no longer has a purpose or task in Jewish life."

But, Ben-Yehuda was determined, and he stated, "I have decided that in order to have our own land and political life, it is also necessary that we have a language to hold us together. We must have a Hebrew language in which we can conduct the business of life. It will not be easy to revive a language dead for so long a time."

And so, he began implementing a plan.

- Encourage the speaking of Hebrew in each home.
- Establish a newspaper and work through it to report the news in Hebrew, creating new words as needed.

- Do everything possible to introduce the teaching and speaking of Hebrew into the schools.
- Produce a dictionary of the Hebrew language to aid in its daily utilization.[5]

His work paid off, by 1921, just a year before he died, the British government recognized the official language of Hebrew and postage stamps were issued in Hebrew for the first time ever, everywhere in the world. And on December 14, 1922 he had just finished working on the Hebrew word nefesh," meaning "soul" or "spirit" and the next day was Friday, Sabbath eve, he started to feel ill, and so he laid down on a sofa to rest, and his wife sent word for doctors. Before long he drifted into a coma, and then suddenly he raised up on an elbow, looked around the room and said, "Speak Hebrew!" Those were his last words and he died at 64 years old. As of 2013, there were about 9 million Hebrew speakers worldwide, of whom 7 million spoke it fluently, which is exactly what God said would happen when you are living in the Last Days. No other language has come back from the dead, but the Hebrew language has. It's just another long string of supernatural events concerning the Jewish People, like this video transcript shares.

"Three years after the Holocaust, three years after 70% of the Jews were destroyed, which was the largest slaughter of any people in human history, the remnant trickled back against the will of the British. With no support from the world, not a desert piece of real estate, with no natural resources, no infrastructure, surrounded by millions of hostile Arabs, with constant warfare, terrorism, and economic blockade.

Think about it, in a few years the desert exported fruits and vegetables to the rest of the world. Israel is the only country in the world with more trees at the end of the 20th Century than at the beginning. In terms of hi-tech per capita the most in the world is in Israel. Since 1948, with no natural resources, constant war, terrorism, economic blockade. The prophets told us that the Hebrew language would be revived...."

Zephania 3:9: "a pure language, that they may all call upon the name of Hashem..."

"When was the last time you saw an English-Phoenician dictionary? Probably not in a while because Phoenician is a dead language. You know the language they speak in Latin America? It's not Latin because Latin, too, is a dead

language. Never before in world history has a dead language been revived and brought back to life before the return of the Jewish people to the land of Israel and the revival of the Hebrew language."

Hebrew was always preserved in Davidic writing and used in the prayer service, but it was not the language that people spoke."

"We have nearly 6,000.000 people today who speak the language that no one spoke 100 years ago. It is resurrected like the Jewish people to their homeland."

"It's unbelievable but people just don't see it. They have gotten used to it. It's Jewish history, it all supernatural.[6]

And boy, that's the problem, isn't it? All these prophetic events concerning the Jewish People are unfolding before our very eyes, the recapturing of Jerusalem, the return to the Shekel, the rebirth of the Hebrew Language. And what's our attitude? Oh well, who cares, hey what time does the game start? It's almost like we're reading this headline and it doesn't even phase us. What if that appeared in the news this morning? Are you ready? Does this information excite you or bore you? Because that's all this information is doing, is letting you know Jesus is coming soon! And if that bores you, you need to ask yourself, why aren't you longing for His appearing like a real bride would and should? I didn't say that God did.

2 Timothy 4:8 "Now there is in store for me the crown of righteousness, which the Lord, the righteous Judge, will award to me on that day – and not only to me, but also to all who have longed for His appearing."

Normal brides are excited about the news of their wedding day and they get even more excited about it as the day approaches. So, if you're not excited about this information that is simply declaring that the Bridegroom cometh, your wedding day is approaching, could it be it's because you really love something else and/or maybe you're not really His Bride after all? Is that a chance you want to take? This is why, out of love, God has given us this update on *The Final Countdown: Tribulation Rising* concerning the *Jewish People & the Antichrist* to show us that the 7-year Tribulation is near, and the return of Jesus Christ is rapidly approaching. And that's why Jesus Himself said…

Luke 21:28 "When these things begin to take place, stand up and lift up your heads, because your redemption is drawing near."

Like it or not, we are headed for *The Final Countdown*. The signs of the 7-year Tribulation are rising all around us! It's time to wake up! The point is this. If you're reading this today and you're not a Christian, then I beg you, please, heed these signs, heed these warnings, give your life to Jesus now! You don't want to be here when God pours out His judgment upon the nations. It's the worst time in the history of mankind, so horrible that unless God shortened the timeframe the entire human race would be destroyed! The only way to escape is through Jesus! Take the way out now before it's too late. Get saved today! But, if you're reading this today and you are a Christian, then it's high time we stop goofing off and being so disinterested and distracted and get busy working together sharing the Gospel with as many as we can! Let's leave here being that faithful, excited, bride, longing for His return! Amen?

Chapter Six

The Jewish People & Their Renewal of the Land

The **8ᵗʰ End Time Prophecy** concerning **The Jewish People** letting us know we're living in the Last Days is that **Israel would blossom as a Rose in the Desert**. But don't take my word for it. Let's listen to God's.

Isaiah 35:1-2 "The desert and the parched land will be glad; the wilderness will rejoice and blossom. Like the crocus, it will burst into bloom; it will rejoice greatly and shout for joy. The glory of Lebanon will be given to it, the splendor of Carmel and Sharon; they will see the glory of the Lord, the splendor of our God."

So here we see God clearly says in the Last Days that the desert and parched land of Israel will be transformed into a beautiful, splendid environment where the flowers will blossom & flourish even in the wilderness areas. In fact, some translations speak of this supernatural beautification of the land of Israel from God with these words…

"The wilderness will rejoice in those days. The desert will blossom with flowers. Yes, there will be an abundance of flowers and singing and joy! The deserts will become as green as the mountains of Lebanon, as lovely as Mount Carmel's pastures and the plain of Sharon."

Clearly, the deserts of Israel will be transformed into a beautiful garden-like environment in the Last Days. In fact, Isaiah, is not the only one who talks about this amazing transformation. So, does Joel and Ezekiel.

Joel 2:21-24 "Be not afraid, O land; be glad and rejoice. Surely the LORD has done great things. Be not afraid, O wild animals, for the open pastures are becoming green. The trees are bearing their fruit; the fig tree and the vine yield their riches. Be glad, O people of Zion, rejoice in the LORD your God, for he has given you the autumn rains in righteousness. He sends you abundant showers, both autumn and spring rains, as before. The threshing floors will be filled with grain; the vats will overflow with new wine and oil."

Ezekiel 36:33-36 "This is what the Sovereign LORD says: On the day I cleanse you from all your sins, I will resettle your towns, and the ruins will be rebuilt. The desolate land will be cultivated instead of lying desolate in the sight of all who pass through it. They will say, 'This land that was laid waste has become like the garden of Eden; the cities that were lying in ruins, desolate and destroyed, are now fortified and inhabited.' Then the nations around you that remain will know that I the LORD have rebuilt what was destroyed and have replanted what was desolate. I the LORD have spoken, and I will do it."

And boy, did He ever! Now, to understand the significance of these prophecies you have to first understand the history and characteristics of the land of Israel. From the very beginning, that land that was promised to the Israelites was totally different from the land they came from. Think about it. They came out of Egypt and the desert to the what? "The Promised Land." And this "Promised Land" was a good land. In fact, it was called "a good land" 16 times in the Old Testament, and "a land flowing with milk and honey" 23 times in the Old Testament. There was something special about that land. And even up to the time of Josephus, a 1st Century Jewish historian, he mentioned how the land was still very prosperous and fertile. Here's what he said:

"For the whole area is excellent for crops and pasturage and rich in trees of every kind, so that by its fertility it invites even those least inclined to work on the land. In fact, every inch of it has been cultivated by the inhabitants and not a parcel goes to waste. It is thickly covered with towns, and thanks to the natural abundance of the soil, the many villages are so densely populated."[1]

Now here's the point. All that changed after nearly 2,000 years of foreign conquerors totally abusing the land. They left it a total complete wasteland. And many prophecy teachers believe it was in response to the Jewish People's disobedience toward God's conditional Mosaic covenant and thus the prophecy and warning of Moses came into play.

Deuteronomy 29:22-28 "Your children who follow you in later generations and foreigners who come from distant lands will see the calamities that have fallen on the land and the diseases with which the LORD has afflicted it. The whole land will be a burning waste of salt and sulfur-nothing planted, nothing sprouting, no vegetation growing on it. It will be like the destruction of Sodom and Gomorrah, Admah and Zeboiim, which the LORD overthrew in fierce anger. All the nations will ask: 'Why has the LORD done this to this land? Why this fierce, burning anger?' And the answer will be: 'It is because this people abandoned the covenant of the LORD, the God of their fathers, the covenant He made with them when He brought them out of Egypt. They went off and worshiped other gods and bowed down to them, gods they did not know, gods He had not given them. Therefore, the LORD's anger burned against this land, so that He brought on it all the curses written in this book. In furious anger and in great wrath the LORD uprooted them from their land and thrust them into another land, as it is now.'"

Until the Last days when the unconditional covenants kicked in and God had mercy on their disobedience and brought them back into the land again and began to reverse the curse, because He's not done with them. But before that time, the conditions of the land were just like a curse, just like God said. Let's listen to some of the people who visited Israel prior to 1948.

- After the scattering of the Jews beginning in 70 A.D. with the destruction of the Temple, the land became utterly desolate, unable to grow much of anything. During nearly 2,000 years of Israel's exile from its land, numerous empires had conquered the Land and countless wars were fought for its possession. And yet, amazingly, no conqueror ever succeeded in permanently settling the land and neither were they able to cause it to bloom again. It was in a horrible state.
- In 1845 Alfon Lamartine in his book, "Recollections from the East" said that, "Outside the walls of Jerusalem we saw no living being, heard no living voice. We encountered that desolation and that deadly silence which we

would have expected to find at the ruined gates of Pompeii. A total eternal dread spell enveloped the city, the highways and the villages."

- In 1855 an American medical doctor, Jonathan Miesse, traveled to the Holy Land and published his recollections in a book titled "A Journey to Egypt and Palestine." (Israel had been renamed Palestine by the Romans and was still called by that name in the 19th Century). Here's what he said, "At present, nearly three thousand years after David, the country is a prey to the wild beasts, and to the wilder Bedouins."

- In 1867 the American journalist Mark Twain made a trip to the area and he published a book about his impressions in 1869 called "The Innocents Abroad." This was the book that made Mark Twain famous. In it he described the area as, "A blistering, naked, treeless land." He said, "The further we went the hotter the sun got and the more rocky, bare, repulsive and dreary the landscape had become." He spoke of the villages as, "Ugly, cramped, squalid, uncomfortable and filthy." He then added that the villages are, "A solitude to make one dreary, unpeopled desert, rusty mounds of barrenness." And then he looked towards the Judean hills in Israel and wrote, "Close to us was a stream and on its banks a great herd of curious looking sheep and the sheep were gratefully eating gravel. I do not state this as a petrified fact – I only suppose they were eating gravel because there did not appear to be anything else for them to eat." Then regarding the Sea of Galilee area, he wrote, "There is not a solitary village. There are two or three small clusters of Bedouin tents, but not a single permanent habitation. One may ride ten miles, hereabouts, and not see ten human beings." Concerning the Valley of Armageddon Mark Twain observed, "A desolation is here that not even imagination can grace with the pomp of life and action." He then described the central highlands of Samaria by saying, "There was hardly a tree or a shrub anywhere. Even the olive and the cactus, those fast friends of a worthless soil, had almost deserted the country." "No landscape exists that is more tiresome to the eye than that which bounds the approaches to Jerusalem." His summary of the land was a dismal one. "It truly is monotonous and uninviting. It is a hopeless, dreary, heart-broken land." "Palestine sits in sackcloth and ashes and why should it be otherwise?" "No man can stand here [in this deserted area] and say that prophecy has not been fulfilled."

- In 1884 another American tourist, Henry M. Field, published a book about his trip to the area and in it he wrote about the treeless, desolate landscape as follows. "The country seemed deserted of human habitations. Its appearance was made still more desolate by being without trees. While riding among the hills, I did not see a single tree. Whether this be owing to the government tax on trees, or the wastefulness of the people in cutting for fuel every young tree almost as soon as it shows its head above the ground, I know not; I only state the fact, that the landscape was absolutely treeless."

- Then in 1905, the Prime Minister of the Netherlands observed, "The Jews have come in vain. Only God can check the blight of the inrushing desert."
- In 1912 a British traveler by the name of Sir Frederick Treves, published a book appropriately titled, "The Land That Is Desolate" and he described the approach to Jerusalem, "The area is practically treeless. Such hedges as exist are mostly of prickly cactus. The villages passed are secretive-looking clumps of flat-topped huts made, it would seem, of a chocolate-colored mud and decorated with litter and refuse." Surrounding the area of Jerusalem, he observed that, "The hills are bare save for some hectic grass and starveling scrub." As for Jerusalem itself he wrote, "The city itself is as the shadow of a rock in a weary land. With the exception of a few pallid olive trees, a patch here and there of indefinite green, and a melancholy cypress, the environs of Jerusalem are a dusty, ungenial limestone waste." He then described Bethlehem as, "A drab city of drab houses on a drab ridge, as monotonous in color and as cheerless looking as a pile of dry bones." And even Nazareth he said was, "A sorry country, for the land is bare, harsh, and treeless. Here is assuredly to be seen the poverty of the earth." And regarding Galilee he described it as, "Abandoned" and Tiberias was, "A wholly dirty town" and "A wretched and stinking place" with "sturdy vermin."
- In 1924 Israel was still being described as "a barren, rocky and forbidding land" by Oliver C. Dalby in his booklet, "Rambles in Scriptural Lands." He characterized Jerusalem as a place where the streets were "narrow and dirty," and where "the buildings are austere and unattractive." "As Jeremiah prophesied, the land became 'a haunt of jackals' and 'a heap of ruins.'"[2]

How many of you would say they were clearly not excelling in the Tourism Industry at that time? Yeah, clearly you didn't want to go there, it was under a curse! Then on top of that, because of these conditions, rainfall had diminished, and with all the trees cut down, top soil eroded and excessive sedimentation in the valleys resulted in water-logging and the creation of swamps. With swamps came an outbreak of malaria which weakened the population and led to the abandonment of villages and formerly cultivated land. The land became repugnant and during the years the Jews were exiled from it, no one really desired it. It became a deserted wasteland and an incubator of disease. In fact, by the beginning of the 19th Century, it was a place people avoided, except for the most fanatical pilgrims, like the Russians who would walk all the way to the Holy Land and die there. But when the Jewish People began to return to the land, everything changed! No foreign conqueror was able to make Israel bloom again no matter how hard they tried. And frankly the foreign conquerors had no respect for the land, no concern for it, no love for it, no wonder it wasn't going to respond. But when the Jewish People came back, they loved the land and they began to immediately work at getting the land back into shape! For them, and them alone, the land began to respond! In fact, when the Jews first began to go back in the early 1900's, the Arabs laughed at them for buying the land. "Who, but a crazy Jew, would want malaria infested swampland?" And of course, today, guess what, the Arabs want the land back because God touched it and has made it beautiful once again, just like He promised He would for the Jewish People, like this:

Gordon Robertson reports: *"In 1867 Mark Twain toured the land of Israel. Known back then as Palestine. Here is how he described it.*

'A desolate country whose soil is rich enough but is given solely to weeds. A silent mournful expanse. There was hardly a tree or a shrub anywhere. Palestine sits in sackcloth and ashes. Desolate and unlovely.' Today Mark Twain wouldn't even recognize this land. Out of rocky soil, out of swamps, even out of deserts. The Israeli's have created gardens, vineyards, and farms with some of the most innovative techniques in the world.

Before Israel even became a state, Jews by the thousands came to live there on communal farms. But when they arrived in the promise land it wasn't exactly flowing with milk and honey. The Coastal Plains were swampy. The Galilean and the Judean Hills were rocky, and the southern half of the country was mostly desert.

Itzhik Moshe, Southern Director Jewish National Fund: *"Since the people of Israel left our homeland over 2000 years ago the area was mismanaged. So, we want to reserve and rehabilitate this holy land."*

Gordon Robertson: *"The early Jewish settlers faced a number of obstacles from bad soil to Bedouin raiders, but they faced an even bigger enemy that threatened to destroy the Jewish state before it even began.*

In the early decades of the 20th century, Israel was a breeding ground for mosquitoes carrying malaria. They overtook the Coastal Plains of the Jordan

Valley, the only land available for Jews to buy since the local Arabs decided that it was inhabitable. In 1920 more than a third of the Jewish residents in Palestine had malaria.

So, with no other choice they went to work. They drained the swamp and sprayed the land and changed the flow of water in irrigation canals to interrupt the mosquitoes breeding. They were so successful that the commission from the League of Nations visited Palestine to learn what they did.

Less than 20 years after Israel's official statehood, Israel was malaria free. Once the threat of malaria was gone, Jewish settlers were focused on making the desert bloom. In the Coastal Plains citrus grows to replace the swamps, and the Jordan Valley, once the center of the malaria epidemic, now became the country's bread basket. The Negev Desert blossomed with the newly planted forest and vineyards and the once most arid part of Israel became a flourishing vegetable industry.[3]

In other words, the desert is blooming again, just like God said it would, in the Last Days, right before our very eyes! And as you saw, when the early Jewish settlers came back to the land, they didn't mess around. They really appreciated getting the land back again, so they immediately began to put into play several different plans, deliberate plans, to get the land to renew again.

The **1st plan** they implemented to help renew the Land was to **Replant the Trees**.

Now again, as we saw, by the beginning of the 20th Century the Jewish homeland was in complete disarray and desolation. Nearly all the trees had been cut down. In fact, one author in the 1800's counted the trees there and reported that there were less than 1,000. From the Sea of Galilee to the south, all the trees had been cut down. They were gone! Now, this deforestation started back in 70 A.D. when the Romans laid siege to Jerusalem and destroyed their Temple. The Roman army single-handedly altered the landscape of the area at that time. They cut down the forests to build stockade towers and battering rams to breach the city's walls and then Emperor Titus ordered that every tree within ten miles of Jerusalem be cut down. In fact, the Jewish Historian Josephus wrote about the effects of this deforestation after the battle:

"And truly, the very view itself was a melancholy thing; for those places which were adorned with trees and pleasant gardens, were now a desolate country every way, and its trees were all cut down. Nor could any foreigner that had formerly seen Judaea and the most beautiful suburbs of the city, and now saw it as a desert, do anything but lament and mourn ever so sadly at so great a change."[4]

Then, on top of that, throughout the centuries, what trees were left, some had been cut down for firewood, others for other military uses from other conquerors, and still others burned whole forests just for hunting purposes. What last remnants of forests were left in Israel were cut down in modern times to fire up the Turkish railway engines. In fact, during this time the Turkish Government even put a tax on trees so there was now an incentive to cut down what trees were left otherwise you'd have to pay a heavy tax on them! So, by the time the Jewish pioneers got there, there was virtually no trees left just like the reports state! But when God says the desert will blossom again into garden-like conditions, it doesn't matter how bad it is, it's going to happen no matter what! And sure enough, that's exactly what happened! The Jewish people literally began to systematically replant, by hand, the destroyed forests, one by one, all by themselves, and simultaneously cleared the land of rocks so it could be re-cultivated. They even founded an organization called JNF or The Jewish National Fund that raised money from the Jewish population from around the world at that time to help repurchase the land and to restore it. Just that one organization alone was responsible for planting over 250 million trees, building 180 dams and reservoirs, and establishing more than 1,000 parks. In fact, they even followed the Bible's lead that told them what kind of trees to plant and where to plant them, so they would flourish in that kind of arid environment. And sure enough, the trees began to take off! And as a result, Israel was the only nation in the world to enter the 21st Century with more trees than what they started off with and one report shared how right now due to this massive tree replanting campaign, there are over 1.2 billion trees in Israel. And believe it or not, this massive reintroduction of trees to the area has actually had an effect on the rainfall of the area. It is estimated that Israel's rainfall has increased now by over 450 percent. As one researcher stated, "God has kept His promise, it's a land of milk and honey once again, and it's a sign that Jesus is coming soon."

Gordon Robertson: *"Today the world is focused upon saving the environment. But Israeli's were green long before it was popular, about a century before."*

Itzhik Moshe: *"It's part of the Israeli dream to create a green land, a green country and in time with experience and research, we studied how to do it."*

Gordon Robertson: *"The prophet Isaiah wrote about a time when the desert would rejoice and blossom as a rose. To the Israeli's that is more than an ancient prophecy. It's a commandment."*

Naty Barak, Netafim Drip Irrigation: *"Israel is a tiny state. Look at a map of our region. We used to always joke, there isn't enough space on the map to write the name Israel. We have to conserve it, to keep it, to maintain it. This is what we have."*

Gordon Robertson: *"To the early settlers in Israel, the word green meant planting trees, and they started in the Negev Desert. A place that gets only 1-7 inches of rain per year. In the 1940's Jerusalem was still under Arab control and Israel's first Prime Minister, David Ben Gurion believed that the Negev was the future of Israel. So, he ordered the creation of a man-made forest there. His esteemed scientists said it couldn't be done. Ben Gurion's response was, 'No problem, we'll get new scientists.'*

The Prime Minister got his new scientists and the Negev Desert began to blossom. Today the Yatir Forest has more than four million trees, including Carib, Pine, Olive and Fig."

Itzik Moshe: *"Israel is among the few countries in the world that at the end of the 20th century has much more trees that at the beginning of the century. Now we have planted more than 240 million trees which is a nice number to this small country."*

Gordon Robertson: *"In the center of the forest is a vineyard planted on the ruins of another one that existed here 2000 years ago. Scientists research the best plants to grow in the Negev and one of their sources was the Bible."*

Itzik Moshe: *"There are plenty of archeological ruins everywhere, water cisterns, dams, and terraces everywhere and we have started construction on some of these ancient farms where we have planted Biblical trees and the trees are surviving without additional irrigation by connecting the same cisterns as our forefathers did 2000 years ago. The fact that we are so flourishing here is a* *sign that this is God's will. This is what is supposed to happen. This is the plan."[5]*

You know, that in the Last Days, God would not only call the Jewish people back into the land, but He'd used the very same people to renew the land and have it blossom as a rose in the desert. Where have I heard that before? Even the secular Jewish People see the prophetic significance of this event. How about us? Or are we still concerned about what time that game starts? But that's not all.

The **2nd plan** the Jewish People implemented to help renew the Land in the Last Days was to **Redirect the Water**.

Again, as we saw, when the Jews returned to the land, they did not find it as a land "flowing with milk and honey." Instead they were faced with trying to eke out a living in a desert wasteland plagued with malaria-infested swamps. They paid exorbitant prices for the land and the Muslims who lived there laughed all the way to the bank. They thought they were crazy. But not for long. The early Jewish settlers immediately began draining the swamps to get rid of the malaria infested mosquitos. Then they imported Eucalyptus trees from Australia to plant around the perimeters of the swamps because those types of trees absorb huge amounts of water. On top of that, just to make sure, they even dug canals to drain the swamps out into the sea. That was just to get rid of the bad water. Then they went about creating good water for the land and here they literally became pioneers in water conservation and water distribution techniques. They figured out a way to get water from the Sea of Galilee in the north, to the major cities in the south, and even further south into the Negev Desert. In 1953 they devised a system of complex giant pipes, open canals, tunnels, reservoirs and massive pumping stations to get the job done and it worked incredibly well. They even took some of the water from the Sea of Galilee and channeled it into various sections of the deserts, which have allowed the deserts to literally begin to blossom with an abundance of flowers. Even to the point where Israel is now a major exporter of flowers and ornamental plants all around the world, just like the Bible said would happen in the Last Days! Then they became masters of conserving what water they did have by developing drip irrigation systems that specifically distributed the precious water at the base of each plant, wasting not a drop. On top of that, to keep up with the growing water needs of the population, the Jewish People became experts in desalination Plants turning saltwater into fresh water. They literally lined their ocean coastlines with desalination plants all along the Mediterranean coast of Israel and they are now providing almost 40 percent of the nation's water needs.

When it comes to water conservation and water technology, they are way ahead of the rest of the world. In fact, as of 2016, Israel was producing 20% more water than it consumed. They went from having NO water, to diseased water, to more than what they need! Can you believe that? And now they even provide water to their neighbors and export their water technology to the rest of the world. In fact, they recently hosted the Israel-California Water Conference in Marina Del Ray, CA with the goal of bringing long-term help to drought-ravaged California. They're even helping us! Meanwhile, Israel keeps becoming greener and more fruitful every year because of their mastery of the water supply:

Gordon Robertson: *"Thousands of years ago Moses had to strike a rock to get water in the desert, but today the Israeli's are taking a slightly different approach using technology and creativity. In Israel, main sources of drinking water are the Sea of Galilee and two underground aqueducts. If rainfall is short, so is the nation's water supply. In 1953 Israel started building the national water carrier. A system of pipelines, canals, and reservoirs carrying water from the Sea of Galilee to the rest of Israel."*

Jonathan Medved, Israeli Venture Capitalist: *"So, we didn't have water, ok, we develop technology. One of the things that Israel has excelled in is what some people would see as 'risk factor' as far as taking curses and turning them into blessings."*

Gordon Robertson: *"For thousands of years the Mediterranean Sea was the center of the ancient world, the cross roads between Europe, Asia, and Africa. Now it's one of Israel's greatest natural resource."*

Jonathan Medved: *"Israel has desalinated so much of its drinking water, the majority of our drinking water's origin, will be the Mediterranean Sea by the end of next year."*

Gordon Robertson: *Today Israel produces 450 million cubic meters of drinkable water a day, a water surplus."*

Jonathan Medved: *In this country we don't have much water, except somehow by the end of this decade, Israel is going to become a net water exporter. Just on today's news there was an item about how Israel is stepping up the export of* *water to Jordan in order to supply water to all the Syrian refugees who are fleeing into Jordan. Today Israel recycles 80% of its waste water. The closest competitor is Spain with 10%. So, we recycle more than eight times more water than any other country on the planet."*

Gordon Robertson: *"Israeli's developed a way to purify waste water using ultraviolet light. This treated water is then used to irrigate crops."*

Naty Barak: *"If you use it for vegetables, then you like to clean it, so you can almost drink it, it is treated to a very high degree. Today 60% of the water that is irrigating fields in Israel is produced water, not natural water."*

Gordon Robertson: *"Today, even the driest parts of the desert are blooming with help from a process called drip irrigation."*

Naty Barak: *"Sometimes with 20 millimeters of rain annual fall, very harsh climate, and still thanks to drip irrigation this has became the vegetable bowl of Israel. 65% of vegetable exports out of Israel are going to Europe."[6]*

In other words, the desert, which is blossoming with a bunch of flowers and fruits and vegetables and all kinds of things, is exactly what the Prophet Isaiah foresaw more than 2,800 years ago. But that's not all.

The **3rd plan** the Jewish People implemented to help renew the Land in the Last Days was to **Revitalize the Agriculture**.

As you just saw, there's a big payoff for Israel's hard work and innovation in renewing the land with trees and water resources. They've now become one of the biggest producers of agriculture on the planet. As one person stated, *"When people think of Jews, they normally think of people who have excelled in the area of finance. But modern Jews in Israel have made their mark in agricultural production and high-tech innovations."* This is because when the Jewish People first came back to the land, they organized themselves into these fortress-like communities called a kibbutz. These were collective farms that provided mutual help for each other as well as shared protection from Arab attacks. As a result of these tight-knit communities and the sharing of their information with each other, the results are phenomenal. The land that was totally desolate at the beginning of the 20th Century is now the bread basket of the Middle East. Israel is not only more than self-sufficient, but it exports agricultural products to both the Arab countries of the Middle East and to the various nations of Europe, and they produce a massive range of crops. We just think it's all desert there but right now they produce wheat, sorghum, corn, all kinds of vegetables, tomatoes, cucumbers, pepper, zucchinis, citrus fruits, avocados, kiwis, guavas, mangoes, grapes, melons, bananas, dates, apples, pears, cherries, oranges, grapefruit, tangerines, you name it, they can grow it! Including, as we saw, flowers! They grow vast quantities of flowers for export. Israel exports 1.5 billion flowers and vegetables to Europe and the U.S., most of which are grown in the desert, exactly like Isaiah said! And what they do grow is some of the biggest and tastiest produce in the world! This is because the water they pump from underneath the desert is "brackish" or in other words, salty. Normally you would think this would be the worst kind of water for plants to grow in. However, it just so happens that this saltiness in Israel's water underground actually improves the fruit. *"What happens when you irrigate the fruits or the vegetables with brackish water is that the plant goes into stress, and so it produces less leaves and more fruit with less water inside which makes it have more meat, and this helps to make it three times sweeter than usual produce.* "It's almost like when God said this land was "a good land" and a land "flowing with milk and honey," that it just needed the "right people" to get back there and make it come alive again, by pumping out that brackish water. Gee, I wonder who that is? The Jewish people maybe? But as you can see, flat out, Israel, the once barren desert wasteland filled with mosquitoes and malaria where pilgrims went and died, is now, in our lifetime, the world's leader in agricultural research and development. To the point where the American Society for Horticultural Sciences recently stated that Israel's desert agricultural technology is *"one of the most significant advances in food production in the past 1000 years."* Even the United Nations, which normally specializes in condemning Israel, has declared that Israel is *"The most agriculturally efficient land on planet earth."* Now, as if that wasn't enough proof that Israel is blossoming as a rose in the desert, and it's becoming again a land flowing with milk and honey, I've got one more for you. *"Israeli cows are the best milk producers in the world and their dairies produce the highest amounts of milk per animal in the world."* They're being called super cows!

Julie Stahl, Israel: *"In the Bible God promised the Jewish people a land flowing in milk and honey. And while it is a sign of abundance it's also literal."*

Moshe Kempinsky, author: *"The term milk and honey is critical. It's used 20 times in scripture."*

Julie Stahl: *"But when the Jewish people returned from 2000 years in exile, they found a barren, desert land. An Orthodox Jewish author Moshe Kempinsky, said that was all in God's plan."*

Moshe Kempinsky: *"God says 'I need something miraculous, I'm going to create a land, that even though it has those kinds of issues, it will be a land filled with dates and milk and honey. So that they know nothing comes here except when it is from Me'."*

Julie Stahl: *"And God has delivered on that promise. Despite the heat, humidity, and limited resources the Israeli cow produces more milk per year than cows in the U.S., European Union, and Australia. And what about the honey? Most believe honey during Bible time probably came from date trees. There are tens of thousands of acres of date trees in Israel. Some three thousand of those trees are planted here.*

Each one of the trees at Kibbutz Kitori produces about 350 lbs. of dates each year. They even managed to sprout a 2000-year-old date seed found by archeologists years ago at Masada. Nicknamed Methuselah, the tree is now 5 years old. Today Israel's dates are still famous throughout the world. Israel exports some twelve thousand tons of dates each year to twenty countries. According to Keminsky, the revival of trees in the land is the first sign of redemption."

Moshe Keminsky: *"Ezekiel 36 says 'shoot forth your branches, give forth your fruit, for your children are coming home'. That's an unusual thing for God to tell a tree. That's what He created the tree to do. God is saying in Leviticus 'It's going to be a desolate land when I take you out but when I bring my people back home this land is going to come forth with blossoms and trees and fruits.'*

Julie Stahl: *"So he says, every day you eat and the milk you drink here is like prophecy being fulfilled."*[7]

In other words, right before your very

eyes! Why? Because in the Last Days God said the land would blossom as a rose in the desert and return to be a "land flowing with milk & honey." Even that specific detail is coming to pass.

As one guy stated, *"Can there be any doubt that this amazing prophecy of the renewing of the land of Israel in the end times has been fulfilled?* Answer, no! It's happening right before our very eyes in our lifetime, which means, we're living in the Last Days! YET, what's our attitude? "So what, who cares, hey, the game is starting, CHOP CHOP! It's like we're staring at this picture and it doesn't even phase us. All these prophetic events concerning the renewal of the land of Israel are unfolding before our very eyes and it is just like a speeding train whistle, letting us know the 7-year Tribulation is near and the Rapture is even closer. The smoke pouring out of the stack is all these signs, and what's our attitude? "Who cares, the game's about to begin, finish up already will you!" If that's you, you need to ask yourself, why are you treating a church service like it's a boring religious service, that you come to once a week, so you can punch in your religious time clock and then hurry up and get back in the world? Could it be it's because you're one of these people Jesus warned about?

Matthew 7:21-23 "Not everyone who says to Me, 'Lord, Lord,' will enter the kingdom of heaven, but only he who does the will of My Father who is in heaven. Many will say to Me on that day, 'Lord, Lord, did we not prophesy in your name, and in your name drive out demons and perform many miracles?' Then I will tell them plainly, 'I never knew you. Away from me, you evildoers!'"

Basically, Jesus is saying, *"Religious people don't go to heaven. Religious people go to hell."* Oh, you went to church services alright, but you couldn't wait to get out, and get back to the world. It was all for the appearances of men, because your heart never belonged to Christ. You were just into a "Christian Religion" and you went straight to hell! I didn't say that, Jesus did! And is that a chance you really want to take? This is why, out of love, God has given us this update on *The Final Countdown: Tribulation Rising* concerning the *Jewish People & the Antichrist* to show us that the 7-year Tribulation is near, and the Return of Jesus Christ is rapidly approaching. And that's why Jesus Himself said…

Luke 21:28 "When these things begin to take place, stand up and lift up your heads, because your redemption is drawing near."

Like it or not, we are headed for *The Final Countdown*. The signs of the 7-year Tribulation are Rising all around us! It's time to WAKE UP! So, the point is this. If you're reading this today and you're NOT a Christian, then I beg you, please, heed these signs, heed these warnings, give your life to Jesus now! You don't want to be here when God pours out His Judgment upon the nations. It's the worst time in the history of mankind, so horrible that unless God shortened the timeframe the entire human race would be destroyed! The only way to escape is through Jesus! Take the way out now before it's too late. GET SAVED TODAY! **Listen to the whistle blowing**! BUT…if you're reading this today and you are a Christian, then it's high time we stop goofing off and getting distracted with this world. Let's get busy working together sharing the Gospel with as many as we can! Let's leave here being true relational Christians longing for His return and excited about the news of His soon return! Amen?

Chapter Seven

The Jewish People & Their Light Unto The World

Revelation 16:17-18,19,20-21 "The seventh angel poured out his bowl into the air, and out of the temple came a loud voice from the throne, saying, 'It is done!' Then there came flashes of lightning, rumblings, peals of thunder and a severe earthquake. No earthquake like it has ever occurred since man has been on earth, so tremendous was the quake. The great city split into three parts, and the cities of the nations collapsed. Every island fled away, and the mountains could not be found. From the sky huge hailstones of about a hundred pounds each fell upon men. And they cursed God on account of the plague of hail, because the plague was so terrible."

Now for those of you who aren't familiar with that passage, it's speaking of the 7-year Tribulation. And as you can see, it's a totally fearful and scary time that you don't want to be a part of, and it's no joke! The Bible says it is an outpouring of God's wrath on this wicked and rebellious planet. Jesus said in **Matthew 24** that it would be a *"time of greater horror than anything the world has ever seen or will ever see again."* And that *"unless God shortened that timeframe, the entire human race would be destroyed!"* But praise God, God's not only a God of wrath, He's a God of love as well. And because He loves you and me, He's given us many warning signs to wake us up, so we'd know when the 7-year Tribulation is near, and the Return of Jesus Christ is rapidly approaching.

Just as the Prophet Isaiah foresaw more than 2,800 years ago, Israel, the once barren desert wasteland filled with mosquitoes and malaria, where pilgrims went and died, is now the breadbasket of the Middle East! In our lifetime, they have gone from being a desert wasteland to the world's leader in agriculture, from having no trees to 1.2 billion trees, even becoming a major world exporter of flowers from the desert, just like the prophet said. They have truly become the land flowing with milk and honey, again, just like God said would happen when you are living in the Last Days! Now as we have seen before, the odds of this are absolutely insane!

"Peter Stoner was chairman of the mathematics and astronomy departments at Pasadena City College and professor emeritus of science at Westmont College in Santa Barbara, California. He wrote a book called Science Speaks to show how Bible prophecy proves that Jesus was truly God in the flesh. In it, Stoner calculated the probability of just 8 Messianic prophecies being fulfilled in the life of Jesus, such as "The Messiah will be born in Bethlehem (Micah 5:2) "The Messiah will enter Jerusalem as king riding on a donkey (Zechariah 9:9) "The Messiah will be betrayed for 30 pieces of silver (Zechariah 11:12) etc. etc.

He actually calculated that the probability of just 8 prophecies being fulfilled in the life of one person was 1 in 10^{17} or 1 in 100,000,000,000,000,000. That's one in one hundred quadrillion! Stoner then illustrated the meaning of this number. He asked the reader to imagine filling the State of Texas knee deep in silver dollars. Include in this huge number one silver dollar with a black check mark on it.

Then, turn a blindfolded person loose in this sea of silver dollars. The odds that the first coin he would pick up would be the one with the black check mark are the same as 8 prophecies being fulfilled in the life of Jesus. The point, of course, is that when people say that the fulfillment of prophecy in the life of Jesus was accidental, they do not know what they are talking about.

Keep in mind that Jesus did not just fulfill 8 prophecies, He fulfilled over 300. The chances of fulfilling 16 prophecies is 1 in 10^{45}. When you get to a total of 48, the odds increase to 1 in 10^{157}. Accidental fulfillment of these prophecies is simply beyond the realm of possibility. The conclusion is obvious. The incredible detail of these prophecies marks the Bible as the inspired Word of God. Only God could foreknow and accomplish all that was written about Jesus being the

Messiah. This historical accuracy and reliability set the Bible apart from any other book or record."[1]

And that would include the prophecies about the Jewish People. So far, just like Jesus, we've seen how they have also fulfilled eight prophecies right down to the tee. So that means mathematically, the same analogy of Texas being covered in silver dollars is applicable to them as well. Just like Jesus, we're not done with the Jewish People! There's way more than 8! There's no way this is happening by chance in our lifetime! It's almost like God's trying to get our attention or something and drive home the point that there's something special going on here and He's not done with the Jewish People, anybody else getting that impression?

The **9th End Time Prophecy** concerning the Jewish people, letting us know we're living in the Last Days is that **Israel Would Become a Light Unto the Nations.** But don't take my word for it. Let's listen to God's.

Isaiah 42:5-6 "This is what God the LORD says – He Who created the Heavens and stretched them out, Who spread out the earth and all that comes out of it, Who gives breath to its people, and life to those who walk on it: 'I, the LORD, have called you in righteousness; I will take hold of your hand. I will keep you and will make you to be a covenant for the people and a light for the Gentiles."

Literally there in the Hebrew (go-ee) "gowy" or "goyim" means nations. And that's why some translations say just that, nations. That Israel will not only be a light unto the Gentiles, but literally a light unto the nations. So here we see God clearly saying in the Last Days that little bitty tiny Israel, a speck in the world scene, will one day, in the Last Days, become a light, a blessing, a luminary source to the whole planet. In fact, that's not the only time that Isaiah talks about this amazing light that Israel will be to the whole world.

Isaiah 49:6 "He says, 'It is too small a thing that you should be My servant to raise up the tribes of Jacob and to restore the preserved ones of Israel; I will also make you a light of the nations so that My salvation may reach to the end of the earth.'"

Isaiah 60:2,3 "But the LORD will rise upon you and His glory will appear upon you. Nations will come to your light, and kings to the brightness of your rising."

So, it's repeated more than once. In fact, this prophecy about Israel becoming a light to the world is something that even the Jewish people are very familiar with and that they themselves quote all the time.

Chris Mitchell, Jerusalem Dateline: *"In just a few weeks Israel will celebrate its 70th anniversary. Here's a look back at where the infant state of Israel was in 1948 and where it is today and how it is fulfilling ancient prophecy.*

On May 14th, 1948, Israel took its place among the nations when David Ben Gurion announced the establishment of the Jewish state."

Amb. Michael Oren, Deputy Min. of Public Diplomacy: *"What was the situation in May of 1948? When we were 600,000 people. About half the size of a mid-sized American city with basically handguns fighting armies that have come within 26 miles of Tel Aviv. It's hard to imagine when they were surrounding Jerusalem, not far from where we are sitting. No economy, no allies, a population that was still languishing in displaced person camps after the Holocaust. Just think about that."*

Chris Mitchell: *"70 years later Israel not only survived, but, thrived."*

Michael Oren: *"Our Economy has one of the highest growth rates in the world. We have one of the most powerful armies in the world. We are a world leader in technology. Israel is regularly listed as one of the 7th most powerful countries in the world. In a historical prospective, I think that Israel's situation is nothing short of miraculous."*

Chris Mitchell: *"Israel's continuing miracle is not only that it has thrived but now helps nations in need."*

Benjamin Netanyahu, Israeli Prime Minister: *"Because we are a light unto the nations, this is a fulfillment of that great prophecy and in fact that is what Israel is doing. Doing it in places like Haiti, or the Philippines, or Mexico."*

Chris Mitchell: *"When Israel sent aid to Mexico after their recent devastating earthquake, Mexicans applauded them on the streets.*

Benjamin Netanyahu: *"They just love Israel and you see that elsewhere, many people around the world say "Why do you do it, what do you get out of it?" And* *the answer is, we aren't getting anything out of it, we are fulfilling our deepest values. Israel is a light unto the nations. "*

Chris Mitchell: *"Whether helping the world through humanitarian outreach, bringing innovation to global investors, or being the responsible stewards of history, these are simply a fulfillment of Israel's mission to the world. The Jewish principal of repairing the world and as the Hebrew prophet Isaiah wrote nearly 2700 years ago, 'to be a light to the nations.'"[2]*

Sounds to me like somebody knows what their destiny is. Not only to be a chosen people by God, but a people God will use in the Last Days to be a light to the world, to benefit mankind. Even their secular leaders admit it! And for those of you who think this isn't even possible, let alone happening, let me share with you just a smidgen of the proof that Israel, little bitty teensy weensy seemingly insignificant Israel is indeed brightening our world:

• There are over 6,000 startups currently in Israel in the areas of Mathematics, Science, Robotics, Chemistry, Physics, Optics, Medicine, Economics, Biotechnology, Computer Science, Computer Hardware & Software and even Mobile Software, Defense, Agriculture, Breeding, Energy, Consumer Goods & Appliances, Games, Food & Drink, Entertainment, Physical Exercise, you name it! In fact, many of the things we use today came from Israeli innovations:

SCIENCE
• Prediction of Quakes.
• Formulation of Black Holes.
• Nanowire – a conductive wire made of a string of tiny particles of silver 1,000 times thinner than a human hair.
• World's smallest DNA computing machine system which is the smallest biological computing device ever constructed.

MEDICAL
• Rewalk – a bionic walking assistance system that enables paraplegics to stand upright, walk and climb stairs. *Do you walk in your dreams? Remember when you saw the world eye-to-eye? Imagine seeing a person walking through a field of flowers. Then switch to a woman in a wheelchair rolling down a sidewalk. What if your shoes were no longer wheels? What if you could stand up to disability? She wheels her chair to a park bench where there are artificial legs waiting for her. What if there was a technology that liberated you? You see her*

strapping on the artificial legs. What if you could walk again? You see her standing and with the help of a couple of canes she is walking. She proceeds to walk away from the park bench. She is walking with the help of ReWalk.com.[3]

- Development of robotic guidance system for spine surgery.
- Discovery of Quasicrystals.
- Discovery of the role of protein Ubiquitin.
- World's smallest video camera which led to the development of the 'Pillcam' the first endoscopy solution to record images of the digestive tract. After nine years, the FDA has approved Pillcam. A digestible pill that will help doctors to detect colon cancer or polyps in patients who struggle with the traditional colonoscopy. Pillcam is a pill equipped with two miniature color video cameras that the patient swallows while wearing a recording device around the waist for 10 to 12 hours. During an 8-hour trip through the intestine and colon Pillcam captures images while transmitting them to a recording device. Images are then sent to a computer screen enabling a doctor to detect polyps and cancer.[4]
- A notation system for recording early diagnosis of Autism.
- Development of Azilect, a drug for Parkinson's disease.
- Development of the Copaxone drug for treating Multiple Sclerosis.
- BabySense – a non-touch, no-radiation device designed to prevent crib death.

AGRICULTURE
- Drip irrigation system.
- Golden hamster – first domesticated for pet use by a Hebrew University of Jerusalem zoologist in 1930.
- Hybrid cucumber seeds.
- Grain cocoons to help farmers keep their grain market-fresh.
- Biological pest control – breeding beneficial insects and mites for biological pest control.
- AKOL – a Kibbutz-based company which gives low-income farmers the ability to get top-level information from professional sources.
- Reusable plastic trays to collect dew from the air, reducing the need to water crops by up to 50 percent.
- Zero-discharge system - an invention that allows fish to be raised virtually anywhere by eliminating the environmental problems in conventional fish farming.
- Judean date palm - oldest seed ever to be revived, restoring an extinct plant.
- The Tomaccio cherry tomato was developed by several Israeli laboratories.

ENERGY

- Rooftop solar hot-water system
- Super iron battery – a new class of a rechargeable electric battery more environmentally friendly.
- The electric car grid.
- Ormat Technologies – designs, develops, builds, owns, manufactures and operates geothermal power plants worldwide, supplying clean geothermal power in more than 20 countries.
- Pythagoras Solar – makes the world's first solar window which combines energy efficiency, power generation and transparency.
- 3G Solar – pioneered a low-cost alternative to silicon that generates significantly more electricity than leading silicon-based solar modules at a lower cost per kilowatt hour.
- Leviathan Energy – innovated the Wind Tulip, a cost-effective, silent, vibration-free wind turbine designed as an aesthetic environmental sculpture, producing clean energy at high efficiency from any direction.

CONSUMER GOODS

- Epilator – (originally "Epilady") – an electrical device used to remove hair by mechanically grasping multiple hairs simultaneously and pulling them out. It was developed and originally manufactured at Kibbutz HaGoshrim.
- Wonder Pot – a pot developed for baking on the stovetop rather than in an oven.
- Micronized coating instant hot water pipes.
- Like-A-Fish – a unique air supply system that extracts air from water, freeing leisure and professional scuba divers, as well as submarines and underwater habitats, from air tanks. The Powerbreather is an innovative sports tool for swimming, triathlon and diving for those who like to sink deep while swimming. Suitable for everything from swimming pools, to heavy flip turns, to smooth or choppy open water. The Powerbreather has two tubes that wrap around your head and has a membrane in the mouthpiece. The two tubes provide fresh air as you breathe in and the membrane allows you to exhale out through your mouth. This innovative snorkel enables a swimmer to breath freely underwater.[5]
- Turbulence – the world's first hyper-narrative interactive movie that allows the viewer to choose the direction of the film's plot by pressing buttons on the PC, Mac or iPad at various moments in the action.

GAMES

- Rummikub – a tile-based game.

- Hidato – a logic puzzle.
- Taki – an Israeli card game.
- Mastermind – a board game.
- Guess Who? – a two-player guessing game.

COMPUTER
- The Intell 8088 – the first PC CPU from IBM that was designed in Israel at Intel's Haifa laboratory.
- ICQ – an Instant Messaging software developed initially in 1996 by the Israeli company Mirabilis and later procured by AOL.
- The first Voice over Internet Protocol (VoIP) based PC to Phone software solution.
- Quicktionary Electronic dictionary – a pen-sized scanner able to scan words or phrases and immediately translate them into other languages or keep them in memory in order to transfer them to the PC.
- Laser Keyboard – a virtual keyboard projected onto a wall or table top for typing on computers and cell phones.
- USB Flash Drive – originally marketed as the DiskOnKey.
  Israel invented the USB flash drive. You know that little stick of joy that can store all your documents, files, and movies, probably used by everyone on the planet. It is surely one of the most useful inventions out there. In the year 2000 the first flash drive was sold. At that time, it only had 8 mb capacity and went on to replacing CDs .[6]
  Umoove – a high tech startup company that invented a software only solution for face and eye tracking.
- WeCU – (pronounced 'We See You') Technologies, is a technology able to pick up, analyze, and identify terrorists in real-time and being implemented in airports around the world.
- GetTaxi – an app that connects between customers and taxi drivers enabling users to order a cab either with their smartphone or through the company's website.
- Mobileye – a vision-based advanced driver-assistance system (ADAS) providing warnings for collision prevention and mitigation. Rear-end collisions are one of the most common accidents caused by driver inattention. The Mobileye system continuously scans the area in front of your vehicle detecting all types of vehicles in your path, including motorcycles. The system calculates the relative speed and critical situations and it issues both a visual and auditory warning of an impending collision with the vehicle ahead. This system can

provide a warning up to 2.7 seconds before impact, both during city and highway driving.[7]

- OrCam MyEye – a portable, artificial vision device that allows the visually impaired to understand text and identify objects through audio feedback describing what such people are unable to see.
- Waze – a GPS-based app for smartphones with support and display screens, which provides turn-by-turn information and user-submitted travel times and route details. It's now available in over 100 countries, was acquired by Google for a reported $1.1 billion. With Waze you always get the fastest route based on real-time traffic shared by millions of fellow Wazers. Navigating is super easy. All your destinations are just one tap away. Once on the road you'll be alerted before you approach incidents. You can help others too by simply driving with Waze, you share the real time traffic information, or you can actively report. When you are meeting others simply send your ETA to inform them of your arrival.[8]
- Which is why one person said, "Despite its short history, tiny size, and turbulent political situation, Israel has produced a staggering number of remarkable inventions and innovations. From technology to agriculture, to defense and TV shows, Israel is home to some of the world's most brilliant minds and by now is well-known as the "Start Up Nation." [9]

Or as God calls it a light unto the nations in the Last Days! In fact, all this amazing innovation Israel is putting out, brings another prophecy into view!

Zechariah 8:23 "Thus says the LORD of hosts, 'In those days ten men from all the nations will grasp the garment of a Jew, saying, 'Let us go with you, for we have heard that God is with you.'"

In other words, stick with the Jewish People! They always have great stuff and make great things for the world and God's blessing is all over them! All this information is not merely to peak your interest or provide that wow factor just in case you ever get on Jeopardy and get asked, "Who invented the Cherry Tomato?" Rather, it's God's way of saying, it's a major mega sign that you're living in the Last Days and you better get motivated!

Israel Defying the Odds, "Israel is the 100th smallest country on the globe and has about 1/1000th of the world's population. It's only 70-years-old, smaller than New Jersey, surrounded by enemies, under constant threat of survival and possesses few natural resources.

And yet Israel is the only country in history that has revived an unspoken language since its founding. Israel has won the second most Nobel prizes per capita. Although Israel holds only 0.2% of the world's population, Jews have received 22% of the Nobel prizes. Constituting an inexplicable 11,250% above statistical probability.

Israel is the only country that entered the 21st century with the net gain of its number of trees. Even more remarkable in an area that's mainly desert. Over 90% of Israeli homes use solar energy for hot water. The highest percentage of any country. Israeli companies are building the largest solar production facility in the world.

Israel operates the world's largest desalination plant and is the #1 country providing usable water from seawater. Israel's scientific research institutions rank 3rd in the world and rank 2nd in space sciences. Israel leads the world in medical patents and has revolutionized modern medicine.

Oramed is changing the diabetes therapeutic paradigm by putting insulin in a pill. ReWalk exoskeleton allows paraplegics to walk. Orocam allows blind people to virtually see. Israel has more patents registered than the U.S., China, India, and Russia combined who have 300 times Israel's population. Israel's innovations have improved the way we work, print, drive, read, eat, drink, talk, exercise, and even play.

Israel is the only liberal Democracy in the Middle East and its third largest party is the Arab party. Israel has provided humanitarian aid & rescue services to over 140 countries. Even to some that refuse to recognize it, like Syria and Lebanon. Israel is the 3rd most educated country in the world according to the OECD. Israel has the 2nd highest number of books per capita. Israel has the 3rd highest rate of entrepreneurship among women in the world and in 1969 Israel elected Golda Meir the 2nd female head of state in modern history.

In proportion to its population, Israel has the largest number of start-up companies in the world. Israel has more start-up than any other country except the U.S. and China. Israel is the only country whose indigenous population returned to its native land after 2000 years of forced exile. There are 26 Muslim states in the world and 18 Christian states, but there is only one Jewish state. Israel, a small place making a big difference."[10]

How can they be defying the odds like that? Because God said in the Last Days that Israel will not only return to the Land, but they will become a light unto the nations. That too is happening before our very eyes! It's time to get motivated! This is why, out of love, God has given us this update on *The Final Countdown: Tribulation Rising* concerning the *Jewish People & the Antichrist* to show us that the 7-year Tribulation is near, and the Return of Jesus Christ is rapidly approaching. And that's why Jesus Himself said…

Luke 21:28 "When these things begin to take place, stand up and lift up your heads, because your redemption is drawing near."

Like it or not, we are headed for The Final Countdown. The signs of the 7-year Tribulation are Rising all around us! It's time to wake up! If you're reading this today and you're not a Christian, then I beg you, please, heed these signs, heed these warnings, give your life to Jesus now! You don't want to be here when God pours out His Judgment upon the nations. It's the worst time in the history of mankind, so horrible that unless God shortened the timeframe the entire human race would be destroyed! The only way to escape is through Jesus! Take the way out now before it's too late. Get saved today!

But if you're reading this today and you are a Christian, then it's high time we stop goofing off and getting distracted with this world, let's get busy working together sharing the Gospel with as many as we can! Let's leave here living for Jesus and longing for His soon return. Amen?

Chapter Eight

The Jewish People & Their Military Conflict

The **10th End Time Prophecy** concerning **The Jewish People** letting us know we're living in the Last Days is that **Israel Would Become a Source of World Conflict.** Wow! Just turn on your news, right? That one's happening right before our eyes! But don't take my word for it. Let's listen to God's.

Zechariah 12:1-3 "This is the word of the LORD concerning Israel. The LORD, Who stretches out the heavens, Who lays the foundation of the earth, and who forms the spirit of man within him, declares: 'I am going to make Jerusalem a cup that sends all the surrounding peoples reeling. Judah will be besieged as well as Jerusalem. On that day, when all the nations of the earth are gathered against her, I will make Jerusalem an immovable rock for all the nations. All who try to move it will injure themselves.'"

In other words, don't mess with Israel! But here we see clearly that God is not only going to make Israel a nation again, on the world scene, in the Last Days, but He's also going to let them become a major ongoing problem on the world scene in the Last Days. And tell me that hasn't happened! As we saw before, in 1948, when the Jewish people became a nation again, the very next day, here comes the conflict! The nations around them declared war with Israel. And the fighting for control has never stopped. Since then, this is why you can turn on the news or read in all the newspapers of how Israel has indeed become what? An international global problem. It has become a center of world conflict. Exactly like the Bible said would happen. When? In the Last Days! In fact, some translations put it even more bluntly. They say, "I will make Jerusalem a 'cup of trembling' and a 'burdensome stone for all people.'" In other words, Jerusalem and the Jewish people aren't just one big ongoing problem in the world, but they will instill fear in people of the world over this ongoing conflict. And is that not what is happening? Are people afraid of what's going on in the Middle East, the ramifications of all this fighting going on over in Jerusalem, and can there be peace in the Middle East? Is this going to lead to WWIII? Uh yeah! Are not the nations around the world getting tired of having to deal with this ongoing burdensome conflict that they can't seem to solve, and nobody wants to deal with it, they're tired of dealing with it? Yeah! In fact, the Bible says this attitude is going to get so bad in the Last Days that Israel will basically be left all alone with all the nations coming against her, but God will rise up to defend her.

Zechariah 12:9 "On that day I will set out to destroy all the nations that attack Jerusalem."

Zechariah 14:3 "Then the LORD will go out and fight against those nations, as He fights in the day of battle."

Israel is basically left alone in the Last Days, as the burdensome stone, and the nations eventually come against her, but God sovereignly protects them because He's not done with them. Don't mess with Israel, again, is the lesson. But do we see signs that the nations around the world are coming against Israel and she's being left all alone in the world scene, trying to defend herself? Uh…yeah! In fact, watch what happened when Israel's current Prime Minister Benjamin Netanyahu confronted the U.N. and nations around the world over their treatment towards Israel and you tell me if they've not been left all alone.

"Now for the inspiring comeback story in world history. After building the most moral and innovative democracy in the entire Middle East you would think that Israel would be supported and held up as an example, but we see that the U.N., a representation of all the nations of the world condemns Israel more than any other country on the planet.

Zechariah 14:2: "And I will gather all nations against Jerusalem to battle."

"The only country in the world that has been called, destruction has been called for by members of the U.N., A national movement, Zionism, was declared racist and illegal by the U.N., that it's capital, which was the oldest capital in the world, was not recognized by any country."

Benjamin Netanyahu: "Last month Khomeini made his genocidal intentions clear. Before Iran's top clerical body, the assembly of experts, He spoke about Israel, home to more than 6 million Jews. He pledged, 'There will be no Israel in 25 years.' Seventy years after the murder of 6 million Jews, Iran's rulers promised to destroy my country, murder my people, and the response from this body, the response from nearly every one of the governments represented here has been absolutely nothing. Utter silence. Deafening silence."

Fox News: *"Then Netanyahu gave them 45 seconds of silence. For years I have heard that in the Last Days Israel will be isolated as a nation. They would be left alone. And we are seeing it happen. They are as burdensome stone to all nations as the prophet said. No one wants anything to do with Israel. And we're seeing all the signs of the end of the age around us.*

The Jews have got Jerusalem back. The first time in 2000 years. In 1967 they got it. This is what Jesus spoke of in Luke 2, Matthew 24, these are fearful times, but Jesus said that when these things come to pass, lift up your head and rejoice. It says the gospel must be preached. So, preach the word, in season, out of season, reprove, rebuke, exhault, with all longsuffering and doctrine, while we still have time."[1]

That time is running out. Israel and Jerusalem have become a burdensome stone that nobody wants to deal with, exactly like God said would happen in the Last Days! You just read the actual clip from the U.N. proving it! It's happening right now! One guy puts it this way. Here's how we're to respond.

"Israel is always pictured as the focal point of world politics in the end times. There is not a day that goes by that Israel is not in the news. The world is very focused on Israel and especially Jerusalem.

The world is wondering what to do about the problems between Israel and her neighboring Arab countries. There is also concern about the problems between Israel and the unhappy Arabs who live today inside her borders.

Over the past several decades the United Nations has tried to answer this 'Middle East problem' and many heads of state have tried to tackle the problem. In fact, every United States administration since the re-establishment of Israel in 1948 has made some attempt to resolve the abrasions between Arabia and Israel. Failure and frustration have abounded. The 'peace process' has especially failed when the subject of who will control Jerusalem is entertained.

And isn't it ironic that as large as the world is and as diverse as the world's problems are, there is so much focus on this tiny country. At its widest point, Israel is only 85 miles wide and is 290 miles long! The population is around 8 million compared to the world's almost 7.5 billion. It's seemingly insignificant, compared to the rest of the world both in size and population.

Yet, Israel remains much of the focus of the United Nations and the world.

The prophet Zechariah prophesied when the world is convinced the "peace talks" have completely collapsed, they will start sending their armies to force "peace". This will be the fulfillment of Zechariah 14:2 which states that a day is coming when all nations will be gathered against Jerusalem to battle.

And when they do, the scenario will be set up for the fulfillment of the greatest event of all of human history, the return of Jesus! Praise the Lord! What an exciting time to live and see these things beginning to take place!"[2]

In other words, it's time to get motivated! We're living in the Last Days! It's not a time to be fearful, it's a time to get excited. JESUS IS COMING BACK!!! And it could happen a lot sooner than you think! Now, I wanted to share a few of reasons why Israel has become this burdensome stone in the Last Days, that's instilling fear in people. First of all, it leads us to another prophecy being fulfilled.

The **11th End Time Prophecy** concerning **The Jewish People** letting us know we're living in the Last Days is that **Israel Would Have a Powerful Military**.

Zechariah 12:6 "On that day I will make the leaders of Judah, like a firepot in a woodpile, like a flaming torch among sheaves. They will consume right and left all the surrounding peoples, but Jerusalem will remain intact in her place."

So now we see another amazing prophecy about Israel in the Last Days and this one has to do with their military might or military strength. Apparently, what God is saying is that even though Israel is teensy weensy in comparison to the rest of the world, nonetheless, in the Last Days they will consume all the people's around them that come against them. The Hebrew word there for consume is "akal" and it means, "To eat, to devour, to burn up, or to destroy!" Hence, they're going to have a powerful military in the Last Days that consumes their enemies just like somebody going through a dry wheat field with a flaming torch! You mess with Israel, you get burned! And boy, has that been the case ever since the Jews were re-established in the Land. If there's one lesson to learn, it's don't mess with the Jewish People! God's hand is on them and you aren't going to win! They will consume you in a fiery ordeal! Outnumbered and against all odds, the Israeli forces have astounded the world by their victories over and over again during multiple wars. Israel's military today is one of the best trained in the world and they have proven this prophecy over and over again in the last 70 years with an effective fighting force. They have emerged victorious against incredible odds from every major military campaign launched against them since the country was re-established in 1948. For instance, within hours of Israel's declaration of independence in 1948, Egypt, Syria, Jordan, Iraq, and Lebanon all invaded Israel. The combined population of those countries was at least 20 million at that time. Yet, Israel had fewer than 1 million. But when all was said and done, the Jewish people not only won the war, but they expanded the size of Israel by 50 percent. The five Arab armies were utterly defeated. Then in 1956 there was an Egyptian-Syrian alliance that was defeated by Israel over the Sinai area. They too lost big time! In 1967 there was the combined effort to overrun Israel by Egypt, Syria, Jordan, Kuwait, Iraq, Algeria, and Lebanon and they were also defeated by the Israelis in what was known as the Six-Day War, when they also gained control of Jerusalem. The Israelis put down yet another combined effort to come against them in 1973 in what was known as the Yom Kippur War. In this war, the Egyptians and Syrians, with around 1000 warplanes, over 4,000 tanks, and 800,000 troops, challenged Israel. Then Iraq, Morocco, Algeria, Saudi Arabia, Jordan, and Kuwait had joined with the Egyptian and Syrian forces. But when all was said and done the once again, seriously outnumbered Israeli army, was again victorious; this time with less than 500 warplanes, 1700 tanks, and 300,000 men. They were outnumbered almost 3 to 1 and they still whooped their enemy's pants off! Today, Israel, more than ever, has the most powerful fighting force in the area that includes an arsenal of nuclear weaponry and some believe they even have hydrogen weaponry.

Their Air Force, Navy and Army are among the most technologically advanced in the world. Pilot to pilot, airframe to airframe, the Israeli Air Force is the best in the world. And on and on it goes throughout the years. Israel's military is not just unbeatable, but they consume their enemies just like God said! Part of this is because, out of sheer survival, they have, and still to this day, have developed some of their most advanced military weapons, weaponry and fighting techniques on the planet! Their military is called the IDF or Israel Defense Forces and between 1948 and 1977, they grew from 90,000 personnel and 12 brigades to 700,000 personnel and 44 brigades. Initially, they fielded only 20 tanks that were obsolete; to some 3,800 tanks just 30 years later, most of which were state-of-the-art. During the same period, the Israeli Air Force grew from a single, ill-equipped fighter squadron, to 20 fighter-attack squadrons armed with cutting-edge combat aircraft. The number of combat sorties they could sustain daily grew from a mere 20 to 1,200 a day and today it's up to 1,850 which is the highest daily sortie rate in the world. Their navy grew from virtually nothing to the dominant force in the region, and all they do even to this day, is continuing to grow and modernize. You don't want to mess with them. One guy said, "Today, Israel stands out as the dominant military power in the Middle East." In fact, they're the ones who invented, the Bullpup Assault Rifle, the UZI Submachine Gun, the Python air-to-air Missile, the Desert Eagle, a short-range pistol and the Wall radar, a unique radar system that allow users to see through walls.[3]

"Imagine a new tactical tool, that can be used during war time to see what is happening on the other side of the wall. Imagine seeing a person with a gun pointing at another with a black hood over his head, kneeling on his knees. As you watch what is happening a helicopter has been radioed the circumstances and is now lowering soldiers for the rescue and to stop the murder.

This weapon is compact and mobile and provides real time intelligence. As everything is being watched on the Wall radar the assassin hears the helicopter and stops what he is doing long enough that the soldiers make it into the building. The Wall radar has the ability to see through walls. The assassin tries to escape, he can run but he can't hide.[4]

But not only that, they have invented Wound Clot bandages that stops bleeding in minutes: made from cellulose (plant cells), they absorb the blood and boost the natural clotting process. They even invented the Injured Personnel Carrier and the Iron Dome Air Defense System, just to name a few military advances.

"The Israeli army is one of the most technologically advanced fighting forces on earth. When they wanted a one man's hands free method of evacuating a wounded soldier, the IPC would allow both hands on their weapons during evacuation. This solution was surprisingly simple. The IPC attaches in seconds and makes it easier to pick up an incapacitated person on the ground. It allows him to be carried much more comfortably for longer and gives you a 100% hands free capability.

The Iron Dome Air Defense System has 20 missiles on it. When the red light flashes it means it is armed and ready. One of the dozen or more Iron Dome batteries is kept ready to intercept missiles and provide Israel a shield from aerial attacks.

Lt. Colonel Cohen oversees its operation. It took three years and about 200 million dollars to develop this defense system. It relies on a radar that instantly tracks when a missile has been fired. Algorithms quickly try to determine what type of projectile is in the air, and whether it is headed for a populated or strategic area. If so, it launches a missile of its own.

It is said that the Iron Dome has taken down over 1000 missiles since being turned on in 2011. What's clear though is that the algorithms capable of directing projectiles while performing a cost benefit analysis on human life are the most advanced in the world.[5]

One guy stated, "Israel today deploys the world's most capable ground-based integrated air-defense system. Nothing equivalent exists elsewhere." They also have the world's second most effective space-based surveillance capability providing real-time coverage of its wartime theater of operations. And it is a world leader in cyber warfare. Then on top of that, Israel's military maintains the world's second-largest inventory of PGM's (Precision Guided Missiles). And their ground forces? Nobody can touch them! The IDF Soldiers are legendary, some of the best trained soldiers in the world! One writer shared, *"I don't think anybody doubts that the Israel Defense Forces are, pound for pound, the best fighting force on Earth."* Hands down, Israel is far and above the most powerful force in the region, just like the Bible said would happen when you are living in the Last Days! You don't want to mess with them! They are going to consume you if you come against them! And when you look at the statistics of their Military Ranking considering their size compared to other countries around the world, it's mind-blowing!

This is from Global Firepower Military Ranking in 2015

Countries Ranked by Military Strength
Things to keep in mind
Nuclear capabilities are NOT taken into account

- #1 ranking – United States – 3.806 million square miles
- #2 ranking – Russia – 6.602 million square miles
- #3 ranking – China – 3.705 million square miles
- #11 ranking – Israel – 8,019 square miles

They are not only ahead of....

- Australia
- Canada
- Mexico
- But they are 11th on the list of the most powerful military on the planet out of 136 countries listed.
- Another more recent article shared, "Israel ranked 8th most powerful country in the world" when you take into account other factors.
- They even go on to say, "For its relatively small size, the country has played a large role in global affairs," Gee I wonder why!
- Now, speaking of size, keep in mind also that Israel's size is tiny by comparison to the rest of the nations on the planet.
- The state of New Jersey is 8,729 square miles
- Israel is less than that with 8,019 square miles
- You can fit 20½ Israel's in the one state of California
- It's tiny yet you're 11th on the list in the world for military strength, 8th most powerful in general out of 136 countries with greater size!
- Total Population – 8,299,706
- Available Manpower – 3,600,000
- Which is why they are hands down the strongest military in the Middle East.
- 1 – Israel
- 2 – Iran
- 3 - Saudi Arabia
- 4 – Syria
- 5 - United Arab Emirates
- 6 – Jordan

- 7 – Oman
- 8 – Kuwait
- 9 – Qatar
- 10 – Yemen
- 11 – Bahrain
- 12 – Lebanon
- 13 – Iraq
- In fact, they have so many military arms that they are now becoming one of the world's largest arms exporters. (As of 2015)
- United States – 10,194
- Russia – 5,971
- China – 1,978
- France – 1,200
- Germany – 1,110
- United Kingdom – 1,083
- Israel – 1,074
- They're 7th in the world just barely behind the 4th spot France.
- Now remember, we're not counting Nuclear Weapons yet. Watch this.
- Russia – 8000 Nuclear Warheads
- USA – 7300 Nuclear Warheads
- Israel – 400 Nuclear Warheads
- France – 300 Nuclear Warheads
- China – 250 Nuclear Warheads
- UK – 225 Nuclear Warheads[6]

I'll say it again, here's little bitty tiny Israel, smaller than the state of New Jersey. 20½ of them could fit inside California, and yet you have the third greatest number of nukes on the entire planet! It's almost like they've become a powerful military just like God said would happen when you're living in the Last Days! If you go up against them, what's going to happen? They are going to consume you! Remember the Hebrew word "akal" for "consume" means "eat, devour, burn and destroy you!" That's exactly what that word means! Now, speaking of burning and consuming, in our lifetime, can we see for the first time the possible fulfillment of this passage of Scripture concerning the disintegration of human flesh to the bone while standing:

Zechariah 14:12 "This is the plague with which the Lord will strike all the nations that fought against Jerusalem: Their flesh will rot while they are still standing on their feet, their eyes will rot in their sockets, and their tongues will rot in their mouths."

Some people would say that this is just some sovereign act of God where He supernaturally causes a plague that instantly removes people's flesh while they're still standing. And it could be. Kind of like that scene from Indiana Jones:

"Indiana Jones is telling his friend, "Don't look at it! Close your eyes and don't look at it. No matter what happens." Suddenly smoke comes out of the altar and flows above the soldiers that are standing there facing it. They get a look of amazement on their faces as they watch the smoke circle around them and then back up to the altar.

One of the soldiers get a shocked look on his face as he watches the smoke going inside of the soldiers, outside the soldiers, circling them as they watch this sight. He calls out, "It's beautiful!" Then the smoke turns into an image of a woman with long white hair. She is so beautiful, but suddenly as she gets closer to the soldiers her skin falls away and there is an ugly skeleton left with its mouth wide open as if to devour them. The man in charge sees her coming at him and screams but it is too late. The image goes into the altar and fire begins to emerge. It goes into each person who was watching the beautiful sight. They are all in pain and agony as the heat is burning them to death.

They fall on their knees, still screaming from the pain. As the flames burn hotter and hotter their skin melts off like wax. As the skin falls to the floor they are still screaming in pain. Finally, they each get so hot that they explode all over the room."[7]

So, could that be it? Is that how, "Their flesh will rot while they are still standing on their feet, their eyes will rot in their sockets, and their tongues will rot in their mouths." Could be? I personally don't want to be there to find out. However, with the modern weaponry that we see today, even in Israel, what does that graphic description look like to you? Kind of like a nuclear holocaust, doesn't it? They just happen to have a ton of nukes! Maybe it will be more like a scene depicted here in the Terminator movies:

"The video begins with a woman walking across a grassy field towards a playground. As she gets to the chain link fence she grabs hold with both hands and stares at the children playing on the swings and the teeter-totters. As you

look closer you see that she is actually watching herself play with her son in the playground. She is trying to warn herself to run and get away from what is coming but no one can hear her cries.

She watches herself and her son having fun playing. She tries to rattle the fence to get someone's attention, but no one can hear her. Suddenly there is a bright flash that actually knocks her and her son down on the ground. The city in the back ground has been hit with what looks like an atomic bomb. They are all trying to cover their eyes, the light is so bright. She suddenly starts burning.

The other mother and her son are also burning, as are the rest of the children there. The blast is overflowing the city and demolishing everything in its path. This is the end. No one can live through this. It hits with such a force that it blows cars and semi-trucks off the road. The tallest buildings are blown over and burned. People are disintegrating all around the city."[8]

Is that what Zechariah saw? Is that how, "Their flesh will rot while they are still standing on their feet, their eyes will rot in their sockets, and their tongues will rot in their mouths." Could be? It might even be from a biological weapon. But either way, in our lifetime, in our generation, we can get a real good idea can't we? This is why, out of love, God has given us this update on *The Final Countdown: Tribulation Rising* concerning the Jewish People & the Antichrist to show us that the 7-year Tribulation is near, and the Return of Jesus Christ is rapidly approaching. And that's why Jesus Himself said…

Luke 21:28 "When these things begin to take place, stand up and lift up your heads, because your redemption is drawing near."

Like it or not, we are headed for *The Final Countdown*. The signs of the 7-year Tribulation are rising all around us! It's time to wake up! So, this is the point. If you're reading this today and you're not a Christian, then I beg you, please, heed these signs, heed these warnings, give your life to Jesus now! You don't want to be here when God pours out His judgment upon the nations. You could be one of those people whose flesh rots off your bones! It's the worst time in the history of mankind, so horrible that unless God shortened the timeframe the entire human race would be destroyed! The only way to escape is through Jesus! Take the way out now before it's too late. Get saved today! But, if you're reading this today and you are a Christian, then would you please stop goofing off like these guys?!

For days, a photo of three golfers putting near what appears to be the setting of Dante's Inferno in Oregon has been making its rounds on the Internet, with commenters doubting it's too-crazy-to-be-real imagery and claiming the picture had been altered. Not so, says amateur photographer and Columbia River Gorge aficionado, Kristi McCluer. And she would know—she snapped the photo of the blazing Oregon fire.[9]

When I first saw this, I thought it was a joke like that volcano we saw before, but it too is legit! It's an actual photo of these guys playing golf in front of a raging forest fire in Oregon, acting like, so what, no big deal! And yet, how many Christians are acting like this spiritually! The planet is getting ready to blow, people's faces are getting ready to melt with fire. God's giving us all these signs, and we're walking around, goofing off playing golf or whatever when the whole time GOD says get busy sharing the gospel! What are you doing? We're on a rescue mission not a golf outing! It's not about you, it's about reaching the lost. So, let's heed these signs ourselves and get busy doing something splendid for Jesus like sharing the gospel, not golfing in front of a forest fire! Amen?

Chapter Nine

The Jewish People & Their Religious Conflict

The **2ⁿᵈ reason** why Israel has become a source of world conflict in the Last Days just like the Bible said is not just because of the military conflict but also **The Religious Conflict**.

You see, to make matters even worse for Israel, it just so happens that the world's three largest religions have headquarters, guess where? Jerusalem! Islam, Catholicism, and Judaism. This is why you can turn on your news almost every single day and what do you hear? Not just conflict in Jerusalem but religious conflict in Jerusalem especially over the Temple Mount!

"Palestinians call for a 'Day of Rage' as they march down the street chanting to protest new security measures at one of the holiest sites in Jerusalem, the Temple Mount. Israeli authorities say they are taking no chances. Smoke bombs are being sent out at the crowd as they are surrounding the Dome of the Rock.

Gun shots are being fired as people are running to and fro. The police are pushing the people back as they chant 'Allahu Akbar', Allah is the greatest. Some are being taken away on stretchers. As the police are going inside the Mosque they are being met by rocks and fire bombs.

Gilad Erdan, Israeli Public Security Min: *"They used firearms inside the Temple Mount, violating the holiness of this important place."*

Israel's decision to continue to employ metal detectors at the entrances to the al-Aqsa compound prompted Muslim leaders to urge worshipers to protest the decision. Violent demonstrations have broken out in East Jerusalem leading Israeli police to fire live ammunition, tear gas and rubber coated bullets at Palestinians protesting against the security measures. Those tensions have spilled into neighboring Jordan where thousands protested in the streets of Amman against the installation of metal detectors.

Palestinians view the increased security measures as an infringement on the status quo at the Holy site, which gives Muslims religious control over the compound and Jews the right to visit but not to pray there. The Holy site houses al-Aqsa mosque, the Dome of the Rock Shrine, and the ruins of the biblical Jewish Temple. Questions about control of the site frequently lead to violent clashes.[1]

Or what the Bible calls conflict. So, as you can see, having these three major world religions being headquartered in Jerusalem with all their differences, and all their different desires over the Temple Mount is adding to the ongoing conflict there just like the Bible said. But many also believe that having all three of these major religions there is also setting the stage for the coming One World Religion that the Bible warned would come on the scene in the 7-year Tribulation. But don't take my word for it. Let's Listen to God's.

Revelation 17:1-6;15-18 "One of the seven angels who had the seven bowls came and said to me, 'Come, I will show you the punishment of the great prostitute, who sits on many waters. With her the kings of the earth committed adultery and the inhabitants of the earth were intoxicated with the wine of her adulteries.' Then the angel carried me away in the Spirit into a desert. There I saw a woman sitting on a scarlet beast that was covered with blasphemous names and had seven heads and ten horns. The woman was dressed in purple and scarlet, and was glittering with gold, precious stones and pearls. She held a golden cup in her hand, filled with abominable things and the filth of her adulteries. This title was written on her forehead: 'Mystery Babylon the great mother of prostitutes and of the abominations of the earth. I saw that the woman was drunk with the blood of the saints, the blood of those who bore testimony to Jesus. When I saw her I was greatly astonished. Then the angel said to me, 'The waters you saw, where the prostitute sits, are peoples, multitudes, nations and languages. The beast and the ten horns you saw will hate the prostitute. They will bring her to ruin and leave her naked; they will eat her flesh and burn her with fire. For God has put it into their hearts to accomplish His purpose by agreeing to give the beast their power to rule, until God's words are fulfilled. The woman you saw is the great city that rules over the kings of the earth."

We have a lot going on in this text, we see that the One World Religion Harlot will not only be "drunk with the blood of the saints," speaking of those who get saved after the Rapture of the Church, but she's also working in conjunction with the Antichrist, controlling the religions of the world, and ruling over the kings of the earth, right? But at some point, it says that the Antichrist turns on her, God allows it as a form of punishment or judgment, and the Antichrist will destroy her. He apparently uses her until he gets what he wants, world domination. She's just a tool. At first, she rides him, seemingly in control, but later he grabs, controls, and kills her. Now I said all that to get to this. In order for this passage to be fulfilled, we need to see some sort of global religious identity working with the governments around the world, trying to control them, as well as promoting all the world's religions to come together as one under its control. Can I tell you something? That's exactly what the Vatican is doing right now! One of the places they want to set up shop is, guess where? In Jerusalem. Why? Because as we saw, it just so happens that the world's three largest religions have headquarters in Jerusalem and reports are saying the Vatican wants to use that to set up a global religion there. Now, first of all, the Vatican is no friend of Israel. In fact, we saw that in WWII, if the Vatican had taken a stand against Nazism, then the outcome might have been quite different for the Jewish people. But they didn't. They had their chance to support the Jews, but they didn't. In fact, during the Holocaust under Pope Pius XII, the Vatican turned a deaf ear to the slaughter of the Jewish people. They've never been a friend to Israel! And believe it or not, the Vatican is no friend of Islam either, even though they currently feign it. They talk all the time about Palestinian support as seen here.

"Thousands of pilgrims gather in St. Peters Square Sunday to witness Pope Francis canonize four Nuns including two from what was 19th century Palestine. Among the onlookers was Palestinian President Mahmoud Abbas who was invited to a private meeting with the head of the Catholic Church Saturday."

126

Romereports.com: *"This affectionate meeting marks the beginning of the meeting between Pope Francis and Palestinian President Mahmoud Abbas. They held a private twenty minute meeting to discuss the recent agreement in which the Vatican recognized the Palestinian state. Also covered was the peace process with Israel and the conflicts ravaging the Middle East and the need to fight terrorism by promoting inter-faith dialog. Pope Francis gave Abbas a copy of Evangelic Idiom and an Angel of Peace Medallion."*

Pope Francis: *"I thought of you. You are an angel of peace."* As they shake hands.

"The Pope's defacto recognition of the Palestinian state builds on the Vatican support of Palestine and the United Nations," says Middle East analyst, Sharif Nashashibi. *"He has made great efforts to build bridges and reach out across the Middle East."*

"Israel has expressed disappointment at the Vatican's recognition of Palestine, but Palestinian pilgrims at the Vatican welcome the move. But even while prayers for peace were offered at the Vatican, in Jerusalem, violence broke out between Israeli's and Palestinians Sunday. Jewish nationalists commemorated Israel's 1967 capture of East Jerusalem with a march through the mainly Muslim quarter in the old city. The violence followed events in the Palestinian territory last week to mark what they call "Catastrophe," the founding of Israel in 1948. The Vatican joins 135 countries in recognizing Palestine as a state and lists the Popes position as a spiritual leader of over a billion Catholics worldwide.[2]

I'm here to tell you it's all a smoke screen! You call the Palestinian leader, who seeks to annihilate the Jews, an "Angel of Peace," did you catch that? But I'm telling you, there's more going on here than meets the eye! I believe the evidence will show that the Vatican and the Catholic Church are chumming up with the Muslims and various world leaders, at various times, to get what they ultimately want, and that is total control of all religions on the planet in Jerusalem. It's all a PR campaign with the Pope chumming up to these guys, it's a smoke screen! But let me give you some of that proof from reading just some of the headlines out there.

"Vatican representative in Israel declare that 'Jews are no longer the chosen people," and *"The Vatican says Israel's existence as a Jewish state has nothing to do with the Bible."*

Excuse me? What Bible are you reading? That's the problem! It's not only flat out unbiblical to say that, but that doesn't sound like you have got Israel's best interests to me! But there's more. *"We cannot speak about the Promised Land for the Jewish people. The concept of the promised land cannot be used as a base for the justification of the return of Jews to Israel and the displacement of Palestinians."*

What? So now you're saying the Jewish people are not only not the chosen people of God, but now you're saying that they have no right to the land that they themselves received unconditionally from God! Who do you think you are, God? First of all, as we saw before, there are no real historical people called the Palestinians in the first place. That was made up by the Romans out of spite of the Jews! And two, the people wandering around over there are the leftover Arabs who got duped by their own Arab leaders and countries to leave their homes when they went to war against Israel and lost. They could take them in, they are their own people, it's their responsibility, but refuse to do so and are capitalizing on their own people's plight! And three, the Bible says God is the One Who forever promised the Jewish people that land because it is His land to give away to them in the first place! It doesn't belong to Ishmael the Arabs, it belongs to Isaac the Jews! Then, as if that weren't enough, the Vatican even went so far as to, "Denounce the Judaization of Jerusalem" and attacked Israel for "trying to transform it into an only Hebrew-Jewish city, excluding the other faiths." In other words, other religions should have it as well. Why? Because again, the Vatican wants all religions to be there, so they can control it all! That's their ultimate goal. Then if that still wasn't enough proof of their real intentions, the Vatican's Cardinal Jean Louis Tauran, president of the Pontifical Council for Inter-religious Dialogue (Inter-religious means One World Religion) declared that, *"Israel must adopt an internationally recognized statute for that part of Jerusalem where the Holy Places of the three monotheistic religions are open to believers."*
In other words, you can't say it's just yours, it belongs to all religions. I'm telling you, this is why the Vatican sometimes even joins forces with Islam, as you saw before to achieve this goal. That's why the Pope "says" he supports a "Palestinian state." It's not because he or the Vatican cares about Islam, frankly they don't and never have. It's all a smoke screen. Let me show you the proof of that. Remember the Crusades? That didn't come from Christians by the way, you don't need to defend that, that came from the Catholic Church. They did it to get control of Jerusalem! But, can you name a time in history when the Vatican sincerely endorsed the Muslim control of Jerusalem? Answer is…No! Never!

Including today! In fact, history is loaded with examples of the Vatican opposing, often violently, Muslim control of the Holy Land. Again, that's what the crusades were all about! It was Pope Urban II, in 1095 AD who was responsible for setting off the Crusades in the Middle Ages and it was always about continued occupation of the holy places and above all getting Jerusalem. Therefore, the Muslims today are just a pawn in the Vatican's hand. Even in the Crusades the Catholic Church showed they were no friend of Muslims or Jews! In the First Crusade alone, Catholic crusaders slaughtered some 70,000 Jews and Arabs in their goal to get Jerusalem from the so-called "infidel" i.e. anybody who tries to control it other than the Catholic Church! The First Crusade was followed by another, and then another, then another, each in an attempt to purge the Holy Land of Muslims of course and Jews as well. History is clear folks, that the Vatican has never supported Muslim control of Jerusalem let alone Jewish control! So, the question is why are they seemingly doing it now? Well, again, I think it's all part of a smoke screen for this purpose. To get Islam to do the "dirty work" for them! Watch this current headline.

This year! "The Pope and Turkish leader meet over Jerusalem."

"Recently, the Pope welcomed to the Vatican an Islamic world leader attempting to re-establish the Caliphate. Pope Francis met with Turkish President Erdogan and the future status of Jerusalem was high on the agenda

They called for an end to racism, xenophobia, 'Islamophobia' and discrimination. The meeting has been hailed as promising 'global peace.'"

So why is the Vatican meeting the Muslim Community? One guy states this:

"There are two reasons the Catholic Church, for now, is making it appear it supports a Palestinian state and greater Muslim influence over Jerusalem.

First, this effort undermines Israel's control over the city. When it comes to diminishing Israel's grip on Jerusalem and its holy sites, Catholic officials are happy to let the Muslims do the dirty work.

Second, the Vatican's endorsement of Palestinian statehood provides ideal cover for their own ambition to wrest control of Jerusalem from the Jews themselves."

This is what the Vatican wants. Historically they never have and never will let Islam gain control of Jerusalem, let alone the Jews. What they really want is control over Jerusalem to make it a site for a global religion.

And they're tricking the Muslims into doing the dirty work for them!

In fact, more headlines, *"The Vatican not only wants to lay its hands-on Jerusalem, but they are demanding control of the religious sites in Jerusalem."*

And this is their goal!

The Roman Catholic Church has been fighting for more than 450 years to win back control over the areas that were seized from them during the Ottoman Empire back in the 1500's, and their recent efforts are paying off because even as recent as 2006, Israel's then Prime Minister, Ehud Olmert and Foreign Minister, Tzipi Livni, negotiated to give away the "holy basin" to the Vatican.

You say, what's that? The "holy basin" is the area in Jerusalem that includes the Old City and its adjacent territories, and they want even more than that. The Vatican uses the expression "Holy Basin," to refer to the area of the Temple Mount, the Mount of Olives, Mount Zion and a variety of other "holy sites. And shocker, former President Bill Clinton recommended these areas be administered under a "special regime." (In other words, the Catholic Church) Obama's plan called for the Old City of Jerusalem to be designated an "international zone." (Open to all religions but somebody's got to control it...I wonder who that will be?) And don't forget, both of these Presidents met with the Vatican. Gee I wonder what they talked about?

And believe it or not, it's even reported that Israel's former President Shimon Peres also agreed to hand over the sovereignty of the holy sites to the Vatican. The Vatican's tactics are slowly methodically paying off. They're gaining back control of Jerusalem for their One World Religion. In fact, the plan was for the Old City having an Israeli mayor and a Palestinian mayor, both under the orders of the Holy See..." And lest you think that's not what they're after, look at this, more headlines.

"Peace negotiations in the Middle East must tackle the issue of the holy sites of Jerusalem because there will be no peace if the holy sites are not adequately resolved."

In other words, you won't have peace in the Middle East until you give the Vatican control of these areas! They're the experts. They know how to bring peace to the planet...yeah right! This is coming, again, from the Vatican's Council for Interreligious Dialogue.

"The holy sites of the three religions – is humanity's heritage. The sacred and unique character of the area must be safeguarded, and it can only be done with a special, internationally-guaranteed statute."

In other words, only the Vatican has the experience to do it right! Just give us control!

And they go on to say, *"Before territorial problems are resolved, we have to assure that never again one party should claim Jerusalem as its possession."*

Again, give us control of Jerusalem and the holy sites and we'll bring peace to all this religious conflict. It's not right for just the Jewish people to have it! We need it for all religions, and we'll head it up for you! That's what's really going on folks! It's a set up! The Vatican wants this ongoing religious conflict that we're seeing in the news everyday so that "out of this conflict" they can rise up and be the "savior of humanity" bringing in a so-called religious peace to the planet. With a new global religious headquarters in Jerusalem! They're tricking the world into getting what they really want. A One World Religion with them, the Vatican, at that top! In fact, some say, there might be another reason why the Vatican is so desperate to hurry up and get control over Jerusalem and the "holy sites." It might be to cover up what could be found. This was interesting.

"In January 2001, Israel TV journalists secretly filmed under the Shrine of Omar, the 7th century Islamic building constructed over the Holy of Holies, the most sacred room of the ancient Jewish Temple.

The video revealed a new and massive tunnel aimed directly at the most sacred core of Solomon's and later, Herod's Temples.

During the Crusades in the early 12th century, it is reported that the Knights Templar dug under the ruins for nine years and found a network of tunnels where the Jewish priests hid their treasures from the marauding Romans in 70 AD.

It was also assumed that the original records of the Jerusalem Church which prove that the Vatican was not practicing Christianity as its founders had intended, was buried in this spot.

If these scrolls were made public, they would jeopardize Rome's legitimacy.

Thus, it is imperative to the Vatican that the Jews be removed from the Temple Mount so that they don't find these important scrolls."[3]

You know that they are not representing, true Christianity and they are a religious sham! But be that as it may, the even bigger desire for the Vatican is they also need total control of Jerusalem and the Holy Sites, so they can perform their deceptive play for all the world to see in the Last Days. Jerusalem has to be the place for that play to take place! Check this out.

"It can't be that the Vatican is only interested in access to the 'Holy Sites' in Jerusalem. It's something else that the Vatican wants. The Roman Catholic Church needs to have certain versions of events be played out for them in order to stand in front of mankind and proclaim, 'Our Messiah has returned.'

Of course, to the Jews, this Messiah will be a false messiah, but that doesn't matter to the Vatican. They know this isn't the end of the story that the Jewish God had in mind, but what they're doing is engineering their own ending to the story.

This is why, for centuries, they have attempted to obtain control of Jerusalem, which started with the Crusades. In order for them to convince the world that the Messiah they put on the world's stage is going to be accepted as genuine, they need to perform this play in the Old City, in Jerusalem.

The story of this production is that this 'Messiah' will merge the three monotheistic religions, usher in peace and harmony in the world, and solve the Middle East conflict. The location for this 'production' will be in none other than the Old City of Jerusalem.

Then, this so-called 'Messiah' will insist that by having a 'world government' as well, then world peace and harmony will be ushered in. This will be a lie, and a fraud, but never mind. It's all part of the Vatican's plan!

Israel will be pressured to accede to these demands by all world bodies and the superpowers on the claim that 'this is the only way to solve the Middle East conflict.'

And in order to get the Jews to go along they will convince them that with this 'Messiah' having appeared for the Jews, it is now time to start rebuilding the Third Temple. This is what The Vatican is after.

And this is why it is critical for the Vatican to control the entire Old City of Jerusalem and 'holy sites' because it is all needed for the "play they have planned" to be performed on the world stage."[4]

In other words, they have to get control of this area to usher in a One World Religion, which is what they want and also promote a false Messiah who controls the world's government. Which is exactly what Revelation 17 said. If they're going to internationalize Jerusalem and basically "fake the Millennial Reign" then there is no place for the restoration of the nation of Israel in its theology, let alone the Jews maintaining control over Jerusalem. In order for the Vatican and the Roman Catholic Church to convince the world the lie of their False Messiah and One World Religion, they have to get control of Jerusalem! You don't perform your play in New Jersey, it won't work in Moscow, Beijing or Sydney, Australia! It has to be Jerusalem! This is what's going on right now as we speak and it's all adding to the major religious conflict over there, that God said would come in the Last Days![5]

Now, for those of you who think this is just some wacky conspiracy theory I made up, where the Vatican is after a One World Religion, even controlling the governments of the world, here is their own commercial they've recently released, and you tell me that's not what they're up to!

The Pope is reading this declaration while we see leaders of different religions agreeing with what he is saying. "Most of the planet's inhabitants declare themselves believers. This should lead to dialogue among religions. We should not stop praying for it and collaborating with those who think differently."

A Buddist says, "I have confidence in the Buddha."

A Rabbi says: "I believe in God."

A Priest says: "I believe in Jesus Christ."

A Muslim says: "I believe in God, Allah."

The Pope speaks again: "Many think differently, feel differently, seeking God or meeting God in different ways. In this crowd, in this range of religions there is only one certainty we have for all, we are all children of God."

Once again, the Buddhist says: "I believe in love."

The Rabbi says: "I believe in love."

The Priest says: "I believe in love."

"I hope you will spread my prayer request this month: That sincere dialogue among men and women of different faiths may produce the fruits of peace and justice. I have confidence in your prayers."

We see all the different religions hugging in love and then at the end of the commercial they all hold their hands out with a baby Jesus, Buddha, Catholic beads, and a Jewish Menorah, a hope for One World Religion.[6]

Nope! Nope! They don't have any plans for a One World Religion. That's just another wacky Crone theory! Straight from the Vatican itself folks! How do you get any clearer than that? And when you understand this ultimate goal, it starts to make sense why the Vatican, historically, has always been a promoter of "Replacement Theology." For centuries the Vatican has been pushing "replacement theology" which states that the Catholic Church has replaced Israel as the "New Israel." They are the "New Jerusalem." They believe they are the "rightful heir to the Kingdom of God" not Israel! If Israel continues to control Jerusalem, then it obviously proves that the Catholic Church's claims are not correct and that the literal interpretation of the Bible is correct. And you can't have that if you're going to pull off a One World Religion! That's exactly what our text said a world religious identity would do in the Last Days with the Antichrist! The Vatican is the headquarters of all this! This is not make-believe, it's all happening right now! In fact, as we saw before, the Jews and Muslims are already falling for the ruse by the Vatican! Both parties are already calling for a United Nations of Religions where some global entity would control the world's religions just like the United Nations controls all the World's Government.

Former King Abdullah of Saudi Arabia has been planning for years to, "find a way to unite the world's major religions in an effort to help foster peace and believes a new international organization will help make that dream a reality."

Chief Rabbi Yona Metzger, one of the two Chief Rabbis of Israel said, "We need a United Relations of Religions, which would contain representatives of the World's Religions as opposed to nations. Uniting the world's faithful is key to world peace. We must promote a respect for the differences among various religions. A Church, a mosque, a synagogue or a holy temple must be embassies of God and we have to spread this idea to our believers." He has suggested that the Dalai Lama could lead the assembly.

Muslim Leader Adnan Oktar recently met with three representatives from the re-established Jewish Sanhedrin, to discuss how religious Muslims, Jews and Christians can work together on rebuilding the Temple." An official statement about the meeting has been published on the Sanhedrin's website, "We are all the sons of one father, the descendants of Adam, and all humanity is but a single family. Peace among nations will be achieved through building the House of G-d, where all peoples will serve." Oktar added that the Temple, "Will be rebuilt and all believers will worship there in tranquility." And, "The Temple could be rebuilt in one year."

Shimon Peres: Former President of Israel even more recently just met with Pope Francis to discuss the idea of creating a UN-like organization that he called "The United Religions" to, bring an end to the wars raging in the Middle East and around the world.

World Trade Center: Even here in America the Pope visited Ground Zero at the World Trade Center and the U.S. Media used it as an opportunity to promote a One World Religion.

The Pope recently visited Ground Zero and recited the following: "On this hallowed ground, the scene of unspeakable violence and pain." Behind him there are seated a Jew, a Muslim, a Buddhist, a Hindu, a Native Indian, a Christian, and many more different religions.

When he is finished speaking another one stands up to speak in their native tongue. The interpreter translates what the lady from India is saying. "May God nourish us, may we work together." The next one to speak is a Buddhist Monk.

He also speaks in his native tongue. Translated he is saying, "Victory begets enmity, the defeated dwell in pain." The next to take the stage is a Hindu priest and what he says is, "Truth is above everything and the highest deed is truthful living."

The next one to speak is a Catholic priest, "For theirs is the kingdom of Heaven, blessed are those who mourn." Another gets up to speak, "Grant us to live with the salutation of peace and lead us to your abode of peace." Now the Jewish Rabbi speaks but it is more like a song with no translation. But a choir then comes on stage and sings "Let there be peace on earth and let it begin with me."[7]

Yup…let's build this One World Religion on the planet, let it begin with me, so we can have peace on earth to end all this conflict and violence and oh yeah, let the Pope and the Vatican run the whole show! Looks like people are falling for the Vatican's deceptive play right before our very eyes, even here in America! In fact, this is the very "play" that the New Age Movement also wants and they too think it's a good thing. Let's see how they "perceive" things "playing out" in the Last Days! First of all, they believe that what is coming, and they're expecting it very soon, is what's called, "The New Jerusalem Covenant." Sound familiar? Daniel says the Antichrist makes a "covenant" with the Jewish People for 7 years which is the very event that starts the 7-year Tribulation, the final week of Daniel's 70th week prophecy! But sometime soon they believe, the following scenario will unfold, depending only on the right set of circumstances:

- Muslim and Jewish areas in Jerusalem will be combined with Christian/Catholic to create the New Jerusalem Covenant.
- The Pope will visit the combined Jewish/Christian/Moslem sector of Jerusalem to announce that all religions should be combined into one. This action will then finally break the Middle East logjam.
- All religions will convene to celebrate three religious festivals simultaneously.
- 1. Festival of Goodwill -- normally in May-June
- 2. Festival of Easter -- normally in April (Celebrates new birth, as exemplified by the Christ -- Jesus Christ to Christians)
- 3. Festival of Wesak -- normally in March (Celebrates birth of the Buddha)

This celebration of these three combined Festivals will create the New World Order Religion and will be the spiritual equivalent of the political United

Nations. Then when the religious communities of the world are thus merged, political governments will simultaneously hold the following political/business conferences:

- 1. Planetary Goodwill Congress
- 2. Planetary Human Resource and Disarmament Congress
- 3. Planetary Environmental Resource and Space Congress

Thus, when the three religious conferences and the three political/business conferences are simultaneously held, a grand merger of all forces will occur worldwide that will move the world in any desired direction. Then, and only then, will it be possible to build a combination Temple/Church/Mosque in Jerusalem.

"Any permanent solution to the Middle East conflict would also have to see the religious portion of the problem solved. Once this religious problem is solved, then the power and influence of the Orthodox Jews in Israel would permanently decline."

They also believe that there will be three types of people on the planet as these events form and take shape.

- 1. Those whose consciousness have been properly raised so they can readily accept him.
- 2. Those whose consciousness have been raised somewhat but not so high that they can readily and immediately accept him, but they might be able to accept him after further enlightenment.
- 3. Those who will never accept him.

So, what happens to those who will never accept him?

"The persons of Group #3 will 'elect to leave for another room.' They do not commit suicide, they will simply "leave this dimension."

As one guy states, "I would not be surprised if this group is actually writing the Peace Treaty/Covenant which the Antichrist will sign with Israel at the proper time. This would then directly fulfill Daniel's prophecy of 9:27.

Daniel 9:27 "He will confirm a covenant with many for one 'seven.' In the middle of the 'seven' he will put an end to sacrifice and offering and in a wing of the temple he will set up an abomination that causes desolation until the end that is decreed is poured out on him."

In other words, he's going to lose! And lest you think this ruse of the Antichrist and False Prophet is nowhere near close to being pulled off, creating a global religion and bringing a so-called peace to the Middle East religious conflict, then you might want to read this transcript of a video with the various world religions saying we all need to be friends with guess who at the top!

The world's most prominent religious leaders call on everyone to make friends across religions:

Ecumenical Partriarch Bartholomew: *"We are called, as we like to say, to look into one another's eyes in order to see more deeply and in order to recognize the beauty of God in every living human being."*

Ayatollah Sayyid Fadhel Al-Milani: *"Our advice is to make friends to followers of all religions."*

Pope Francis: *"It's very important, because my religious life became richer with his explanations, so much richer. And I guess the same happened for him."*

Rabbi Abraham Skorka: *"It was through our religious calling that we found each other in life."*

Bhai Sahib Mohinder Singh: *"No matter from which side of the mountain you're climbing, we should be helping each other. So that we can get all to the same place. So, there is need for people to make friends."*

Grand Mufti Shawki Allam: *"And don't focus on or search for differences between religious groups."*

H.H. The Dalai Lama: *"Personal contact, personal friendship then we can exchange a deeper level of experience."*

Sri Sri Ravi Shankar: *"Honor other religions like you do your own."*

Ayatollah Sayyid Hassan Al-Qazwini: *"We need to get together and know one another. Just to discover and explore those commonalities."*

Archbishop Antje Jackelen: *"That starts a process where prejudices go away, where new insights are born and where basically hope is born."*

Archbishop Justin Welby: *"It's not complicated. I would say to everyone: Start with sharing what we all share, which is the pleasure of conversation."*

Chief Rabbi Jonathan sacks: *"One of the wonderful things about spending time with people completely unlike you is you discover how much you have in common. The same fears, the same hopes, the same concerns."*

Ven.Khandro Rinpoche: *"I think I'll keep it very simple, it's probably time to talk less, listen more."*

Mata Amritanandamayi (Amma): *"May universal friendship become a reality."*[8]

As well as a Universal One World Religion with the Vatican and Pope at the top! But all this is going on right now, while we're all concerned about the economy and who won what game and not just the satanic New Age Movement, but even the Vatican is promoting this "satanic play" or Last Days scenario that they are going to foist upon the whole world in Jerusalem. They have to gain control of Jerusalem to make it all work! This is why you can turn on the news and read in all the newspapers of how Israel has indeed become what? An international global problem. It has become a center of world conflict, a religious conflict. Exactly like the Bible said would happen. When? In the Last Days! This is why, out of love, God has given us this update on *The Final Countdown: Tribulation Rising* concerning the Jewish People & the Antichrist to show us that the 7-year Tribulation is near, and the Return of Jesus Christ is rapidly approaching. That's why Jesus Himself said...

Luke 21:28 "When these things begin to take place, stand up and lift up your heads, because your redemption is drawing near."

Like it or not, we are headed for The Final Countdown. The signs of the 7-year Tribulation are Rising all around us! It's time to Wake up! This is the point. If you're reading this today and you're not a Christian, then I beg you, please, heed these signs, heed these warnings, give your life to Jesus now! You don't want to be here when God pours out His Judgment upon this planet! It's the worst time in the history of mankind, so horrible that unless God shortened the timeframe the entire human race would be destroyed! The only way to escape is through Jesus! Take the way out now before it's too late. GET SAVED TODAY!

But if you're reading this today and you are a Christian then it's high time we stop goofing off and getting distracted with this world. Let's get busy working together sharing the Gospel with as many as we can! Let's leave here living for Jesus and longing for His soon return. Amen?

Chapter Ten

The Jewish People & Their Relocation Conflict

We just saw how the Vatican, right now, is trying to gain control of Jerusalem and the Temple Mount and other "holy areas" to stage their play to create a One World Government and a One World Religion, just like Revelation 17 says!

As one guy states, *"Jerusalem is a thermometer for measuring the nearness of our Lord Jesus Christ. The more the tension rises between Jews and Muslims— and the more that the Catholic Church interferes in Jerusalem—the closer we are to this awesome, history-altering event! Stay tuned for the Second Coming of Jesus Christ!"*[1]

But, as we saw, somebody had to come along and mess things up for the Vatican! His name is President Donald Trump!

The **3rd reason** why Israel has Become a Source of World Conflict in the Last Days, just like the Bible said, is because of the **Relocation Conflict**. Let's go back to that text that explains why there's a conflict in the first place.[2]

Zechariah 12:1-3 "This is the word of the LORD concerning Israel. The LORD, who stretches out the Heavens, who lays the foundation of the earth, and who forms the spirit of man within him, declares: 'I am going to make Jerusalem a cup that sends all the surrounding peoples reeling. Judah will be besieged as well as Jerusalem. On that day, when all the nations of the earth are gathered against her, I will make Jerusalem an immovable rock for all the nations. All who try to move it will injure themselves."

In other words, again as we saw before, don't mess with Israel! But here we see clearly that God is not only going to make Israel a major ongoing problem on the world scene in the Last Days, but notice specifically where! Not once, not twice, but three times in just three verses God said this source of world conflict would be where? In Jerusalem! Not Tel Aviv, not Haifa, not even Beersheba, but specifically Jerusalem! And this is exactly what has happened in recent events with our current President Donald Trump! His acknowledgment of Jerusalem as Israel's capital, by moving the U.S. Embassy there. Here's just one report.

Fox News Reports: *"The U.S. embassy officially opened today. Listen to what Israeli Prime Minister, Benjamin Netanyahu had to say at today's ceremony."*

Benjamin Netanyahu: *"Last December President Trump became the first leader to recognize Jerusalem as our capital. And today the United States of America is opening its embassy right here in Jerusalem. Thank you, thank you President Trump for having the courage to keep your promises."*

President Trump: *"We will move the American Embassy to the eternal capital of the Jewish people, Jerusalem."*

Fox News: *"Trump making good on his campaign promise may unravel the peace process in the Middle East."*

Nabil Shaath, Senior Palestinian official: *"That totally destroys any chance that he will play a role as an honest broker. That takes away honest, takes away broker, takes away chaperone of peace, takes away the deal of the century and makes them beyond us, gone into the files of history."*

Fox News: *"Every U.S. president since 1948 has located the U.S. Embassy in Tel Aviv to avoid igniting further conflict between Palestinians and Israelis over their shared land. Israel recognizes Jerusalem as its capital and welcomes the U.S. move. But Palestinians claim east Jerusalem as the capital of their future state. According to a royal statement, Jordan's King Abdullah II told Trump that moving the U.S. Embassy "will provoke Muslims and Christians alike." His concerns have been shared by Arab League and Palestinian Authority President*

Mahmoud Abbas and leaders across the Middle East and Europe. There have already been protests in the Gaza Strip and the West Bank. The U.S. Consulate in Jerusalem has warned employees, their families and fellow Americans.[3]

Of what? Of the conflict this decision has created! But as you can see, our President, Donald Trump frankly had the guts to do what nobody else would do! Historically he's the only one to pull it off! Then Presidential candidate Bill Clinton promised to recognize Jerusalem as the capital of Israel and move the US Embassy from Tel Aviv to that city, but he didn't. Then Presidential candidate George W. Bush promised to do the same but didn't. And of course, Presidential candidate Barack Obama refrained from making any promise of recognition, Presidential candidate Donald Trump renewed the promise and did it!

As one guy said, *"The promises of Clinton and Bush proved to be insincere, meaningless hot air. Obama's unwillingness to take a stand signaled that he would become the most anti-Israel president in American history.*

But President Trump has kept his promise, and he is to be commended for doing so. He made his proclamation on December 6, 2017 and in it he stated,

'This [recognition] is nothing more or less than a recognition of reality. It is also the right thing to do. It's something that has to be done.'"[4]

Why? Because as we saw before, Jerusalem is the capital of the Jewish People and it has to come back into play on the world scene in the Last Days! Bible prophecy tells us that is where Jesus is coming back to set up shop and rule and reign over the entire planet in the Millennial Kingdom! So, what President Trump did was the right thing to do both politically and prophetically! One guy puts it this way.

"In other words, it's a slap in the face! So here comes President Trump saying, 'That's a bunch of baloney!' And he does the right common-sense thing!"

In fact, back in May of 2017 President Trump showed even more support of Israel and the Jewish People by becoming the first sitting President to visit the Western Wall while he was in office.

CBSN Reports: *"While President Trump will be making history in the Holy Land, he will be the first sitting president to visit the Western Wall. It is* *considered the most Holy site in Judaism. The Wall, in the disputed Jerusalem is the holiest site where Jews can pray. Trump appears to slip a prayer or note between its stones, as is custom. It's his first visit abroad as president, which has drawn controversy."[5]*

In other words, conflict, which again is the theme of the prophecy we opened up with, but it didn't conflict with the Jewish People! Their Transportation Minister is now naming the new Western Wall train station after Trump!

Transportation Minister Israel Katz said, *"The Western Wall is the holiest place for the Jewish people, and I decided to call the train station that leads to it after President Trump – following his historic and brave decision to recognize Jerusalem as the capital of the State of Israel."[6]*

In fact, the bulk of the Jewish People are absolutely thrilled with Trumps decision and they are repeatedly saying that it comes with prophetic implications!

Israel Rabbis – A group of 250 Israeli rabbis sent a letter to President Trump thanking and praising him for his decision. Specifically, they said, "We are confident that you will be remembered in the history of the Jewish people forever as one who stood at the forefront and was not afraid. You are fulfilling prophecies. You will be remembered in the history of the Jews people. We are privileged to be seeing the rebuilding of Jerusalem", wrote the rabbis. "Children play in its streets (Zechariah 8:4) and we are confident in the fulfillment of all the prophecies. With this recognition, we see the fulfillment of another step in the completion of the prophecy of Isaiah that the nations of the world will recognize the centrality of Jerusalem," said Rabbi Eliyahu. Rabbi Asaf Fried, an official spokesman for the United Temple Mount, saw Trump's action as similar to the role played by the Persian king, Cyrus, who ended the Babylonian exile and helped with the building of the Second Temple.

Israel Leaders – Benjamin Netanyahu — The Prime Minister of Israel received the President's proclamation with great joy and appreciation, saying, "The President's decision is an important step toward peace, for there is no peace that doesn't include Jerusalem as the capital of the State of Israel." He then added, "President Trump has inscribed himself in the annals of our capital for all time. His name will now be linked to the names of others in the context of the glorious history of Jerusalem and our people." Netanyahu then likened President Trump to the Bible's King Cyrus, the Persian king who rescued the Jewish people from Babylonian captivity, a comparison that some evangelicals have been making since Trump's election campaign. This is also why some would say it is significant that President Trump is the 45th American president and that the prophecy about King Cyrus delivering the Israelites from captivity appears in the 45th chapter of Isaiah. As one person stated, "You can't make this stuff up!" But, be that as it may, Cyrus is the only Gentile in the Old Testament who is called 'anointed' by God and evangelicals who subscribe to this belief say that Cyrus is a perfect historical antecedent to explain Trump's presidency: "A nonbeliever who nevertheless served as a vessel for divine interest." And this is why even President Trump admitted that Evangelicals seem even more excited over His decision than the Jews.

TBN Exclusive, Mike Huckabee interviewing President Trump*: "The embassy was moved from Tel Aviv to Jerusalem. I was there. It was as surreal a moment as I have ever witnessed. You made that promise, you kept that promise. What was it that made you do, what other presidents promised as well, what made you decide that I'm going to do this because I said I would?"*

President Trump: *"Well the embassy was a big thing, as it was for many Presidents before me. Everybody campaigned that they would move the embassy to Jerusalem and nobody did it. And I never understood why. I never did. I knew there would be pressure, but I never understood. But I do understand now. Because two weeks before I did it, the word was out that I was going to do it. I was called by so many countries saying please don't do it. It had actually got to a point where I said I will call you back in a week. Because I didn't want to hear them say don't do it, and I do it. It was a campaign promise that I thought was very important. And you know who really likes it the most is the evangelicals. I get more calls of thank you from evangelicals and I see it in the audiences and everything else than I do from Jewish people. The Jewish people appreciate it, but the evangelicals show more appreciation than the Jews. It's incredible."*

Mike Huckabee: *"It's not a surprise Mr. President because evangelicals are the people of the Book and they believe that you kept a promise that was fulfilling a 3000-year commitment to recognize Jerusalem as the capital."*

President Trump: *"I think it was a nice thing to say because it really affects Jewish people in theory more, but as you say, people of the Book. People of the Bible, but the evangelicals really appreciate it and that makes me feel good.*

Nobody did it, I never could understand why. As soon as that second week was up, and I did it, it was something very special, it was an important event."[7]

"Jerusalem became the capital city of the Jewish people some 3,000 years ago when David conquered the city from the Jebusites (2 Samuel 5:6-7).

During the 1,878 years that the Jewish people were evicted from the land (70 AD to 1948), Jerusalem never served as the capital of any Arab or Muslim nation.

And when the Muslim leaders of the Middle East say they want a "two-state solution," they are lying. Their desire is not simply a separate Palestinian State. Their goal is the annihilation of Israel.

Gaining a separate Palestinian State would serve only as a stepping stone toward their final attack on Israel, just as they have used their acquisition of Gaza as a launching pad for missiles. This is the reason why Israeli Prime Minister, Benjamin Netanyahu, has often said, 'If the Arabs put down their weapons today, there would be no more violence. But...if the Jews put down their weapons today, there would be no more Israel.'

The steadfast refusal of most of the world's nations to recognize Jerusalem as Israel's capital and move their embassies there is an incredible insult to the Jewish people.

It is really an expression of anti-Semitism since no other nation has been treated in such a horrible way.

It is equivalent to some nation saying to the American people, "We do not recognize Washington, D.C. as your capital, so we are going to place our embassy in Chicago."[8]

Why? Because it's part of Bible Prophecy and evangelicals know it! Jerusalem has to be the capital of the Jewish People in the Last Days because that's where Jesus Christ is going to come back and set up shop and rule and reign over the entire planet in the Millennial Kingdom! And President Trump is acknowledging that and it's happening on TV right now! It's wild! But as you can imagine, and/or have already seen in the media, there's a ton of people all over the world, including the Pope, who are upset over Trump's decision adding to the conflict.

Ayman Odeh — The Israeli-Arab political leader in the Israeli parliament, declared, "Trump is a crazy pyromaniac who is capable of setting the entire region on fire with his madness."

Theresa May — The British Prime Minister provided a typical bureaucratic response when she characterized Trump's move as, "unhelpful to peace in the region."

Emmanuel Macron — The new Prime Minister of France dismissed the announcement as "a unilateral decision."

The Arab League — Denounced the decision, calling it "dangerous and unacceptable" and a "flagrant attack on a political solution." They proceeded to call upon the nations of the world to recognize the State of Palestine and East Jerusalem as its capital. (East Jerusalem includes the Old City, which is the location of the Temple Mount and the Western Wall.)

The Palestinian Authority — Mahmoud Abbas, the President of the PA, denounced the decision, saying that it would "motivate extremist groups to wage holy war." The chief Palestinian negotiator, Saeb Erakat, said Trump's decision "disqualified the United States to play any role in any peace process." He added, "President Trump just destroyed any policy of a two-state solution."

Recep Erdogan — The President of Turkey said his country would not tolerate the recognition of Jerusalem as Israel's capital. "Jerusalem is our red line. Any steps against Jerusalem's historic status and holiness are unacceptable."

Pope Francis – Even the Vatican and Pope Francis got in on the negative response to Trump's decision. Pope Francis slammed President Trump for recognizing Jerusalem as the Capital of Israel and said, "He cannot silence his deep concern over President Donald Trump recognizing the disputed city as Israel's capital. Then he called for all to honor United Nations resolutions on the city, which is sacred to Jews, Christians and Muslims. As one guy said Pope Francis obviously needs to spend more time reading his Bible and less time appeasing radical Islam. But here's what was on the video:

Leaders around the world have warned against the United States' decision to declare Jerusalem as Israel's capital.

Stephane Dujarric, United Nations spokesman: *"And we always have regarded Jerusalem as a final status issue that must be resolved through direct negotiations between the two parties based on relative security resolutions."*

Federica Mogherini: *"The European Union supports the resumption of meaningful process towards a two states solution. We believe that any action that would undermine these efforts must absolutely be avoided."*

Nabil Shaath, Senior Palestinian Official: *"President Trump will have destroyed every chance to get the deal of the century that he has been talking about."*

Sigmar Gabriel, Acting German foreign minister: *"A solution to the Jerusalem problem can only be found through direct negotiations between the two parties. Everything that worsens the crisis is counterproductive in these times."*

Theresa May, British prime minister: *"Jerusalem should ultimately form a shared capital between the Israeli and Palestinian states. That is, we continue to support the two-state solution. We recognize the importance of Jerusalem and that position has not changed."*

Ahmed Aboul Gheit, Arab League secretary general: *"Proceeding with this is dangerous, would have consequences."*

King Abdullah II, King of Jordan: *"There is no alternative to the two-state solution and Jerusalem is key to any peace agreement and key to the stability to the entire region."*

Haider Al-Abadi, Iraqi prime minister: *"This move would unleash turmoil in the region and the world alike. The U.S.'s decision will also have a prejudice against the rights of Palestinians, the Arab and Islamic world."*

Binali Yildirim, Turkish prime minister: *"Either way, this will be an unlawful decision and the ongoing problems in the region will reach a stalemate."*

Naftali Bennett, Israeli education minister: *"Jerusalem has been the Jewish capital for 3000 years. It was never, and will never be the capital of anyone else."*

Pope Francis: *"I make an urgent appeal to everybody to respect the status quo of the city, in accordance with the pertinent resolutions of the United Nations."*[9]

Worldwide Response: In Times Square there were chilling calls to massacre Jews after Trump's announcement followed by explicit, blood-curdling calls for violence against Jews. First the Muslim chants began with the regular angry anti-Israel flavor but soon took on a different tone as the crowd began calling for a Muslim holy war against the Jews. The chanting began with, "We don't want no two-state, we want '48". This is an explicit refusal of the two-state solution, which would create a Palestinian state. The number '48' is a reference to the 1948 United Nations Partition Plan which led to the modern State of Israel. Then the crowd began chanting an even more inciteful slogan, "With spirit and blood we'll redeem al-Aqsa, there is only one solution; intifada revolution." Al-Aqsa is the mosque on the Temple Mount, and "Intifada" means a violent confrontation. Then the rally got really ugly when the crowd began calling not only for an end to Israel, but for a massacre of the Jewish people. Demonstrators started chanting, "Jews remember Khaybar, the army of Muhammed is returning." Khaybar was the name of a Jewish-majority city about 90 miles north of Medina in Saudi Arabia which existed in the time of Muhammed. Muslims slaughtered the city's Jews in 628 AD and thus is used as a battle cry when attacking Jews or Israelis. Here's what the video shows us.

"People are gathered in the street and Anti-Israel protesters calling for violent intifada against Jews. "Our message to the Palestinian Authority: You have to stop all kinds of peace processes. No peace process and negotiations with the occupation in Palestine. Oslo has to be stopped and to be finished. We have to start a new Intifada. Intifada! Intifada! Intifada! Intifada! With our souls and our blood, we will redeem you, oh Al-Aqsa! The Palestinian vanguard, with their incredible courage. The Palestinians fight with whatever they can. They fight with rocks, they fight with rockets from Gaza, they fight with guns, their children fight. Every single Palestinian is in it to win it! We should be just as angry that they (the U.S.) have an embassy in Tel Aviv or Jaffa as we are about Jerusalem because every inch of Palestine is Palestinian land. It is up to all of us here, including everyone in the crowd, to keep this resistance going, if we want to see Israel fall within our lifetime. Khaybar, Khaybar, oh Jews, Khaybar, Khaybar, Khaybar, oh Jews. The army of Muhammad will return! The army of Muhammad will return! The army of Muhammad! The army of Muhammad!"[10]

Now what's wild is the Jewish writer writing this article concerning this video admitted the prophetic significance of what was taking place. He quoted, **Jeremiah 29:18** "I will make them a horror to all the kingdoms of the earth, a curse and an object of horror and hissing and scorn among all the nations to which I shall banish them."

- Then there was a rally in front of the US Embassy in London where approximately 3,000 pro-Palestinian protesters began by chanting "Down down USA" and "Hands off Jerusalem", but the chants quickly became "Khaybar Khaybar, ya yahud, Jaish Muhammad, sa yahud."
- Then a rally in Vienna erupted centered around the Arabic call to kill the Jews.
- On the same night, a rally of 200 pro-Palestinian protesters in Malmö, Sweden culminated in a call to "shoot the Jews." The rally was followed by 20 men firebombing a nearby synagogue, trapping several people inside the building, and then firebombing a Jewish cemetery.
- Then the Islamic Al Jazeera Network shared its reader's response to the Embassy move to Jerusalem.
- **Aya Mohammad**: *"Jerusalem is the capital of my country Palestine forever even if this stupid clown with yellow hair announced the opposite. Jerusalem was, is and will be the capital of Palestine."*
- **Marcella Jager**: *"Jerusalem is the city of peace for all 3 Abrahamic religions. Trump has no respect for that and would rather ignite a war for his own political purposes. Get this clown out of the White House."*
- **Megh Myrm**: *"For me, Jérusalem = Palestine's capital. I don't even recognize the existence of the criminal and hitlarian state of "Israel."*
- **Amru Zulkifli**: *"It's important to the three faiths, Christianity, Islam and Judaism. So, what about mark it as international zone where every people can visit? No need to be selfish. No need to make people think ooh, we're now in Jewish capital? Just let it be capital for Abrahamic religions."*

Then Headlines erupted all over the world!
- "Palestinian Envoy says US Recognition of Jerusalem Is 'Declaring War'"
- "Gaza Burns U.S. & Israeli Flags Ahead of Trump Recognition of Jerusalem"
- "Trump to Recognize Jerusalem as Israel's Capital Sparking Arab 'Day of Rage' Plans"
- "Turkey's President Erdogan Calls for an Islamic Summit Next Week on Jerusalem"
- "Iran 'will not tolerate' Trump Jerusalem 'violation'"

- "Iran Warns of Intifada against Israel"
- "Arab World Blasts Trump's Announcement on Recognition of Jerusalem as Israel's Capital"
- "Saudi Arabia King Salman Warns against Embassy Move to Jerusalem"

The United Nations — The entire UN followed suit by passing a non-binding resolution that condemned Trump's recognition of Jerusalem (That vote was 128 to 9) and later it voted again (14-1) to condemn Trump's decision. Even Britain got in on the action. *"Britain joined 13 other members of the UN Security Council to vote in favor of a resolution calling for Donald Trump to rescind his declaration that Jerusalem is the capital of Israel, showing the depth of global opposition* (i.e. conflict) *to the move. The United States cast its first veto in more than six years to block the Egypt-drafted resolution. And Nikki Haley, the US ambassador to the UN, denounced the resolution as "an insult" and it "won't be forgotten" and as she said prior to this kind of behavior "we're taking names."*

CBSN News Reports: *"President Trump has issued a warning to members of the United Nations that he is watching very closely. On Thursday's vote of his decision to recognize Jerusalem as the capital of Israel and according to a letter issued by U.S. Ambassador Nikki Haley obtained by CBS News, "The President and the U.S. will take this vote personally." Haley also tweeted, "At the UN we're always asked to do more and to give more. So, when we make a decision, at the will of the American ppl, abt where to locate our embassy, we don't expect those we've helped to target us. On Thurs there'll be a vote criticizing our choice. The US will be taking names."*

"Will those in favor of the resolution contained in Doc. S/1027/1060 please raise their hand." The count was taken. "Thank you, those against." The hands were counted when included Nikki Haley. "14 votes in favor, 1 vote against." "The General Assembly is now voting."

"The US, as it held off the United Nations, sent off a stinging rebuke for its decision to recognize Jerusalem as the Israeli capital. In an act of defiance, 128 countries called on Washington to withdraw its recent move. Amb. Nikki Haley insisted nothing had changed."

Nikki Haley: *"To its shame, the United Nations has been a hostile place for the sake of Israel. Both the current and the previous Secretary Generals have objected to the UN's disproportionate focus on Israel. It's a wrong that* *undermines the creditability of this institution and that in turn is harmful for the entire world.*

I've often wondered why in the face of such hostility Israel has chosen to remain a member of this body and then I remember that Israel has chosen to remain in this institution because it is important to stand up for yourself. Israel must stand up for its own survival as a nation. But it also stands up for the ideal of freedom and human dignity that the United Nations is supposed to be about.

Standing here today, being forced to defend sovereignty and the integrity of my country, the United States of America, many of the same thoughts have come to mind. The President's decision reflects the will of the American people and our right as a nation to choose the location of our embassy. There is no need to describe it further.

Instead there is a larger point to make. The United States will remember this day in which it was singled out for attack in the General Assembly for the very act of exercising our right as a sovereign nation. We will remember it when we are called upon once again to make the world's largest contribution to the United Nations. And we will remember it when so many countries come calling on us, as they so often do, to pay even more and to use our influence for their benefit.

America will put our Embassy in Jerusalem. That is what the American people want us to do and it is the right thing to do. No vote in the United Nations will make any difference on that."[11]

Her comments were met with appreciation by Israeli Prime Minister Benjamin Netanyahu. *"Thank you, Ambassador Haley. On Hanukkah, you spoke like a Maccabi. (Refers to one of the Maccabees derived from the Hebrew word (makkabah) meaning "hammer") You lit a candle of truth. You dispel the darkness. One defeated the many. Truth defeated lies. Thank you, President Trump. Thank you, Nikki Haley."* he tweeted.

Israeli Ambassador to the UN Danny Danon blasted the resolution saying, *"Members of the Security Council can vote another hundred times to criticize our presence in Jerusalem, but history won't change. While the Jewish people celebrate the holiday of Hanukkah that symbolizes the eternal connection to Jerusalem, there are people who think that they can rewrite history,"* he said.

"It's time for all countries to recognize that Jerusalem always was and always will be the capital of the Jewish people and the capital of Israel."

And of course, this instigated the newly reinstituted Jewish Sanhedrin to give their stern warning to the UN and World behavior. *"In a special session of 71 elders, the court of the Sanhedrin called on the nations of the world to take their prophesied role in building Jerusalem by not voting against the declaration of President Trump in the United Nations, emphasizing that this was an auspicious moment that will decide their fate, whether for blessing or curse."*

The Declaration reads: *"The nations should now take this opportunity to advance their required role in building God's House in Jerusalem, the House of Universal Peace, on Mount Moriah, as prophesied in the Bible in order to bring about the long-awaited world peace. Nations that vote for this evil decree via their representatives are instruments of destruction and their fate is sealed, as has been the case throughout history for those nations who have chosen the path of evil. The nations that support the US president's declaration will gain merit. We emphasize that this vote does not affect the prophecies concerning Jerusalem as the City of God since God's word is eternal. It is Jerusalem's fate to be a Light Unto the Nations. Any nation that desires life will act intelligently and support the declaration of the United States."*

Rabbi Hillel Weiss, the spokesman for the Sanhedrin, explained the proclamation in simpler terms. *"Every child who learns the Bible knows that if you bless Israel, you will be blessed, and if you curse Israel, you will be cursed,"* citing Genesis 12:3. He also explained that, *"Israel is God's tool in this world for testing the hearts of men. By their actions towards Israel, men and even entire countries show their feelings towards God. Right now, the world is being called upon, nation by nation, to display this."*

And of course, the Jewish article ended by quoting, **Zechariah 12:3** "When all the nations of the earth gather against her. In that day, I will make Yerushalayim a stone for all the peoples to lift; all who lift it shall injure themselves."

Gee, where have I heard that before?! In other words, Israel and specifically Jerusalem will be a source of world conflict in the Last Days!

The Bible says, at the End of the Age, God will set the stage for the final fulfillment of Bible prophecy by making Jerusalem a "cup of trembling" to all the nations surrounding it! And it's happening right now!

As one person said, *"As you can see, condemnation for the President's decision to recognize Jerusalem as Israel's capital and move the Embassy there, is widespread, virtually coming from the entire world."*

And that's exactly what the Bible said would happen! Ever since our President did that, the nations around the world are "trembling" over that issue and that announcement! Which means we're watching Bible Prophecy happen right before our eyes! One that was written nearly 2,500 years ago! AND…some would also point out that President Trump's recognition of Jerusalem as Israel's capital was 50 years since Israel recaptured the city of Jerusalem in the Six Day War back in 1967. Some would say since every 50 years in Israel is a "Jubilee Year", this action certainly fits because the Jubilee year is where all the land automatically returns back to the original Jewish owner. Coincidence? I don't know, but one person gives the reason for this conflict.

"What our political leaders have failed to understand is that the Israeli-Arab conflict is not a political one capable of a political solution. It is, instead, a spiritual conflict that can be traced back 4,000 years to the time of Abraham when his family split between the descendants of his two sons, Ishmael and Isaac.

Ever since the re-establishment of the State of Israel in May of 1948, the nation has been the focal point of world politics, and the status of Jerusalem has been the center of the controversy.

The United Nations originally wanted to internationalize the city. The Vatican has laid claim to it. The Arabs demand that they be given exclusive sovereignty over it. The European Union, joined today by the UN, wants to divide it between the Jews and the Arabs.

And President Trump's act of recognition has inflamed the debate and the hatreds that are rooted in satanic anti-Semitism. In that regard, his action has led to a partial fulfillment of Zechariah 12:2-3, but not to its complete fulfillment.

The fulfillment of the prophecy must await the day when all the nations of the world, including the United States, turn against Israel. That reality means we have two possibilities: 1) That Trump will ultimately reverse course, or 2) That a successor will do so.

But either way, this is a conflict that will only be resolved when Jesus Christ, the King of Kings, and Lord of Lords returns to rule over all the world from Jerusalem."[12]

Wow! And that's why you can turn on the news and read in all the newspapers, even with our current administration, how Israel has indeed become an international global problem, a center of world conflict, including Jerusalem. Exactly like the Bible said would happen when you're living in the Last Days! Folks, this is why, out of love, God has given us this update on *The Final Countdown: Tribulation Rising* concerning the Jewish People & the Antichrist to show us that the 7-year Tribulation is near, and the return of Jesus Christ is rapidly approaching. That's why Jesus Himself said…

Luke 21:28 "When these things begin to take place, stand up and lift up your heads, because your redemption is drawing near."

Like it or not, we are headed for The Final Countdown. The signs of the 7-year Tribulation are Rising all around us! It's time to WAKE UP! So, the point is this. If you're reading this today and you're not a Christian, then I beg you, please, heed these signs, heed these warnings, give your life to Jesus now! You don't want to be here when God pours out His Judgment upon this planet! It's the worst time in the history of mankind, so horrible that unless God shortened the timeframe the entire human race would be destroyed! The only way to escape is through Jesus! Take the way out now before it's too late. GET SAVED TODAY!

But if you're reading this today and you are a Christian, then it's high time we stop goofing off, getting distracted with this world. Let's get busy working together sharing the Gospel with as many as we can! Let's leave here being LIVING FOR JESUS and longing for HIS SOON RETURN. Amen?

Chapter Eleven

The Jewish People & Their Resource Conflict

In the last chapter we saw a third reason for conflict and that was the recent **Relocation Conflict** with President Trump's decision to move the U.S. Embassy to Jerusalem, which in effect acknowledges Jerusalem as Israel's capital. So, of course, what's going on? The whole world is in conflict over it! This is why you can turn on the news and read in all the newspapers, even with our current administration, how Israel has indeed become an international global problem, a center of world conflict. The nearly 2,500-year-old prophecy from Zechariah is coming to pass, right before our eyes which means, we're living in the Last Days! But that's not all.   *Zechariah 12:2-3*

The **4th reason** why Israel has become a source of world conflict in the Last Days, just like the Bible said, is because of the **Resource Conflict**.

You see, it just so happens that Israel is located in the heart of the world's oil reserves and other major mega resources, that most people don't know about, that makes it a great strategic significance to all the countries in the world. In other words, they want it, .and it's going to create a conflict for control. In fact, many are wondering if in fact, this resource issue in Israel will be the "hook in the jaw" that tempts Russia to come down from the North to start the Gog and Magog War. But don't take my word for it. Let's listen to God's.

Ezekiel 38:1-18 "The word of the LORD came to me: 'Son of man, set your face against Gog, of the land of Magog, the chief prince of Meshech and Tubal; prophesy against him and say: 'This is what the Sovereign LORD says: I am against you, O Gog, chief prince of Meshech and Tubal. I will turn you around, put hooks in your jaws and bring you out with your whole army – your horses, your horsemen fully armed, and a great horde with large and small shields, all of them brandishing their swords. Persia, Cush and Put will be with them, all with shields and helmets, also Gomer with all its troops, and Beth Togarmah from the far north with all its troops, the many nations with you. Get ready; be prepared, you and all the hordes gathered about you, and take command of them. After many days you will be called to arms. In future years you will invade a land that has recovered from war, whose people were gathered from many nations to the mountains of Israel, which had long been desolate. They had been brought out from the nations, and now all of them live in safety. You and all your troops and the many nations with you will go up, advancing like a storm; you will be like a cloud covering the land. This is what the Sovereign LORD says: On that day thoughts will come into your mind and you will devise an evil scheme. You will say, I will invade a land of unwalled villages; I will attack a peaceful and unsuspecting people, all of them living without walls and without gates and bars. I will plunder and loot and turn my hand against the resettled ruins and the people gathered from the nations, rich in livestock and goods, living at the center of the land. Sheba and Dedan and the merchants of Tarshish and all her villages will say to you, 'Have you come to plunder? Have you gathered your hordes to loot, to carry off silver and gold, to take away livestock and goods and to seize much plunder?' Therefore, son of man, prophesy and say to Gog: 'This is what the Sovereign LORD says: In that day, when my people Israel are living in safety, will you not take notice of it? You will come from your place in the far north, you and many nations with you, all of them riding on horses, a great horde, a mighty army. You will advance against my people Israel like a cloud that covers the land. In days to come, O Gog, I will bring you against my land, so that the nations may know me when I show myself holy through you before their eyes. This is what the Sovereign LORD says: Are you not the one I spoke of in former days by my servants the prophets of Israel? At that time, they prophesied for years that I would bring you against them. This is what will happen in that day: When Gog attacks the land of Israel, my hot anger will be aroused, declares the Sovereign LORD.'"

In other words, you are going to get it for messing with Israel! Now for those of you who may not be familiar with this passage this is the infamous

Ezekiel passage dealing with the Last Days Gog & Magog prophecy. The Last Days war mentioned in the Bible. It continues on throughout Chapter 38 and 39 which shows their absolute utter destruction. Why? As we saw before, it deals with a confederation of nations that God's not too pleased with because they're trying to come against Israel and destroy it, rob it, and plunder it! Not a good thing to do! Again, don't mess with Israel! Now, the key to understanding just how close we are to fulfilling this passage of Scripture, that many believe will be a WWIII scenario, is figuring out who in the world these nations are that are coming against Israel. How many of you took your last vacation in Beth Togarmah? Or Meshach and Tubal? Or Gomer? Or how about Put? These nations today are Russia, (or Magog), (Gog is the personage of Magog or Russia). Then we have Turkey, (which is Meshach, Tubal, Gomer, Togarmah) then there's Iran (which is Persia), some add Afghanistan and Pakistan, then Sudan, some add Ethiopia and Somalia (or Cush) and finally Libya (or Put). So, the Bible predicted nearly 2,600 years ago through the prophet Ezekiel that Russia, Turkey, Iran, Sudan, Libya, and some would add Afghanistan, Pakistan, Ethiopia, Somalia, basically the Muslim nations surrounding Israel right now, would try to apparently invade Israel and take her out! Whew! Good thing we see absolutely no sign of that prophecy coming to pass anytime soon! Really? What's in the news? Russia (or Magog) and Putin (a Gog-like figure) is the one right now arming these nations with weapons to go against Israel. On top of that, Russia is on the move in the North again over the Ukraine issue as well as Syria. Many believe it's starting to fulfill this passage of Scripture. Just turn on your news!

We also see in our text the reason why Russia comes down from the North with these Muslim nations attacking Israel in the first place. It's not because they're bored on a Saturday afternoon! No! It was for plunder. They "devise an evil scheme" and say, "Hey, let's go Invade Israel and plunder and loot and carry off silver and gold and livestock and goods." And not just a little "plunder" but the text said *much* plunder. This is the 'hook in the jaw' that God uses as an act of judgment upon these nations to get them to invade the land, so He can take them out! And boy does He ever! Here's what happens to them!

Ezekiel 39:4-6,8-10,17,21-22 "On the mountains of Israel you will fall, you and all your troops and the nations with you. I will give you as food to all kinds of carrion birds and to the wild animals. You will fall in the open field, for I have spoken, declares the Sovereign LORD. I will send fire on Magog and on those who live in safety in the coastlands, and they will know that I am the LORD. It is coming! It will surely take place, declares the Sovereign LORD. This is the day I have spoken of. Then those who live in the towns of Israel will go out and use the weapons for fuel and burn them up, the small and large shields, the bows and arrows, the war clubs and spears. For seven years they will use them for fuel. They will not need to gather wood from the fields or cut it from the forests, because they will use the weapons for fuel. And they will plunder those who plundered them and loot those who looted them, declares the Sovereign LORD. Son of man, this is what the Sovereign LORD says: Call out to every kind of bird and all the wild animals: Assemble and come together from all around to the sacrifice I am preparing for you, the great sacrifice on the mountains of Israel. There you will eat flesh and drink blood. I will display my glory among the nations, and all the nations will see the punishment I inflict and the hand I lay upon them. From that day forward the house of Israel will know that I am the LORD their God."

So here is the question. Do we see any signs of this hook, i.e. desiring the resources of Israel, being put in the jaw of Russia and these other Muslim nations setting them up for judgment, and are they devising an evil scheme to go get these resources any time soon? Uh yeah! Again, just turn on your news! I want to share with you some of that proof. In fact, some of these resources Russia wants, are recent discoveries by Israel!

The **1st resource** that Israel has that these nations want is **Israel's Land Mass.**

You see, it's not by chance that of all places on the planet that God called Abram, later changed to Abraham, out of the Ur of the Chaldeans, it was to the land of Canaan or modern-day Israel.

Genesis 12:1-5 "The LORD had said to Abram, 'Leave your country, your people and your father's household and go to the land I will show you. I will make you into a great nation and I will bless you; I will make your name great, and you will be a blessing. I will bless those who bless you, and whoever curses you I will curse; and all peoples on earth will be blessed through you. So, Abram left, as the LORD had told him; and Lot went with him. Abram was seventy-five years old when he set out from Haran. He took his wife Sarai, his nephew Lot, all the possessions they had accumulated and the people they had acquired in Haran, and they set out for the land of Canaan, and they arrived there."

So again, why of all places did God call Abram to Canaan? Well it makes sense when you look at it.[1]

As you can see, not only was it a "good land" as we saw before "flowing with milk and honey," but as you can see, it's a strategic area for missions. The Promised Land is only 60 miles wide in some places. At its western edge is the Mediterranean Sea. To the east is an impassable desert. So, its location makes it a land bridge between three continents. Africa's only land link to Europe and to Asia is through here and vice versa. So, if God wanted to make Himself known throughout the ancient world, this would have

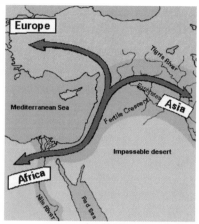

been the ideal place to do it from. Why? Because you can reach all Europe, Asia, and Africa all from that one spot! It's a strategic land bridge that connects them all! And that's why Israel was to be a Light Unto the Gentiles! That "all peoples on earth will be blessed through you," that is the Messiah would come and the news of the Messiah would spread rapidly from that one location! God knew exactly what He was doing when He placed him there! But, historically, Israel has also been a strategic area for invasions. Since Israel is the strip of land that connects Asia, Africa, and Europe all together, it makes it great not only for missions but for trade. It's the ultimate trade route for all these continents. And so, if you wanted to own or control these trade routes, you had to own or control this area. And that's what we see throughout history, even Biblical history.[2]

CONVERGENCE ZONE

As you can see that the Assyrian Empire needed to go through there, the Babylonians went through there, the Persian Empire had to go through there, Alexander the Great and the Macedonian Empire went through there.[3]

Copyright Stratfor 2015 www.stratfor.com

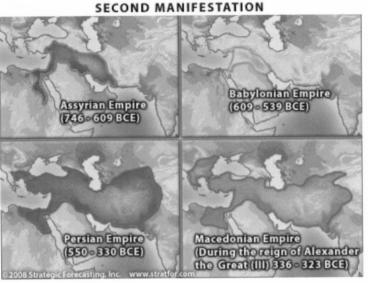

SECOND MANIFESTATION

Assyrian Empire (746 - 609 BCE)

Babylonian Empire (609 - 539 BCE)

Persian Empire (550 - 330 BCE)

Macedonian Empire (During the reign of Alexander the Great (III) 336 - 323 BCE)

© 2008 Strategic Forecasting, Inc.   www.stratfor.com

Even the Roman Empire needed go through there to control the area, and so it is today! This is why Israel is such a valuable land today. This is why she is such prime real estate. If you want to invade other countries and control the trade routes, you have to go through Israel! And this is exactly why Ezekiel said this as well.

Ezekiel 5:5 "This is what the Sovereign LORD says: This is Jerusalem, which I have set in the center of the nations, with countries all around her."

In other words, it's a strategic land mass and this is why so many countries throughout history, even today have wanted to get their hands on it, like this video shares.

Stratfor.com: *"Founded in 1948, Israel is located on the eastern shore of the Mediterranean Sea. The country borders the Gaza Strip, the West Bank, Lebanon, Syria, Jordan and Egypt. Israel's territory has historically been a magnate of great powers from the Romans to the British. For Mediterranean power it serves as a strategic land bridge and for Eastern power control of Israel is necessary to secure its flank. Israel contains parts of four distinct topographical regions.*

The Negev is an extension of the Sinai Desert and accounts for more than half of Israel. The coastal plain begins at the Gaza strip and continues northward towards the border with Lebanon. The Hill Region extends from the foot hills of Mt Hermon to south of Jerusalem. The Jordan Rift Valley follows the length of the Jordan River and continues down to the Red Sea. Israel also claims 2/3rds of the Golan Heights, a strategic plateau.

The country's core is the Coastal Plain and the Hill Region. Over three million Israeli's ten million live in the greater Tel Aviv area. Israel currently has the ability to defend itself but must obtain a posture of constant military readiness. "[4]

Gee, I wonder why? Maybe because it's a strategic land mass that so many people want!

The **2nd resource** that Israel has that these nations want is **Israel's Gas & Oil**.

You see, it just so happens that Israel's location is not only a strategic land mass for invasions and trade routes, but it happens to be in the heart of the world's oil & gas reserves making it a major strategic significance to all the countries in the world who are dependent upon gas & oil for survival, which is basically everybody. And think about it! Back when Abraham came over from the Ur of the Chaldeans, people weren't driving cars and dependent upon oil and gas, but we are now! Do you think that's by chance? No way! God knew we would need oil and gas and God also knew it would be there for our future time and sure enough it's adding to the major conflict going on over there just like He said would happen nearly 2,500 years ago! In fact, it's become a major hook in the jaw for countries, including Russia, because Israel not only has "some" gas and oil, but they've got a ton of it! Let's start with the gas. Believe it or not, Israel just recently discovered one of the largest gas deposits on the planet. One of them is called the Leviathan Gas Field.

Bloomberg Reports: *"Israel is located in a region that is extremely rich in oil and gas, but it has had practically none of its own until recently. Offshore discoveries could make the country self-sufficient in energy."*

Elliott Gotkine Reports: Israel's Gas Bonanza: *"The Middle East produces nearly (30.4%) a third of the world's oil and about (14.4%) fifteen percent of its gas. Almost none of it comes from Israel. But on the eastern edge of the Med that is changing. Here is why. Named after the Biblical sea monster, Leviathan, is a monster gas field, the biggest discovery in a decade. It contains 20 TLN Cubic Feet of natural gas. That is enough to power Israel for the next 100 years. U.S. based, Nobel Energy, together with its partner, local Delek Drilling, stand to make billions."*

Gideon Tadmore, Delek Drilling Chairman: *"So it is a big deal, not only for ourselves, as a commercial company, which is for sure a game changer, but I think the implication is very significant also to the Israeli economy and for the state of Israel in large."*

Elliott Gotkin: *"Now Israel could export the gas to Asia, it could export it to Europe. These areas are dependent on Russia flexing its own diplomatic muscle in the process."[5]*

In other words, becoming a major player in resources, specifically gas! Did you catch the dynamic that was going on there? Israel having so much gas is affecting what country? Russia, or Magog! They're going to get hit hard economically! Of all nations on the planet, it just happens to be Russia, from the North, and do you think they're going to just sit idly by and let this happen? No way. This is why many believe this recent discovery might be a part of the Last Days hook in the jaw for Russia to invade Israel and put a stop to it, as this researcher shares.

"Recently, President Vladimir Putin contacted Israel's Prime Minister Benjamin Netanyahu and made an offer he believed couldn't be refused. Putin offered to guarantee the safety of Israel's newly discovered Leviathan gas fields using the full might of the Russian military. Netanyahu politely declined.

The very next week on the direct orders of Vladimir Putin, fighter jets, tanks, sophisticated battlefield communications equipment and Special Forces began landing in Syria. Even more alarmingly, Russia has also deployed advanced anti-aircraft missile batteries to bolster their force.

The question though, is against whom exactly are these highly advanced missiles deployed? ISIS does not have an Air Force so who are they meant to deter? These missiles are clearly to deter Israel and they will seriously impact the IAF's ability to act in Syrian and Lebanese air space should they so desire.

This impressive Russian arsenal is further augmented by the ominous presence of a Russian nuclear submarine, off Syria's coast in the Mediterranean. This provides Russia with the ultimate deterrence, if it were needed. Clearly Russia is in Syria for the long game, not the short.

Russia's aims in Syria are obvious, resources. Their real access to the Middle East is through Syria, therefore Putin will not let Assad fall.

This Russian objective relates to Israel and the "hook" that God Himself will place in Gog's jaw. At some point Gog will have an "evil thought" and will determine to invade the beautiful land to "take a spoil."

It seems increasingly likely that this "evil thought" centers on the Leviathan gas fields, an oil field so vast it could dwarf the existing Saudi and Iraqi fields making Israel, or whoever owns them, the richest nation on planet Earth. These oil fields sit easily within Russia's legitimate grasp.

We truly live in the days of awe. We are blessed to see what we see today. We are witnessing the real time build-up of the horde that will seek to vanquish God's very own inheritance, as described in Ezekiel 38 and 39.

Multitudes of the past have gazed upon these days from afar through the lens of Scripture, yet we are privileged to see these events in real time as our present-day reality. This "horde" is forming now.

The alliances necessary for Ezekiel 38 and 39 are coming to pass. Russia and Iran are already very close, and Turkey has become natural allies to Iran due to a hatred for Israel. The President of Turkey openly despises Israel, and he is a vicious hater of Israel.

Then there is little Israel, sitting all alone in the Middle East. Little Israel sitting on an oil field of immense size and almost incalculable value. Little Israel hated and scorned by all nations of the world, openly despised, seemingly without a true friend or a real protector. Little Israel, isolated, alone, very exposed.

Or so Gog thinks. God Himself on that day will stand up and fight on her behalf, and woe to Gog and his allies, for mighty is the Lord God who will save her.

Blessed be the Lord God, who has revealed these things to his servants! He has not left us alone but has revealed to us what is shortly to come to pass. Though the world will look on these things in days to come with fear and dread we should not. We know the end from the beginning!

Israel is rapidly approaching her appointment with destiny and so are we!"[6]

What about
Psalm 83 war?

In other words, GET READY FOR THE RAPTURE!!! The Gog and Magog war could happen at any time! But that's not all. Israel not only has a ton of gas fields like the Leviathan, not to mention the Tamar, Dalit, and Dolphin fields just to name a few, but they also have major mega resources of oil! The more they drill, the more they find! And these are recent discoveries!

RT News Reports: *"Recently discovered oil reserves in the Eastern Mediterranean is set to be the latest point of tension in the troubled region. At least four major competitors are staking their claim. Israel, Lebanon, Turkey, and Cyprus all want a piece but with no clearly defined Maritime borders, the fight could be lengthy, bitter or even bloody."*

One Investor*: "I've been begging for a year, please Lord don't let me down. Don't let me down."*

RT News: *"And finally, his prayers have been answered. The oil company he invested in reported hitting bingo underground."*

"We are still talking about the largest amount of oil ever to be discovered in the State of Israel."

RT News: *"But it's not only Israel laying claim to the reserves. Greek Cyprus, Turkey and Lebanon, all say that the oil is theirs. And while international laws say a country can drill in the international shelf off its coast, the fact that Israel and Lebanon have never agreed upon maritime boundaries makes it unclear where Israel ends, and Lebanon begins."*

Daniel Reisner, Herzog Fox & Neeman Law Firm: *"I know that Lebanon has its version of where they think the borderline will pass if and when we negotiate, and I know Israel has its own version."*

RT News: *"Because the two countries are enemy states it is unlikely there will be any agreement any time soon. There's a joke in Israel that when Moses led the Jews out of Egypt, he took a wrong turn on his way to the Promised Land bringing them to the one spot in the Middle East that has no oil. But that punch line may need to change because Moses may not have been that wrong after all."[7]*

In other words, it's like God knew what He was doing the whole time when He sent Abraham there! It's a set-up for the Last Days! It's like it's going to start a war, become a hook in the jaw or something! And the oil they're finding is not just in the Mediterranean as we just saw. But Israel is discovering oil on land as well including the hotly contested site of the Golan Heights! Can anybody guess who wants to get their hands on those resources? That's right! Once again it rhymes with Russia! Can you say Magog?

"Will the discovery of huge amounts of oil in Israel lead to war in the Middle East? Billions of barrels of oil have been discovered in Israel, and this discovery could essentially make Israel energy independent for many decades to come.

But there is just one problem. This discovery was made in the Golan Heights. If you are not familiar with the Golan Heights, it is an area that Israel took from Syria during the Six-Day War of 1967.

The government of Israel considers the Golan Heights to be part of Israeli territory, but the United Nations does not recognize Israel's claim. Instead, the UN still recognizes Syrian sovereignty over that area.

So now that massive amounts of oil have been discovered there, what will this do to tensions in the region? Could this discovery of oil help set the stage for World War III?

And do you think that Syria and Israel's other Arab neighbors are going to enjoy sitting there as Israel pumps "their oil" out of the ground?

Just as Israel's offshore Mediterranean gas discoveries have created an entire energy industry, so the Golan Height's oil find could also generate a new industry around it as well.

But it is also going to give renewed motivation to those that wish to take the Golan Heights back from the Israelis. If oil can be extracted, it will be a huge bonanza for Israel and an enormous reason for whoever rules in Syria, to launch a war on Israel.

Depending on the size of the oil find under the Golan, the whole configuration of oil-control in the Middle East could be affected. Who has it, who owns it, who sells it, who buys it, and who sets the price?

This is why Putin has made recent attacks on Syria in an effort to jack up oil prices by "increasing uncertainty" in the region and long-term, Putin wants to extend his influence in the Middle East. WHY?

Hopefully this will allow him to keep oil prices at a level that would bring rescue to the Russian economy, which, as an oil exporter, has been languishing under low-cost oil.

And if you think that's a stretch, The Russian Times is even talking about this discovery saying it has the potential to produce billions of barrels.

"We are talking about a significant quantity." Everybody and his brother want a piece of the pie. As usual, war is a strategy for getting it."[8]

In other words, it's going to create a war! Gee, I wonder what war that will be? But the article ends with an even more blunt summation. It appears that the prophetic scenario in Ezekiel 38-39 is beginning to take shape as Russia moves more military assets into and close to Syria. As Ezekiel predicts, Magog (Russia) will invade Israel with its prime motivation: to seize spoil and carry off plunder… (Ezek.38:12). "Oil, something the entire world depends on, definitely qualifies as plunder." In other words, the hook in the jaw is here right now for the first time in history of mankind, that Ezekiel warned about nearly 2,600 years ago. Get ready for the Gog and Magog war!

The **3rd resource** that Israel has that these nations want is **Israel's Water**.

Now as we already saw before, there's another new recent resource that Israel just happens to have, and that everybody in that region certainly needs, and that's water! When they came back into the land they not only devised a massive system of complex giant pipes, open canals, tunnels, reservoirs and massive pumping stations to get access to what little water they did have, but they became masters of conserving that water and leading experts in desalination plants turning saltwater into fresh water, to the point where as of 2016 Israel now produces 20% more water than it consumes. They went from having no water, to diseased water, to more than what they need! Can you believe that? And now they even provide water to their neighbors and export their water technology to the rest of the world. Which, guess what? Has become a very valuable resource that many want to get their hands on, so much so that many are saying is going to lead to war! Shocker! I wonder what war that is? Let's take a look.

RT News Reports: *"Water is life, so they say, but rivalry over supplies can lead to bitter conflict. You can see that since the mid-20th century the planet has seen nearly 180 conflicts connected to water resources. This includes both large and small scale clashes. A lot of these in the Mid-East and Africa. You might be surprised that it is water rather than oil that is fought over in the coming years.*

The Bible tells us that within a short distance from here, Jesus turned water into wine. 2000 years later the miracle might be turning the wine back into water. The problem is in some cases there is very little water to go around. Examples of possible conflicts with Syria's major water sources travel through Turkey and Iraq making it vulnerable while Jordan is reliant on a river where Syria built a dam. Egypt recently expressed concern over the country using the upper Nile to generate electric power."

Paula Slier Reports: *"In the dry landscape of the Middle East, water is a prize more precious than diamonds. In its absence famine and drought are quick to follow. This is a region that very seldom needs an excuse for war and water shortage just might tip the balance."*[9]

In other words, it becomes a hook in the jaw that creates a war! Over what? Water! It just so happens that Israel has tons of it, thanks to their innovations and inventions and desalination plants in the Last Days. Could this be another hook in the jaw for these nations surrounding Israel to invade her, and try to take control, with the help of Russia? I think so and so does the news! Again, this is happening in our lifetime! Israel has never had water like this, but they do now! Just in time for Ezekiel 38 and 39 prophesies mentioned some 2,600 years ago!

The **4th resource** that Israel has that these nations want is **Israel's Minerals.**

This one usually gets overlooked. But speaking of water and resources, it just so happens that Israel is also sitting on another valuable piece of real estate called the Dead Sea that people want to get their hands on. It's not dead at all! The Dead Sea contains a plethora of valuable minerals that all kinds of people are getting rich off of! Including one company called AHAVA. The Dead Sea isn't really dead folks, that's a myth!

AHAVA, Active Dead Sea Minerals: *"The Dead Sea, the lowest place on earth and one of nature's greatest wonders. The earth's crust cracked creating the*

Great Rift Valley, Underground Salty Spring. The special climate conditions combined with a burst of underground salty springs created the ancient valley.

A hypersaline lake like no other in the world, with 34% solid mineral content. Ten times more than any other sea or ocean. This mineral content held a power like no other. This is the natural magnificence of the Dead Sea. It's beauty and healing properties became known around the world. Coveted by many who voyaged to its captivating shores to bask in its skin revitalizing waters.

Even Queen Cleopatra made the Dead Sea her own private spa. For thousands of years millions of visitors have come to witness the breath-taking landscape and to experience the wonders of the Dead Sea region. Natures greatest spa. But this is only the beginning of the legend. In 1988, driven by their love for the region, and a deep passion to unearth its mysteries, the founders joined together to establish the mineral skin care brand AHAVA.

Today AHAVA is the Dead Sea minerals beauty authority and its products are marketed in over 30 countries through prestige chains, department stores and beauty spas in addition to local and international concept stores. In the lowest place on earth the wonders of nature are packed and delivered to the world."[10]

So, as you can see, there's a TON of valuable minerals in the Dead Sea. And not just for beauty and health care needs like AHAVA, but what did it say at the beginning? The Dead Sea has the richest source of minerals in the world! And many of those minerals just happen to be the kind that a lot of countries would love to get their hands on, you know, it's a hook in the jaw like this man shares!

"God dug a tremendous hole in the earth many years ago to store a treasure for His people which staggers the imagination. Yes, the lowest elevation on the earth's surface is the Dead Sea.

But the way God arranged things, the Jordan River and its tributaries have been washing minerals down into that hole which God prepared, for thousands of years, and in recent years it has been found to be the most valuable depository of strategic chemicals in the world.

It is estimated that the potential value of the potash, bromine and other chemical salts of its water is FOUR TIMES the wealth of the United States.

Any would-be dictator would take high risks to capture a treasure like this which could furnish enough fertilizer for the whole world, and with its other chemicals provide the explosives needed to subdue all its enemies!

Why do you think Russia has spent billions of dollars in helping the Arabs fight Israel? Just because she likes the Arabs? No, there is little love lost between them. Russia wants the riches of Israel and its strategic location for world domination. The Soviets would have little trouble taking it from the Arabs.

(In other words, they're just using them) But the Godless gang in the Kremlin never took into consideration how our Creator has it all written down in His Book what He plans for Israel, and the disposal of her enemies.

When the nations of the earth will be beating a path to Israel's door for those chemicals which mean life to them, God will judge and crush them!

YET, even as we speak, the men in the Kremlin are plotting to do the job themselves. They are preparing for a tremendous invasion force to go down over the mountains of Syria to seize Israel.

For years people have laughed at the prophecy that after God destroyed that great army in the mountains that are in the northern part of Israel, that Israel would not have to buy fuel for seven years. She would be burning the weapons of her enemy.

Only recently has it been known that the tanks and weapons of this army are made of non-metallic materials which burn like coal, to thwart the Israeli metal-seeking atomic missiles!

Reuters News Agency has reported that Russia has made large purchases of special archery equipment, so powerful and accurate that it can shoot an arrow through a man's heart at 100 yards and it will keep on going! And it is no secret that Russia has also bought up large numbers of horses recently, of a type best adapted for military invasion through mountains.

How wonderful the way improbable Bible prophecies are coming true these days! Who would have dreamed of a literal fulfillment of Ezekiel's prophecies of bows and arrows and horses figuring into this great battle when Russia and her satellite armies are destroyed by God in a cataclysm from the sky!

Christians, this is not a pipe dream. These are carefully authenticated facts, which fit perfectly into the pattern of Bible prophecy. Let's get busy while there's still time, with tracts and personal witness, rescuing those who still need to receive Christ as Savior before it is too late.

And if you're unsaved, the day of grace is still here, but it may be gone tomorrow or even today. So, repent of your sins now while you still have time because the prophesied Ezekiel 38 war is about to come to pass!"[11]

In other words, if you're not saved you better get saved now! The prophesied Gog and Magog War is upon us and you don't want to be left behind! Why? Because the Bible is clear. It's about to get a whole lot worse for Israel before it ever gets better, like this shows.

In 90 seconds: Jerusalem in Prophecy

01 seconds: "Jerusalem means 'City of Peace'"

03 seconds: "Yet its history runs with rivers of blood."

08 seconds: "In 4,000 years, Jerusalem has suffered over 115 conflicts."

11 seconds: "It is a city fraught with tension and conflict."

16 seconds: "This tension and conflict was prophesied in your Bible."

20 seconds: "God says, 'I will make Jerusalem a cup of trembling.' Zechariah 12:2"

27 seconds: "Jerusalem is claimed by three major religions. Judaism, Christianity, Islam."

33 seconds: "Soon these religions will clash and fight for control of the Holy City."

37 seconds: "Bible prophecy says that 'Jerusalem's immediate future will again flow with blood.'"

44 seconds: "Bible prophecy says: 'East Jerusalem will be taken violently from

Israel.'" Zechariah 14:2, Jerusalem will be besieged. Ezekiel 4:1-8, European armies will surround Jerusalem. Luke 21:20"

53 seconds: "These events will trigger, and occur during, World War III."

58 seconds: "But there is good news..."

60 seconds: "Jerusalem will again know peace."

64 seconds: "God says that He 'will again choose Jerusalem.' Zechariah 2:12"

67 seconds: "Jerusalem will be the headquarters from which Christ will rule the Earth."

70 seconds: "And many nations shall come, and say, Come and let us go up to the mountain of the Lord, for the law shall go forth of Zion, and the word of the Lord from Jerusalem. Micah 4:2"

90 seconds: BE READY[12]

Be ready is right! Time is running out and you have no excuse! You don't want to be left behind when the carnage comes! All the signs are given by God to lovingly wake us up before it's too late! Ezekiel 38-39, Zechariah 12, prophesied nearly 2,500 and 2,600 years ago! This is why you can turn on the news and read in all the newspapers of how Israel and Jerusalem have indeed become an international global conflict, and Russia and the Muslim nations are breathing down her doorstep. It's all signs we're living in the Last Days! And folks, this is why, out of love, God has given us this update on *The Final Countdown: Tribulation Rising* concerning the Jewish People & the Antichrist to show us that the 7-year Tribulation is near, and the Return of Jesus Christ is rapidly approaching. That's why Jesus Himself said...

Luke 21:28 "When these things begin to take place, stand up and lift up your heads, because your redemption is drawing near."

Like it or not, we are headed for The Final Countdown. The signs of the 7-year Tribulation are rising all around us! It's time to WAKE UP! So, this is the point. If you're reading this today and you're not a Christian, then I beg you, please, heed these signs, heed these warnings. Give your life to Jesus now! You don't want to be here when God pours out His Judgment upon the nations. It will be the worst time in the history of mankind, so horrible that unless God shortened the timeframe the entire human race would be destroyed! The only way to escape is through Jesus! Take the way out now before it's too late. GET SAVED TODAY!

But...if you're reading this today and you are a Christian...then it's high time you stop goofing off and getting distracted with this world. Let's get busy working together sharing the Gospel with as many as we can! Let's leave here living for Jesus and longing for His soon return. Amen?

Chapter Twelve

The Jewish People & Their Rebuilt Temple Part 1

The **12th End Time Prophecy** concerning **The Jewish People,** letting us know we're living in the Last Days, is that **Israel Would Rebuild the Temple**.

The actual Temple that the antichrist will go up into and declare himself to be god! But don't take my word for it. Let's listen to God's.

2 Thessalonians 2:1-4 "Concerning the coming of our Lord Jesus Christ and our being gathered to Him, we ask you, brothers, not to become easily unsettled or alarmed by some prophecy, report or letter supposed to have come from us, saying that the day of the Lord has already come. Don't let anyone deceive you in any way, for that day will not come until the rebellion occurs and the man of lawlessness is revealed, the man doomed to destruction. He will oppose and will exalt himself over everything that is called God or is worshiped, so that he sets himself up in God's temple, proclaiming himself to be God." *or separation*

As we saw before, this text tells us that in the Last Days, the antichrist is going to go up into the rebuilt Jewish Temple, halfway into the 7-year Tribulation, and declare himself to be what? To be god, right? So, this is the point. Do we see any signs of the Jewish People getting ready to rebuild this Last Days Temple that the actual antichrist will be going up into declaring himself to be god! Uh yeah! Signs and the desire are all over the place as we speak! And I wanted to share that with you.

The **1ˢᵗ way** we know the Jewish People are getting ready to Rebuild the Last Days Temple now, is that **The Jewish People are Ready to Build the Temple.**

You have to understand, the Jewish People aren't just back in the land again and being established as a nation again, right now, they are really preparing to rebuild that Temple again. And it's not a hundred years down the road, it's right now! So much so that they are airing tons of commercials advertising that fact and that desire! Here's yet another recent one they came out with recently. You tell me if they don't want to build a Temple!

"There is a young man walking across the floor. He has a breathing apparatus around his neck and is carrying a crate full of what looks like tools. He lays the crate down and proceeds to put the apparatus on his face. He walks over to the wall and then takes a spray can of paint out of the crate and starts spraying something on the wall. It's dark in this building and he knows he is trespassing, so he has to hurry and get it painted before someone catches him.

Suddenly, he hears someone yell, "Hey you!" He stops painting, picks up the crate and runs out of the building. The watchman comes in with a flash light. He shines it on the wall to see what this painter has put on the wall. It isn't words at all. It is a beautiful painting of the new Temple to be built.

The people are ready, are you?"[1]

No kidding! Are you ready for what? For the Jewish people to build the actual Last Days Temple that the antichrist will go up into halfway into the 7-year Tribulation and declare himself to be god! This is wild folks! Airing right now in Israel as we speak! But that's the tip of the iceberg! This media campaign is apparently working so well that it is actually spurring the Jewish People on to ascend the Temple Mount in record numbers, where they believe this new Temple needs to be built, in spite of massive unrest from the Muslim community. There has been a "75 percent rise in religious Jews visiting the Temple Mount compared to the previous year." "The Temple Mount, in the Old City of Jerusalem, is the holiest site in Judaism. A fierce debate has raged for generations over whether Jews are even allowed to set foot on the Temple Mount itself." In fact, here's a map showing the obvious massive increase.[2]

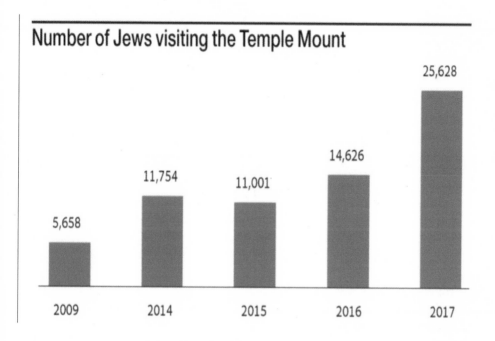

Number of Jews visiting the Temple Mount

Looks like there's a recent uptick in visits to ascend the Temple Mount where they want the new rebuilt Temple to be! In fact, the article goes on to say, "In addition, the number of organized groups from schools, yeshivas, (Orthodox Jewish Seminary) pre-military academies and other institutions has grown." And again, you have to understand that this desire to ascend the Temple Mount where they want the new Temple to be doesn't come without risk. They're not just taking a casual stroll. That's because the Jewish People are actually banned from praying or prostrating themselves on the Temple Mount and entry to the Dome of the Rock is restricted to Muslims only. You and I can't even get in there! Here's what the rules actually state:

"Jewish prayer on Temple Mount is completely forbidden. Jews may enter only to visit the place, and only at limited times. Muslims are free to pray on the Temple Mount; however, Christians and Jews may only visit the site as tourists. They are forbidden from singing, praying, or making any kind of 'religious displays.'"

Attempts to violate these rules causes major problems! In 2000, Ariel Sharon, then the leader of Israel's opposition party, took a delegation to the top of the Temple Mount, which Muslims rioted over and sparked what was called the Second Intifada, which resulted in the deaths of more than 4,000 people. Then in 2014, a Muslim shot Rabbi Yehuda Glick near the Temple Mount because he wanted the Jews to pray freely at the top of the Temple Mount. Most of the time what happens on so-called peaceful days is that Muslims pray at the "top" of the Temple Mount while they look over the edge to see Jews praying at the Western Wall down below. But every year, Jerusalem Day is celebrated, a Jewish national holiday commemorating the reunification of Jerusalem and the establishment of Israeli control over the Old City in the aftermath of the 1967 Six-Day War. If you recall, this was when Israel recaptured Jerusalem fulfilling yet another Bible Prophecy as we saw, but initially they also took control of the Temple Mount. The paratroop commander at that time, a guy named Mordechai Gur cried into his field radio – *"The Temple Mount is in our hands!"* And the brigade's chief communications officer, Ezra Orni, retrieved an Israeli flag from his pouch and asked Gur whether he should hang it over the Dome of the Rock. Gur said to go on and go up. Major Arik Achmon, chief intelligence officer for the Brigade accompanied him into the Dome of the Rock. They climbed to the top of the building and victoriously fastened the Israeli flag onto a pole that was topped with an Islamic crescent. But that didn't last long because the then Defense Minister at that time, Moshe Dayan, watching the scene through binoculars from Mount Scopus, urgently radioed Gur and demanded: Do you want to set the Middle East on fire? So, Gur told Achmon to remove the flag. But Achmon couldn't bear the notion of lowering the Israeli flag, and so he instructed one of his men to do it instead. So basically, this is what Jerusalem Day is all about. This is what they are celebrating each year, when the Jewish people, not only got Jerusalem back, but the Temple Mount back, but was returned shortly thereafter. And every year when they celebrate it, they are in essence saying we the Jewish People are the rightful owners of the Temple Mount and it causes a major ruckus!

"The horn blows through the city of Jerusalem, it is Jerusalem Day. At this moment we are entering the Lions Gate. We are inside the old city." The voice of Gen. Motta Gur, commander of paratroopers declares, "The Temple Mount is in our hands!" This declaration was retrieved from the Official IDF archive material as it happened on June 7th, 1967.

Jerusalem Day, 2015, Rabbi Yisrael Ariel, founder, Temple Institute, IDF paratrooper and liberator of the Temple Mount says, "Today, Jerusalem Day, I had the merit to enter The Temple Mount, 48 years ago, almost 50 years ago. No one demanded me to present my identity card before I could enter the Mount. Jews entered as rightful owners.

I am compelled to mention there were soldiers who entered and paid with their lives for this Holy Place. Where do they come up with this degradation to demand of a Jew, who is the rightful owner of this place to present an identity card while at the same time others enter freely? Thus, each one of you who has come here today, I say this to everyone:

Everyone who is here today he is to be considered as one of the paratroopers who liberated the place of the Holy Temple. The paratroopers who were here, some of them are no longer with us. But all who are here today are proof that we are rightful owners of this place. This is the fulfillment of the commandment to conquer the Mountain, plain and simple.

We are actually fulfilling the positive Torah commandment. 'You shall seek out His presence and come there' Deut. 12:5. May we merit with God's help to enter into the courtyard of the Holy Temple." During the time he is speaking the IDF Chief Rabbi General Shlomo Goren stands with Torah scroll and shofar at the entrance to the site of the Holy of Holies.

They are proceeding to walk towards the Temple Mount. On each side of them were the Muslim chanting Allah Akbar. They are trying to interrupt their walk and get them to turn around. There are also police walking with them to keep this walk from getting violent.

Then over a loud speaker the words, "The Temple Mount is in our hands! Well done! Cease firing! All forces to cease firing!" The horn starts blowing again.

The Rightful owners ascend the Temple Mount. Demand the right to pray![3]

Ascend the Temple Mount! Demand your right to pray! Why? Because that's where the new Temple needs to be, and Jerusalem Day celebrates the Jews being the rightful owner of that place! In fact, speaking of "rightful owners," not that long-ago Israel blasted 33 countries that ignored the Jewish historical ties to the Temple Mount. Israel, on Wednesday, dispatched sharp letters to the 33 countries, including France, Russia, Spain and Sweden, which supported a resolution by the United Nations that ignored Jewish historical ties to the Temple Mount and the Western Wall in Jerusalem. The resolution, which the Jewish

People are calling "outrageous," is sponsored by six Arab states, Algeria, Egypt, Kuwait, Morocco, Tunisia and the United Arab Emirates on behalf of the Palestinians, and referred to the Western Wall plaza by its Muslim name, Al-Buraq Plaza and the Jewish name for the holy site, the "Temple Mount," was excluded from the text and replaced with the Muslim reference, the al-Aksa Mosque and al-Haram al-Sharif. The resolution also noted that every aspect of the Jewish religion, history and archaeology were presented as fiction, referring to "Jewish fake graves," and "so called Jewish ritual baths." Only six countries, the US being one of them, voted against the resolution." So, Jerusalem Day is a hotly contested topic! But that's not the only Jewish holiday that stirs up a ruckus over the Jewish People's desire to retake the Temple Mount and rebuild the new Jewish Third Temple that the antichrist is going into. So is another holiday called Tisha B'av.

It's celebrated the 9th day of the month of Av (Jul. 21-22, 2018). *"It's the saddest day on the Jewish calendar, on which we fast, deprive ourselves and pray and is the culmination of the Three Weeks, a period of time during which we mark the destruction of the Holy Temple in Jerusalem."*

That's what they're recalling every time they celebrate this holiday. But it's not just recalling the past but it's also looking forward to the future when they get to rebuild the Temple again. Here's proof! Here's yet another commercial airing in Israel as we sit here for Tisha B'av this holiday specifically showing their desire to rebuild the Temple!

"A young man is laying in bed when his alarm goes off. He looks at his phone to see what time it is and the words 'Tisha B'av Today is showing on his phone. He gets up and puts on his clothes and begins to walk out the door. When he opens the door, a bright light is waiting for him to walk into.

It's like a dream. As he walks down the street, he is in awe of what he sees. So many people are walking here and there. It is very unusual. Some are holding signs that say, 'Happy 9th.' A man he passes even hands him an invitation that says 'Kohen Cadol invites everyone for a special Tisha B'av celebration! Happy 9th!!' He wonders what is going on.

So many people are celebrating. As he walks further through the city, he finally sees what the commotion is all about. In front of him is the new Temple. Then he sees two men blowing horns in celebration. Suddenly, he is back in his bed, the

alarm has just gone off, he picks up his phone and then his Dad walks in the
room telling him to get up, it's time to go.

He sits up in his bed and looks around. He realizes all that he has just seen is just
a dream. But then he grins. It was a wonderful dream of what is to come.

Time to wake up and make the dream come true."[4]

Time to wake up and make what dream a reality? Rebuild the Third
Jewish Temple that the actual antichrist will go up into and declare himself to be
god halfway into the 7-year Tribulation! Being broadcast right now in Israel as
we're all worried about who wins what game and how's that economy doing?
Again, the antichrist does this, he commits the Abomination That Causes
Desolation halfway into the seven-year Tribulation in this Temple! If we see the
Jewish People desiring to build that Temple now and it's going to take a little
time to build, you don't build it overnight, then how much closer is the Rapture
of the Church which takes place prior to all this? Folks, we are living in the Last
Days and it's time to get motivated!

The **2nd way** we know the Jewish People really are getting ready to rebuild the
Last Days Temple now, is that **The Muslim Fear is Rising Over the Temple.**

As we just saw, the Muslim community is up in arms over this Jewish
desire to rebuild the Third Jewish Temple. And the reasons are pretty obvious!
This would obviously replace the Dome of the Rock which is where the Jewish
Group called The Temple Mount. The faithful believe the original Temple and
the Holy of Holies is there on the Temple Mount. This would also replace the Al-
Aqsa Mosque, which is not the same as the Dome of the Rock. One is a mosque
the other is a shrine, but both are on the Temple Mount. So, any talk of building a
Jewish Temple on the Temple Mount sets the Muslim community off like a
rocket! And if you're paying attention to the Muslim media and Palestinian
broadcasts going on over there, and unfortunately hardly anybody is, they are
clearly saying this could happen any day!

"Over the past few months, PA officials have been claiming Israel's goal is to
destroy the Al-Aqsa Mosque and replace it with a new Temple on its ruins."

Mahmoud al-Habash, the former Palestinian Authority (PA) Minister of
Religious Affairs, claimed on Thursday, *"Israel plans to blow up the Al-Aqsa*

Mosque in Jerusalem to prepare the way for a new Temple to be built on its ruins."

He claimed, *"The plot to destroy the Dome of the Rock, is being planned by 'extremist Jewish organizations' and may be carried out by a drone carrying large amounts of explosives or a small plane flown by a Jewish suicide bomber."*

So, he called on Muslims from all over the world to come to Jerusalem and to protect the Al-Aqsa Mosque from destruction. Here's some of their actual news reports.

Palestinian Media Watch: *"The excavation's purpose is to destroy the Al-Aqsa Mosque. In fact, its foundations have been removed. Chemical acids were injected into the rocks to dissolve them. The soil and the pillars were moved so the mosque is hanging in midair. There is an Israeli plan to destroy the Al-Aqsa Mosque and to build the Temple."*

PA Minister of Religious Affairs, Mahmoud Al-Habbash: *"Israel plans to remove the Al-Aqsa Mosque. Israel is following a systematic, gradual plan supported by the Israeli government and protected by the Israeli army, and its aim – I'm telling you – is not to divide al-Aqsa, not to divide Al-Aqsa."*

Host: *"To impose their sovereignty over Al-Aqsa."*

PA Minister of Religious Affairs Mahmoud Al-Habbash: *"Its aim is to remove the Al-Aqsa Mosque."*

Host: *"As the final goal."*

PA Minister of Religious Affairs Mahmoud Al-Habbash: *"As the final goal – they don't want to see the shining, golden elegant Dome of the Rock."*

Khaled Mismar, PLO official accuses Israel of Planning to destroy the Al-Aqsa Mosque and erect "what they call the 'Temple.'" *"Now they want to divide up the Al-Aqsa Mosque (i.e. the Temple Mount); furthermore, they want to destroy the Al-Aqsa Mosque and erect what they call 'the Temple' over al-Aqsa."* [5]

So, whether or not people really want to believe the Jewish People are getting ready to rebuild the Temple, talk to the Muslims. They're convinced it could happen any time! In fact, to make matters even more alarming for the Muslim community, the Israel Minister of Housing and Construction, Uri Ariel, publicly expressed his wish to see the construction of a "Third Temple" in the Al-Aqsa Mosque compound in occupied Al-Quds (East Jerusalem).

According to the Alray Palestinian News Agency, **Uri Ariel** said. *"The first Temple was destroyed in 586 BC, the second Temple in 70 A.D. and ever since the Jews have been mourning its loss."* He then went on to say *"Al-Aqsa Mosque is currently in place of the temple, despite the temple being much holier than it. Al-Aqsa Mosque is only the third most holy mosque in Islam."*

"Now that Israel has once again become a Jewish sovereign state, there have been calls to rebuild the Temple," he added. Here's the Muslim news report of that event.

Press TV Reports: *"Israel says it's planning to replace al-Aqsa Mosque in Jerusalem with a Temple. The Israeli Minister urges the building of the third[1] Temple to replace the Holy Site. The Al-Aqsa is considered the third holiest site in Islam. Palestinians denounced the plan as desecration. They say it's part of Israel's ongoing attempt to distort the Arab and Islamic history. Palestinians argue that Jerusalem is the capital of the future Palestinian independent state and that its heritage should remain intact. Israeli minister says that the first and second temples were destroyed many years ago and the third one needs to be built now."[6]*

And what Temple will that be? Oh yeah! That's right! The one the antichrist is going up into halfway into the 7-year tribulation and declare himself to be god! Folks, it's all going down soon, we better wake up! In fact, the accusations don't stop there. The Muslims have gone on to even accuse the Jewish People of creating the recent earthquakes in an attempt to destroy Al-Aqsa mosque." This was only a few months ago!

MEMRI (Middle East Media Research Institute) reported that these "experiments" are part of Israel's attempt to cause man-made earthquakes in order to collapse Al-Aqsa mosque and the Dome of the Rock.

"These actions are preparation for a major criminal action against these holy sites to destroy them in preparation for creating a Holy Temple in the attempt to Judaize Jerusalem."

"We cannot trust the Israeli occupation, since it plans to use technology and science in order to complete its planned expansion, while blaming nature and natural causes."

Earlier this year, speaking of crazy, a councilman in Washington, D.C., a Democrat named Travon White Sr., suggested on Facebook that *"rich Jews control the weather."*

Are you kidding me?! And don't misunderstand me, I'm not taking the side of the Muslims or supporting some wacky conspiracy theories against the Jews that are basically anti-Semitic. Of course not! I just bring this up to show you that even though people here in the West might try to downplay this desire of the Jewish people to rebuild the Last Days antichrist Temple, now the Muslim community sure thinks its legit! In fact, many people don't even realize that this is such a deep-seated desire for the Jewish People, that is, to rebuild the Temple, that they even have it embedded in their wedding tradition. How many of you have ever been at a Jewish wedding or have seen what they do at one? At some point they what? A glass is placed on the ground, and with a stomp, the groom crushes the glass, and the guests shout, 'MAZAL TOV!' Why do they do that at every Jewish wedding? Is it because they have too much glass and need to get rid of it somehow? Let's take a look and find out.

"At the conclusion of every Jewish wedding, a glass is broken by the groom in remembrance of the destruction of the Holy Temple."

The family and friends come to the synagogue, they dance, they celebrate the occasion, but the ceremony has them walking down the aisle with the husband wearing a customary white robe, meeting his beautiful bride at the front of the congregation. As she walks down to meet him, she walks around him then stops in front of the Rabbi. They share a small glass of wine. The ring is put on her finger and the Rabbi puts the glass down on the floor in front of them. The husband then smashes the glass with his foot.

"How many more glasses need to be broken? It's time to build."[7]

Time to build what? One last time, the Last Days rebuilt Jewish Temple that the actual antichrist will go up into halfway into the 7-year Tribulation and declare himself to be god! It's embedded in every Jewish wedding ceremony with the breaking of the glass, yet how many of us realize that these are all signs for us here today. Our wedding day as the Bride of Christ is fast approaching! We too will hear a shout and a trumpet call, but it won't be in the 7-year Tribulation when these events take place, but at the Rapture of the Church which takes place prior. Are you ready for your own wedding day? Are you listening to the Lord? What more does He have to do to get our attention? Right now, Jesus is building our "huppah" or Bridal Chamber. This is what He meant here.

John 14:1-3 "Do not let your hearts be troubled. Trust in God; trust also in Me. In My Father's house are many rooms; if it were not so, I would have told you. I am going there to prepare a place for you. And if I go and prepare a place for you, I will come back and take you to be with Me that you also may be where I am."

In other words, when He's done building the Bridal Chamber, the Father's going to inspect it and tell the son, "Okay Son, go get your bride" just like in a Jewish wedding ceremony. He'll typically come when she's not expecting it and "surprise" and "whisk her away!" Literally "abduct," which is where we get our word "rapture" from. It's the final stage of the Jewish Marriage ceremony called the "nissuin" or "the taking." And that's what Paul was talking about here.

1 Thessalonians 4:16-18 "For the Lord Himself will come down from heaven, with a loud command, with the voice of the archangel and with the trumpet call of God, and the dead in Christ will rise first. After that, we who are still alive and are left will be caught up together with them in the clouds to meet the Lord in the air. And so, we will be with the Lord forever. Therefore encourage each other with these words."

You bet it's an encouragement! Because as we saw, the words "caught up" is where we get our word "Rapture" from. What it literally means is a "catching or snatching away" just like an abduction with a bride. Do you think that's by chance? No way! Yes, we don't know the day nor the hour, but after 2000 years, you'd think Jesus is getting pretty close to finishing that Bridal Chamber, amen? We better get ready! Now once the couple returned to the father's house, they would consummate the marriage and celebrate their wedding feast for the next seven days (during which the bride remained closeted in her Bridal Chamber). And so it is, that we too, the Bible says, are whisked away and closeted in our Bridal Chamber, during the 7-year Tribulation. We're up in

Heaven at the Father's house enjoying our Wedding Day while the unbelieving world is unfortunately undergoing His wrath. Therefore, the point is this. You better make sure you're ready to go. You better make sure you're really a Bride of Christ. Make sure before it's too late. Receive the greatest wedding present of all, the gift of eternal life, now! Don't be left behind like these people.

Acts News Network: Time to build the Third Temple

"Temple worship ceased 2000 years ago with the destruction of the Second Temple. Orthodox Jews worldwide pray daily for the restoration of the Holy Temple and for the Shekhinah (Divine) presence to dwell in it and for the resumption of the full order of sacrificial worship including animal sacrifice. For more than 15 years on the eve of the Jewish New Moon, thousands march around Jerusalem's ancient gates praying for the Third Temple and to celebrate the coming of the Messiah. The Temple Institute in Jerusalem is producing sacred vessels required for Temple Rituals."

Rabbi Yehuda Click: *"In our architectural plans that we are planning for the Third Temple, we included air conditioning, we included computers, parking lots, up to date, more beautiful, based on the spirit, based on the word we read from the prophets."*

"The building of the Third Temple is currently prohibited. Management of the Temple Mount is under the Islamic Waqf. Some believers in Jesus correlate the construction of the Third Temple with the emergence of the "man of lawlessness" – the antichrist, for others it signals the return of the Lord."

Hopewell Baptist Church: *"One day Jesus is coming. You may be at church, you may be at work, you may be asleep. God grant that you will be ready when He makes His personal appearance. My God, what if his appearance occurred on a Sunday morning. My prophetic word this morning is GET READY, GET READY, GET READY!!!"*

The scene is a church on a Sunday morning. The Rapture has occurred. Half the congregation is still in the church. It is chaos in the sanctuary. How could they have been left. There is crying and praying. They know that they were not ready. But not only is part of the congregation left but so are some of the ministry still standing there in shock.

"It's going to be joyful for those who are raptured but it is going to be sad for those who are left behind."

Conversations taking place sound like this; "Life as we know it will change." "You swore to me that you would get yourself together and start coming to church with me." A wife tells her husband. His reply is, "It'll be okay."

This is a Sunday morning rapture.[8]

Boy isn't that the excuse every time. I'll go to church services next Sunday. I'll get saved next Sunday. I'll get right with God next Sunday. What you don't realize is that this Sunday might be your last chance! This is why, out of love, God has given us this update on *The Final Countdown: Tribulation Rising* concerning the Jewish People & the Antichrist to show us that the 7-year Tribulation is near, and the Return of Jesus Christ is rapidly approaching. That's why Jesus Himself said…

Luke 21:28 "When these things begin to take place, stand up and lift up your heads, because your redemption is drawing near."

People, like it or not, we are headed for The Final Countdown. The signs of the 7-year Tribulation are rising all around us! It's time to wake up! The point is this. If you're reading this today and you're not a Christian, then I beg you, please, heed these signs, heed these warnings, give your life to Jesus now! You don't want to be here when God pours out His Judgment upon this wicked and rebellious planet! It's the worst time in the history of mankind, so horrible that unless God shortened the timeframe the entire human race would be destroyed! The only way to escape is through Jesus! Take the way out now before it's too late. GET SAVED TODAY! But if you're reading this today and you are a Christian then it's high time you stop goofing off and getting distracted with this world. Let's get busy working together sharing the Gospel with as many as we can! Let's leave here living for Jesus and longing for His soon return. Amen?

Chapter Thirteen

The Jewish People & Their Rebuilt Temple Part 2

The **3rd way** we know the Jewish people really are ready to Rebuild this Last Days Temple now, is that **The Jewish Leaders are Ready to Build the Temple.** But don't take my word for it. Let's listen to God's.

Revelation 11:1-8 "I was given a reed like a measuring rod and was told, "Go and measure the temple of God and the altar and count the worshipers there. But exclude the outer court; do not measure it, because it has been given to the Gentiles. They will trample on the holy city for 42 months. And I will give power to my two witnesses, and they will prophesy for 1,260 days, clothed in sackcloth." These are the two olive trees and the two lampstands that stand before the Lord of the earth. If anyone tries to harm them, fire comes from their mouths and devours their enemies. This is how anyone who wants to harm them must die. These men have power to shut up the sky so that it will not rain during the time they are prophesying; and they have power to turn the waters into blood and to strike the earth with every kind of plague as often as they want. Now when they have finished their testimony, the beast that comes up from the Abyss will attack them and overpower and kill them. Their bodies will lie in the street of the great city, which is figuratively called Sodom and Egypt, where also their Lord was crucified."

According to our text, the Book of Revelation clearly reveals that a Jewish Temple is clearly going to be rebuilt, i.e. in existence during the 7-year Tribulation, right? It's right there in the text. And that's big news because the last Jewish Temple was destroyed in 70 A.D. by the Romans, which is exactly what Jesus prophesied would happen. What else did it say? It said the Two Witnesses and the antichrist are going to be associated with this Temple and it's located where? Where did it say? The Holy City, where their Lord was crucified, right? And where Jesus was crucified? In Jerusalem, right? So, the Bible clearly says, in yet another passage, that in the Last Days, there will be a rebuilt Jewish Temple specifically in Jerusalem. Here's the point. Do we see any signs of the Jewish people really getting ready to rebuild this Last Days Temple any time soon in Jerusalem? Uh yeah! The signs are all over the place and the desire is going through the roof, including now with the Jewish leaders. I'm talking about whether it be the Jewish Rabbis, leaders in the religious community, or even the leaders in the Jewish government, everybody's talking about building this temple again. Let me share some of that proof with you. Let's start with the Rabbis.

Rabbi Ben Greenberg: *"Please God, help us bring about Your Third Temple. You have been with us throughout our long exile. You have sheltered us under the wings of your Divine presence. You have protected us. You have led us to refuge when our neighbors would have us no more. Now, You have brought Your people back into Your land. You have restored our sense of national worth. We defend ourselves with Your help. We govern ourselves with Your help. We look to Yerushalayim and see a city once again bustling with the sounds of children playing and brides and grooms dancing on their wedding day. We look to Har HaMoriah, the Temple Mount, and see a vacuum of what could be. What we see are the ruins of Your glory on earth. The House of Prayer for all People, the one location on the planet where genuine closeness to You could be felt. We know not how your Beit HaMikdash, the Temple, will be restored whether through human or Divine intervention or combination of both. Those matters remain hidden to us. When the Temple is restored may we hear Your promise as Shlomo HaMelekh, King Solomon, heard it thousands of years ago: "I have heard your prayer and your supplication, that you have made unto Me. I have hallowed this house, which you have built, to put My name there forever and My eyes and My heart shall be there for all time." Amen. With hope, Rabbi Benjamin Green."*

Rabbi David Lau: *He's Israel's Chief Rabbi and he recently urged that the Jews can rebuild the Temple in Jerusalem saying, "The structure could fit atop the Temple Mount without need to remove Muslim houses of worship." He would* like to see the Jewish temple rebuilt on the Temple Mount in Jerusalem and to build it, there was no need to remove any of the Muslim shrines on the Temple Mount, where there was plenty of room for Jews, Christians, Muslims, everyone, he told the Knesset Channel on Tuesday. And this of course made Pope Francis happy who has been meeting with the Jewish Rabbis including Rabbi Lau.

Romereports.com: *"After visiting the Holocaust memorial, Pope Francis met with the Chief Rabbis of Israel, Rabbi Rosen and Rabbi Lau. In his speech the Pope summarized the relationship between the Jews and Catholics since the second Vatican council."*

Pope Francis: *"It is a bond whose origins are from on high, one which transcends our own plans and projects, and one which remains intact despite all the difficulties which, sadly, have marked our relationship in the past."*

Romereports.com: *"Pope Francis concluded his speech with an appeal to keep these bonds alive. He also called for greater mutual understanding between the two religions."*

Pope Francis: *"Together, we can make a great contribution to the cause of peace. Together, we can bear witness, in this rapidly changing world, to the perennial importance of the divine plan of creation."[1]*

Rabbi Ben-Dahan: *"There is a reason Palestinian Authority President, Mahmoud Abbas claims that the Temple in Jerusalem never existed; there's a reason why he makes sure every archeological discovery found linking the Jewish people to the Temple Mount will disappear. He understands that the Temple Mount is the beating heart of the Jewish people. The Temple Mount and the Temple are the heart of the nation of Israel, and without a heart there is no body."* He then added that the rebuilding of Jerusalem would not be complete until the Temple, too, is rebuilt and the Temple Mount redeemed. *"We are all here to declare that we have returned to Jerusalem and God-willing we will prepare the hearts of the people to return to the Temple Mount as well and to rebuild the Temple. We aren't embarrassed to say it: We want to rebuild the Temple on the Temple Mount."*

Rabbi Yehuda Glick, a notable Temple Mount activist, said, *"The time had come to replace mourning with action. For 2,000 years we lived out the verse in* *the Book of Lamentations 'You shall surely weep at night.' No more! We must stop weeping and start to take action."*

Rabbi Chaim Richman, International Director of the Temple Institute, declared: *"Everyone that has ever attended a Jewish wedding knows that we break a glass, but how many internalize the message. The broken glass isn't supposed to let guests know when to shout 'mazal tov', on the contrary it is a catalyst to move people into a new level of consciousness that fuses mourning with celebration – giving hope for a time in which we will finally rebuild the Holy Temple in Jerusalem. Every single bridegroom announces the proclamation that he and his future household will not forget Jerusalem, because it is incumbent on every one of us, at all times, to prepare for the rebuilding of the Holy Temple. With the work of the Temple Institute over the last three decades, preparation for the Temple is no longer a dream, it's a reality, in which everyone can play a part."[2]*

Whoa! Sounds to me like they're ready to build that thing! And take part in what? Oh yeah! Rebuilding the Last Days Temple in Jerusalem that the actual antichrist will go up into and declare himself to be god! In fact, most people don't even realize that Rabbi Richman was just here in the U.S. and he just finished up a U.S. Tour called, The Holy Temple in Jerusalem – From Destruction to Rebuilding."

It was, *"To Give Insights and Progress Towards the Rebuilding of the Holy Temple in our Time and Its Meaning for All Mankind."*

Yeah! It means we're living in the Last Days and he's over here even in the U.S. reminding us of that! In fact, it makes you wonder if the antichrist who's going up into that Temple is somewhere alive and well on planet earth. Now, lest you think that the Jewish People really aren't going to be able to pull this off, the rebuilding of the Temple, this is why many Rabbis are not looking to just Pope Francis for help to build the Temple but of all places, they're looking to our current President, Donald Trump.

Rabbi Yosef Berger: *He believes, "Trump will build Third Temple in Jerusalem." "US President Donald Trump's unabashed support for the Jewish state and his public recognition of Jerusalem as its capital have many Israelis electrified. The current American leader's positive attitude toward Israel seems nearly illogical, especially after decades of far more hostile trends. That's why a prominent Israeli rabbi believes the reason for this unprecedented (at least in* *modern times) shift is that Trump has a big role to play in the building of the Third Temple and the coming of Messiah."*

Rabbi Asaf Fried: *"Words of prophecy are coming forth from the Bible and becoming facts." "While Muslims jeer, Israelis cheer President Trump's Jerusalem declaration, prompting Jewish religious activists to suggest building the Third Temple is closer to reality than ever before." "What he did was an enormous step in bringing the Temple," said Asaf Fried, official spokesman for the United Temple Movement, an association of organizations working towards making the Third Temple a reality. He added, "This necessarily had to come from a non-Jew in order to bring them into the process, so they will be able to take their part in the Temple." Fried sees Trump's role similar to the one played by Cyrus, the Persian king who ended the Babylonian exile and helped build the Second Jewish Temple. Fried describes Trump as a modern-day Persian King Cyrus the Great. He pointed to Proverbs 21:1, which says, "Like channeled water is the mind of the king in Hashem's [God's] hand; He directs it to whatever He wishes." There have been amazing advances towards bringing the Temple this year. It was clear that Trump was part of that process, guided by Hasehm [God]," said Fried.*

So that's what the Rabbis are saying. That our President is being guided by God to do what he's doing.

In fact, so much so they believe this, that they have made actual Temple coins with President Trump's head right along King Cyrus. As we saw before, they just produced a new silver half-shekel for Temple purposes with our President's head on it! Here's the actual coin again. And again, the Mikdash (Temple) Educational Center from whom I bought this actual silver shekel from said this about it.

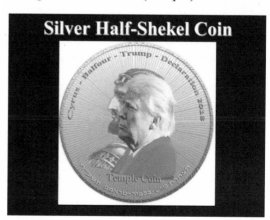

Silver Half-Shekel Coin

"The Temple Movement and Jewish Sanhedrin Issues Half-Shekel Coin with Profile of Trump and Cyrus, the likes of which the Torah mandates every Jewish male must donate to the Temple, with a weight of 9.5 grams in real silver. On the face of the coin is a

picture of the Temple with the inscription 'Half Shekel.' On the other side is the figure of US President Donald Trump, alongside Cyrus, King of Persia, who made the building of the Second Temple possible."

But now they just came out with new Gold Temple Coin hot off the press, with Trump and Cyrus's heads on it. Here it is!

Gold Temple Coin

Again, this is from the Mikdash (Temple) Educational Center from whom I bought this actual Gold Temple Coin from. *"The 70 years Israel Redemption Temple Coin is in honor and praise of Israel's 70ᵗʰ Independence Day."* The Sanhedrin, the Mikdash Educational Center, and the Temple Mount Zion Organizations have minted this new Temple Coin with Biblical verses on the coin declaring the proclamation of Cyrus, king of Persia.

Ezra 1:2 "And He – HASHEM, the Lord of the World – charged me to build Him a house in Jerusalem."

This declaration took place exactly 70 years after the people of Israel were sent into exile and the prophet Jeremiah promised that with the passing of seventy years, *"I will bring you back to your place."*

"Therefore, this coin expresses our joy and gratitude that the American Embassy will be transferred to Jerusalem in honor of Israel's Independence Day. It is the fulfillment of the Trump Declaration recognizing the centrality of Jerusalem as the Capital of the State of Israel. The menorah, the symbol of the State of Israel, stands in the center of the coin together with the ancient Persian symbol, and the seal of the United States of America. Thus, this coin calls for the continuation of the ingathering of the Jewish exiles from all corners of the globe, to the Land of Israel, to Jerusalem and to the Temple, which will bring peace in the world, through the establishment of the Third Temple and the realization of the

prophetic vision. On the backside is a dove, the universal symbol for peace, holding an olive branch in his beak, flying towards the Temple."

Folks, we better wake up! These temple coins are talking about the real live Temple that will be in existence when the antichrist goes up in it halfway into the 7-year Tribulation and declares himself to be god! In fact, the Jewish Rabbis go on to say they think this is all divinely inspired and that this will bring forth the Messiah.

Rabbi Kenneth Cohen: "Mr. Trump – rebuild the Third Temple. You are the most powerful man on earth. When it comes to the Middle East, every president has tried to build his legacy by forcing an unrealistic settlement on the parties in conflict. I would like to suggest that you build your legacy in a way that wasn't attempted for a few thousand years. Mr. Trump, you have developed some of the most amazing building projects in your career. Rebuilding the Third Temple would be your most ambitious project by far. The Temple was a place that actually brought peace to the world. The Rabbis of the Talmud have stated that had the nations of the world known how much they benefited from the Temple, they would never have destroyed it. By building the third Temple, you will help bring back morality and holiness to the world. It will cause everyone to want to get closer to God and elevate himself to be a more righteous and caring individual. Knowing that Temple service will be restored to the holiest place on earth will have a ripple effect throughout the world. I realize that we might have a little problem with the Al-Aksa Mosque as well as the Dome of the Rock. Our modern technology will allow us to move these buildings to Mecca without causing any damage to these ancient structures. As for the details as to how to do the actual construction, the Temple Institute is ready to assist you. Rumor has it, that there is even a red heifer waiting for service. So many people laughed at you when you decided to run for President. They are not laughing anymore. I know you like challenges and you want to make your mark on the world. As crazy as all of this sounds, Mr. Trump, you just might be the one to pull this off. Oh, and by the way, an added bonus for getting the job done, will be the coming of the Messiah."

Rabbi Gematria: Some Jewish leaders have pointed out that the gematria (numerical value) of Donald Trump's name equals that of the phrase 'Meshiach Ben David' (Messiah, Son of David). They view the gematria of Trump's name as an indication of him playing a role in the 'redemptive process' – a role in preparing the conditions for the Messiah's arrival. The calculations they bring up are the fact that Trump was born 700 days before Israel became a nation, won the election on Prime Minister Netanyahu's 7th year, 7th month and 7th day in office, and served his first full day in the White House at the age of 70 years, 7 months and 7 days old. While we should be careful of reading too much into these numbers, it would seem that God Himself has had His hand on the unusual rise of Donald Trump and if so, would have a particular purpose for his Presidency."[3]

Yeah, like help the Jewish People rebuild the Temple! And according to the Jewish Rabbis, this will pave the way for the coming of the Messiah! Isn't this wild?! This is all going on right now in the news as we're all distracted by the economy, sports, social media, and other things! Now, speaking of getting help to build the Temple from leaders around the world, the Jewish Rabbis are also getting involved in their own government and are starting to get the "ear" of figures like Benjamin Netanyahu. "A high profile Temple activist joins the Netanyahu Government" and that of course is Temple mount activist Rabbi Yehudah Glick. He's been brought into the Israeli parliament as a member of Netanyahu's ruling coalition. And boy is he making an impact! Here's a picture of him...

And if you'll recall previously, he was the guy who got shot by the Muslim in 2014 with four bullet wounds to the chest, just for suggesting that the Jews get to pray on the Temple Mount like the Muslims do. It looked like it was the end for Rabbi Glick, but in what doctors described as a miracle – none of the bullets hit any vital organs. And after one month and nine surgeries, he recovered, and it spawned the birth of several new organizations devoted to Jewish prayer rights on the Temple Mount. So, basically the Muslim attack backfired! Well, now he's in the Israeli parliament to "influence the nation of Israel." And that "influence" is to what? To rebuild the Temple! And lest you think it's not working...you're wrong. Ever since our President moved the U.S. Embassy to Jerusalem, even Benjamin Netanyahu, is now starting to say, "It's time to rebuild the Temple!"

Benjamin Netanyahu at the US Embassy in Israel: *"Thank you all. And of course, I want to welcome Jered Kushner and Ivanka Trump. Your presence here today is a testament to the importance of the occasion, not only for the Trump Administration but in a very personal way.*

For you and the pursuit of peace and for President Trump himself. Thank you. Dear friends, what a glorious day. Remember this moment. This is history. President Trump, by recognizing history you have made history. So, to me this spot brings back personal memories, but for our people, those profound collective memories of the greatest moments we have known on this city on the hill.

In Jerusalem, Abram passed the greatest test of faith to be the father of our nation. In Jerusalem, King David established our capital 3000 years ago. In Jerusalem, King Solomon built our temple, which stood for many centuries.

In Jerusalem, Jewish exiles from Babylon rebuilt the temple, which stood for many more centuries. In Jerusalem the Maccabees rededicated that temple, and restored Jewish sovereignty in this land.

And it was here in Jerusalem some 2000 years later that the soldiers here in Israel spoke these immortal words, 'the temple mount is in our hands.' Words that lifted the spirit of the entire nation. We are in Jerusalem and we are here to stay."[4]

And do what? Rebuild the Last Days Temple! It's all in the news, right now, the current news, as we sit here, dealing with our President and the current administration, all saying, "Let's build this Temple again!" And what Temple will that be? Oh yeah! That's right! The one that the actual antichrist will go up into halfway into the 7-year tribulation and declare himself to be god! We better wake up!

The **4th way** we know the Jewish People are getting ready to rebuild this Last Days Temple now, is that **The Non-Jewish Leaders are Ready to Build the Temple**.

You might think there's no way the Jewish People are going to get the Muslims or other nations to go along with this, even with President Trump's help and Benjamin Netanyahu's blessing, it's just impossible! Really? This is the other strange thing going on. Non-Jewish Leaders from around the world are jumping on the bandwagon to rebuild this Last Days Temple as well. Makes you wonder if God's not controlling it all.

Proverbs 21:1 "The king's heart is in the hand of the LORD; He directs it like a watercourse wherever He pleases."

Daniel 2:19,20,21 "Then Daniel praised the God of heaven and said: 'Praise be to the Name of God for ever and ever; wisdom and power are His. He changes times and seasons; He sets up kings and deposes them."

Daniel 5:21 "The Most High God is sovereign over the kingdoms of men and sets over them anyone He wishes."

Romans 13:1 "For there is no authority except that which God has established. The authorities that exist have been established by God."

And that's true not only with President Trump, but even other non-Jewish Leaders from around the world, are all of a sudden Pro-Israel, in favor of building this Last Days Temple, starting with Vladimir Putin! *"Rabbis are urging Trump and Putin to help rebuild the Temple in Jerusalem."*[5]

Within days of the election victory, long time Temple Mount advocate and now prominent member of the Israeli Knesset Rabbi Yehudah Glick, issued a call inviting Trump to visit the Temple Mount. This call was followed days later by an open letter from the re-convened Jewish Sanhedrin addressed to both the U.S. President Donald Trump and Russian President Vladimir Putin – asking them both to fulfill the Cyrus mandate of rebuilding the Temple. The Sanhedrin is calling on Russian President Vladimir Putin and President Donald Trump to join forces together and fulfill their "Biblically-mandated roles" by rebuilding the Jewish Temple in Jerusalem.

Compared to President Trump, Russian President Vladimir Putin might seem like an even more unlikely Cyrus. Many would instead view him as a potential 'Gog' – one of Israel's great end time enemies. However, the Sanhedrin are basing their letter to Putin on positive reports concerning his attitude to the Temple Mount.

He visited the Western Wall and disclosed that he was personally praying for the rebuilding of the Temple.

"Putin is walking down the hallway with the Rabbis and police walking towards the Synagogue. They come to a stop and he exchanges kisses of welcome with the Rabbis. As they enter the building he kneels and crosses himself at the replica of the Temple Mount. Cameras are going off all around him as he kneels once again to light a candle and places it on the stand.

He again stands and crosses himself. He stands with the other Rabbis while their pictures are being taken again. Then they walk to the model of the Third Temple. The Rabbis explain what he is looking at. It is all spoken in Hebrew and Russian. He is shaking his head yes."[6]

Now if you noticed there at the last, Putin was there with the Rabbis shaking his head repeatedly over something, but it was before what? They were talking over a model of the Temple Mount. There was a little mini Dome of the Rock replica there and Putin shaking his head yes, over something! I don't speak Russian or Hebrew, but it's reported that, "During his third official trip to Jerusalem, Putin paid a late-night visit to the Western Wall. And when he arrived at the holy site, the Russian leader stood in silence for several minutes, offering up a personal prayer, after which he read Psalms from a Russian-Hebrew prayer book. An Israeli bystander called out in Russian, "Welcome, President Putin." Putin then approached the man, who explained the importance of the Temple Mount and the Jewish Temple. Then Chadrei Charedim, an Orthodox Hebrew news site, reported that Putin responded, *"That's exactly the reason I came here – to pray for the Temple to be built again."* So, because of this, the Sanhedrin sends him a letter calling on him to fulfill his prayer, to help build the Temple again, along with Trump! In fact, they go on to say, *"The leaders of Russia and America can lead the nations of the world to global peace through building the Temple, the source of peace,"* Rabbi Weiss explained. *"We are poised to rebuild the Temple."* One Rabbinical Tradition states, *"Maimonides teaches that the Temple will be built by Messiah himself, and in fact its construction will be one of the signs that he is indeed the Messiah."* So that brings up the question, "Is this Cyrus type figure the prophesied antichrist on earth?" Don't know? But one researcher stated, *"While the Sanhedrin is looking for a Cyrus type figure to arise and help build the Temple now, many Christians tend to link the rebuilding of the Temple not with a Cyrus but rather with the antichrist himself.* The Scriptures are clear that the coming antichrist will defile this temple. In his day, King Cyrus helped build a temple in Jerusalem at divine instruction, which was later defiled by Antiochus, a type of antichrist. Could it be that God will likewise in the end times raise up a new Cyrus figure that will help facilitate the rebuilding of the Third Temple - which will later be defiled by the antichrist before the real Messiah finally returns to take His rightful place in the Temple? Could be! Folks, it's all going down as we sit here, we better wake up and stop getting distracted! But you might be thinking, "Okay, that's fine and dandy with Trump and Putin's support, but you know there's no way the Muslim's are ever going to go along with this? Really? Talk about "directing a watercourse wherever He pleases!" Some Muslim Community Leaders, right now, are saying they actually want to help build this Temple too. Starting with this guy, Adnan Oktar.

"He's a well-known famous Turkish Muslim leader who hosted a prominent group of Israeli rabbis over one of their stated goals, to rebuild the Jewish Temple in Jerusalem. The meetings included other Muslims and so-called Christian representatives as well. So, it's kind of like a One World religion thing. But here's his bio…

Muslim Leader Adnan Oktar

"Adnan Oktar, is a controversial but highly influential Muslim intellectual and author with over 65 million of his books in circulation worldwide. Oktar recently met with three representatives from the re-established Jewish Sanhedrin, a group of 71 Orthodox rabbis and scholars from Israel, to discuss how religious Muslims, Jews and so-called Christians can work together.

The objectives of this alliance include waging a joint intellectual and spiritual battle against the worldwide growing tide of irreligiousness, (in other words people who don't go along with a One World religion) *unbelief and immorality.*

But even more unusual is their agreement with regard to the need to rebuild the Jewish Temple, a structure that Oktar refers to as the "Masjid (Mosque)" or the "Palace of Solomon."

An official statement about the meeting has been published on the Sanhedrin's website and a historian to the Sanhedrin regarding issues related to Islam, emphasized the rebuilding of the Temple is a very good development for all mankind.

Oktar said Muslims, Jews and Christians share many common values and the current opposition was a ploy of satan. He said people of reason who are full of love should come together and encourage peace.

Oktar has also stated that the Temple of Solomon "Will be rebuilt and all believers will worship there in tranquility."

And during his meeting with the Sanhedrin, Oktar expressed his belief that the Temple could be rebuilt in one year at the most.

"It could be built to the same perfection and beauty. It could be rebuilt in a year in its perfect form."

And since the meeting took place, two of the rabbis who met with Oktar explained, "The building of the Temple is one of the stages in the Messianic process."[7]

In other words, let's all build this One World Religion Temple and the Messiah will show up. But here's the actual news broadcast of one of their meetings.

Holy Land Uncovered Reports: *"Welcome back to Holy Land Uncovered, our next discussion can only take place in the Holy Land. Have you ever heard of the initiatives to build a Third Temple in Jerusalem? Well, even if you might have heard of such an initiative this still might really surprise you. How about Turkish Muslims promoting the Third Temple project along with Jewish Orthodox Rabbis. Meet doctor Oktar Babuna who came here from Turkey. Thank you so much and welcome to Israel. Rabbi Yehuda Glick will also join us shortly. Oh, here he is, welcome to you as well. The Temple Mount is one of the biggest flash point sites in the region that often ignites violence and clashes. Your message here is holy sites should be centers of reconciliation and not conflict."*

Dr. Babuna: *"For the people who are living in this country it is sacred for Jews, for Muslims, and for Christians and that makes it prone to violence. It is no* *benefit for anybody. It's a prayer house, where God's name is mentioned, and it has to be rebuilt so people of all the nations can pray there. All nations, God says, to pray shoulder to shoulder to serve God. It states this from the Torah."*

Reporter: *"Rabbi Glick, you have met with the doctor here in the studio. Were you surprised by the initiative?"*

Rabbi Glick: *"Yes, I am actually in a long-term connection with him and I think they are doing a wonderful activity. They are led by a very special leader from Turkey, Adnan Oktar. I think that it shouldn't surprise us that the people believe in God and know that God is inclusive and not exclusive. And he wants us all to join together and turn the Temple Mount into a house of prayer for all nations and I think that, I am sure that, we are at the beginning of a Biblical era where more and more religions from around the world will join this one initiative of turning the Temple Mount into a place where it should be a world center for peace and following the one and only God."*

Reporter: *"What we are seeing here is the images of the Temple, the Third Temple Mount, which is very interesting, but I have to ask, is this doable or is it just a fantasy? With so many regulations, objections and funding of course?"*

Rabbi Glick: *"With love and discussions it is very, very doable. Actually, it is a promise from God as we read the statements from the Torah. We will pray there, it is a prayer house of God. Nothing can stop that. It has pure gold carving with original form, it will be revealed as a prayer house for all the nations, shoulder to shoulder. It's doable because it is not going to damage either the Dome of the Rock or the Al-Aqsa. There is enough land, and this can be a prayer house for Jews, Christians and the Muslim."*

In other words, they want to turn it into a One World Religion Temple! WOW! So, they've fallen for the One World Religion lie! The Pope must be happy! But here's the point! Who would have thought that the Muslim community would be chumming up with, and agreeing with, the Jewish Rabbis about rebuilding the Last Days Temple, let alone go along with a One world Religion! It's almost like…**Proverbs 21:1** "The king's heart is in the hand of the LORD; He directs it like a watercourse wherever He pleases." In other words, God's directing these Last Days events for His purposes! One researcher states: *"As believers we should be watching these developments, praying for God's prophesied purposes to be accomplished, and checking our own spiritual lives to* *make sure that we're ready to meet the soon coming King."* In other words, stop goofing off, we're living in the Last Days, make sure you're a Bride of Christ! Why? Because on top of all this, there's even talk now about how the Jewish Rabbis know the actual location of the Ark of the Covenant and they are just waiting for the right time to bring it out! And that right time is when the Temple goes up! Check this out...

Rabbi Richman: *"There are inquiries about the Ark of the Covenant from all over the world because of the popularity of the issue for many people. It's an issue that has a lot of significance. And now a very famous book has been written about it, there have been television specials, postulating this theory or that, but I would have to say what I would consider impeachable, unbroken transmission of knowledge of the Jewish people. There is no question about the Ark of the Covenant, that it remains in the same chamber as it was hidden by King Josiah towards the close of the First Temple.*

That chamber that was personally designed by King Solomon who saw in a prophecy that the Temple would be destroyed. It was hidden there together with other items. We know where they are. An attempt was made a number of years ago to obtain them but was not successful. But we certainly believe that when the proper time comes, we shall be able to gather these things for their position in the rebuilt Temple."

In other words, when they get permission to build that Temple, the Ark of the Covenant is coming out. And based on what we saw today, that time is just about here! That's Rabbi Richman from the Temple Institute! What more does God have to do to get our attention? One last time I belabor the point! What Jewish Temple are we talking about here? That they're ready to put the Ark of the Covenant in? The Temple that the actual antichrist is going to go up into halfway into the 7-year Tribulation and declare himself to be god! And so, if we see the Jewish and even non-Jewish leaders from around the world, even the Muslims, ready to rebuild this Temple now, how much closer is the Rapture of the Church that takes place prior to all this? This is why, out of love, God has given us this update on *The Final Countdown: Tribulation Rising* concerning the Jewish People & the Antichrist to show us that the 7-year Tribulation is near, and the Return of Jesus Christ is rapidly approaching. And that's why Jesus Himself said...

Luke 21:28 "When these things begin to take place, stand up and lift up your heads, because your redemption is drawing near."

Like it or not, we are headed for The Final Countdown. The signs of the 7-year Tribulation are Rising all around us! It's time to WAKE UP! And so, the point is this. If you're reading this today and you're not a Christian, then I beg you, please, heed these signs, heed these warnings, give your life to Jesus now! You don't want to be here when God pours out His Judgment upon this wicked and rebellious planet! It's the worst time in the history of mankind, so horrible that unless God shortened the timeframe the entire human race would be destroyed! The only way to escape is through Jesus! Take the way out now before it's too late. Get saved today! But, if you're reading this today and you are a Christian, then it's high time we stop goofing off and getting distracted with this world. Let's get busy working together sharing the Gospel with as many as we can! Let's leave here living for Jesus and longing for His soon return. Amen?

Chapter Fourteen

The Jewish People & Their Rebuilt Temple Part 3

The **5th way** we know the Jewish people really are ready to rebuild this Last Days Temple now, is that **The Temple Organizers are ready to Build the Temple**. But don't take my word for it. Let's listen to God's.

Matthew 24:10-22 "At that time many will turn away from the faith and will betray and hate each other, and many false prophets will appear and deceive many people. Because of the increase of wickedness, the love of most will grow cold, but he who stands firm to the end will be saved. And this gospel of the kingdom will be preached in the whole world as a testimony to all nations, and then the end will come. So, when you see standing in the holy place 'the abomination that causes desolation,' spoken of through the prophet Daniel – let the reader understand – then let those who are in Judea flee to the mountains. Let no one on the roof of his house go down to take anything out of the house. Let no one in the field go back to get his cloak. How dreadful it will be in those days for pregnant women and nursing mothers! Pray that your flight will not take place in winter or on the Sabbath. For then there will be great distress, unequaled from the beginning of the world until now – and never to be equaled again. If those days had not been cut short, no one would survive, but for the sake of the elect those days will be shortened."

In other words, it's going to be horrible and you don't want to be there!

But, according to our text, Jesus clearly reveals that a "holy place" or a rebuilt Jewish Temple is going to be in existence in the 7-year Tribulation, because the antichrist is going to go up into it and desecrate it, right? It's right there in the text. Do we see any signs of the Jewish people really getting ready to rebuild this Last Days Temple any time soon in Jerusalem? Uh yeah! In fact, so much so that they have actual organizations dedicated to doing exactly that! Let's take a look at just two of them.

The Temple Institute: It was founded in 1987 in the Jewish quarter of Jerusalem's Old City. It is dedicated to every aspect of the Biblical commandment to build the Holy Temple of God on Mount Moriah in Jerusalem. Rabbi Yisrael Ariel is the founder and head of the Temple Institute, and he served in the paratrooper brigade which liberated the Temple Mount in the Six Day War of 1967, and he was one of the first soldiers to reach the Mount.

He stated, "Through the years, the more I studied the more I began to understand that we had only ourselves and our own inaction to hold accountable: God does not intend for us to wait for a day of miracles. We are expected to act. We must accomplish that with which we have been charged: to do all in our power to prepare for the rebuilding of the Holy Temple, and the renewal of the divine service."

Their short-term goal is to rekindle the flame of the Holy Temple in the hearts of mankind through education, but their long-term goal is to do all in their power to bring about the building of the Holy Temple in our time. Towards this end, the Institute has begun to restore and construct the sacred vessels for the service of the Holy Temple. They are made according to the exact specifications of the Bible, and have been constructed from the original source materials, such as gold, copper, silver and wood. These are authentic, accurate vessels, not merely replicas or models. All of these items are fit and ready for use in the service of the Holy Temple. Among the many items featured in the exhibition are musical instruments played by the Levitical choir, the golden crown of the High Priest, and gold and silver vessels used in the incense and sacrificial services. And after many years of effort and toil, the Institute has completed the three most important and central vessels of the Divine service: the seven-branched Menorah, made of pure gold; the golden Incense Altar, and the golden Table of Showbread. The director of the International Department is headed by Rabbi Chaim Richman. Rabbi Richman has been associated with the Temple Institute since 1989. He states, *"The Torah testifies that the Holy Temple in Jerusalem was the spiritual center for all mankind. All of Israel's prophets foretell that in the future, the Holy Temple will once again stand on Mount Moriah, and at that time all nations will worship there together. In our time, there is a great spiritual awakening concerning the importance of the Temple. The Temple Institute views this awakening as Divinely-inspired, and actively seeks to share the desire and knowledge of the Temple with people around the world, thereby laying the foundation for the spiritual revolution that will precipitate the rebuilding of the Holy Temple and the fulfillment of this prophecy in our time. The major focus of the Institute is the beginning of the actual rebuilding of the Holy Temple. "*

The Temple Mount and the Land of Israel Faithful Movement: They are an Orthodox Jewish movement, based in Jerusalem, whose goal is to rebuild the Third Jewish Temple on the Temple Mount in Jerusalem and re-institute the practice of ritual sacrifice. The movement was founded by former Israel Defense Forces officer Gershon Salomon. Members of the movement are referred to as the "Temple Mount Faithful." The group was established in 1967 and were the first significant group to advocate the Jewish takeover of the Temple Mount, and during the 1970s and 1980s Salomon stated, "Whoever controls the Temple Mount has rights over the Land of Israel." But here's how it all started. Gershon Salomon was grievously wounded in battle against the Syrians. He experienced a miraculous deliverance from his would-be Syrian executors and felt God calling him to dedicate his life to the rebuilding of the Temple. As Israel conquered the Temple Mount in 1967, Gershon – still on crutches – joined his fellow Israeli soldiers on the sacred grounds. What he witnessed that day would change his life forever. As Gerson and his fellow soldiers toured the Temple Mount, they encountered a neatly dressed Jordanian guide. Addressing them in English, the guide proceeded to give the Israelis a tour of the site, explaining where the Temple, the menorah and the altar originally stood. When asked by the group of soldiers why he was showing them all this, the Jordanian guide answered, "We have a tradition from our fathers and they from their fathers that one day the Jews would wage a war and conquer this mountain and rebuild the Holy Temple." Then addressing the Israelis, the guide went even further saying, "I assume that you're starting tomorrow?" Gershon further relates that the tour guide seemed to suddenly disappear, and the whole experience appeared so miraculous that he and other soldiers assumed the guide must have been an Angel. Facing towards the Holy of Holies, Gershon solemnly pledged that day to work ceaselessly for the rebuilding of the Temple. Among their stated objectives are, "Liberating the Temple Mount from Arab (Islamic) occupation, consecrating the Temple Mount to the Name of God so that it can become the moral and spiritual center of Israel and of the entire world, and the rebuilding the Third Temple in accordance with the words of all the Hebrew prophets (Ezekiel 40-44). This temple will be a house of prayer for the people of Israel and all nations (Isaiah 56:7). The first stone of the Third Temple will soon be laid.[1]

Wow!! Sounds to me like somebody's pretty serious about building that Temple, how about you? The organizations are here to do it! In fact, it gets even more wild when you see firsthand on location, just how ready these organizations like the Temple Institute and Temple Mount Faithful really are. And since yours truly was just there, let me share with you some of the actual photos I took while I was there at the Temple Institute, and you tell me if they're not serious about this endeavor.

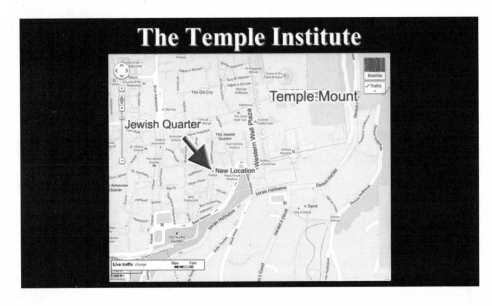

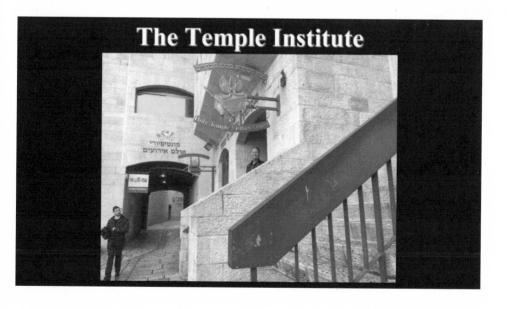

The Temple Institute

The Temple Institute

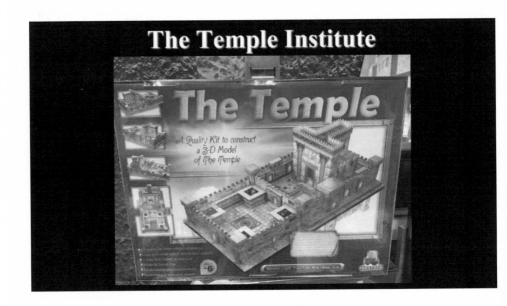

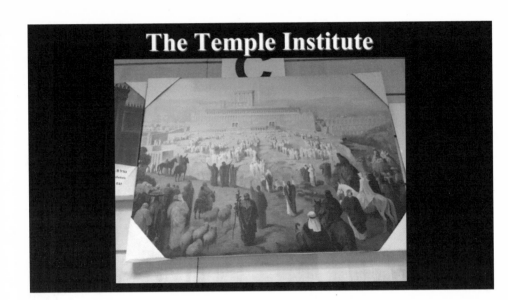

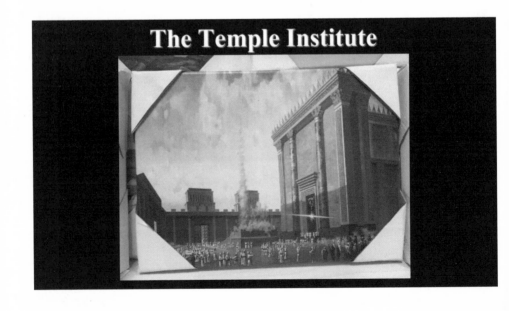

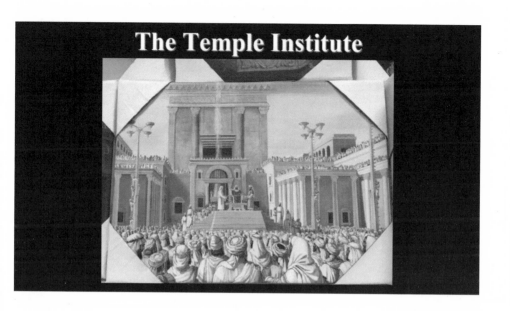

214

The Temple Institute

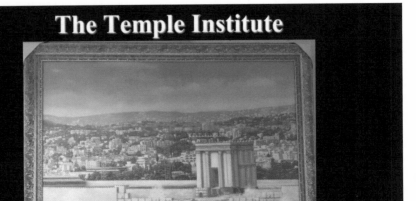

The Temple Institute

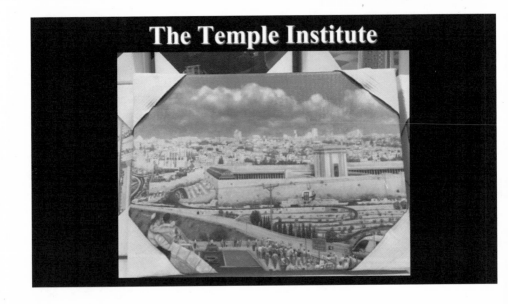

The Temple Institute

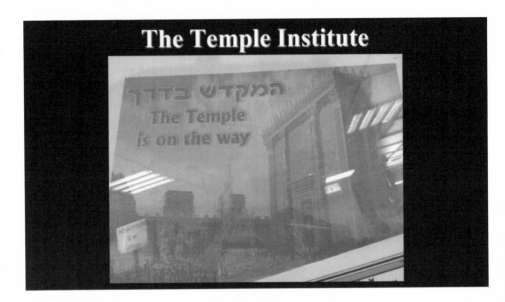

Make no mistake about it! These guys are ready to build the Last Days Temple! And that's just in the gift shop! Again, these are the same guys who are pumping out all these commercials saying, "We are ready to build the Temple." In fact, here's another one saying they're ready, being aired in Israel.

"The students are in their robes, studying the Torah. The elder is praying in front of the class. In the next room are the Jewish children playing. But one of the older ones in the class stands and looks at the smaller ones playing. Then he takes out a wooden chest and pushes it out onto the floor. He stands on the chest and proceeds to call out to the little ones. They all stop what they are doing to look at him.

They all stand and give him all their attention. There is a picture on the wall behind him. As he is talking, he starts pointing to the picture. It is a picture of the Temple. They look at the picture and smile. He then opens the chest and he takes out plastic belts and hands one to each child. They buckle them on and then put on plastic hard hats. They are ready to get to work on rebuilding the Temple. They then go into the room where the older students and men are. They each take the hand of one man and they lead them out of the room. The oldest boy that started the idea of putting on the tool belt is now standing in front of one of the older students and holds out his hand, encouraging him to stand. He too stands, takes the boys hand and they join the others as they walk out of the room. The old teacher turns around and there isn't anyone in the classroom. They have all gone through the door with the bright light.[2]

The Children Are Ready."

Yes, once again, the children are ready. The question is, "are you?" And why do I ask? Because once again, what are we talking about here? This is the Temple that the actual antichrist will go up into halfway into the 7-year Tribulation and declare himself to be God! The Rapture is around the corner, are you ready?

The **6th way** we know the Jewish People really are ready to rebuild this Last Days Temple now, is that **The Finances are Ready to Build the Temple.**

You see, you might be thinking, "Well hey, there's no way they're going to be able to pull this off, rebuilding the Temple, because we're not just talking some average everyday edifice here. These guys aren't going to build this thing with Stucco and plywood! They want this Temple with real gold, tons of it, and real silver and precious stones, the whole nine yards! I mean the expenses for this thing are going to be astronomical! How are they going to get enough finances for that?" Well, that's why you need to pay attention to the methods they're using to raise the money for just that! First of all, you can go to their website and support them the Old-Fashioned way.

Temple Institute Donations

In fact, they have many huge donations from Christian Institutions from around the world, and it just keeps going! So much so that they've even got categories of different levels of giving. For instance,

Giving Categories

- The Mitzvah Level – ($18 USD)
- The Levitical Choir Level – ($36 USD) – Here you'll receive a beautiful high-resolution photograph of a ten-string lyre and a message of gratitude from the Temple Institute.
- The High Priest Garments Level – ($54 USD) Here you'll receive a beautiful high-resolution photograph of the Garments of the High Priest and a detailed description of all the elements of the High Priest's garments and a letter of gratitude.
- The Incense Offering Level – ($120 USD) Here you'll receive a beautiful high-resolution photograph of the Golden Incense Chalice and a short description of the Chalice and how it is used by the priests in the daily incense offering and a letter of gratitude.
- The High Priest's Crown Level – ($180 USD) Here you'll receive a beautiful high-resolution photograph of the Golden Crown of the High Priest and a brief description of the Golden Crown and a letter of gratitude.

- The Ark of the Covenant Level – ($260 USD) Here you'll receive a beautiful high-resolution photograph of the Ark of the Covenant and a brief description of the Ark and a letter of gratitude.
- The Platinum Family Membership – ($500 USD) Here you'll receive a platinum membership card which includes free entrance for you and your whole family to the Temple Institute Visitor Center.
- Exhibit Tour w/Rabbi Richman – ($1000 USD) Here you'll receive an exclusive tour of the Temple Institute's Visitors Center conducted by Rabbi Chaim Richman.
- Exclusive Tour of the Temple Mount – ($5000 USD) Here you'll receive a special tour of the Temple Mount and Temple Institute's Visitors Center with Rabbi Chaim Richman.
- Preview of the Architectural Plans – ($50,000 USD) Here you'll receive an exclusive preview of the current architectural plans with Rabbi Richman along with a tour of the Temple Mount and Temple Institute's Visitors Center.

Now they're even going beyond those traditional methods of fundraising, to even more popular trends of giving. Like the "bucket challenge" thing remember that? And all those other crazy goofball fundraising gimmicks where people poured water over their heads! Well, they did that to, only theirs was called, "The Shofar Challenge."

The Temple Institute: *"I am here with the Shofar Challenge. What is the challenge? Blow the Shofar and proclaim this year and donate to The Temple Institute's Build the Third Temple crowd funding campaign. Proceeds go towards creating the architectural plans for building the Holy Temple. If you can't blow the Shofar you can still donate to our Build the Third Temple Campaign and nominate three others to accept the challenge within the next 24 hours.*

What's it all about? It's about taking responsibility for the ultimate goal of rebuilding the Holy Temple. For almost three decades the Temple Institute has led the way in Temple research and education and preparation of the sacred vessels ready for use in the Holy Temple. We call upon our supporters worldwide to blow the Shofar and proclaim the clear message that the people of Israel have returned to the land of Israel and truly long for the Holy Temple.

In these days the Shofar is blown daily, so let's take it one step further. We challenge you to blow the Shofar or at least try to blow, upload it and then challenge three others to do the same. Take the challenge and please donate and help to make the dream of 2000 years come closer to reality this year and rebuild the Temple. I nominate the following to blow the Shofar and contribute to the Temple Institutes' build the Third Temple Campaign. Professor Jeffrey Wolf, Rabbi Toby Singer, Rabbi Efram Goldberg, Jonathan Felstein, Josh Hasting."[3]

As you guys can see, they are using all kinds of methods, even modern methods, as well as traditional methods, to drum up the finances needed to rebuild this Last Days Temple! They're going to get the job done! In fact, you heard him mention another modern fundraising method, the crowd funding campaign. Everybody does that nowadays. Whether it's for an emergency, or hospital bills, house burned down, businesses, you name it! And theirs has been very successful!

"The Temple Institute has created a $100,000 Indiegogo campaign to raise financing to construct the Third Temple, which it says will be a "house of prayer for all nations" and will usher in "a new era of universal harmony and peace" as prophesied in the Bible."

One headline stated, "Want world peace? Build The 3rd Temple."

The campaign slogan says, "Don't make history, make the future, build the Third Temple" and then it added, "After a millennia of yearning, the Temple Institute is paving the way for the rebuilding of the Temple, including the recreation of 60 sacred Temple vessels ready for use once the Temple is rebuilt."

And the campaign statement continued, "It is not enough to wait and pray for the Third Temple. It is a Biblical obligation to build it."

"This generation of children is "ready" to see the center of Jewish worship rebuilt, once and for all."

That was the description of their crowdfunding campaign, And, in no time at all, they actually surpassed their initial goal by receiving 900 pledges from 30 different countries worldwide and received 10,000 shares on Facebook. and Rabbi Richman explained why they were doing this. *"We are constantly looking for ways to include as many people as possible in our mission to rebuild the Holy Temple. This is not about one group or organization; it's about bringing about a spiritual reunification of mankind. And today with the help of the internet our message is resonating across the globe. Our decision to use Indiegogo for this campaign was an extension of our success on YouTube, Facebook and Twitter."*

So again, they're using modern technology in our lifetime, never before in the history of the Church, to actually help raise the funds to build the actual Temple that the antichrist is going up into declaring himself to be god! But you might still be thinking, "Well okay, that's a lot of money. I'll give you that. But you're going to need a whole lot more than that if you're going to be able to pull off building this Third Temple and all its precious amenities." And if you were to say that, you're right! And maybe that's why this recent discovery happened! It's almost like God brings everything about when it's the right time.

This article says… *"Billions of Dollars of Gold Discovered Under Eilat Mountains in Israel to be Used to Rebuild Third Jewish Temple."* And they quote, **Genesis 2:12** "The gold of that land is good; aromatic resin and onyx are also there." A treasure-trove of raw gold worth billions of dollars is believed to be sitting under Mount Eilat in southern Israel, breaking Israel News has learned. In an exclusive interview, Rabbi Yehuda Glick, the Executive Director of The Temple Mount Heritage Foundation in Jerusalem, revealed the news, which had been kept under wraps for the last several years. Explaining the discovery, Glick said that everything began with Friedman, a Temple Mount researcher, who had been studying each of the 12 unique stones set on the breastplate of the High Priest as described in the Bible. Each stone represents one of the 12 tribes of Israel and during his studies, Friedman realized that without a geological background he could not properly appreciate the depths and meanings behind each of these stones. So, Friedman and Glick, knowing the Bible verses concerning gold in the Land of Israel, realized this was a project which had to be pursued. *"Because of the extensive Biblical proof, we presented the exact location where the gold was to be found, we won the license to begin digging."* And they struck it big! Here's Yehuda Glick talking about it.

"We are here in Jerusalem, on Jerusalem Day, with Rabbi Glick and Rabbi you are telling me…"

Rabbi Glick: *"I want to share with you something that is very new actually, we haven't really told people about it yet. You are one of the very first people to hear about it. We, with a group of geologists, after about five years of exploring, we have located a place, in the Mountain of Ilat, where there is a large quantity* *of very high-quality gold in the ground. We have found, both by taking pieces of the ground and sending it to laboratories, and also sending our results of our finding to different geologists around the world. We also have satellite photography of the area and we know exactly where the canal of gold is, like 100 meters in the ground. It's an investment but we know for sure that there is more than a billion dollars' worth of gold there. We're talking about more than a million ounces of gold that is spread around there. The first time we have convinced the ministry of Israel to give us an exclusive license to that area, we have the exclusive license to do the digging as soon as we manage to raise the money needed for the investment. Within 30 days we can go down there and start drilling, and we will come back with what you call deposit reports, within a year we can do that and then we can start digging. We need the exclusive license to do it."*

Reporter: *"Are you serious?"*

Rabbi Glick: *"Serious? Yes, I'm serious. God said in the book of Genesis, "and the gold of that land is good.""[4]*

And apparently, that gold is going to be used to help build the Temple! And why do I say that? Because they go on to say....

When asked what these modern-day Biblical explorers plan to do with their billions in gold, Rabbi Yehuda Glick replied, *"Ultimately, we expect to use the gold in the rebuilding of the Third Temple. Whether we use the gold itself for creating vessels and decoration or by selling the findings and using the money to buy the materials and manpower needed to rebuild the Temple, we look forward to that great day!'"*

What great day is that? When the antichrist will go up into it halfway into the 7-year Tribulation and declare himself to be God! Is this wild or what? They've got all the finances they need and then some to rebuild that Last Days Temple now!

The **7th way** we know the Jewish People really are ready to rebuild this Last Days Temple now, is that **The Plans are Ready to Build the Temple**.

Now, as you read about the crowdfunding campaigns, one of the things they're going to be doing with this money, is the creation of the architectural plans for the rebuilding of the Temple. Which is pretty basic…you can't build a Temple without the plans…unless of course you want to end up with things like I build with no plans and last for about 14 seconds when a cat brushes up against it and it falls over! But seriously, you have to have plans before you can start, right? Well guess what? Thanks to the financing…they've got them! In fact, here's a transcript of a video of Rabbi Richman of the Temple Institute reading some of the new plans for the Temple, and I'll explain what they include.

Imagine two men sitting at the table with the plans for the Third Temple laid out in front of them. Rabbi Richman is pointing out all the different spots on the plan and is explaining to the other gentleman all the things that will be built into the Temple. The plans are bigger than the table top and they are three sheets deep. It is going to be beautiful when completed.[5]

They go on to say, "Now is time for one of the most ambitious projects yet: completing the architectural plans for the actual construction of the Temple.

"The Temple Institute has engaged with an architect to map out as practically as possible the modern Third Temple's construction."

"The Third Temple will be equipped with every modern amenity: full computerization, underground parking, temperature control, elevators, docks for public transportation, wheelchair access, and much more."

"With every detail of the future Temple's requirements listed in the written and oral law, our architects are not only designers, but Torah scholars who will ensure that everything is built to the highest modern standards, while adhering to the letter of Jewish law."

"As you can see, our bold campaign to raise the finances for the preparations of architectural plans for the Third Temple has been successful, thanks to the hundreds of people who have supported this effort."

"This development will make the Third Temple a reality."

Then they go on to say, *"This past Tisha B'Av we released a short video showing for the first time, the actual detailed architectural plans and 3D renditions of the actual Holy Temple Sanctuary."*

The Architectural plans for the third Holy Temple have begun:

Stage One: The Sanctuary, is huge. With the sun shining on it, it looks like it is made of gold. The altar is in front and the smoke is coming from it as sacrifices are being made. Hundreds of people are standing around in the courtyard. The Priests dressed in white with red ties around their waists, are blowing the horns. After passing the priests at the entry we go inside the double doors into a hallway. The hallway has two square arches that we need to walk through to get to a chamber where a priest is standing on a perch that is hanging from the ceiling. In the middle of the room is a large vase that is hanging on a golden rope from the ceiling. There are also several golden decorations hanging from a pole that is attached to the wall. There are several floors in this Temple and many stairways going up. The next hallway we go down, on the wall are what looks like picture frames but inside these are blue crowns with the Star of David in front and gold designs embossed all around them. As we walk down another hallway, we come into a large empty room but on one wall there is a portion painted in red with what looks like two golden doves facing each other. This covers the wall ceiling to floor. Another large room has several priests in it, some on their knees. There are gold emblems on each of the walls with a red and blue curtain at the far end. In front of the curtain is the Menorah. In another room we find the priests working with the cups, and rolls of fabric. The ladders take us up to the top of the Temple with a deck circling the top. We end up in a room at the very top with the red wall with the two golden doves.

The Temple Institute: Building the Holy Temple. The Future is in our Hands.[6]

The **8th way** we know the Jewish People really are ready to Rebuild this Last Days Temple **now**, is that **The Cow is Ready to Build the Temple**.

Of course, I'm talking about the infamous red heifer! In fact, here's a video transcript of Rabbi Richman of the Temple Institute explaining this next ambitious project of theirs.

Rabbi Richman: *"For almost 30 years the Temple Institute has been accomplishing the impossible. We created a Menorah made of solid gold for the Holy Temple. Everyone thought it couldn't be done. After 10 years of research we created a breastplate of the High Priest. Everyone thought it was impossible. For the first time in 2000 years we have produced pure olive oil for the Menorah. Over 60 vessels have been restored by the Temple Institute. Everyone thought it* *couldn't be done. All these things people told us were impossible. Now we are restoring the commandment of the red heifer. Everyone thought it was impossible. But all the commandments of the Torah are possible. Thank you for being part of the Holy work of the Temple Institute."[7]*

The Temple Institute, The future is in Our Hands. Raise a Red Heifer in Israel.

Now you might be thinking, "Okay, so what? So, they want to raise a red heifer in Israel. That's their next project. What's the big deal about that?" Well, it is a big deal if you read the Bible! The Bible says without a red heifer you can't have that Temple!

Numbers 19:1-4 "The LORD said to Moses and Aaron: This is a requirement of the law that the LORD has commanded: Tell the Israelites to bring you a red heifer without defect or blemish and that has never been under a yoke. Give it to Eleazar the priest; it is to be taken outside the camp and slaughtered in his presence. Then Eleazar the priest is to take some of its blood on his finger and sprinkle it seven times toward the front of the Tent of Meeting."

According to the Bible, a pure red heifer is needed to perform the necessary purification and cleaning rituals that are a part of the service of the Temple. But the problem is, ever since the Temple was destroyed by the Romans in 70 AD, pure red heifers no longer exist, until now. All of a sudden, several years ago, red heifers started popping back onto the scene! And even though some of the first ones ended up having a blemish and were disqualified, it just so happens they're starting to appear on the scene again after all these years! That should get your attention, first of all! Then, even if it didn't happen naturally, we just happen to be living in the times when we have the technology to artificially make one through genetic engineering and cloning! But even so, God doesn't need modern technology to meet the need! Thanks to the Temple Institute, guess what they just produced on one of their farms? That's right! A pure red heifer and this one does qualify! Here's the announcement from Rabbi Richman!

Rabbi Richman: *"For 2000 years we have been waiting for a perfect red heifer. People think that finding a real red heifer is impossible. But the truth is that there are thousands of red cows. Go to Google and you will see red angus in America, you'll see red cows in the Scottish Highlands, you'll see red cattle in Norfolk, Ireland, just to mention a few.*

There are many red calves throughout the world. But the challenge is not to find a particular red cow, the challenge is to raise a perfect red heifer according to the exact Biblical requirements here in the land of Israel. It's time to stop waiting and start doing. The Temple Institute has embarked upon an unprecedented, historical project to raise a herd of red cows here in the land of Israel.

After decades of intensive study and research the Institute has partnered with an Israeli cattleman and using state of the art technique under strict rabbinical supervision, we are going to raise a herd of red cows here in Israel. We are going to select a proper candidate from this herd for the fulfillment of the Biblical requirements of the commandments of the red heifer.

Make no mistake this project is nothing less than the first stage of the reintroduction of Biblical purity into the world. The prerequisite of the rebuilding of the Holy Temple. For 2000 years we have been mourning the destruction of the Holy Temple. But the future is in our hands. You can become part of history. Help us make this project become a reality."[8]

The Temple Institute: The Future is in our Hands. Raise a Red Heifer in Israel.

This literally just happened at the time of this writing! All that they need to build the Last Days Temple is here, including a red heifer! It's almost like we're living in the Last Days and it's time to get motivated! They go on to say, *"The Temple Institute has announced the birth of a flawless all-red heifer that could pave the way for the fulfillment of a major end times Biblical prophecy."*

"In Jewish theology, the red heifer is essential to the rebuilding of the Third Holy Temple in Jerusalem and will be needed to be sacrificed to complete the ritual of purification for the Temple."

"It is claimed there have only been nine true red heifers, and the 10th will herald the construction of the Third Temple. Several red heifers have been born in the past but have been disqualified for not meeting the Biblical requirements."

But now, there is a red heifer in Israel. As Rabbi Richman shares, *"If there has been no red heifer for the past 2,000 years, perhaps it is because the time was not right; Israel was far from being ready. But now what could it mean for the times we live in, to have the means for purification so close at hand? If there are now red heifers, is ours the era that will need them?"*

It goes on to say, *"Truly these developments show that the prophetic clock is ticking, and piece by piece the Temple is getting ready to be rebuilt."*

"Jews believe this event is part of the process that would mark the coming of the Messiah and the final judgment," as these Jewish guys share as well.

"Who knows, maybe this red cow will be the one used when the Messiah will come. I think they have the message of the red heifer, and it is for all mankind, not just the Jewish people. I believe that when it happens, the non-Jewish people also believe in the red heifer and the coming Messiah, they are waiting just like we are. I think it's the beginning of the times when we need to do what we have to do to get ready for it."[9]

In other words, wake up and stop goofing off! We need to realize we're living in the Last Days and it's time to get motivated! Virtually everything is ready for the Holy Temple. What more does God have to do to get our attention? If we see for the first time in 2,000 years the Jewish People having the desire, the leadership, the organization, the finances, the plans, and even a genuine red heifer needed to rebuild that Last Days Temple now, then how much closer is the Rapture of the Church which takes place prior? We are so close folks, it's not even funny! And this is why, out of love, God has given us this update on *The Final Countdown: Tribulation Rising* concerning the Jewish People and the antichrist to show us that the 7-year Tribulation is near, and the Return of Jesus Christ is rapidly approaching. And that's why Jesus Himself said...

Luke 21:28 "When these things begin to take place, stand up and lift up your heads, because your redemption is drawing near."

Like it or not, we are headed for The Final Countdown. The signs of the 7-year Tribulation are Rising all around us! It's time to wake up! And so, the point is this. If you're reading this today and you're not a Christian, then I beg you, please, heed these signs, heed these warnings, give your life to Jesus now! You don't want to be here when God pours out His Judgment upon this wicked and rebellious planet! It's the worst time in the history of mankind, so horrible that unless God shortened the timeframe the entire human race would be destroyed! The only way to escape is through Jesus! Take the way out now before it's too late. Get saved today! But if you're reading this today and you are a Christian, then it's high time we stop goofing off and getting distracted with this world, let's get busy working together sharing the Gospel with as many as we can! Let's leave here living for Jesus and longing for His return. Amen

Chapter Fifteen

The Jewish People &Their Rebuilt Temple Part 4

The **9th way** we know the Jewish People really are ready to Rebuild this Last Days Temple now, is that **The Jewish Sanhedrin are ready to Build the Temple**. But don't take my word for it. Let's listen to God's.

Numbers 11:16-17 "The LORD said to Moses: 'Bring me seventy of Israel's elders who are known to you as leaders and officials among the people. Have them come to the Tent of Meeting, that they may stand there with you. I will come down and speak with you there, and I will take of the Spirit that is on you and put the Spirit on them. They will help you carry the burden of the people so that you will not have to carry it alone."

In other words, these guys have been raised up to help you rule and govern the Jewish people, so you don't burn out! Praise God for delegation, amen? And we also see this delegation here in this passage.

Deuteronomy 16:18 "Appoint judges and officials for each of your tribes in every town the LORD your God is giving you, and they shall judge the people fairly."

For those of you who don't realize it, this is basically the birth of what's called the Jewish Sanhedrin. The word "Sanhedrin" comes from a Greek word that means, "assembly" or "council" and notice at the very outset, they were instituted around the Tent of the Meeting which is the early version of the temple that was portable. But basically, they were the Supreme Court of Israel made up of 70 men and the high priest. And that's why they would meet in the Temple in Jerusalem. They convened every day except for Jewish festivals and the Sabbath, and they had powers that lesser Jewish courts did not have. For instance, they were the only ones who could try the king or extend the boundaries of the Temple and Jerusalem, and were the ones to whom all questions of law were finally put. They had the last word! In the New Testament we see that the Sanhedrin were the ones involved in the mock trials that led to the crucifixion of Jesus.

Matthew 26:59-60 "The chief priests and the whole Sanhedrin were looking for false evidence against Jesus so that they could put Him to death. But they did not find any, though many false witnesses came forward."

As you can see, the Jewish Sanhedrin were around in the Old Testament and New Testament and were the ones making important decisions on religious matters, government issues, and matters concerning the Temple and even the Messiah. If the Jewish people are going to have a Temple again, and they have to do everything according to law, which they are commanded to do, then what do they need to have on the scene again? They need to have a Jewish Sanhedrin again, right? Well, the problem was that ever since the destruction of the Temple in 70 A.D. by the Romans, the Jewish Sanhedrin went out of existence, until now! Now, there were a few attempts through history to revive them, but nothing stuck, until 2004.

A group of 71 rabbis in Israel undertook a ceremony in Tiberias, where the original Sanhedrin was disbanded and re-established themselves. They refer to themselves as the "nascent" Sanhedrin or the "developing" Sanhedrin, and regard themselves as a provisional body awaiting full integration into the Israeli government as a "Supreme Court" just like in Bible times. And they've not only already started to rule again on Jewish legal issues and matters pertaining to the Jewish Law, but wonder of wonders, guess what they also want to rebuild? That's right! A New Third Temple! In fact, one of the Sanhedrin's members is none other than Rabbi Yisrael Ariel.

As we saw before, he's the founder of the Temple Institute, who is preparing and making preparations for the rebuilding of the Third Temple now! In fact, let me show you some of the Sanhedrin's behavior concerning the Temple.

Rabbi Yisrael Ariel

- The new Sanhedrin formed a committee to collect opinions as to the exact location of the Temple on the Temple Mount.
- Some of its members ascended to a portion of the Temple mount that was added by Herod and considered by rabbis associated with the Temple Mount Faithful movement to be permitted to Jews.
- This visit culminated in a declaration that the "Jewish people should begin collecting supplies for the rebuilding of the Temple."
- For Passover, they led a drive to offer the Passover sacrifice on the Temple Mount.
- Several members of the new Sanhedrin ascended to the Temple Mount again and began saying short prayers on the mount, with the apparent support of the Israeli government.
- And this is why today, most Jews see the new Sanhedrin as an attempt to re-establish the Temple.
- And what makes this goal even more clear is how, thanks to the help of the Temple Institute, the plans for The Hall of Hewn Stones, the traditional meeting place of the Great Sanhedrin, have now been completed as well.

Plans for the Sanhedrin Temple: The Temple plans are all laid out. The model of the Temple looks like how the actual Temple will look when it is completed. As we look down into the entry of the Temple there are four entrances. Many people are going inside. The Sanhedrin are meeting in one of the chambers. They are all seated while one is speaking or teaching. In a larger hall there are again many that are seated undergoing instructions. This room is larger and has a chair similar to a throne where possibly laws were made to help make the decisions in their hearings. In another chamber they are all dressed in white with their red ties around their waists. They seem to be praying in this room. The main chamber has chairs in a circle all around the room. The Sanhedrin are all seated in the circle. There are two of them writing down the activities that are going on. Again, there is the main priest that is doing the instructing. After seeing the images in paintings, we can now see computer generated pictures. The large room that we saw before, now has a large circular fountain in the center. When you look towards the ceiling it is a dome shape painted like the blue sky with white clouds. In another large room the floor is designed with tiles that are circular. Around the wall there are many chairs, two floors of chairs. Many people can be seated in this room. There is one big desk where several Priests will be able to sit to conduct business. If you go out one of the doors you will enter a library. It seems like when you exit one very large meeting room you enter another one. The blueprints are all ready to start building. All the details have been made. They are ready to start building the Temple now. [1]

Wow! Somebody's been putting those finances to good use! But that's still not all! "The Sanhedrin called on the Arabs to take on their role in building the Third Temple as Prophesized by Isaiah."

Isaiah 60:6 "Herds of camels will cover your land, young camels of Midian and Ephah. And all from Sheba will come, bearing gold and incense and proclaiming the praise of the LORD."

"The Jewish Sanhedrin, released a letter in Hebrew, English and Arabic inviting the Arabs as the sons of Ishmael to take their role in supporting the Third Temple as prophesied by Isaiah."

"This move is far more than symbolic. It is intended to bring the entire world one step closer to the global peace that will characterize the Messianic era."

The letter reads: *"Dear brothers, the distinguished Sons of Ishmael, the great Arab nation, With the gracious help of the protector and Savior of Israel, Creator of the world by covenant, we declare that the footsteps of Messiah are evidently heard and that the time has come to rebuild the Temple on Mount Moriah in Jerusalem in its ancient place.*

We, the Jews who advocate the building of the Temple, are applying to your Honorable ones, to give gifts to the Temple as prophesied by the prophet Isaiah concerning your essential role in keeping the Temple and supporting it with lamb sacrifices and incense in order to receive God's blessings.

If a single sacrifice is brought into the Third Temple, the shofar announcing the Messiah will start to blow."

Oh, but that's still not all! *"The Sanhedrin urged candidates for Jerusalem Mayor to Prepare for the Third Temple."* (This was November 8th, 2018)

"Jerusalem will have a new mayor next week and more than any other election this year will decide the religious nature of Israel's capital."

"The Jewish Sanhedrin addressed a letter to the two candidates emphasizing the role of the Third Temple in current policy."

"With God's merciful approval, one of you will be chosen as head of the city, may it be built and made ready for its ultimate purpose...which is the building of the Temple."

"Every Jew and all of humanity are commanded to ascend to the Temple Mount." "We expect you, as candidates, to relate to this role the city has as home of the Temple."

And then as if that wasn't enough, "The Sanhedrin invited 70 Nations to the Hanukkah Dedication of the Altar for the Third Temple." (This was dated November 29th, 2018)

"The Jewish Sanhedrin released a declaration to 70 nations to be read at a ceremony in Jerusalem on the last day of Hanukkah as an invitation to the nations to participate in the Temple and to receive its blessings."

The ceremony will include the consecration of a stone altar prepared for use in the Third Temple.

The altar is currently in the form of loose stone blocks ready to be transported to the Temple Mount and stored in a manner that will enable them to be transported and assembled at a moment's notice."

"When complete, the altar will be nine feet square on each side and five feet tall and includes a ramp for the priests to ascend. The details of their composition are the result of a long study performed by the members of the Sanhedrin in conjunction with the Temple Institute."

Rabbi Hillel Weiss explained the significance of the ceremony being held on the last day of Hanukkah. *"According to Jewish tradition, the tabernacle and Aaron the Priest were consecrated for service on the last day of Hanukkah. It is fitting that we should invite the nations to the ceremony since Hanukkah is about bringing light to the darkness. The Jews were meant to do this for the entire world."*

"The Jews were brought back to Israel for the purpose of spreading the light to the nations. We see God's hand clearly in the miracle of the Jewish state that arose again two thousand years after its destruction."

But that's still not all! The Jewish Sanhedrin then even went and picked a guy and recommended him to be the actual High Priest in preparation for the Third Temple!

"Rabbi Baruch Kahane, shown here offering the Omer (barley) sacrifice to God in the heart of the Old City of Jerusalem. He has been recommended as High Priest by the Sanhedrin."

"This is a significant step towards reinstating the Temple service with the selection of Rabbi Baruch Kahane as the next Kohen Gadol (high priest)."

Rabbi Hillel Weiss, spokesman for the Sanhedrin, explained the necessity for choosing a High Priest, even in the absence of a Temple.

"The only obstacle preventing the Temple service today is the political issue. If that should suddenly change, as it very well could, we would be required to begin the Temple service immediately. It is therefore necessary that we have a candidate prepared to fill the role of the High Priest, especially now that we have kohanim prepared to serve in the Temple."

Rabbi Yisrael Ariel, founder and head of the Temple Institute and member of the Sanhedrin also shared how it was necessary for the Sanhedrin to choose a Kohen Gadol or High Priest.

"This is certainly something we should do now as religious Jews. Choosing a high priest and all of the preparations for the Temple Service are incumbent upon us according to the Torah."

"It is not a matter of opinion. We have to choose a Kohen Gadol, and make all the preparations, regardless of whether there is a Temple standing right now or not."

Rabbi Kahane *"Things could change overnight. In any case, it is clear that we need to be prepared, to prepare the priests, to have everything ready." "If the government decided to permit it, the structures can be prepared almost overnight."*

In other words, they're ready to go! And finally, they go on to say, *"The world can rest assured that, as the moment those changes should occur, the Jewish people are prepared."*

For what? Prepared to build the Temple that the actual antichrist will go up into halfway into the 7-year Tribulation and declare himself to be god! Is this wild or what? They are ready to build that Temple now!

The **10th way** we know the Jewish People really are ready to Rebuild this Last Days Temple now, is that **The Jewish Priests are ready to Build the Temple.**

And again, this is another thing the Jewish People need to have if they're going to build the Temple.

Exodus 28:1-2 "Have Aaron your brother brought to you from among the Israelites, along with his sons Nadab and Abihu, Eleazar and Ithamar, so they may serve Me as priests. Make sacred garments for your brother Aaron, to give him dignity and honor."

In other words, what we see here is the classic text where we have recorded for us the birth of the Jewish Priesthood for service in the Temple. And again, if you're going to have a Temple, you not only need a High Priest like Aaron, but you need all the other priests performing all the other priestly duties and there's a ton of them if you read through the Old Testament. So, the question is, "Do the Jewish people really have Priests, let alone enough Priests to perform all these duties once the Temple is rebuilt?" Uh yeah! In fact, they keep all the eligible Priests from around the world in a huge database!

"A Rabbi, who is actually the one who started all of this stuff to prepare to rebuild the Temple, has a synagogue right in the middle of the Arab quarter, and there Ariel, who heads up the Temple Institute with Rabbi Richman, these two Rabbis, study how to make these implements, how to prepare these priestly garments.

For example, they have to be made out of one-piece of cloth. They have all the priestly garments. One day I was sitting next to the Rabbi. He was working on his computer. I asked him, 'What are you doing on your computer, Rabbi?' He said, 'I'm studying the Torah.' I asked him, 'Rabbi, do you have anything else you use that computer for?' He said, 'Yes I do. I have a data base on this computer.' I said, 'A data base, for what?' He said, 'For every single Jewish man in the world who is qualified to be a Priest.' And they have called them into Jerusalem to study the priestly duties."[2]

In fact, so much so, they have called them to study those priestly duties, what they have built, for the first time in 2,000 years, a Jewish Priest School to train them in!

"The Temple Institute has initiated the next stage towards building the Temple: compiling a list of Jewish Priests who will be eligible to prepare the red heifer and serve in the Temple."

"Rabbi Richman, the International Director of the Temple Institute, announced on Monday that the registry will include men who have a clear patriarchal heritage from the priestly class (descendants of Aaron), were born and raised in Israel, and have observed the laws of purity incumbent upon Priests."

"This includes not coming into proximity with the dead, so Priests, or kohanim, who were born in hospitals, have visited hospitals, or have entered cemeteries are not eligible."

Now, let me stop there for a second. Notice it wasn't just for a call for Priests, but Priests who are undefiled or clean. And as one guys says, *"Has the Summoning of the 144,000 Begun?"*

And that's because if you read the Book of Revelation, you'll see in Revelation Chapter 7 that God calls to Himself 144,000 male Jewish evangelists, in the 7-year Tribulation, 12,000 from each of the 12 Tribes of Israel. And it goes on to say that they were not only male, and Jewish, but that they were undefiled or pure.

Revelation 14:4-5 "These are those who did not defile themselves with women, for they kept themselves pure. They follow the Lamb wherever He goes. They were purchased from among men and offered as firstfruits to God and the Lamb. No lie was found in their mouths; they are blameless."

This why some people are starting to say, on top of everything else, *"If an "undefiled" priesthood is being sought out as we speak with the utmost urgency, could this be the beginning of the summoning of the 144,000?"*

And one of the Tribes mentioned in that list in Revelation is Levi! Makes you wonder! But, be that as it may, the training of these Priests is in full swing! *"Once the Temple Institute has compiled a list of candidates with verified eligibility, it will begin to train them in the complex preparation of the ashes of the red heifer."* That's why, *"The Temple Institute established, The Nezer HaKodesh Institute for Kohanic Studies to instruct Jews from the priestly caste in the Temple service."* This comes after four years of extensive pilot programs. In the new program, students will learn the halacha (Torah law) relevant to the Temple service. The Temple Institute's courses of study include:

- The Role and Application of Modern Technology in the Third Temple

- The Mathematics of the Holy Temple
- The Temple Service: Theory and Practice
- Holy Temple Administration
- The Sacred Temple Vessels: Aspects of Engineering and Design
- The Topography of the Temple Mount and the Structure of Ezekiel's Temple.

"We are extremely excited to announce this new step towards the restoration of the Holy Temple service," says Rabbi Richman. "We call upon all those who may fit the bill to contact the Temple Institute immediately."

In fact, here is his announcement!

Rabbi Chaim Richman, Director, International Dept, Temple Institute:

"Shalom, I'm privileged to share an exciting announcement with you today. In advance of this week's special Torah reading. The Temple Institute is now inaugurating an historic and unprecedented program that will select and identify Priests who stand with Biblical purity that enables them to attend to the preparation of the red heifer.

This is the second stage of the Institutes for reaching efforts to restore Biblical charity to the World. A continuation of our on-going program of raising red heifers in Israel. Kohanim are male Jews who are of patriarchal decent of Aaron and thus members of the priestly tribe. If you are a Kohanim born and residing in Israel and have exercised caution according to the laws of Biblical purity you may be eligible to participate in this program. For more information or to help in these efforts, contact us at redheifer@templeinstitute.org.

Avraham Kahana, Kohen Education Director, Nezer Hododesh Institute for Kohanic Studies: *My name is Avraham Kahana, of the Temple Institute. I am a Kohen, not because I was now chosen to be a Kohen, but because my father is a Kohen, and my grandfather was a Kohen, and my great-grandfather was a Kohen, all the way back to Aaron the High Priest, who was the very first Kohen of the nation of Israel.*

Everyone from the tribe of Levi, from the family of Aaron the Kohen is a Kohen and was chosen by God to serve Him in the Holy Temple. 30 years ago, the Temple Institute was established, and has reproduced many of the sacred vessels for use in the Third Holy Temple. Having completed the sacred vessels, we now need to focus on those who will use the vessels.

Who will perform the service in the Holy Temple? The Kohanim! We need to train Kohanim and prepare them to perform the Divine service in the Holy Temple. Toward that end we have established the Nezer HaKodesh Institute for Kohanic Studies for the purpose of training Kohanim to be completely prepared to serve in the rebuilt Holy Temple.

Towards this goal we are conducting actual practice drills of the Temple service in anticipation of the Holy Temple: the daily Tamid service, the Water Libation, the Passover Offering, Shavuot – the Twin Loaves Offering, and the First Fruits! These are just some of the drills that we continue throughout the yearly cycle of the sacred seasons.

Every Kohen who is a student of Nezer HaKodesh will study and participate in the drills. The Rabbis who teach the Kohanim the proper performance of the Temple service include Rabbi Yisrael Ariel, Head of the Temple Institute, Rabbi Azarya Ariel, Dean of the Institutes Research Center, and Rabbi Yehoshua Freedman, researcher at the Temple Institute, who instruct the Kohanim in both the halachic principles and in their practical application.

Our goal is to reach far beyond the Institute's walls, and our current group of students, so that all kohanim, and the entire nation of Israel and the whole world will come and learn the proper way of performing the Service, so that we will be ready for the Holy Temple!³

Well, good thing they've got that database, so they know who to call around the world! Isn't this wild? Everything is falling into place as we sit here! In fact, they go on to say, *"For first time in 2,000 years, Jewish Priests will undergo training to ascend the Temple Mount and enter the Holy of Holies, where God's presence is said to dwell."* And again, what Temple, and what Holy of Holies are these priests being trained right now to serve and enter in? Oh, that's right! The actual Temple that the actual antichrist will go up into halfway into the 7-year Tribulation and declare himself to be god?

We are living in the Last Days folks! It's time to get motivated!

The **11ᵗʰ way** we know the Jewish People really are ready to Rebuild this Last Days Temple **now**, is that **The Jewish Ceremonies are ready to Build the Temple**.

You see, apparently all that schooling is paying off for the priests, because now they are doing full blown reenactments of the Temple Services! Here's just one of them mentioned in the Bible.

Exodus 12:21-24 "Then Moses summoned all the elders of Israel and said to them, 'Go at once and select the animals for your families and slaughter the Passover lamb. Take a bunch of hyssops, dip it into the blood in the basin and put some of the blood on the top and on both sides of the doorframe. Not one of you shall go out the door of his house until morning. When the LORD goes through the land to strike down the Egyptians, he will see the blood on the top and sides of the doorframe and will pass over that doorway, and he will not permit the destroyer to enter your houses and strike you down. Obey these instructions as a lasting ordinance for you and your descendants.'"

Which includes today! But this is the infamous passage dealing with just one Jewish ceremony in the Bible called Passover. Now, as a side note, before I get into the Jewish aspect of it, Passover actually has significance for you and I as the Christian, because Jesus is our Passover "spiritually" (1 Corinthians 5:7; Revelation 5:12). And He was killed at Passover time, with the Last Supper being a Passover meal (Luke 22:7–8). And by "spiritually" applying His blood to our lives by faith, we trust in Him to save us from death. But for the Jewish people, they still think that this ceremony, along with their ancestry, is going to give them good standing with God. It's not. Unfortunately, they miss the spiritual meaning that was fulfilled in Jesus. But, be that as it may, Passover is still the most widely celebrated Jewish holiday and one of the three "pilgrimage" festivals mentioned in the Bible for the Jewish people to travel to Jerusalem and observe at the Holy Temple. So, guess what? They're doing Passover Sacrifice again in preparation for the New Temple!

Euronews Reports: Jerusalem 3//26/2018

People have come from all over to attend the Passover ceremony. They watch as the priests blow the horns and sing. Then they wash their feet. This is a great celebration, the music is playing, they are singing, and everyone is dancing

Rabbi Richman: *"We have to understand the significance of the Passover Offering. It is so profound that it is imperative and bound up with the very identity of who the Jewish people are in this world. This is not the first time that we have had this seminar but early indications is that this will probably be the most important and most well organized, and it's a reflection of the fact that more and more Jewish people here in the land of Israel, and I hope all over the world, are waking up to the fact that, you know, Passover is a beautiful time.*

It's a time for families to be together. We have matzo ball soup and seder, and all that. But there is something terribly wrong. There is something missing. That is the Passover offering, which it is so completely bound up with the core identity of who we are in this world.

So, this is more than anything, it's such an incredible timing of the times we are living in, having such an awakening as a people to who we have to be when we grow up. And the calling of the rebuilding of the Holy Temple and bringing the offerings there and reclaiming our heritage. This is just a really beautiful sign of the times we are living in and hopefully this will be the very last time we have to have a drill and a practice of the Passover offering.

God willing, we are drawing closer and closer to the time of the rebuilding of the Temple. Here we have real Kohanim wearing priestly garments, we have a Rabbinical choir, we have Rabbis that are giving classes now about every aspect of how the Passover is offered. Because we need to know how to do this. We need to be connected to our heritage. And you know all of this today is a clear indication of the tremendous awakening, resurgence, renewal and revitalization of Temple consciousness."[4]

"The Temple Institute, in conjunction with the Sanhedrin and other Temple organizations, held a reenactment of the service as it would have been performed in the Temple."

"The ceremony was intended to be educational for the spectators and a dry-run for the priests who participated. Events like this help prepare for the actual Temple. Not only does it raise public awareness, it also helps instruct Kohanim, Jews of the priestly class."

"Joshua Wander, a resident of the Mount of Olives who has attended several of the Temple Institute's events, noted that it also helps fix lapses in practical knowledge."

"When we did the reenactment of the Passover offering, we discovered that it is difficult to roast a whole animal without burning the outside and leaving the inside raw. We found out that you have to wrap it up and seal it, which had to be done carefully since it is forbidden to break any of the bones."

So, they're learning lessons after 2,000 years of not doing it! And these reenactments are huge! We're not just talking a couple people here! *"Thousands to participate in Priestly Blessing at Western Wall on Passover."*

And listen to these comments! The Jewish People got all fired up!

*"Jerusalem city council member **Arieh King** said he hoped that the Temple Mount would soon be free of what he termed "the abomination" currently at the site."*

"We wish even in our days that we won't see it there anymore and we'll see the altar, the Kohanim and ourselves there."

"Then Rabbi Yisrael Ariel, head of the Temple Institute said the event was preparation for when the Temple Mount would be 'flattened and cleaned' and the Temple rebuilt."

And that wasn't the only ceremony they're reenacting! "Rabbi Weiss, the spokesman for the Sanhedrin said,

"We recently reenacted the Omer Wave Offering, which has ramifications for when Israel can eat the current wheat harvest. And for the first time since the Second Temple they had the Golden Vessel Libation Ceremony."

This was September of this year (2018). They go on to say, "*In the Temple, this ceremony would take fifteen hours with accompanying celebrations lasting all night until the Temple Service began again the next morning.*"

Then they also reenacted the giving of the shoulder, two cheeks, ceremony that you give to the priests.

Deuteronomy 18:3 "This is the share due the priests from the people who sacrifice a bull or a sheep: the shoulder, the jowls (two cheeks) and the inner parts."

Then there was the reenactment of the First Fruits' Ceremony (that was May of 2018) overlooking the Temple Mount, just as it was performed in the Temple.

"The event was organized by the Mikdash (Temple) Educational Center, the United Temple Movements and the Jewish Sanhedrin."

"And Rabbi Baruch Kahane led a group of four priests dressed in the Biblically mandated garments required for the Temple Service and has played a central role in educating the Kohanim in all aspects of the Temple service."

"The reenactment was intended as part of this essential stage of preparing for the future when the Third Temple will be built, and these rituals will again be performed."

The First Fruits Ceremony

The First Fruits Ceremony

They go on to say, as you can see, *"A model of the ark of the covenant, the menorah, the altar, and a rack for the show breads were arranged as an educational illustration."*

And here's what's wild! I was at the Temple Institute, and they've got the Golden Menorah built, the Golden rack for the Showbreads built, and they even have a portable altar that can be moved to the Temple. But can you imagine if they not only had just a "replica" of the Ark of the Covenant built, as you can see in that picture. But can you imagine if they actually had the real deal, the actual Ark of the Covenant? Well, as the story goes, they do have it, right under the Temple Mount! They say they're just waiting for the right time to bring it out!

"Now if anybody wants to debate that, I wish I could submit the two men that saw it, but they have now passed from this world, but they were two very prestigious Rabbis. Rabbi Guron was the Rabbi at the Western Wall June 7, 1967, who sounded the shofar and put the first prayer in the Western Wall after the Jews had reunited the city of Jerusalem. Rabbi Getz, he was the chief Rabbi of the Western Wall.

These two men in 1982 went in at Warren's Gate underneath the Temple Mount area and they both told me, I have it recorded on video. They saw the Ark of the Covenant under there. I asked them both, 'Why did you not bring the Ark out?' And they said, 'We don't have a place to put it. As soon as we have a Temple, we will bring it out and put it in the Holy of Holies.'"[5]

Wow! And apparently that time is getting close. Why? Because it's common sense! If we see for the first time in 2,000 years the Jewish People having the desire, the power, the organizations, the finances, the plans, the red heifer, the Sanhedrin, the Priesthood, the Ceremonies, and very possibly, the actual Ark of the Covenant ready to go to rebuild the end times Temple right now, then how much closer is the Rapture of the Church which takes place prior? We are so close it's not even funny! And again, what is the point? This is the Temple that the actual Antichrist will go up into halfway into the 7-year Tribulation and declare himself to be God! We're that close! And folks, this is why, out of love, God has given us this update on *The Final Countdown: Tribulation Rising* concerning the Jewish People & the Antichrist to show us that the 7-year Tribulation is near, and the Return of Jesus Christ is rapidly approaching. And that's why Jesus Himself said...

Luke 21:28 "When these things begin to take place, stand up and lift up your heads, because your redemption is drawing near."

Folks, like it or not, we are headed for The Final Countdown. The signs of the 7-year Tribulation are Rising all around us! It's time to wake up! The point is this. If you're reading this today and you're not a Christian, then I beg you, please, heed these signs, heed these warnings, give your life to Jesus now! You don't want to be here when God pours out His Judgment upon this wicked and rebellious planet! It's the worst time in the history of mankind, so horrible that unless God shortened the timeframe the entire human race would be destroyed! The only way to escape is through Jesus! Take the way out now before it's too late. Get saved today! But if you're reading this today and you are a Christian, then it's high time we stop goofing off and getting distracted with this world. Let's get busy working together sharing the Gospel with as many as we can! Let's leave here living for Jesus and longing for His soon return. Amen?

Chapter Sixteen

The Jewish People & Their Rebuilt Temple Part 5

The **12ᵗʰ way** we know the Jewish People really are ready to rebuild this Last Days Temple now, is that **The Articles are ready to Build the Temple**. But don't take my word for it. Let's listen to God's.

Daniel 9:24-27 "Seventy 'sevens' are decreed for your people and your holy city to finish transgression, to put an end to sin, to atone for wickedness, to bring in everlasting righteousness, to seal up vision and prophecy and to anoint the most holy. Know and understand this: From the issuing of the decree to restore and rebuild Jerusalem until the Anointed One, the ruler, comes, there will be seven 'sevens,' and sixty-two 'sevens.' It will be rebuilt with streets and a trench, but in times of trouble. After the sixty-two 'sevens,' the Anointed One will be cut off and will have nothing. The people of the ruler who will come, will destroy the city and the sanctuary. The end will come like a flood: War will continue until the end, and desolations have been decreed. He will confirm a covenant with many for one 'seven.' In the middle of the 'seven' he will put an end to sacrifice and offering. And on a wing of the temple he will set up an abomination that causes desolation, until the end that is decreed is poured out on him."

So once again, we see in Daniel's amazing 70ᵗʰ week prophecy, that in the final week, the 7-year Tribulation, the antichrist will not only be the one who makes a covenant with the Jewish people which starts the 7-year Tribulation, but in the middle of that week, or 7-year Tribulation, he will go up into a rebuilt Jewish Temple, apparently, and declare himself to be god, or what's also called the abomination of desolation, right? It's right there in the text. Daniel wrote that nearly 2,600 years ago! So, here's the point. Do we see any signs of the Jewish people really getting ready to rebuild this Last Days Temple any time soon in Jerusalem, that the antichrist will go up into and declare himself to be god? Uh yeah! In fact, so much so that they are in the process of finishing up virtually every single article they need for this Temple to be in full swing. You not only need the Priests, and the spiritual leadership, the Sanhedrin, but you need every single article to perform these services! Let me show you just how many they have completed!

- **Copper Laver:** The copper laver and stand, which stands in the Temple courtyard between the sanctuary and the outer altar, is the first of the Temple vessels to greet the priests each morning. There the priests wash their hands and feet before proceeding to attend to the daily tamid offering.
- **Measuring Cup:** Measuring cups are used for measuring flour, wine and oil, of which specific amounts are prescribed to be used as ingredients in various offerings.
- **Copper Vessel:** The copper vessel is used for preparing the meal offering. Meal offerings are made using various amounts of flour, oil and spices.
- **Lottery Box:** On Yom Kippur, the High Priest reaches into the lottery box and chooses lots. This is what determines which goat will be used as an offering to G-d, and which will be sent off as the scapegoat, as an atonement for the sins of the people. During the First Temple, the lots were fashioned of wood. In the time of the Second Temple, they were of gold. The lots pictured are fashioned of both wood and gold.
- **Mizrak:** This is the device that the priest collects the blood from the sacrifice into, and then spills the blood onto the corner of the altar.
- **Large Mizrak:** The large mizrak, and the smaller mizrak, are used to gather the blood of the sacrifice, and to spill it onto the corner of the altar. The large mizrak is used when sacrificing larger animals, (cows and bullocks).
- **Three-Pronged Fork:** The three-pronged fork is mentioned in 1 Samuel 2:13. According to Hebrew Scholars, the fork is used to turn over the offerings on the altar fire, or to lift up unconsumed portions of the offering so that the woodpile can be rearranged.
- **Silver Shovel:** The silver shovel is kept on the southwestern corner of the altar. This shovel is used for the removal of ashes left on the altar, the first task performed by the priests each morning at the break of dawn.

- **Silver Decanter:** The silver decanter is used for the wine libation. Wine is poured on the altar twice daily, morning and evening, accompanying the daily service.
- **Silver Libation Vessels:** One of the main aspects of the Holiday of Sukkot (Tabernacles) is the Biblical commandment, "And you shall be glad on your holiday, and you shall be only joyful" (Deut. 16:14). Indeed, the pilgrims who arrived in Jerusalem at the Temple's courtyard came to rejoice. The focus of this rejoicing was the ceremony surrounding the commandment to pour water on the altar – the water libation.
- **Silver Cup:** The silver cup, with the golden flask, is used in the Festival of the Water Libation, which takes place during the Holiday of Sukkot. At dawn, the Priests and Levites, accompanied by the throngs of participants, wind their way down to the Spring of Shiloach. Water is drawn from the spring and carried up to the Temple in the golden flask, where it is poured into the silver cup, as it rests atop the altar.
- **Sickle:** On the 16th day of Nissan, in a public gathering on the outskirts of Jerusalem, the first of the barley crop is harvested using sickles. This barley is then brought to the Holy Temple to be used in the Omer offering.
- **Omer Offering Implements:** Once the barley is brought to the Temple Courtyard, priests beat, roast, grind, and sift the grain. A handful of the resulting flour is burned on the altar. The remainder is eaten by the priests.
- **Abuv:** The Abuv is a three-tiered stand. The top level holds a perforated copper pan, and below it is a receptacle for hot coals. It is used for roasting the newly harvested barley of the Omer offering, performed on Passover.
- **Golden Menorah:** The menorah, made from a single piece of solid gold, stands in the southern side of the Sanctuary. Each morning a Priest prepares and rekindles the wicks. The central wick, known as "the western candle" is required to burn perpetually. The oil and wicks of this candle are changed in such a fashion as to ensure that it will never be extinguished.
- **Oil Pitcher:** The oil pitcher is used to replenish the oil for the menorah. The design is based on an ancient coin from the Second temple period. This pitcher contains 3.5 lug, (2 liters) of oil.
- **Small Golden Flask:** The small golden flask is used to pour olive oil into the menorah. The Priest pours oil into this flask from the larger pitcher, which contains enough oil necessary for all seven lamps. This smaller flask is then used to replenish the oil of each individual lamp.
- **Menorah Cleansing Vessel:** The daily service of the Temple includes the cleaning of the seven oil cups of the Menorah, using a vessel that includes tongs and a brush.

- **Table of Showbread:** In the northern side of the Sanctuary stands the table of the showbread. The table is made of wood, overlaid with gold. Upon it are placed the twelve loaves of showbread. Each Sabbath, the loaves are simultaneously removed and replaced by fresh loaves, so as to ensure that these loaves remain "perpetually" on the table. Miraculously, the week-old loaves being replaced also retain their heat and freshness. These loaves are distributed among the priests.

- **Frankincense Censer:** Once a week, on the Sabbath, the twelve loaves of the showbread are removed by the priests and replaced with new loaves. At the same time, the two portions of frankincense are also replaced. The two portions of frankincense are carried inside the gold Frankincense Censer. Still inside the censer, they are placed on the table of the showbread.

- **Incense Altar:** Centrally located in the Sanctuary, between the menorah to the south, and the table of the showbread to the north, stands the incense altar, directly in front of the Holy of Holies, to the west. The incense altar, made of wood covered with gold, is employed in what is considered to be the most beloved aspect of the Temple service in G-d's eye: the incense offering. In order to allow for every priest to perform this most prized of offerings, a daily lot is drawn. Only those priests who have never offered incense upon the altar are allowed to participate.

- **Incense Chalice:** The incense chalice, which holds "half a portion" (approx. 200 grams), of the incense offering ingredients. The chalice is carried into the Sanctuary of the Temple, where the golden incense altar stands. Upon entering the Sanctuary, the priest sounds the small ring-shaped bell seen on the top of the chalice cover.

- **Incense Shovel:** This shovel is used to remove burning coals from the outer altar. The Priest then carries the coals on this shovel into the sanctuary, where the coals are used on the golden incense altar.

- **Silver Trumpets:** In the Holy Temple, silver trumpets are used during the Divine service, as well as for announcing the arrival of the Shabbat, the New Moon, the three Festivals, and for other various occasions.

- **Gold-Plated Shofar:** The gold-plated shofar, (ram's horn), is blown in the Holy Temple on Rosh Hashana.

- **Silver-Plated Shofar:** The silver-plated shofar, (ram's horn), is blown in the Holy Temple on fast days.

- **Harp:** The harp, or nevel, is a prominent instrument used by the Levites in their orchestral accompaniment to the Divine service.

- **Lyre:** The lyre, or kinnor, like the harp, is frequently mentioned in the book of Psalms, as being a feature of the Levitical orchestra, which performs in the Inner Courtyard of the Holy Temple.
- **High Priest Crown:** One of the four "golden garments" of the High Priest is the crown, fashioned from one single piece of pure gold. The crown is worn across the forehead, extending from ear to ear. It is held in place by a string dyed in the same blue color as used in all the High Priest's garments. The crown bears the inscription: "Holy to G-d," and is worn by the High Priest at all times while he is officiating in the Temple.
- **Garment of High Priest:** Here we see the weaving of the sacred Ephod garment for the uniform of the High Priest. The Temple Institute has also completed the complicated task of joining the ephod to the remembrance stones and affixing the breastplate. This complex project has been based on extensive research by the Institute. With G-d's help this task has been completed and the results have been made public.
- **Ark of the Covenant:** The Ark of the Covenant is the only object that is placed within the Holy of Holies. Once a year, on Yom Kippur, the Day of Atonement, the High Priest enters the Holy of Holies, asking G-d to forgive the transgressions of the entire house of Israel. Made of wood covered with gold, it contained within it, during the period of the First Temple, the two tablets of the Law brought down from Mount Sinai by Moses, as well as a vessel containing manna, and the staff of Aaron. Fearing its capture by the invading Babylonians, King Josiah had it removed from the Holy of Holies and hidden in a chamber deep beneath the Temple Mount. A tradition of its exact location is maintained to this day.[1]

Looks to me like somebody's got just about everything they need, virtually every single article, ready to go for service in this Last Days rebuilt Jewish Temple, how about you? And again, what Temple is this. Oh yeah! That's right! The one that Daniel prophesied about nearly 2,600 years ago that the antichrist will go up into and declare himself to be God halfway into the 7-year Tribulation. But that's not all.

The **13th way** we know the Jewish people really are ready to rebuild this Last Days Temple now, is that **The Miscellaneous Items are ready to Build the Temple**.

You see, if you thought what we've seen so far, over the last several chapters prove beyond a shadow of a doubt just how ready the Jewish people really are ready to rebuild this Last Days Temple right now, think again! It gets even more detailed! They have just about everything you can think of! And again, a lot of it, is current events, just now happening! Let me show you what I mean.

The **1ˢᵗ miscellaneous item** the Jewish People have ready to go right now for the Last Days Temple, is **The Temple Calendar**.

This is from (March 12, 2018) "A Third Temple Calendar has just been launched." And they go on to quote.

Exodus 12:2 ""This month is to be for you the first month, the first month of your year."

"The 'King's Calendar' is a new calendar specifically designed for use in the Third Temple. It was created by Reuven Prager, a Levite who takes his Biblical identity seriously, and who has also

used his skills as a tailor to create the banner of the tribe of Levi.

As part of his passion for the Temple, Prager decided 36 years ago that he wanted to create a calendar for the Third Temple. But the project was so complicated and requires so much research that the first calendar is only coming out now.

The King's Calendar tracks all the activities that took place in the First and Second Temples and which will be performed again when the Third Temple is built.

This includes the Biblical feasts that are observed today, but the calendar also has many surprises, holidays and events that are only observed when a Temple stands in Jerusalem.

"It's a mind-blowing calendar for the Third Temple era and the first of its kind."

The **2nd miscellaneous item** the Jewish People have ready to go right now for the Last Days Temple, is **The Temple Bread**.

This is from (August 23, 2018) *"Hands-on Reenactment of Temple Bread Baking is now occurring in Israel."*

While many read and study about the breads of the Beit Hamikdash (Temple) in the Bible, few have the opportunity taste or to see them come to life. But thanks to Les Saidel and his Artisan Baking Institute, hands on workshops are now available for the Biblical baking of Temple breads and it is the only one in existence.

"Tourists have come from all four corners of the world for this workshop," he told Breaking Israel News.

Over the last five years, Saidel has researched bread during Temple times, even creating replicas of the baking utensils, as well as the Showbread Table, used in the Temple offerings. Saidel explains the ingredients and methods to mixing and baking the dough that was used almost two thousand years ago and also explains the importance of such a workshop. *"By going through the steps of baking bread as well as better understanding the purposes for bread in the Temple, the Jewish people will be better prepared in Third Temple times."*

The Temple Bread

"If Moshiach arrived tomorrow, we wouldn't know how to bake the breads. So, we need to map our resources and be ready," he maintained. *"Perhaps,"* said Saidel, *"this learning and eagerness could actually hasten Moshiach (the Messiah)."*

The **3ʳᵈ miscellaneous item** the Jewish People have ready to go right now for the Last Days Temple, is **The Temple Oil.**

Rabbi Richman: *"The Temple Institute and the Association of Temple movements, together with all of Israel take another historic step towards the resumption of the Divine service in the Holy Temple with the unveiling and the presentation of the first pure olive oil for the Temple Menorah to be produced in purity in 2000 years and the special vessels to hold them.*

Created in purity an unprecedented step towards the resumption in purity in our time is a true Hanukah miracle. Monday Night, the 30ᵗʰ of Kislev, December 22ⁿᵈ

The Temple Oil

the procession begins at 5:30 pm Zion Gate. 6:00 pm meet at the Golden Menorah R Yehudah HaLevi Stairs opposite the site of the Holy Temple. 6:30 pm The Temple Institute's Holy Temple Visitors Center in a joyous song filled procession.

Olive oil will be deposited in the Temple Institute's Holy Temple visitors center. Join us on the 7th night of Hanukah Monday December 22nd in the Jewish quarter of Jerusalem's old city to witness the first pure olive oil in 2000 years. Be there for the continuation of the story of Hanukah and the nest step to rebuilding of the Holy Temple in our time."[2]

This is from October 2, 2018. *"The Temple Institute has now announced that is has produced pure olive oil fit for use in the Menorah of the Temple for the first time in two thousand years. Initially, they produced only four and a half liters of the precious olive oil and it was an extremely complex process due to the necessity of keeping it pure according to Jewish law. But now they have whole farms! Farmers are now harvesting olives, like a stream of liquid gold, in preparation for the Third Temple Sacrifices."*

Every olive in the press, at Achiya Farms was planted and harvested in Israel's Biblical heartland, right outside of ancient Shiloh, Israel's first capital and the location where the holy Ark of the Covenant stood for nearly 400 years. Today, a small team of farmers are re-planting the land, fulfilling what they say is the Biblical prophecy described in Ezekiel:

Ezekiel 36:8 "But you, O mountains of Israel, will produce branches and fruit for my people Israel, for they will soon come home."

"We are doing the work that our ancestors did in the time of the Temple, of course with the expectation that the day will come when we will take our olive oil to Jerusalem for use in the Third Temple," said Farm Manager Itamar Weis. "This is holy work that we are doing."

Sacrifices were suspended with the destruction of the Second Holy Temple by the Romans in 70 A.D. The expectation is that they will return when the Temple is rebuilt. And Achiya Farms, one of the largest olive presses in the country, is preparing for such a time. According to CEO David Zitzer, *"The farm's oil will be suitable for bringing a personal meal-offering when the Third Holy Temple in Jerusalem is rebuilt."*

The **4th miscellaneous item** the Jewish People have ready to go **right now** for the Last Days Temple, is **The Temple Perfume**.

This is from November 6, 2018 and they go on to quote:

2 Chronicles 13:1 "Every morning and evening they present burnt offerings and fragrant incense to the LORD. "

"During the days of the Temple, the priests would burn ketoret (incense) every evening and morning on the golden altar in front of the holy Ark of the Covenant."

Many Jewish people

The Temple Perfume

believe that the incense offering was considered the most precious part of the Temple service in God's eyes and that the one who would have the privilege to offer the incense would be rewarded by God with wealth and prosperity forever, in this world and the next.

Therefore, Sarah and Shimon Barda created the world's first Jewish perfume based on the incense offering. They use some of the incense offering's original herbs and flowers, and many other natural scents, to create a whole line of perfumes, including creams and deodorants.

The couple investigated and collected thousands of plants and established a laboratory and manufacturing facility that sells a wide-range of natural products. Their products all center on ingredients of Israel and the Bible. Shimon worked in the fashion business in France, but he and his wife always had a dream of owning and running their own perfume business. After moving to Itamar in the Samarian Mountains, he was inspired to make it happen. Shimon and his wife said referring to their line of cosmetics, *"If you really want to connect with the Land of Israel, this is one way to do it."*

The **5th** miscellaneous item the Jewish People have ready to go right now for the Last Days Temple, is **The Temple Music**.

This is from August 21, 2018 *"The Return of David's Harp is Heralding the arrival of the Third Temple."*

Psalm 33:2 "Praise the LORD with the harp; make music to Him on the ten-stringed lyre."

"The Temple of Solomon was filled with the music of 4,000 harps and a remarkable couple have been on a lifelong journey to return that music in time for the Third Temple."

The Temple Music

Micah and Shoshanna Harrari of www.harrariharps.com settled in Tiberias on the shores of the Kinneret (Sea of Galilee) where Micah set up a carpentry shop. Shoshanna had always wanted a harp for some reason she didn't entirely understand. *"I am the daughter of a Kohen so I am sure there is some ancient connection,"* she explained. Micah was a trained musical instrument craftsman, and perhaps inspired by the Kinneret whose name means 'harp,' he announced to his wife that the time had come for him to fulfill her musical dream. They learned that archaeologists had discovered cave drawings of a harp in Megiddo. The drawings were believed to be 3,000 years old, meaning the Megiddo lyre would have been the instrument young David played to soothe a troubled King Saul. Thus the "The Harp Project" an ongoing non-profit endeavor to create harps and lyres for the Third Temple had begun. Soon they were contacted by Rabbi Yisrael Ariel, founder of the Temple Institute, *"He told us that one day there would be a Temple and there would need to be harps ready for the Temple service."*

As donations came in, the Temple Institute commissioned more harps from the Harraris. In fact, Micah and Shoshanna Harrari recently released a video depicting this long-awaited fulfillment of the Psalm.

'And I will bless those that bless thee' Genesis 12:3

"After 2000 years the prophetic sound of the harp of David is heard once again in Israel. These Biblical harps will return to the Temple in Jerusalem one day. Where 4000 harps and lyres were played by the Kohanim and Levites in musical prayers during the Three Pilgrim Festivals.

Sponsoring the harps for the Temple, had given good hearted people across the globe the opportunity to partner with them. In the reconstruction of the sacred Biblical instrument to be played once again in the Temple. Along with the destruction of the Second Temple and exile of the Israelites came also the exile of the Biblical harp.

On the way to Babylon we hung them upon the willow tree. **Psalm 137:2** *and the sweet sound of the harp of David was all but forgotten. These ancient harps did not exist until 1982 when Micah Harrari built one for his wife Shoshanna, unintentionally restoring the Biblical harp of David. An article published in the Jerusalem Post initiated interest in people all around the world to order a harp for themselves.*

So, they began building them in a harp shop in the Judean hills. Around the same time the Temple Institute in the old city of Jerusalem began collecting all the sacred objects that were used in the first two Temples. To be used once again in the future Temple. Thanks to the Temple harp project and generous funding from people like you these Biblical harps are being built one by one, two by two, to be kept safe in the Temple Institute, awaiting their true purpose to bring forth melodious prayers to our creator."³

The **6ᵗʰ miscellaneous item** the Jewish People have ready to go right now for the Last Days Temple, is **The Temple Request.**

This is from the Temple Mount & Land of Israel Faithful Movement.

"Gershon Salomon recently sent a letter to Pope Francis in the Vatican calling him to immediately return without delay the golden Temple Menorah and all the other temple vessels hidden in the Vatican that the Romans robbed from the Second Holy Temple in Jerusalem.

"It is the time for you to return the Holy Temple Menorah, the Vessels and the Treasures to Israel with no delay to be used in the Holy Temple of God that is soon to be built."

The Romans brought the Temple Menorah along with the other temple vessels to

Rome and on the Roman Triumphal Arch of Titus that exists in Rome today, we can see the Jewish prisoners who were captured in Jerusalem carrying the seven-branched Temple Menorah and the additional holy vessels that the Romans robbed from the Holy Temple in Jerusalem. These vessels were put into the palace of the Roman Caesars and then later put in the Vatican after Constantine. For many years these vessels, including the Temple Menorah, were shown in the Vatican. Jewish travelers who visited the Vatican during the Middle Ages and even during the past few centuries personally saw these vessels along with the Temple Menorah inside the Vatican.

Years ago, the temple vessels suddenly disappeared, and as we learned, they were hidden in the basement of the Vatican, especially after the foundation of the State of Israel in the year 1948. The papal authorities were afraid that Israel would build the Third Holy Temple and that the Israelis would ask the papal authorities to return the vessels so that they can be used in the rebuilt Holy Temple. After 1967, when the G-d of Israel, together with the Israeli army, liberated the Holy Temple Mount and Jerusalem, the possibility that Israel would issue a request to the Vatican to return the temple vessels became even more probable especially after the year 1990 when the Temple Mount and the Land of Israel Faithful Movement prepared the cornerstone, weighing six and a half tons according to biblical law, and brought it to the southern gates of the Holy Temple Mount in Jerusalem in order to begin the rebuilding of the Third Holy Temple. It was the first cornerstone ever prepared for the building of the Third Holy Temple since the destruction of the Second Holy Temple in 70 AD. The chairman of the Temple Mount and Land of Israel Faithful Movement, Gershon Salomon, calls the Israeli parliament and government to build the Third Holy Temple with no delay. This is a godly call to 'our generation,' the 'last days' generation and we are honored and privileged to be the generation who will fulfill the expectation of the G-d of Israel and fulfill it in our lifetime. Gershon will not stop his activities for this purpose until the vessels are safely and promptly returned to Jerusalem. If the request is ignored again, the Temple Faithful Movement will ask an international court to command them to do so. (Gee, I wonder if some world ruler in the future will do this for the people of Israel and work out a deal where they get these articles back as well as permission to start building a new Temple?)

The **7th miscellaneous item** the Jewish People have ready to go right now for the Last Days Temple, is **The Temple Stone**.

"A Prophetic Lost Stone from the High Priest's Breastplate is believed to be found after a 1,000-year Journey."

Exodus 28:9,12 "Take two onyx stones and engrave on them the names of the sons of Israel and fasten them on the shoulder pieces of the ephod as memorial stones for the sons of Israel."

Sometimes incredible stories are actually true, and in this case, experts agree that a small onyx stone, claimed to be given to a Knights Templar over 1,000 years ago and handed down through one family from generation to generation, is actually what the present owner claims: a gem from the breastplate of the High Priest in Jerusalem. In addition to the 12 stones mounted on the breastplate were two sardonyx stones fixed in gold settings on the shoulders of the High Priest. Experts believe this is one of those stones. If this is so, it may play an important role in returning to the service of the Temple. Dr. James Strange, a noted professor in religious studies and archaeology, traveled to South Africa and met with the family, intending to humor them. Instead, he was astounded by what they showed him.

"I was indeed amazed at the gemstone," Dr. Strange told Breaking Israel News. *"I was unaware that anyone in the late Middle Ages had the technology to cut a hemisphere in such a stone and even more astounding than the cut of the stone was the inexplicable inscription inside the stone, visible through the clear surface: two letters in ancient Hebrew."*

"There is no modern or ancient technology known to me by which an artisan could produce the inscription, as it is not cut into the surface of the stone."

The family also had documentation that traced its descent from a Crusader-period male ancestor who had been in the Holy Land in the Middle Ages and claimed the stone was a reward for his help in freeing Jerusalem around 1189 AD. Meticulously recorded family trees and genealogical reports corroborate the story. And it has been strongly transmitted to each member of the family through the centuries that it was God's hand that inserted the mysterious inscription inside the stone and experts agree. The sardonyx stone is kept in a papyrus casket in which it was carried. The present owner has contracted with a South African businessman to find investors who are willing to purchase the stone and bring it home to Israel and donate it to the Temple.

"Of all the unusual artifacts that they say has been in their family for 1000 years and object of all the attention is a stone with an inscription dating back to 1000 B.C. It has been languishing in a South African bank vault for many years. The descendants that have brought the Sardonyx stone to South Africa in the 1700's now say they want to sell it, although they prefer to remain anonymous. But the stone itself is surrounded by controversy. Some would believe it is a priceless museum piece. While others say the inscription, which takes the form of Hebrew letters B and K is nearly a quirk of nature."

Prof Moshe Sharon, Wits University: *"If it is man-made then it raises the question of what kind of technology these people had in order to burn these letters into the heart of the stone. Because there is no interference with the surface, the face of the stone itself. It's absolutely clean."*

"Letters in the stone are almost identical to the archeological find from 1300 to 300 B.C. but only an electron microscope with reveal the truth."[4]

The **8th miscellaneous item** the Jewish People have ready to go **right now** for the Last Days Temple, is **The Temple Sheep**.

"For the first time in 2,000 years streaked, speckled and spotted sheep are born in Israel."

Genesis 30:39 "And they bore young that were streaked or speckled or spotted."

Dubbed, "Jacob's Sheep," a rare breed that was originally raised by Jacob, have now been born in the land of Israel for the first time in over two millennia and made their auspicious appearance last month in the Jordan Valley. One Torah expert believes they will play a role in bringing forth the Third Temple.

Gil Lewinsky, emphasized the importance of sheep to the people of Israel, explaining to Breaking Israel News that, *"The Jews need the sheep to serve God in the Third Temple and their wool is also used in making the clothes for the kohamim (male priests) and they are the breed that was offered up as a sacrifice in the First and Second Temples."*

It is for this reason that Gil applied to the Agriculture Ministry to change the status of the sheep. For the first time, the ministry has declared a breed of sheep a protected species.

The **9th miscellaneous item** the Jewish People have ready to go right now for the Last Days Temple, is **The Temple Veil**.

"Israeli women are now weaving the Holy of Holies veil for the Third Temple."

If the Jewish Temple is ever to be rebuilt in Jerusalem, the massive curtain – 66 feet high by 33 feet wide and 2 inches thick – that once hung in the Second Temple and was consumed by fire in A.D. 70, will need to be recreated. That task is already underway in the Jewish community of Shiloh, located in

The Temple Veil

biblical Samaria about 40 minutes north of Jerusalem, reports Israel Today. For more than two years women from the community have been working to assemble the materials and learn the techniques needed to weave the veil that will hang between, and separate, the Holy Place and the Holy of Holies.

Exodus 26:31 "Make a curtain of blue, purple and scarlet yarn and finely twisted linen, with cherubim worked into it by a skilled craftsman."

In some ways Shiloh, as the place for "the women of the veil chamber" to pursue their task, is a natural one. Ancient Israel's Tabernacle, the precursor to the First Temple built in Jerusalem by King Solomon, stood in Shiloh for over 300 years. And it was to Shiloh that the tribes of Israel came for annual festivals. The Gospel of Matthew records that upon Jesus death, the great veil of the Temple "was torn in two, from top to bottom."

Matthew 27:50-51 "And when Jesus had cried out again in a loud voice, He gave up His spirit. At that moment the curtain of the temple was torn in two from top to bottom. The earth shook and the rocks split."
Now that veil is being reconstructed. The weavers of the veil see their work as a "holy activity" that hastens the time of Israel's redemption. *"Step by step, patiently, we are preparing."*

The **10th miscellaneous item** the Jewish People have ready to go right now for the Last Days Temple, is **The Temple Altar.**

This is what we saw in the last chapter. *"The Jewish Temple Altar for the Third Temple is rebuilt and ready for use."*

The altar is a central component to the Biblical sacrificial service. The larger altar sat in the outer courtyard of the Temple and was approximately 16

The Temple Altar

feet tall and 52.5 feet wide, with four "horns", or raised corners, and a ramp.

Exodus 40:29 "He set the altar of burnt offering near the entrance to the tabernacle, the Tent of Meeting, and offered on it burnt offerings and grain offerings, as the LORD commanded him."

The Temple Institute in Jerusalem has announced that it has finished building an altar suitable for Temple service. The altar, which took several years to build, can be operational in little more than a moment's notice. According to the Bible, the altar may not be made out of stones hewn by metal implements. It is constructed from bricks fired to withstand the immense heat of the Temple's eternal flame and the weight of the sacrificial animals.

What makes the altar so unique is that it can be disassembled and reassembled easily, allowing it to be transported quickly and efficiently from its current location, on display at the institute, or to the Temple Mount when the time comes. According to the Temple Institute, *"The people of Israel are required to build an altar exclusively on the site of the original altar on Mount Moriah, the Temple Mount. When circumstances become favorable, this new altar can be quickly re-assembled on the proper location, enabling the Divine service to be resumed without delay."*

"It is now ready for use." "With Passover around the corner, and the Passover Sacrifice a central component of the traditional celebration, perhaps that time will come soon!"

And that's why on December 10th the Sanhedrin hosted a Dedication of the Altar for the Third Temple. On Monday, the Sanhedrin hosted the dedication of the altar for the Third Temple, marking the event with a full-dress reenactment of the Korban

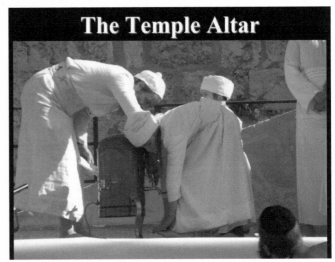
The Temple Altar

Tamidi (eternal offering).[6]

Lighting the fire
on the Altar for
the Third Temple
for the first time.

Kohanim in
training

Blasts on silver trumpets end the service

The Kohanic (priestly) blessing

Heeding the Sanhedrin's call to the 70 Nations to participate in the consecration of the altar, for the Third Temple, as Guatemalan Ambassador Mario Adolfo Bucaro Flores stated during his speech, *"This is a truly historic moment. My government is pleased to be partners with the Sanhedrin and with Israel in bringing [the] Messiah."*

The **11ᵗʰ miscellaneous item** the Jewish People have ready to go **right now** for the Last Days Temple, is **The Temple Sacrifice**.

This is from December 11, 2018 *"Temple Mount Activists Celebrated New Altar and planned to Practice an Animal Sacrifice." 'What we still have to do is awaken the people,'* says one activist

Activists who hope to see the Temple rebuilt on Jerusalem's Temple Mount unveiled a new altar Monday they say is intended to be placed on the Mount and used to offer sacrifices. For the past decade, these activists, who are preparing for a rebuilt Temple by recreating some of the ancient tools used in Temple rituals, have been practicing offering sacrifices. On Monday, the activists wanted to practice using the altar but had to suffice with only part of the service because the Jerusalem municipality would not let them slaughter an animal in a public park. So far, the practice sessions have included slaughtering an animal and offering it on a temporary altar of wood. On Monday the activists wanted to enact the complete ritual of slaughtering the animal and offering it and had even received a permit from the police. But the municipality's legal adviser rejected their request to slaughter an animal in a public park outside the Old City walls, thus the sheep earmarked for this purpose was taken to another location to be slaughtered. Rabbi Baruch Kahane served as the High Priest, instructing the other priests in their functions. Just as in Solomon's Temple, the different tasks to be performed were assigned by lottery. The priests wore Biblically accurate garb appropriate for use in the Temple. Incense was made for the reenactment and a small quantity was burned on the replica Golden Altar. Among the priests were young boys who were being trained in the Temple service. Even though the sheep was slaughtered at another location, the sections of meat were arranged on the ramp leading up to the altar in the ritually prescribed manner and one piece was thrown onto the fire on the altar to be burned completely.

"There is slow but sure progress, and if the authorities allow it, tomorrow we can do the whole service."

Rabbi Hillel Weiss, the spokesman for the Sanhedrin, *"We are on the cusp of the revelation of the Moshiach (Messiah)."*

The 12ᵗʰ **miscellaneous item** the Jewish People have ready to go right now for the Last Days Temple, is **The Temple Crown**.

This is from December 7, 2018 *"A Campaign has been launched to construct the Messianic Golden Royal Crown."*

Psalm 21:3 "You welcomed him with rich blessings and placed a crown of pure gold on his head."

"Rabbi Yosef Berger, the rabbi of King David's Tomb on Mount Zion, has initiated a special project to create a golden crown to be presented to the messiah-king upon his arrival in Jerusalem."

Rabbi Berger, a direct descendant of King David, explained *"that the founding of the State of Israel and the Six-Day War were overt miracles and that*

we are today living in the beginning of the messianic era. Creating such a crown, he said, and uniting the 70 nations of the world around the project, will hasten the arrival of the king. For 2,000 years, Israel has waited for the moshiach (messiah)," Rabbi Berger said. *"As a symbol of our belief that this period of waiting has ended, we should prepare a crown, since the first act of the moshiach will be to restore the Davidic Dynasty, which will be visibly unlike any other kingship that has ever existed."* The rabbi emphasized *"that a king of Israel would ensure that the exile would end, the ingathering of the exiles would be complete, the Temple would be rebuilt, and the Temple service reinstated."* The rabbi also noted that amazing efforts have been made to prepare for the Third Temple and all of the utensils stand ready, but no preparations have been made for the messiah who will build the Temple. *"Creating a crown for the king is unprecedented,"* Rabbi Berger said. *"When all 70 nations unite in an act of love expressly intended for the king in Jerusalem, this will surely be answered by Hashem."* Rabbi Berger said. *"By preparing an actual crown, we are taking the first step toward bringing the inner vision of a king into reality."*

[Video Transcript]
"For 2,000 years, Israel has waited for the Moshiach (Messiah). As a symbol of our belief that this period of waiting has ended, we should prepare a crown. Since the First act of the Moshiach will be to restore the Davidic Dynasty, which will be visibly unlike any other kingship that has ever existed. Join Israel365 and Rabbi Yosef Berger, the Rabbi of King David's tomb on Mount Zion, to create a golden crown to be presented to the Messiah-King upon his arrival in Jerusalem.

Donors of $180 or more will receive a special commemorative Temple coin. We are today living in the beginning of the Messianic era. Creating such a crown and uniting the 70 nations of the world around the project, will hasten the arrival of the king. Donate now:"[6]

Folks, virtually everything is ready to go for the Temple. Everything you can think of including crowning the guy who they think will be their Messiah. Gee, I wonder who that will be? What more does God have to do to get our attention? If we see for the first time in 2,000 years the Jewish People having the desire, the power, the organizations, the finances, the plans, the red heifer, the Sanhedrin, the Priesthood, the Ceremonies, and virtually every article needed as well as the miscellaneous items[7] needed to rebuild the end times Temple right now, then how much closer is the Rapture of the Church which takes place prior? We are so close it's not even funny! This is why, out of love, God has given us this update on *The Final Countdown: Tribulation Rising* concerning the Jewish People & the Antichrist to show us that the 7-year Tribulation is near, and the Return of Jesus Christ is rapidly approaching. And that's why Jesus Himself said…

Luke 21:28 "When these things begin to take place, stand up and lift up your heads, because your redemption is drawing near."

Like it or not, we are headed for The Final Countdown. The signs of the 7-year Tribulation are Rising all around us! It's time to wake up! Here is the point. If you're reading this today and you're not a Christian, then I beg you, please, heed these signs, heed these warnings, give your life to Jesus now! You don't want to be here when God pours out His Judgment upon this wicked and rebellious planet! It's the worst time in the history of mankind, so horrible that unless God shortened the timeframe the entire human race would be destroyed! The only way to escape is through Jesus! Take the way out now before it's too late. Get saved today! But, if you're reading this today and you are a Christian, then it's high time we stop goofing off and getting distracted with this world. Let's get busy working together sharing the Gospel with as many as we can! Let's leave here being living for Jesus and longing for His soon return!

Chapter Seventeen

The Jewish People & Their Spiritual State

The 13th End Time Prophecy concerning **The Jewish People** letting us know we're living in the Last Days is that **Israel Would Become Spiritually Deceived.** That's the sad commentary of this text. Let's go back to our opening text that we saw last time but look at it from a different angle.

Daniel 9:25-27 "Know and understand this: From the issuing of the decree to restore and rebuild Jerusalem until the Anointed One, the ruler, comes, there will be seven 'sevens,' and sixty-two 'sevens.' It will be rebuilt with streets and a trench, but in times of trouble. After the sixty-two 'sevens,' the Anointed One will be cut off and will have nothing. The people of the ruler who will come will destroy the city and the sanctuary. The end will come like a flood: War will continue until the end, and desolations have been decreed. He will confirm a covenant with many for one 'seven.' In the middle of the 'seven' he will put an end to sacrifice and offering. And on a wing of the temple, he will set up an abomination that causes desolation, until the end that is decreed is poured out on him."

So once again, we see in Daniel's amazing 70th week prophecy, that in the final week, the 7-year Tribulation, the antichrist will not only go up into a rebuilt Jewish Temple, halfway into the 7-year Tribulation and declare himself to be god, or what's also called the abomination of desolation, but what is the very event that starts the 7-year Tribulation in the first place? The antichrist makes a covenant with the Jewish people, right? It says it right there in the text. Daniel wrote that nearly 2,600 years ago! And the point is, do we see any signs of the Jewish People really being in such a "spiritually weakened state" that they would actually be deceived into making a peace treaty with the antichrist himself starting the very 7-year Tribulation? Uh yeah! In fact, so much so that they are ready to cut the deal anytime! But let me show you some proof they really are in a spiritually weakened state!

The **1st way** we know the Jewish People really are in a spiritually weakened state to fall for the antichrist's deception is, **They are Seriously Secular**.

You see, the problem is, most people think the Jewish people are all super spiritual, and they've got the dangling hair thing going on, reading the Torah, going to the Western Wall every day. Not so! It's kind of like people making the same false assumption that everybody who lives in America must be a Christian because we're a Christian nation, right? Yeah, I wish that were true! But it's the same thing with the Jewish People! Just because they're over there in Jerusalem doesn't mean they're religious. They need to be saved just like anybody else because they too are secular and have rejected Jesus like everybody else, even up to this very day.

Matthew 27:22-25 "What shall I do, then, with Jesus Who is called Christ? Pilate asked. They all answered, 'Crucify Him!' 'Why? What crime has He committed?' asked Pilate. But they shouted all the louder, 'Crucify Him!' When Pilate saw that he was getting nowhere, but that instead an uproar was starting, he took water and washed his hands in front of the crowd. 'I am innocent of this man's blood,' he said. 'It is your responsibility!' All the people answered, 'Let His blood be on us and on our children!'"

Boy has that ever unfortunately come to pass. But as you can see the Jewish People rejected Jesus at His first coming and unfortunately even on up to today, like the rest of the secular world, they are still rejecting Him. In fact, let me show you how secular they are. Here are the different secular states of your average Jewish Person.

Jews by Birth – These are those that are direct descendants of Abraham. In recent years this has been anyone whose mother is Jewish, but most modern

Jewish groups will recognize anyone who has one parent as being Jewish. These people are referred to as "Jews by birth."

Jews by Choice – These are those people who are converts to Judaism. The requirements for conversion are different depending on the group within Judaism that one is converting to. In general, the requirements are circumcision for males, immersion (like baptism) for men and women, and to understand and accept the duties of classical Jewish religious law.

Modern Judaism – Modern Judaism is somewhat of a hodge-podge of belief and practice. There's an old saying that goes, "Two Jews, three opinions." Judaism is by no means a monolith; it has changed and will continue to change for years to come. Chances are if you go to a handful of Jewish websites, you'll find dozens of explanations of what it means to "be Jewish" and "live Jewishly." These days, the Jewish experience varies from extremely religious to atheistic and all points in between, and their observances, practices and ways of life often reflect this diversity. But in general, they believe in what's called the "13 Articles of Faith."

1. God exists
2. God is one and unique
3. God is incorporeal
4. God is eternal
5. Prayer is to God only.
6. The prophets spoke truth.
7. Moses was the greatest of the prophets.
8. The Written and Oral Torah were given to Moses.
9. There will be no other Torah.
10. God knows the thoughts and deeds of men.
11. God will reward the good and punish the wicked.
12. The Messiah will come.
13. The dead will be resurrected.

Worldly Judaism – Of the approximately 15 million Jewish people worldwide, not all consider themselves to be religious or even practice Judaism. Many profess to be atheists, agnostics, or secular. Still others have embraced New Age and Eastern philosophies. This is because they believe Judaism is a religion of deed, not creed, making it possible to be an atheist and yet an Orthodox Jew at the same time because one happens to attend an Orthodox congregation. What an individual believes about God or the afterlife is not nearly as important as how one lives.

Religious Judaism – Religious Judaism is usually broken down into three broad "denominations" each itself containing a variety of beliefs and practices: Orthodox, Reform, and Conservative. None of the three "denominations" emphasize a personal relationship with God. They are much more interested in living according to tradition than in a personal relationship with their Creator.

Orthodox Judaism – These Jews adhere to a strict application of the laws and ethics in the Talmud or "Oral Law" and as developed by later Rabbinical teachers. An Orthodox Jew will generally adhere to the 13 Articles of Faith and are expected to observe all 613 mitzvoth (commandments). However, there are certain core practices considered essential to being Orthodox. These are the minimums to be considered Orthodox.

1. Refraining from murder, idolatry, and certain biblically-prohibited sexual practices.
2. Refraining from activities that violate the Jewish Sabbath and Jewish holidays.
3. Observing the Jewish dietary laws.
4. Observing the laws of family purity.
5. Observing circumcision for males.

Orthodox Judaism falls into two broad categories: Modern Orthodox and Hasidim. The Modern Orthodox are usually more academic, while the Hasidim are more mystical. Hasidic men usually wear black or dark gray suits and always wear skullcaps.

Reform Judaism – Reform Judaism (not "Reformed" Judaism) have embraced modern life, liberalism, and humanism and have set aside the belief and practices of Orthodox Judaism. In this form, synagogues are called "temples" and doctrines such as the coming of Messiah and bodily resurrection have been spiritualized. What remains in Reform Judaism is a liberal ethical system based on a monotheistic philosophy which generally maintains a more inclusive position regarding ideas like feminism and homosexuality.

Conservative Judaism – These Jews are an intermediate form of Judaism between Orthodox Judaism and Reform Judaism. They retain the feasts and many of the Jewish traditions, but make allowances for modern culture, while "conserving," as far as possible, traditional Judaism.

Messianic Jews – These are the Jews who have accepted Jesus Christ as their Personal Lord and Savior (some would call them a completed Jew) and they do emphasize a personal relationship with God.[1]

As you can see, so much for everyone being a Religious Jew in Jerusalem who is desperately seeking Jehovah God! They are far from it! They are spiritually all over the place and secular just like here in America! In fact, just like in America, they have even got so secular they are now doing this!

"Israel's abortion law is now among world's most liberal." *"Despite its conservative leanings, the government approves free pregnancy termination for nearly all women, and it barely causes a ripple."*

"It has some of the most liberal abortion coverage in the world. Among the many additional treatments to be offered to Israelis in 2014 are free-of-charge abortions for women ages 20-33."

"No medical reason for the abortion is required."

"Israeli Kibbutz to Become Worldwide Medical Marijuana Hub."

"Gan Shmuel is one of Israel's oldest kibbutzim. It was founded in 1913 when Jewish pioneers built a two-story house near an orchard close by. They kept animals on the ground floor and lived above."

"Eventually, the kibbutz thrived, but nothing in its rich history prepared it for what's about to come: Gan Shmuel will soon become a major worldwide center for the production and distribution of medical marijuana."

"Working with a Canadian firm, they will soon begin building a 45,000 square foot greenhouse that will produce up to five tons annually and hopefully expand to 24 tons a year before too long. An additional 11,000 square foot laboratory will serve for research and development of effective new brands of weed."

"Israel has an ideal climate for growing cannabis, and this will instantly make Gan Shmuel the largest player in the Israeli market. The rest will be exported globally."

"In the start-up nation, the standards just keep getting higher."

This is why when you talk to your average Jew, they are not only seriously secular in their beliefs and practices, but they have no clue who in the world Jesus is!

A reporter is on the street in Tel Aviv asking the question: "Who is Jesus?" These are the answers that he received. "The Christian prophet." The interviewer then asks his friend. "Do you want to add something?" His answer is, "No he's doing a good job." Then the original guy adds, "The prophet, the God for the Christians. He was a good man; may God rest His soul. He was a righteous man, like our Moses. You need to respect them, like there is Mohammad and Jesus. There is our God and Moses our teacher. He was a good man. We went to summer camp together."

Another person is asked, "Who is Jesus for you?" Her answer is, "Jesus is the founder of the Christian religion." Her friend adds, "I think what they are asking is why we Jews don't believe in Jesus, that he is the Messiah." She then replies "I am a religious woman. I believe in what Judaism gave us. Jesus arrived thousands of years after. He was a Jew who went to a different religion, founded a different religion."

The next person was asked, "Who is Jesus according to Judaism? What status does he have?" This man answers, "Jesus was born to a Jewish mother, so in principal he was a Jew and the Christians took him as their leader. They claim he wasn't born from a mother." The interviewer says, "You mean a father. They say his father was God." "Yes," the man agreed, "But we know he was born from a father." The interviewer asks him, "Where do we know this from?" He answers, "It is discussed in the Babylonian Talmud." The interviewer asks, "Really? What is written about it?" He answers, "She was with someone, I don't remember the name. It is written she was with someone (son of Pandera)."

The next person interviewed is a woman from Jerusalem: She is asked, "Who is Jesus to you?" She answers, "A figure for people who cannot think on their own. It's a story for people who have not been taught critical thinking." The interviewer asks, "Do you think that about all religions or just about Christianity?" She answers, "Yes, I do."

The person answers, "If the redemption had arrived, there would be no need to work and do the commandments. But Judaism says that we still need to fulfill the commandments because no one here lives in total joy so it is clear the redemption hasn't come yet."

The next and last girl he approached was asked, "Who is Jesus to you?" Her answer is, "Oh, a cousin. No, I don't know. I guess for me he is nothing."[2]

Wow! That is sad! But as you can see, the average Jewish person, they not only miss out on Who Jesus really is and how He's their One and Only true Messiah, but He's considered nothing to them and it's this same secular mindset, in our lifetime, that is setting the Jewish People up to fall for the coming deception of the false messiah, the antichrist, even to the point where when he suggests making a 7-year peace agreement, they'll say. "Sure, why not!" And unknowingly, be a part of the very event that triggers the actual 7-year Tribulation, prophesied nearly 2,600 years ago by the Prophet Daniel! *Darby* *See field*

The **2ⁿᵈ way** we know the Jewish People really are in a spiritually weakened state to fall for the antichrist's deception is, **They are Seeking Signs.**

And if you listen to Jesus, that's something you should never do! In fact, He says it's wicked!

Matthew 12:38-39 "Then some of the Pharisees and teachers of the law said to Him, 'Teacher, we want to see a miraculous sign from You.' He answered, 'A wicked and adulterous generation asks for a miraculous sign. But none will be given it except the sign of the prophet Jonah.'"

The sad irony is that here you have the word of God right before you, Jesus, proven repeatedly that He is the Messiah through miracles and fulfilling prophecy from the word of God and you still want a sign. No wonder Jesus called that generation wicked! The truth was right in front of them, but they still rejected it for an endless string of so-called signs. Well, unfortunately the same thing is happening to this generation of Jewish People. They too are seeking for signs of the Messiah's coming instead of going to the word of God!
Let me show you some of that proof.

The **1st sign** they're seeking is **The Stone**.

And these are all current events. This is from July 17, 2018.

"A Stone Fell from the Western Wall. Could this be a Seed to Grow the Third Temple?" They go on to quote out of context:

Habakkuk 2:11 "The stones of the wall will cry out, and the beams of the woodwork will echo it."

"A massive stone fell from the structure on Monday and narrowly missed a

Sign of the Stone

Jewish woman who had come to pray at dawn. The stone, weighing several hundred pounds, landed on one of the two platforms used for prayers."

"The strange occurrence led many to assign spiritual significance to the falling stone. Rabbi Shmuel Rabinovitch, the Chief Rabbi of the Western Wall, clearly felt this was the case."

"This is an unusual and most rare incident and the fact that it happened a day after the 9th of Av fast, in which we mourned the destruction of our temples, requires soul-searching."

The **2nd sign** they're seeking is **The Snake**.

This is from November 1, 2018.

"A snake wriggling out from between the stones of the Western Wall in search of a meal brought with it a message straight from Jewish mystical teachings."

"Connecting the archetypal enemy of man with the High Priest in the Temple, and also, perhaps, serving as a harbinger of the Messiah." They go on to quote out of context:

Genesis 3:1 "Now the serpent was more crafty than any of the wild animals the LORD God had made. He said to the woman, 'Did God really say, 'You must not eat from any tree in the garden?'"

"Women who went to the Western Wall on Wednesday were shocked to see a snake crawling out from between the ancient stones."[3]

"The Coin Snake, common to the region, is not venomous but it is similar in appearance to the deadly viper also found in Israel. The snake brought with it a powerful message."

"The serpent made its Jerusalem appearance during a hotly contested mayoral election, connecting it to the destruction of the Second Temple."

"The snake appeared during this time of dispute and divisiveness at the site of the Temple which was destroyed because of widespread hatred and divisiveness."

"Still another commentator saw a connection between the reptilian appearance and current events, referring to a recent head-on automobile accident near the Dead Sea that killed a family of eight and the horrific murder of 11 Jews in a Pittsburgh synagogue."

"We are truly in the dangerous times that directly precede Mashiach (Messiah)."

"A snake seen crawling between the stones of Israel's Western Wall show that a prophecy about the Messiah's coming is about to be fulfilled."

The 3rd sign they're seeking is **The Sinkhole.** ✔

This is from November 5, 2018.

"Sinkholes on the Temple Mount: Is this a Prophetic Awakening?"

The Temple Mount has been the scene of several strange phenomena lately; large sections of the ancient stones suddenly falling away, a snake crawling out from between the rocks, and now, a sinkhole has appeared adjacent to the Gate of Mercy, or Golden Gate as it is known in Christian literature."

"A pre-Messiah earthquake is prophesied to drastically change the topography of Jerusalem." They go on to quote out of context:

Zechariah 14:4 "On that day his feet will stand on the Mount of Olives, east of Jerusalem, and the Mount of Olives will be split in two from east to west forming a great valley, with half of the mountain moving north and half moving south."

"It may be that this dramatic geologic development has already begun."

"The sidewalk had sunk visibly and was cracking as if the ground was opening up underneath the paving stones."

The **4ᵗʰ sign** they're seeking is **The Strange Mist**.

This is from October 3, 2018.

"On Sunday, a group of Jews praying on the Mount of Olives witnessed a large white cloud rise up out of the ground from the Temple Mount."

"The phenomenon was recorded by Josh Wander, a Mount of Olives resident. A sunrise prayer session was organized on a plaza overlooking the Temple Mount for the holiday of Hoshana Rabbah, the last day of the week-long holiday of Sukkot (Feast of Tabernacles)."

"Just after sunrise, I was recording a Facebook live video of the prayers when I panned my camera to the Temple Mount."

"All of a sudden, I noticed a cloud or fog that erupted from the northeastern corner of the mount." "He has never seen anything like this before."[4]

But there you have it! A major sign apparently! Wander reluctantly described the mist with a word he rarely uses. "It looked supernatural," he said.

"I am certainly not the kind of person who sees signs in nature, but this was just too out of the ordinary to ignore. It looked eerie and the location, the site of the Holy of Holies, is too significant."

Rabbi Yosef Berger stated about this mist, *"If you had told me that it happened any other day of the year, I would not have assigned it any significance."*

"But to have this cloud appear on Hoshana Rabbah is highly significant and makes me happy, knowing the geula (redemption) is at hand."

They go on to quote out of context:

Isaiah 44:22 "I have swept away your offenses like a cloud, your sins like the morning mist. Return to Me, for I have redeemed you."

Really? That's your sign that you're about to be redeemed? This is the problem! You're not only looking for signs but you're taking scripture out of context and little do you know it's setting you up for the antichrist's deception! Here's why the Bible says seeking signs is dangerous!

2 Thessalonians 2:9-10 "The coming of the lawless one will be in accordance with the work of satan displayed in all kinds of counterfeit miracles, signs and wonders, and in every sort of evil that deceives those who are perishing. They perish because they refused to love the truth and so be saved."

what about Darby / Scofield? — Is that ever out of context? —

I'll admit that mist thing was strange. But still you don't put your hope in a sign! Rather it's to be in the revealed word of God! It's right before you, stick with that! But because the Jewish people, in our lifetime have this secular mindset for signs instead of the actual word of God, like with the First Coming, it is setting them up, unfortunately, to fall for the deception of the coming false messiah, the antichrist, even to the point where when he suggests making a 7-year peace agreement, and working with him. They'll say. "Sure, why not! Hey, give us a sign, will you?" And he will, a counterfeit one, and they'll fall for it because they refuse to love the truth. And unknowingly, they'll become a part of the very event that triggers the 7-year Tribulation, prophesied nearly 2,600 years ago by the Prophet Daniel![5]

The **3ʳᵈ way** we know the Jewish People really are in a spiritually weakened state to fall for the antichrist's deception is, **They are Socializing Sodom.**

Now this is another one of the sad truths we see in Scripture.

Revelation 11:7-8 "Now when they have finished their testimony, the beast that comes up from the Abyss will attack them and overpower and kill them. Their bodies will lie in the street of the great city, which is figuratively called Sodom and Egypt, where also their Lord was crucified."

Where was Jesus crucified? In Jerusalem. But here we see again the text we saw before in other studies where in the 7-year Tribulation, the Two Witnesses get killed by the antichrist in Jerusalem. It also shows us the spiritual state of those in Jerusalem at that time. And what were they likened unto? Sodom and Egypt! Egypt in Scripture typifies sin and Sodom speaks clearly of homosexuality! So, here's the question. This happens in the middle of the 7-year Tribulation, so do we see any signs of the Jewish people not only being full of sin like everyone else, i.e. compared to Egypt (yes, the secular mindset), but do we also see any signs of them apparently accepting and welcoming even the sin of homosexuality so much so to be compared to Sodom? Uh, unfortunately yes! In fact, they had one of the biggest Gay Pride Parades recently in Tel Aviv!

I24 Reports: *"Back here in Israel, hundreds of thousands of people are right here in Tel Aviv getting ready for their Gay Pride Parade. More than 200,000 people have taken to the streets. The party starts early in the morning and goes all night long. The Parade is the biggest*

Pride event in the whole world. Gay pride takes to the streets of conservative Jerusalem. The parade took place under heavy police guard."

One of the participants says: *"I came here today to march for equality, equality in all paths of life. And main for me, as a transsexual woman, it comes to the most basic things like walking in the streets without fearing for my life, which happens a lot as there are endless violent events."*

Another participant says: *"Jerusalem is a complex city, but it is also the capital city and therefore it belongs to everybody. The gay community is present in each community: religious, secular, Jews."*[6]

In Israel, right now! Looks to me like somebody has not only become Egypt with their secular mindset but they've also become like Sodom just in time for the 7-year Tribulation! But it gets even worse! Listen to how far it's gone!

"Lesbian, gay, bisexual, and transgender rights in Israel are the most tolerant in the Middle East, and among the most tolerant in Asia. Although same-sex sexual activity was legalized in 1988, the former law against sodomy had not been enforced since a court decision in 1963."

"Israel became the first country in Asia to recognize unregistered cohabitation between same-sex couples, making it the first country in Asia to recognize any same-sex union and even recognizes same-sex marriages performed elsewhere."

"Discrimination on the grounds of sexual orientation was prohibited in 1992 and same-sex couples are allowed to jointly adopt after a court decision in 2008. LGBT people are also allowed to serve openly in the military."

"In 2014, the Ministry of Health issued a statement about conversion therapy that 'It may also cause harm to the individual.' In 2018, the Health Ministry approved new regulations that allows gay and bisexual men to donate blood, regardless of when they last had sex."

"Tel Aviv has frequently been referred to as one of the most gay-friendly cities in the world, famous for its annual Pride Parade and gay beach, earning it the nickname 'The gay capital of the Middle East.'"

"According to LGBT travelers, it was ranked as the best gay city in 2011."

"And opinion polls found that a majority of Israelis support the legalization of same-sex marriage, as well as adoption and surrogacy rights for same-sex couples."

And yet as recent as November 23, 2018, and article came out in Breaking Israel News that stated, "Scientists Admit the Biblical Account of Sodom is Accurate," i.e. it was destroyed for the sin of homosexuality.

"A recent scientific study confirmed what students of the Bible have known all along: a catastrophe from the heavens destroyed all life in the area of the Dead Sea thousands of years ago."

"Some form of catastrophe 3,700 years ago brought to a sudden end and wiped out all of the estimated 40,000 to 65,000 people who inhabited the area at the time."

"Studies of the remains of the settlements in the region showed signs of extreme, collapse-inducing heat and wind. Pottery was discovered to have been exposed to heat so intense that it melted into glass."

"Pottery fragments discovered at the site contained tiny, spherical mineral grains that apparently rained down on the area." "The event was clearly catastrophic, and the Bible gives the city's name: Sodom."

I'll say it again, looks to me like the unthinkable has happened. Somebody has not only become just like Egypt, but they've also unfortunately become like Sodom just in time for the 7-year Tribulation. The spiritual significance of this is that it's the exact same spiritual state prophesied about Jerusalem and the Jewish People nearly 2,000 years ago, where the antichrist will kill the Two Witnesses in Jerusalem! That sad spiritual state is here right now! Egypt and Sodom! If that happens halfway into the 7-year Tribulation and we leave prior, then how much closer is the Rapture of the Church which takes place prior? We are so close it's not even funny! This is why, out of love, God has given us this update on *The Final Countdown: Tribulation Rising* concerning the Jewish People & the Antichrist to show us that the 7-year Tribulation is near, and the Return of Jesus Christ is rapidly approaching. And that's why Jesus Himself said...

Luke 21:28 "When these things begin to take place, stand up and lift up your heads, because your redemption is drawing near."

Like it or not, we are headed for The Final Countdown. The signs of the 7-year Tribulation are Rising all around us! It's time to WAKE UP! And so, the point is this. If you're reading this today and you're not a Christian, then I beg you, please, heed these signs, heed these warnings, give your life to Jesus now! You don't want to be here when God pours out His Judgment upon this wicked and rebellious planet! It's the worst time in the history of mankind, so horrible that unless God shortened the timeframe the entire human race would be destroyed! The only way to escape is through Jesus! Take the way out now before it's too late. Get saved today! But if you're reading this today and you are a Christian, then it's high time we stop goofing off and getting distracted with this world. Let's get busy working together sharing the Gospel with as many as we can! Including the Jewish people! Because they need to be saved just like anybody else and they too can escape the horrible events of the 7-year Tribulation if only they would accept Jesus as their Lord and Savior now, like this man did.

"Here's what you need to do. First you have to shave your head and you dress all in black, you have to wear a white robe, you eat only kosher food, you become a vegetarian, you face Jerusalem, you have to face India when you pray, you pray only in Hebrew, and you have to grow a beard. If you do all those cultural things, you'll discover the god of the universe.

I'm thinking this is crazy that someone thinks that they can force their culture on God and God's going to be impressed by what you wear and what direction you face when you pray, what you eat, all these sorts of things. It seems to me that if there was a God out there who could be known. He should be able to be recognized no matter where I face, no matter how I'm dressed, because He's God.

Growing up we always understood that we had our Bible and the Gentiles had their Bible, The New Testament. That they were two completely separate books. The only people I knew that were believers in Jesus were people in our public school that were Italian Catholic. So, I imagined that Jesus was Italian. So, the understanding that He was Jewish was a shock and then to hear that the New Testament was written by Jews, I couldn't believe it.

My expectation was that the New Testament was like my grandparents had told me. A book about how to persecute the Jews and that you should stay away from it. But of course, when you are told to stay away from something curiosity gets the best of you and you have to see it. When I opened the New Testament, I expected to find a hand book on how to persecute the Jews.

My grandparents warned me that it was written by people who killed the Jews. That's what I was expecting to see. Then when I open it, I find it is written by Jews about Jewish people. The New Testament was a fascinating book. So, as I opened this book in the library, I looked around to make sure none of my friends saw me take the Bible off the shelf. I opened it and here the first sentence is 'This is the genealogy of Jesus the Messiah, the son of David, the son of Abraham. Three people were mentioned, and they are all Jewish. I was very shocked. And as I continued to read, I read of a Jewish man that was born in a Jewish village, in a Jewish country and one day walks into a Synagogue and announces that he the Messiah.

The more I read the words of Jesus the more I became attracted to Him. It was as beautiful as anything I had ever read in any other parts of life. As I came to think that Jesus was the Messiah, it was clear that that was about the most Jewish thing I could do. This is not a renegade to our people, this is the one that was promised in our Bible. the 53rd chapter of Isaiah, it is astonishing, if you would just read that chapter, without the Bible being around you would say this is some Christian Bible, this is Jesus.

What you realize though is that it is in the middle of our Bible, our Jewish Bible. When I first came to faith, I dared not tell my father because this was the time period of the 1970's, of gurus and cults and he was very concerned about me joining some crazy sect and going off someplace. So, I waited for months and when I finally told him he was very skeptical. On his own then he started to read about Jesus as well, and about a year and a half later I told him that one of the fellows that wrote the book Ibid was speaking and he agreed to come out to hear that person.

One of the most amazing moments of my life was when the speaker said, 'Would everyone here that is a Jewish believer in Jesus, raise your hand,' and I raised my hand. My father also raised his hand. I looked at him and said, 'Pop he didn't say would all the Jews raise their hands, he said all the Jewish believers in Jesus raise their hands.' And my dad said, 'Yes, I heard what he said.' The decision to come to faith in Jesus as the Messiah was not something that was a momentary lark or a passing fad. I could see changes in myself that I knew were not within myself. I had tapped in to a truth of our Jewish people that was very powerful."[7]

And it's that truth they need to hear from us today if they're going to be saved. Let's be that faithful remnant, in these Last Days, amen?

Chapter Eighteen

The Jewish People & Their False Messiah & Treaty

The **14th End Time Prophecy** concerning **The Jewish People** letting us know we're living in the Last Days is that **Israel Would Place Their Hope in the Wrong Messiah**. But don't take my word for it. Let's listen to God's.

Romans 11:25-32 "I do not want you to be ignorant of this mystery, brothers, so that you may not be conceited: Israel has experienced a hardening in part until the full number of the Gentiles has come in, so all Israel will be saved, as it is written: 'The deliverer will come from Zion; he will turn godlessness away from Jacob. And this is my covenant with them when I take away their sins.' As far as the gospel is concerned, they are enemies on your account; but as far as election is concerned, they are loved on account of the patriarchs, for God's gifts and his call are irrevocable. Just as you who were at one time disobedient to God have now received mercy as a result of their disobedience, so they too have now become disobedient in order that they too may now receive mercy as a result of God's mercy to you. For God has bound all men over to disobedience so that he may have mercy on them all."

In other words, everybody's going to have an opportunity. But for now, the Jewish people are experiencing a "hardness in part" or some translations say a "blindness in part." This passage is just one of many examples in the Bible that clearly tell us that God is not done with the Jewish people. They are currently under a temporary blindness until what? What did it say there? Until the time or the fullness of the Gentiles, i.e. non-Jewish people, come in, or in other words, get saved. God knows who's going to get saved so once that number comes in, He's going to once again focus on the Jewish people. He's going to rescue them and fulfill His promises He made way back to David and even the Patriarchs. He's not done yet! Therefore, here's the point. Until that time occurs, the Jewish People are unfortunately going to be blinded to the true identity of the antichrist, their hearts are going to be hardened to the truth and thus not just strike a treaty with him, but apparently they're even going to look upon him as some sort of savior to place their hopes in, thinking that he's going to do what everybody else has failed to do, give them peace. They are blinded or hardened to the truth about the real identity of the antichrist. And by the way, this "blindness" is what the 7-year Tribulation is all about. It is God's very tool to open their eyes to the real Messiah.

Zechariah 12:10 "And I will pour out on the house of David and the inhabitants of Jerusalem a spirit of grace and supplication. They will look on Me, the One they have pierced, and they will mourn for Him as one mourns for an only child and grieve bitterly for Him as one grieves for a firstborn son."

So here we see the good news and the bad news for the Jewish people. Their eyes are finally opened to the truth, in the 7-year Tribulation, to who Jesus really is and how He's the one and only real Messiah for them and us. The blindness or hardness is gone, but it comes at a horrible price. The Bible says, the Antichrist, the one they initially put their hope in, will show his true colors and hunt two-thirds of them down and kill them.

Zechariah 13:8-9 "In the whole land, declares the LORD, two-thirds will be struck down and perish; yet one-third will be left in it. This third I will bring into the fire; I will refine them like silver and test them like gold. They will call on My Name and I will answer them; I will say, 'They are My people,' and they will say, 'The LORD is our God.'"

Praise God, their eyes are finally opened, and the hardness is gone, but it comes on the heels of another Jewish Holocaust! Very sad! This is the point, when this happens in the 7-year tribulation, we have already gone at the Rapture. Do we see any signs right now that the Jewish people are really expecting some sort of messiah/savior figure to place their hopes in, that the antichrist is going to fool them into thinking he is? Uh yeah! Slightly! Okay, what I'm about to share with you, the bulk of it, is just from over the last year alone, and just one news source in Israel. This is hot off the press, okay? But it is a massively condensed summation of over 250 pages worth of articles of the Jewish people expecting a Messiah, right now, found last year in just one news source! Now, as we saw before, the Jewish People are not only expecting a Messiah, but so much so that they are getting ready to build the actual crown to put on the head of the guy who they think will be their Messiah.

But they've also completed the Messiah Torah Scroll for the Messiah to read when he arrives, specially made for Him!

"Rabbi Yosef Berger, one of the rabbis in charge of King David's Tomb in Jerusalem's Old City, took an enormous step towards making his year-long dream a reality."

"Rabbi Berger's dream was to write a Torah Scroll to present to the Messiah upon his arrival. Since David's Tomb, the burial place of the Messiah's ancestor, is located on Mount Zion, Rabbi Berger is uniquely positioned to personally present the Torah to the Messiah."

Messiah Torah Scroll

"The Rabbi believes that by writing a Torah scroll, and keeping that scroll on Mount Zion, it will fulfill the requirements to usher in the Messiah."

The reason why they are so expecting of the Messiah, to the point where they want to hurry up and create the crown for his head and make the Torah Scroll for him to read, is because, once again, instead of sticking with Scripture, they are looking to all different kinds of wacky indicators that the Messiah's about to appear. Now, again, I'm skipping over large portions of this crazy behavior, be it looking for the Messiah in Secret Torah Codes, which is a bunch of baloney, or even looking for the Messiah in special needs children. Let's take a look at these:

Messiah in the Torah Codes: *"These are the supposed secret messages encoded within the Hebrew text of the Torah and can supposedly be revealed by arranging specific letters from the text in a certain way so as to reveal a 'secret message.' According to Rabbi Matityahu Glazerson, a so-called Torah Codes expert, hidden clues in the Torah indicate that the Left-Wing party in Israel will be defeated as a precursor to the Messiah. So, using a Torah program, he searched for equidistant letter sequences in the Torah, containing the words "erev rav", "left" and "Moshiach" as well as the words "ketz smole" ("end of the left").*

All these phrases were adjacent to the letters tav (ת), shin (ש), ayin (ע), chet (ח). And it turns out that the numeric equivalent of these letters is the current year according to the Hebrew calendar. But that's not all, Rabbi Glazerson also found Lag B'omer, a Jewish festive day in the Torah codes that could indicate the soon appearance of the coming Moshiach (the Messiah).

Once again, using a special computer program to search for series of letters in the Torah in order to extract hidden meanings, Rabbi Glazerson searched for the words 'Lag B'Omer,' and found them in the Book of Exodus interconnected with the letters yud (י) and chet (ח) leading into the word Iyar (רייא) and the code for the 18th of Iyar appears as a continuation of the word, Moshiach (Messiah). And he also pointed out that all these codes were surrounding the verse that commanded Israel to keep the Sabbath. Therefore, he says, 'In order for the Messiah to come, we need to keep the Sabbath.'

But that's still not all. Rabbi Glazerson then went on to say at the end of last year that according to the Torah Codes, the Messiah will come that year. Unfortunately, the year 5778 ended last September, when Rosh HaShana, the Jewish New Year, ushered in 5779. When asked to explain the discrepancy, Rabbi Glazerson told Breaking Israel news. 'The year 5778 was significant but the actual date of the Messiah is still in question.' (Well duh!) 'It may take longer if we do not merit it, but the soonest it can come is this year." (Well double duh!) And then he actually went on to say, 'Whether or not the Messiah will come this year was decided in heaven last week during the fast of the 10th of Tevet.'"

Messiah in Special Needs Children: *"New messages from autistic children in Jerusalem shows how the Messiah is about to be revealed. Daniel, one of the special needs kids, transmits his messages via facilitated communication (FC), a technique used as a way of communicating with those who cannot speak normally. He is said to be gifted with the power of prophecy and warns that the final stages preceding Messiah are imminent and they will be difficult.*

So why do they listen to him? Because, according to some rabbinic opinions, autistic children qualify as a form of prophetic communication since the Talmud teaches that, 'Since the Temple was destroyed, prophecy was taken from the prophets and given to children.' And Rabbi Brody said, 'One-on-one, he has answered questions for me that I have struggled with for years. I feel this is straight from heaven.'

Many of the autistic children are aware of previous lifetimes. And Rabbi Samuel related how one girl knew that in a previous lifetime, she was born a Jew but rejected her faith when she married a non-Jew. 'She needed to return to this world just to repair this blemish in her faith,' So Rabbi Samuel explained. 'For that, being autistic was just enough since it allowed her to have the most simple and clear faith in the God of Israel.'

So, Daniel goes on to describe how to prepare for the final stages of the Messiah. 'Most people don't want to understand that we are near the end,' Daniel said. 'The Messiah is about to be revealed but we have to undergo something very difficult first. God is going to destroy two-thirds of the world. I don't think this is going to be due to a nuclear war, though that may be part of it.'

Then Rabbi Eldad Shmuel, one of the rabbis who organizes and attends a group of autistic children said, 'They have been saying more and more that the geula (redemption) is very close. But before it comes, there will be a horrible war – the likes of which has never been seen. Entire cities, huge, urban centers, will be destroyed. The United States will be unrecognizable after the war. 'But they say if you do teshuvah, (repentance) God will take care of you: food, water, electricity and all that is needed. The end-of-days will be like when the Jews left Egypt. The Jews will not suffer.'"

Messiah in Near Death Experiences: *"Israeli teen returns from 15 minutes of clinical death with spiritual messages concerning the coming Messiah. A 15-year-old secular Israeli boy named Natan had a near death experience and returned to life describing Biblical prophecies about the End of Days. In a video posted on YouTube, Natan is shown speaking to an Orthodox Jewish audience in a synagogue in Israel, just days after his near-death experience.*

He relates his understanding of what was revealed to him in the next world during the 15 minutes that he was pronounced clinically dead. Natan's near death experience happened on the first night of this past Sukkot (Feast of Tabernacles), which was also the night of the final Blood Moon. At the home of his uncle, where he went to visit for the holiday, Natan began feeling unwell. He described suddenly shivering and felt cold in his arms and legs. Then he decided to go and rest and, in those moments, felt his soul exit his body through his nose.

Among the various spiritual messages received by Natan, the young boy speaks about the messiah standing on the Mount of Olives and determining who is worthy to be saved.

Rabbi: *'What do you see? What do you hear? What do you smell?'*

Natan: *'You smell a good smell, simply a good smell. It just can't be described in this world what that good smell is that you smell. A good smell. And you see the light, and you just want to stay there forever. For always.'*

Rabbi: *'Those who didn't keep Torah and mitzvot?'*

Natan: *'They will die.'*

Rabbi: *'Those who kept Torah and mitzvot?'*

Natan: *'Those who kept Torah and mitzvot – it depends. It depends if they did Torah with gemilut chassadim. There are those who are observant, but they don't really care about it, they are casual about it. But if someone really strict – and studies Torah and does acts of kindness, he will be saved. I also saw the moment that Har Hazeitim splits in two, then the Mashiach will stand at the entrance, but he won't, he won't see who is religious, who has a beard, and who a person is. What he will see if, he sees according to a person's holiness, he will smell each person, he will smell if someone has holiness, if he is pure, if he did mitzvot, if he performed acts of kindness.'*

In describing the qualities of the Messiah, Natan said, 'The Mashiach (Messiah) is first of all someone who can't sin. Someone who repented. and he will be someone who we actually know very well but everyone will be very, very surprised that he is of all people the Mashiach.' Then Natan goes on to describe the power of the Messiah to discern a person's holiness. 'He won't see who is religious, who has a beard and who a person is. What he will see according to a person's holiness, he will smell each person, he will smell if someone has holiness, if he is pure, if he did mitzvot (God's commandments), if he performed acts of kindness, and things like that." (Dude you better blow your nose!) "[1]

Messiah in Netanyahu: *"Is Netanyahu Holding the Keys for the Messiah? Israel's Prime Minister, Benjamin Netanyahu first met Rabbi Menachem Mendel Schneerson, in 1984 when Netanyahu was Israel's ambassador to the United Nations. But before Netanyahu returned to Israel in 1988 to join Likud, (right-wing political party in Israel) the Rabbi gave him so-called prophetic advice about his political trials. 'He's going to come out of it, and he'll stand tall, on G-d's side. He will make it through this, and he will continue, and he'll be able to hand his keys over to Moshiach (the Messiah), and we'll have the complete and true Redemption.'*

Then Rabbi Yitzchak Kaduri, met with Netanyahu in 1997 during his first term as prime minister and he whispered this message into the politician's ear. 'You will serve a very long time and after your term in office, the Messiah would arrive.' Before his death, Kaduri also said that he expected the Jewish Messiah to arrive soon, and that he had met him a year earlier. Then in May, Rabbi Levi Sudri, noted many parallels between the current prime minister and Jonathan, the son of Biblical King Saul.

Sudri suggested that Netanyahu is serving the function of Moshiach ben Yosef (Messiah from the house of Joseph) the first half of a two stage Messianic process. He explained that as the reincarnation of Jonathan, Netanyahu is paving the way for the more transcendent Moshiach ben David who will immediately follow.' And lest you doubt, 'The name 'Netanyahu' (והינתנ) is composed of the same letters as the name, 'Jonathan (יהנותנ).'

Then, if that wasn't enough "proof" Rabbi Moshe Ben Tov, known for his ability to perceive the past and present of people by gazing at the mezuzah on their door, (That's a decorative case placed on the Jewish doorpost that contains a parchment inscribed with Hebrew verses from the Torah) he then stared at the mezuzah in the Prime Minister's office, and gave this message, 'It is very important that your love of Israel continue until the Moshiach comes because you are going stay in office and are going to meet him,' He then said, 'You are the one who will give him the keys to this office.'

However, 'Perhaps the most powerful message connecting current political events to the Messiah came from a 31-year old Israeli woman named Talia Caroline Eliyahu who was going through a spiritual crisis after giving birth. She sensed a dark presence in her home one night as she awoke to change her baby's diaper. When she returned to sleep, she dreamt of a large chariot with many people in it, including a member of her family.

She followed the chariot into a large room where many people were being beaten. And in that room, she encountered her deceased grandmother who said, 'You are partly here and partly there.' She also saw many holy rabbis that she recognized, some alive and some already deceased. And one of the rabbis she recognized was Rabbi Kook, a well-known mystic from Tiberias who supposedly stated, 'When the government of Netanyahu crumbles, it is time to get ready for the Moshiach.'

Messiah in Nature: "According to Torah scholars, the End of Days will be marked with unusual natural phenomena such as stars and earthquakes. And this past year alone, Breaking Israel News reported on various natural phenomena heralding the Messiah, including snowfall in the hottest desert, seismic activity, eclipses, volcanoes, hurricanes, heavy rains, tsunamis, blood moons, blood red rivers and asteroids as a sure sign that the Messiah's coming is imminent.

In fact, several Rabbis are pointing to the recent rare lunar eclipse and continued earthquakes as a divine pre-Messianic wake-up call. Because after all, the Talmud specifies that lunar eclipses are a bad omen for Israel since Israel is spiritually represented by the moon. If the lunar eclipse takes place in the east side of the heavens, then it is a bad omen for all the nations in the east, and if it occurs in the western hemisphere of the sky, it is a bad sign for all the nations in the west.

And according to Rabbi Lazer Brody here's your proof, 'The total time of the eclipse they had was 6 hours, 13 minutes, and 613 is the exact number of the Torah's commandments. Coincidence? No such thing.' Then another mystic rabbi, Rabbi Yekutiel Fish, suggested that the increased geyser activity in Yellowstone National Park may be the precursor to the pre-Messiah war of Gog and Magog. He also saw a connection between recent heavy rains and the Messiah and quoted supposed proof from, 'a section of the Talmud (Tractate Chulin 63a) describing an undefined bird, possibly a sea crow or vulture named a Shrakrak.

The Talmud states that when the Shrakrak sits on something and cries out, mercy comes to the world in the form of rain. But should this bird sit upon the ground and make its call, then the Messiah is about to come.' Then Rabbi Yosef Berger, the rabbi of King David's Tomb on Mount Zion, even noted that the recent surge of fires across America also have prophetic significance concerning the Messiah. He believes you can see the actual Biblical pillars of smoke and fire from a raging wildfire in Arizona.

Jukin Media: *As two people are sitting in their car across the river from the fire burning in Arizona they are watching as the fire burns brightly and edges towards the water. He says, "Wow, there it goes." She adds, "It's a water spout from the fire." Again, he says, "Wow!" The water spout looks like a tornado and it keeps getting bigger and bigger.[2]*

He goes on to say, 'When this vision of a pillar of smoke and fire appeared on the other side of the world, a great tsaddik (righteous Jew) passed away in Israel. In the Zohar, (the writings that are the basis for Jewish mysticism) it is written that before the Messiah appears, a hidden righteous man will be essential to prepare the way for him to be revealed, and a pillar of fire appears when tzaddikim leave the world and there have been many cases throughout history where this has been witnessed.' Then Rabbi Ben Artzi said, 'The Creator is purifying the world from the filth of the snake in order to prepare the way for the Messiah to be revealed in the world.' And Rabbi Levi Sudr said, 'What is happening below the surface is that something wonderful is being born: the Moshiach (Messiah).' And Rabbi Trugman concluded, 'It is clear that we are living in an age that is very close to the Moshiach.' Which is why Rabbi Fish emphasized that, 'The only thing we can do is pray and do tshuva (repent).'

Messiah in Rabbinical Opinions: *"Orthodox scholar Rabbi Yitzchak Breitowitz explained that there are alternative scenarios for the messianic figure. 'Moshiach as a person will be killed in the horrendous wars of Gog and Magog. But he then said Moshiach can take another form. It doesn't have be the form of a person. It can take the form of a movement and a philosophy.' Rabbi Yosef Berger said, 'In the days before Moshiach (Messiah), Hashem (God, literally 'the name') will bring back the ten plagues of Egypt to punish the enemies of Israel, but to an even greater degree.'*

And then former Chief Sephardic Rabbi of Israel, Rabbi Mordechai Eliyahu states that, 'According to the Talmud, there are 36 hidden righteous Jews whose identity is known to a select few. If there is fewer than 36 in any one moment, the world would cease to exist.' Rabbi Yitzchak Kaduri, the most famous Jewish Kabbalist (mystic) in Israel, announced that the world was about to enter a period of increased natural disasters, explaining that these disasters would be directly related to the geula (redemption) process.

It was also at that time, during the afternoon prayers of Yom Kippur, that the rabbi, who was 104 years old at the time, went into a deep meditative state, causing great concern among his students. After 45 minutes, the rabbi lifted his head and smiled, announcing, 'The soul of the moshiach (Messiah) has attached himself to a person in Israel.' But then Rabbi Pinchas Winston said, 'The Messiah might have already come, and we didn't notice. You may not see Messiah until after it happens, if you even see it then.

That being said, it means that Moshiach must come sometime within the next nine years.' Still another Rabbi said, 'Did England just push the Messiah further away?' This is from Rabbi Yosef Dayan, a member of the Jewish Sanhedrin, he was aghast when he heard the story of the death of the 23-month-old Alfie Evans who died as the direct result of an order from a British court to halt the life-support he was on. He and others believe that the death of babies, before and after birth, is delaying the arrival of the Moshiach (Messiah). 'Some actions actually serve to bring the Messiah closer, but everyone that does an abortion and kills a baby is actively delaying the Messiah.'

Then another Rabbi, Rabbi Chaim Kanievsky, was asked if this year was a favorable time for the coming of the Messiah and he said, without hesitation, 'Of course.' And then even more specifically he stated that, 'The Messiah is alive today and when Israel merits it, he will immediately reveal himself.' But then he went on to say that, 'The Messiah will be born this Saturday, if he hasn't been born already and righteous Jews need to prepare special clothes to be worn only for greeting the Messiah upon his arrival.'

Then he added, 'Yell it from loudspeakers, the Messiah is at the door and it is up to each one of us to usher in his arrival. Gather your family and come to Israel. Otherwise, there won't be enough room for you on the airplanes.' Still more he said, 'It very well could be the Messiah will come this week. He can come at any moment. He is here with us already. Don't travel.' And then he stated, 'Don't be sad. The Messiah is already here. He will reveal himself very soon.'

And finally, he shared, 'The only way to be saved is through learning Torah, and through works of loving kindness and there is no other way.' And lest you doubt where his supposed inspiration is coming from, 'Rabbi Kanievsky blesses marijuana as kosher for Passover.' He said it can be eaten or smoked despite the strict dietary laws of the holiday.'

As three Rabbis gather around one that is holding marijuana, they are nodding their heads up and down and look into the green leaves. It is all done in Hebrew. They are blessing the weed for further use."[3]

And maybe that's why, "Israel's High Court won't hear man claiming to be the Messiah." Yeah, maybe they're afraid he's been smoking something!

Man Claiming to be Messiah

"Dov Sobol has repeatedly turned to Israeli courts, demanding recognition of God's purported 'messages' to him."

"The High Court of Justice on Tuesday declined to debate the messages of a self-styled "Messiah to the world" who says he's receiving messages from the "Creator of the world," despite the petitioner noting the very great "responsibility for the fate of the world" that rests on his shoulders."

Dov Sobol, has even asked the High Court to force Prime Minister Benjamin Netanyahu to read his book, "in order to save the world from its future troubles and to bring world peace."

But apparently, they aren't taking any chances because, *"Police in Israel are Actively Preparing for Messiah's Arrival."*

"No one knows the day or the hour, but the Israeli police seem to believe the Messiah is coming soon."

"The Israeli commissioner of police, Roni Alsheikh, stated at a recent Jewish celebration that his department is preparing for the arrival of the Messiah."

"When the Messiah comes, everyone will want to [approach] him so it will get very crowded," "That will be a time when we will need to start preparing for the security operation necessary upon the arrival of the Messiah."

Again, I may not be the sharpest knife in the drawer, but it sure looks to me like the Jewish people are ready to receive some sort of messiah figure to place their hopes in, how about you? In fact, close to 6,000 Jewish Rabbis and community leaders attended an annual International Conference with emissaries who serve the Jewish people from over 75 countries around the world, whereupon they began singing, "We want Moshiach now! We don't want to wait!" Talk about high expectations! And, keep in mind, I skipped over a ton of other supposed indicators such as, whale sightings, shark swarms, oil discoveries, precious gems, and of course the Embassy move, you name it! Just about everything you can think of has become an indicator that the Messiah is almost here! But here's the point. With all those wacky speculations they're looking at as supposed proof for the coming of the Messiah, do you think they are in any spiritual conditions to recognize the false messiah when he comes? Not even close! And that's why when you ask the average Jewish person today about how they will know when the real Messiah comes, they have absolutely no clue.

The Ask Project: *"How will we know the Messiah has come?"*

Israeli: *"We will hear the shofar (ram's horn)."*

Reporter: *"The sound of the shofar? So that means every Rosh Hashana the Messiah comes?"*

Israeli: *"No, we will hear it all around the world."*

Reporter: *"The shofar will be heard all around the world. That's the sign?"*

The Reporter asks another Israeli: *"How will we know the Messiah has come?"*

Israeli Netanel Sfat.: *"Not about Christianity, right? Not about Christianity you mean Judaism."*

Reporter: *"What are you talking about?"*

The Israeli turns to his friend to ask: *"How will we know the Messiah has arrived? How will we know the Messiah has arrived? The Messiah is already here."*

Reporter: *"Who? Who is the Messiah?"*

Israeli: *"The Messiah is the reality that the nation of Israel exists. The Messiah doesn't have to be a person."*

Reporter: *"The fact that Israel exists is the Messiah?"*

Israeli: *"Yes."*

Another lady on the street is asked by the **Reporter:** *"How will we know that the Messiah is coming?"*

Tsahala Kfar Yona: *"What a question! When he comes, we will know. Obviously. I have no answer to that. There is the belief in my heart that he will come when he comes, when he comes, everyone will know."*

Again, the **Reporter** asks the question to another Israeli: *"How will we know when the Messiah comes?"*

Israeli: *"What? I don't know Jewish literature sorry."*

Reporter: *"You don't believe?"*

Israeli: *"No."*

Reporter: *"You don't believe in the Messiah at all?"*

Israeli: *"No."*

The Reporter asks another man on the street: *"How will we know when the Messiah comes?"*

Robert: *"How will we know? It says that it is when the kingship returns to Israel and politically and militarily Israel is secure. Then you will know that the Messiah has come."*

Reporter: *"So if we install a kingship now, that means that the Messiah has come?"*

Robert: *"No, we don't install it. It's not up to us to bring him down. We will know by the success of the Messiah. When the Messiah is successful in bringing about world peace and when Israel is recognized by the nations, then we will know that the Messiah has come. He has to prove himself."*[4]

And that's exactly what the antichrist will do. And I quote, "We will know if the Messiah is real if he brings about world peace and Israel is recognized by the nations around the world." This is what Daniel 9:27 says he will do! He will make a peace treaty with Israel and they will be recognized around the world and this, as you just heard, is what the Jewish People want and are expecting right now. But this is the very event that starts the 7-year Tribulation! Which makes you wonder, if the Jewish People are this ripe to place their hopes in a false messiah to save them, then could it be that the actual Antichrist is alive and well already somewhere on planet earth? Makes you wonder! And that leads us to….

The **15th End Time Prophecy** concerning the Jewish people letting us know we're living in the Last Days is that **Israel Would Place Their Hopes in a Deceptive Treaty**. And again, this is the event that starts the 7-year tribulation!

Daniel 9:27 "He will confirm a covenant with many for one 'seven.' In the middle of the 'seven' he will put an end to sacrifice and offering. And on a wing of the temple he will set up an abomination that causes desolation, until the end that is decreed is poured out on him."

But again, as you can see here in our text, we saw that this was the classic text that specifically tells us the exact event that starts the 7-year Tribulation in the Last Days. And what was it? It's when the antichrist makes a covenant or "peace treaty" with the people of Israel, right? But not only that, what was the specific time frame about this covenant? It's going to specifically be for what? Seven years, right? Again, this is why we have a 7-year Tribulation, not a 42-year Tribulation, or 2 year, or 19 weeks and 3-day Tribulation. It's the final week of Daniel's 70th week prophecy! Okay, now here's the point. Can anybody guess just where in the world, right now, everybody is wanting to make a peace treaty with? Uh, Israel…shocker! Little bitty tiny Israel! Not Russia, not China, but little bitty tiny Israel. Because they are fulfilling the prophecy of them becoming a source of worldwide conflict and it's leading to the fulfillment of this prophecy from Daniel. One day, because of all this conflict going on that we see every day on TV, the people of Israel are going to strike a relationship with the antichrist, of all people, and seek a peace treaty with him! It's right there! So, the question is, "Are there any signs that the Jewish people really are trying to make a peace treaty or covenant with other people? We see they have a desire to place their hope in a false messiah, but how about a treaty? Uh, slightly! In fact, let me show you just a few of the failed attempts that other people and governments have tried to make with Israel in our lifetime, exactly like the Bible said would happen in the last days!

- UN Security Council Resolution 242, 1967
- Camp David Accords, 1978
- The Madrid Conference, 1991
- Israeli-Syrian Talks 1991
- Oslo Agreement, 1993
- Israel-Jordan Treaty of Peace, 1994
- Camp David, 2000
- Taba Talks, 2001
- Saudi Peace Plan, 2002
- Road Map Peace Plans, 2003
- Geneva Accord, 2003
- Sharm el-Sheikh Summit, 2005
- Franco-Italian-Spanish Middle East Peace Plan, 2006
- Israel-Hamas Ceasefire, 2008
- Direct Talks Peace Plan, 2010
- Israeli Peace Initiative, 2011[5]

Okay, maybe it's just me, but it sure looks like somebody's trying to get a peace treaty going on with, of all people, Israel, how about you? Uh yeah. And again, you have to understand the significance of this. One of these treaties, maybe it's one that's even being hashed out now behind the scenes, we don't know, but one of them is going to be with the antichrist himself. And unlike all the other failed ones we just saw, he alone is going to pull it off. And it's not going to lead to peace in the Middle East. It's going to lead to your absolute worst nightmare! It's the very event that starts the 7-year Tribulation! That's how close we are! In fact, many people believe that maybe even one of the recent treaties being hashed out right now as we speak, behind the scenes, with various political rulers, could actually be the treaty Daniel is talking about. Let's take a look at some of those recent attempts from current world rulers.

The **1st recent attempt** for a peace treaty with Israel is the **Trump Peace Plan**.

Now, in actuality, it's really not so much President Trump's Peace Plan as it is his son-in-law Jared Kushner's Peace Plan. In fact, some headlines around the world are saying just that, "Jared Kushner's Peace Plan" and he's over there, "Kushner (not Trump) meets to discuss Mideast peace." And apparently, "Israel says it would welcome the United States as a mediator, led by Jared Kushner, Trump's White House adviser and son-in-law, in what's being called, "The deal of the century." But he, along with his colleague Jason Greenblatt (a Jewish man) are really the one's putting this deal together. Trump's just getting the credit for it. And this has led many to speculate, not so much Donald Trump, but could Jared Kushner be the antichrist? It's a recent deal of the century calling for peace? But that's not all.

The **2nd recent attempt** for a peace treaty with Israel is the **British Peace Plan**.

Believe it or not, even Prince William is getting in on the action to seek peace with Israel, to the point where some are starting to ask the question, "Will Prince William 'Confirm' a Covenant with Israel?" Here's a recent historic trip he made to Israel. I wonder what he's up to?

The Daily Dose: *"Prince William will set foot in Israel for the first time. It will be the first ever official visit to Israel of any senior member of Great Britain's Royal Family. Kensington Palace confirmed release of part of the itinerary that the Prince will hold meetings in Tel Aviv and Jerusalem, and he will also be visiting Jordan and the West Bank on this trip.*

Although we have been told that this trip will be non-political, there have been a lot of politicians on it so far. And this evening, first in front of the Union Flag and national anthem followed by the Israeli Flag and national anthem the Duke stood next to Prime Minister Benjamin Netanyahu. Then Prince William took a step on that delicate political tight rope that he has been navigating in that regional world."

Prince William: *"Never has hope and reconciliation been more needed. I know I share the desire with all of you and our neighbors for a just and lasting peace."*[6]

But that's still not all. The **3rd** **recent attempt** for a peace treaty with Israel is the **French Peace Plan**.

Now for those of you who don't know, Emmanuel Macron is the new French President who is very young, very charismatic, and a European leader that is a staunch globalist. He's not only pro-European Union but he's also a one-worlder to the point where *Frontpage Magazine* had a headline reading, "The Globalist Empire Strikes Back in France." This is because Macron was a Rothschild investment banker with zero political experience, but he was also backed by chief globalist George Soros, and was even trained in the Jesuit school system. He also represents socialism, no borders, immigration, Islam exaltation, and godlessness. He arrived on the scene in France with the same "hope and change" rhetoric of Barack Obama, who by the way endorsed him. And of all things that he's doing on the political world scene, it's this, "France's President Emmanuel Macron has called for renewed peace talks between the Israelis and Palestinians, indicating he will help in the process." This was after his first formal meeting with Israel's Prime Minister Benjamin Netanyahu in Paris.

פריז
יום ראשון, ה-16 ביולי,2017

PARIS
Dimanche 16 juillet 2017

It's his statements in the media that are even more telling of his true motives. First of all, "Emmanuel" in Hebrew means, "God with us" and based on some very strange statements he's making in the media, some are saying, "Could Emmanuel Macron be an Apocalyptic leader?" And the reason why is because Macron has gone on record as stating, "He wants to govern like a Roman god," and he has even been referred to as "The Sun King reborn" and given the nickname "Jupiter." Who by the way, is the Roman god of the sky and thunder, and the king of all the gods in ancient Roman religions. Apparently, this is why

European publications are depicting him as walking on water and asking the question, "Is He Europe's Savior?"

But he also has a reputation for being ruthless. "The Financial Times, quoted a source who has known Macron well for years, detailing how, 'He seduces everyone. And then he kills.'" Whoa! Now wait a minute! That's what the real antichrist is going to do with the Jewish People! First, he seduces them with a peace treaty, then he kills them! I'm sure that's just a coincidence! Now, before I go any further, let me clarify. I am not here to predict who the antichrist is and I'm certainly not saying that any of these guys is the actual antichrist. And that's because as Christians we are not going to be here, so we're not looking for the antichrist, we're looking for Jesus Christ. Amen? I just bring this up to show you how ripe things are on the world scene for somebody, some political ruler, whoever he is, to approach Israel with a deceptive treaty and promise them peace and security. And that brings up another Bible prophecy that the Apostle Paul talked about, sharing how this desire for "peace and security," that all these guys are pushing for, is as he said would happen in the last days.

1 Thessalonians 5:1-3 "Now, brothers, about times and dates we do not need to write to you, for you know very well that the day of the Lord will come like a thief in the night. While people are saying, 'Peace and safety,' destruction will come on them suddenly, as labor pains on a pregnant woman, and they will not escape."

According to this text, the Apostle Paul tells us one of the signs that we know we are getting close to the Lord's return is when all of a sudden, you see people all over the planet crying out a specific phrase. And notice what that phrase was, it was "Peace and Safety" right? Not "Peace and Happiness" not "Joy and Prosperity" not even "Stop Eating Chicken," as cool as that would be, but specifically the phrase "Peace and Safety." Okay, now, pay attention because nothing's by chance in the Scripture! It just so happens that the Greek word here for "safety" is "asphaleia" and it literally means "security" as in "security from enemies or security from danger." So literally you could say in that text, "Peace and Security" and still be totally right on. Now here's the point. Put this Bible prophecy passage from Paul about "Peace and Security" being the exact phrase that people would be crying out for in Last Days, just prior to Jesus' return. Combine it with Israel coming back on the scene to become a "center of conflict for the whole world," where everybody wants to now make peace, and can anybody guess just what all the world's leaders are crying out for in regard to Israel and this problem? Peace and Security! It's the exact same phrase Paul said people would cry out for in the Last Days before sudden destruction! In fact, it's been going on for quite some time now.

Meeting at the United Nations: *"The objective is to have a Palestinian state since the war of 1967 that will lead to..."*

Hillary Clinton: *"Peace and security..."*

Barack Obama: *"One lesson from history is that 'Peace and Security' does not come easy."*

"Peace and stability that all people on all sides long for..."

"Two states for two peoples living side by side in 'Peace and Security' is not just a slogan but a real necessity for the stability of the entire region."

"Israel and Palestinians can live side by side in 'Peace and Security.' This is our vision, and this is our commitment."

Dan Gillerman: *"Our hopes and dreams for Israel are to live in peace, to live in 'Peace and Security'"*

Barack Obama: *"Two states living side by side in 'Peace and Security. True peace for all Israeli's. We will also pursue peace between Israel and Lebanon."*

"Peace and Security..."

Barack Obama: *"Israel and Syria..."*

Benjamin Netanyahu: *"Peace and Security..."*

Barack Obama: *"And a broader peace between Israel and it's many neighbors. We must decide if we are serious about 'Peace and Security', to recognize Israel's legitimacy and it's right to exist in 'Peace and Security'"*

Barack Obama: *"It is how we will find a new pathway to 'Peace and Security'... That is the work we must do."*

Tony Blair: *"Peace and Security and co-existence...."*

Benjamin Netanyahu: *"We have to move towards peace, economy, security and peace...then peace can succeed."*[7]

Not "Joy and Prosperity" not "Deliverance and Happiness" but wonder of wonders it just happens to be the exact Biblical phrase, right now, that the Bible warned would come upon the scene in the Last Days... "Peace and Security." Now, if you're paying attention, they're still saying that exact same phrase even in our current administration. Here's the recent NATO meeting that President Trump attended and notice what's coming out of their mouths!

CBSN reports from a welcoming ceremony at NATO: *"Today we have achieved an unprecedented period of 'Peace and Security.' We are here today so* *that the future generations can enjoy that same 'Peace and Security.' We owe our success to our community, to our soul, to our ability to change as our world has changed.*

And above all to the men and women of our armed forces who put themselves in harms way to keep us safe. Some gave their ultimate sacrifice. So, to the thousands of our soldiers, sailors, and air crew serving in operations around the world, let me say, we owe you and your families a great debt of gratitude. You embody what NATO is. Your skill, your professionalism, your determination, you are what makes 'Peace and Security' possible. You allow us to look to the future with confidence."[8]

Now for those of you wondering why the world leaders in conjunction with the United Nations keep saying that phrase, 'Peace and Security' well, believe it or not, I discovered the reason why when we were shooting the documentary on the Seal Judgements when we visited the U.N. As it turns out, that is one of the three pillars as to why the United Nations exist, "To provide the world with 'Peace and Security'!" Listen to it for yourself!" We recorded the U.N. lady saying it.

The video opens with the view of the Statue of Liberty and then a panoramic view of New York City. As Pastor Billy walks up to the United Nations building, he passes the flags of all the nations that stood next to the entry. There was a statue of a gun that had the barrel twisted in a knot. There was a plaque that read 'One child, one teacher, one book, and one pen can change the world.' Written by Malala Yousafzai, United National Youth Assembly, 12 July 2013. He then enters the building to walk down its halls.

State of Palestine: *"Justice for the Palestinian people, including the Palestine refugees, leaving Palestine to Israel seeking 'Peace and Security' as well as the goal of Israeli peace."*

Benjamin Netanyahu: *"I don't seek applause. I seek the security and peace and prosperity, and the future of the Jewish state."*

John Kerry: *"That's what we were standing up for. Israel's future as a Jewish and Democratic state, living side by side in 'Peace and Security' with its neighbors."*

President Trump: *"In nearly seven decades since Harry Truman spoke those words, the NATO has been the word of international 'Peace and Security'..."*

Now here's what's wild, while touring the U.N. the tour guide used that exact phrase on several occasions. So, obviously I couldn't resist. I asked her about her phrase 'Peace and Security'. This is her answer.

Pastor Billy: *"I have a question. The phrase you had used earlier about that room, 'Peace and Security', is that a phrase? Is that something you came up with or is it a joint effort? Just curious. 'Peace and Security', you hear that a lot."*

Tour guide: *"Right."*

Pastor Billy: *"Did the U.N. come up with that?"*

Tour guide: *"'Peace and Security' is one of the Three Pillars of the U.N."*

So, as you just heard 'Peace and Security' is the first of the Three Pillars of the U.N. 'Peace and Security' "Development" and 'Human Rights'. Two thousand years ago the Bible told us that exact phrase would be used before sudden destruction comes upon them. Can you believe it? Once again, The Bible gets it exactly right.[9]

I'll say it again, not "Joy and Prosperity" not "Deliverance and Happiness" but wonder of wonders it just so happens to be the exact Biblical phrase, right now, that the Bible warned would come upon the scene in the Last Days, "Peace and Security." And when you see people all over the planet specifically crying out that phrase, straight from the goals of the U.N. be it Trump, Kushner, Prince William, Macron, whoever, what did the Bible say would happen? BANG! Sudden destruction will come upon them and they will not escape! You'll be in the 7-year Tribulation! What more does God have to do to get our attention? It's all lined up! The Lord's Return is getting close and we better wake up! This is why, out of love, God has given us this update on *The Final Countdown: Tribulation Rising* concerning the Jewish People & the Antichrist to show us that the 7-year Tribulation is near, and the Return of Jesus Christ is rapidly approaching. That's why Jesus Himself said...

Luke 21:28 "When these things begin to take place, stand up and lift up your heads, because your redemption is drawing near."

Like it or not, we are headed for The Final Countdown. The signs of the 7-year Tribulation are Rising all around us! It's time to WAKE UP! So, the point is this. If you're reading this today and you're not a Christian, then I beg you, please, heed these signs, heed these warnings, give your life to Jesus now! You don't want to be here when God pours out His Judgment upon this wicked and rebellious planet! It's the worst time in the history of mankind, so horrible that unless God shortened the timeframe the entire human race would be destroyed! The only way to escape is through Jesus! Take the way out now before it's too late. GET SAVED TODAY! But, if you're reading this today and you are a Christian, then it's high time we stop goofing off and getting distracted with this world. Let's get busy working together sharing the Gospel with as many as we can! Let's be that faithful remnant, in these Last Days, amen?

Chapter Nineteen

The Jewish People & Their International Antisemitism

The **16ᵗʰ End Time Prophecy** concerning **The Jewish People** letting us know we're living in the Last Days is that **Israel Would Face another Holocaust.** This is the horrible news we see in the Book of Zechariah. But don't take my word for it. Let's listen to God's.

Zechariah 13:8-9 "In the whole land," declares the LORD, "two-thirds will be struck down and perish; yet one-third will be left in it. This third I will bring into the fire; I will refine them like silver and test them like gold. They will call on my name and I will answer them; I will say, 'They are my people,' and they will say, 'The LORD is our God.'"

As we saw before, this passage tells us that one day, the good news is, the Jewish people will eventually lose their blindness like Paul talked about in **Romans 11,** and they will get right with God. But the bad news is that two-thirds of them are going to be struck down by the antichrist, and that happens halfway into the 7-year tribulation when he goes up into the rebuilt Jewish Temple and declares himself to be god. He shows his true colors because the Jewish people are never going to worship him as god, so he seeks to slaughter them for it. This event was what Jesus was talking about in Matthew 24.

Matthew 24:15-21 "So when you see standing in the holy place 'the abomination that causes desolation, spoken of through the prophet Daniel – let the reader understand – then let those who are in Judea flee to the mountains. Let no one on the roof of his house go down to take anything out of the house. Let no one in the field go back to get his cloak. How dreadful it will be in those days for pregnant women and nursing mothers! Pray that your flight will not take place in winter or on the Sabbath. For then there will be great distress, unequaled from the beginning of the world until now – and never to be equaled again."

This is when the slaughter takes place. Now, here's the point. If this slaughter of the Jewish people by the antichrist, 2/3rds of them, is talking about the global number of Jews, there are about 15 million Jews in the world right now. So, if you do the math that number would be about 10 million people! Which means, it's an even bigger holocaust than what Hitler did! Almost double! That's what is coming for the Jewish people! It's horrible! It's sad! And this is why we need to witness to them now! But again, the question is, "Is there any sign of this horrible event, another Jewish Holocaust, ever happening again in our lifetime, especially when WWII wasn't that long ago, with all the evils that Hitler did?" Unfortunately, yes. Anti-Semitism is not just on the rise, it is at an all-time high all around the world!

TURKEY: "Turkey's President Erdogan issues veiled threat of Jewish genocide, referring to a statement of Muhammad about Muslims killing Jews." He tweeted out, 'Those who think they own Jerusalem better know that tomorrow they won't even be able to hide behind trees' which is a reference to a widely circulated Muslim prophecy about hunting down and killing every Jew.

The prophecy says in part, 'The last hour would not come unless the Muslims will fight against the Jews and the Muslims would kill them until the Jews would hide themselves behind a stone or a tree and the stone or a tree would say: Muslim, or the servant of Allah, there is a Jew behind me; come and kill him.'

Then Erdogan went on to say that, 'The US is responsible for the bloodshed in Jerusalem following President Donald Trump's decision to recognize Jerusalem as the capital of Israel. Those who turn Jerusalem into a prison for Muslims and members of other religions will never be able to clear the blood off their hands. President Trumps' statement does not bind us, nor the world of Islam.'"

THE PLO: "Palestinian officials and groups have been very clear about their desire to destroy Israel, but many in the media won't report on it. For instance, the Palestine Liberation Organization (PLO) President, Mahmoud Abbas recently tweeted: 'Our goal is the end of Israel. We don't want peace. We want war and victory.' And as of the writing of this article, not a single major US news outlet had reported on the tweet. Yet, Israeli Prime Minister Benjamin Netanyahu not only pointed out that the tweet was inspired by a quote from Yasser Arafat, Abbas' predecessor, but this talk of peace is a lie. Let's see who is telling the truth.

PA Chairman Abbas: *"Mr. President, I affirm to you that we are raising our children and our grandchildren in a culture of peace."*

Israeli Prime Minister Netanyahu: *"I heard President Abbas yesterday say that they teach, Palestinians teach their children peace. That's unfortunately not true."*

The following broadcasts are from the official Palestinian Authority TV controlled by the Palestinian Authority.

Official PA TV January 20, 2017. PMW Palwatch.org: Children are gathered around a table doing a skit for an audience. The words they are saying is as follows:

Children: *"My rock, my rock has turned into an AK-47 (rifle)."*

PA TV Host: *"Bravo!"*

Child: *"As we slaughtered them in your streets, Beirut, for you Yasser Arafat, for you we shall die. Tomorrow we will take our vengeance, and their leader will be carried in a coffin. We, Fatah, are a storm, and our blood is food for the revolution."*

Another child: *"Fight the Jews, kill them, and defeat them."*

A little girl: *"To war that will smash the oppression and destroy the Zionist's soul."*

Another little boy repeats: *"To war that will smash the oppression and destroy the Zionist's soul."* It will be repeated over and over.

PA TV Host: *"Bravo!"*

Another child: *"Pick up your rifle, resist and terrify them. Destroy, shock, burn and set fire."*

Another little girl proclaims: *"O Sons of Zion, O most evil among creations, O barbaric monkeys, wretched pigs."* This is repeated over and over again.

Then another child: *"Allah's enemies, the sons of pigs. They raped the women in the city squares. Where is the nation of Islam and the Jihad fighters?"*

PA TV Host: *"Bravo, applause!*

Satan: *"I've built my plan on the burning hate and loathing of Muhammad and his supporters, that fills the hearts of the Jews."*

A little girl: *"Our enemy, Zion, is Satan with a tail."* And this is repeated over and over.

PA TV Host: *"Thank you very much. I really like this poem. We say that Palestine exists, and Palestine will return to us, and there is no such thing as Israel. Bravo!"*[1]

Still other reports are saying, *"The Palestinians goal is to wipe Israel off the map."* And apparently, *"Selling land to Jews will get Palestinians killed."* *"A Palestinian man suspected of selling land to Jews was recently murdered near his home in central Israel. His father was murdered 30 years ago under similar circumstances."*

IRAN: Iran's Supreme Leader, Ayatollah Ali Khamenei, on Saturday once again called for Israel's destruction. He said, "The only cure for Israel is annihilation." The latest provocation came in a series of tweets in which he launched a tirade against the Jewish state and called to arm the Palestinian Arabs in Judea and Samaria. "This barbaric, wolf-like and infanticidal regime of Israel, which spares no crime, has no cure but to be annihilated," read one tweet.

This is certainly not the first time that Khamenei has called for Israel's destruction. He previously said on Twitter that the Israeli government was 'the most wicked terrorist' in the world and Israel was, 'an illegitimate and blank regime,' and further called the United States a 'smiling enemy' that is not to be trusted."

EGYPT: A TV Host from Egypt stated, "The Jews are using the Holocaust to suck the blood of Germans." The video footage of host Gaber al-Karmoty first appeared on the Egyptian ON TV network and it showed him going on an anti-Semitic rant and in another video, he celebrates on air the downing of an Israeli jet by handing out chocolates.

MEMRI TV: *"I am happy. I was happy yesterday, but I was very worried about the war on terrorism in Egypt. But today, I'd like to express my joy at the downing of the airplane. Is it possible to show the video of the downing of the Israeli plane? This has been on my mind. Israel was, remains, and forever will be the No. 1 enemy of Egypt and the Arab world, regardless of all the diplomatic matter, and so on and so forth.*

But I wanted to say is that I am happy. Since I like to do things in an 'outside the box' manner, we sent brother Khattab to buy a little something to celebrate the Israeli airplane's crash in Syria. I hope that it was really the Syrian army that downed the plane, and that this will continue to happen. I would like to hand out these chocolates. Come over, people, so that the cameras can capture this. Come over, chief. Go ahead and take one, chief. This is just a small token. Everybody, take a chocolate to mark the downing of the Israeli airplane."[2]

He then lamented the fact that publishing cartoons of the Prophet Mohammad was permissible but that the Holocaust was "off limits." The Egyptian media is rife with anti-Semitic discourse."

HOLLAND: Dutch Soccer Fans Chant "Jews Burn the Best" as well as, "My mother burned Jews in the SS," during a weekend match. Dutch media revealed the chants also included, "Hamas, Hamas, Jews to the gas" and a longer one filmed by someone in the stands showed the fans roaring, "My father was in the commandos, my mother was in the (Nazi) SS, together they burned Jews, because Jews burn the best." Anti-Semitism has been rampant in Holland, but this new incident has taken the Jew hatred to a whole new level. Then in another incident Pro-ISIS demonstrators call for 'Death to Jews' including other chants advocating for 'dirty Jews from the sewers to be killed.'

BELGIUM: Belgian cafe posts sign banning Jews from entering store. The sign in Turkish and French announced, 'Dogs are allowed in this establishment, but Jews are not under any circumstances.' Along with the sign, the cafe owners hung a Palestinian flag and a kaffieh, a Palestinian shawl. The Israeli flag was also in the window, but it was crossed out with a giant red 'X'. Then an Orthodox Jewish woman stated that another shop owner in Antwerp refused to sell her merchandise 'out of protest.'

SPAIN: Videos are being spread around Spain of Muslim women stabbing dolls of Orthodox Jews, calling for genocide and the murder of all Jewish people. One video featured three visibly Muslim women chanting, "Catch and kill all the Jews. Strike them and make the Jews bleat like animals. Exterminate the Zionists. Exterminate them, exterminate them, the world will be better off." As they chanted, one of the women in the video stabbed a doll in the image of an Orthodox Jew with a knife, giving a physical representation to their shrill call to murder.

And so, is it any surprise with this behavior that in Europe there have been many anti-Semitic murders over the past few years. In fact, a recent poll conducted found that 29% of respondents in Spain have anti-Semitic attitudes, with 48% agreeing with the statement: 'The Jews still talk too much about what happened to them in the Holocaust.' And it's this kind of behavior that prompted Chief Rabbi Meir Bar-Hen to declare, 'Europe is lost. His community is doomed' and 'Don't think we're here for good, and I encourage them to buy property in Israel. This place is lost. Don't repeat the mistake of Algerian Jews, of Venezuelan Jews. "Better get out early than late" because authorities in Spain do not want to confront this.

FRANCE: France's Multiculturalist Agenda Makes Jews Pack their Bags. As more French Jews face anti-Semitic attacks, many are leaving for Israel. Most of the attacks have come from Muslims, whether immigrants or French-born, many of whom have not assimilated into French society – if not rejecting French society entirely. Compounding the dangerous situation, France's left-wing government refuses to acknowledge the scope of this crisis, apparently more afraid of losing Muslim votes, they depend on, than in defending France's half-million Jews.

A poll conducted found that 74% of French Jews are considering leaving France and one report said, "It's more accurate to say that French Jews are fleeing France rather than just moving to Israel." The Jewish people are not only being murdered there but they are the object of chants such as, 'gas the Jews' and 'kill the Jews.' In fact, a French deputy mayor even said she was opposed to changing the name of a locality under her jurisdiction. The town is named 'Matajudios,' which literally means 'kill Jews' or 'death to the Jews.' She said, "It's absurd, this name has existed for ages. No one means to harm the Jews."

Then a French-Jewish Holocaust survivor was found dead, burned in Paris, and everything suggests it was an antisemitic crime. "An 85-year-old French-Jewish Holocaust survivor was found dead on Friday in an incinerated apartment in Paris, and suicide has been ruled out. The victim had reportedly filed police complaints against a local resident who had threatened to burn her."

SWEDEN: "Swedish MP Says Jews Aren't True Swedes." Bjorn Soder, deputy speaker of the Swedish parliament, says, "Jews should abandon their identity if they wish to be considered Swedes." He said they need to do this, 'In order to assimilate.' Then, "A Swedish parliamentary candidate suggests deporting all Jews from Israel." Oldoz Javidi, a candidate for the Swedish parliament suggested transferring Israeli Jews to achieve peace.

Javidi has Iranian roots and is a candidate with the Feminist Initiative party. Swedish Jews criticized her words as anti-Semitic saying, "Moving Jews against their will to solve a problem? Sounds like a final solution to me." Then the leader of Sweden's Jewish community said, "This is exactly like in 1930s Germany from which their grandfather had fled."

It goes on to say that rise in anti-Semitism has been felt in France, Germany, Belgium and Holland and the overall number of anti-Semitic incidents in the world jumped 383% with Europe showing a 436% increase. And so is it any wonder that the Swedish government recently officially recognized the Palestinian Authority (PA) as the "state of Palestine", leading Israel to recall its ambassador there.

SWITZERLAND: Violent attacks committed against Jews in Zurich. In Zurich, a German man threatened three Orthodox Jews with a knife. According to the Swiss daily Blick, the assailant shouted anti-Semitic insults while pursuing his victims with his weapon. A bystander stopped the man, who was detained by the Swiss police and then released.

GERMANY: Germany has experienced a wave of violent anti-Semitic attacks. Three Germans and six Syrians were detained for assaulting a Jew in a park. The unidentified 19-year-old victim was wearing a Star of David.

IRELAND: Ireland begins legal steps to ban Israeli settlements from selling goods, calling it a crime to do business with them. This was just recently.

O24 News Reports: *"Irish MP's want to criminalize trade with Israeli settlements. This bill's sponsor assures that the law is on their side. This is the Control of Economic Activity (Occupied Territories) Bill 2018. Ireland is entitled to end its support which the EU says are in violation of International Law. Simply saying that if we are sure that certain goods are being produced as a result of war crimes, we should not be trading in them."*[3]

ENGLAND: UK: Labour candidate Nasreen Khan says, "Hitler wasn't the bad guy" and "What have the Jews done good in this world?" Writing under a video titled "The Palestine you need to know." she said, "It's such a shame that the history teachers in our schools never taught us this, but they are the first to start brainwashing us and our children into thinking the bad guy was Hitler."

Then she said, "Stop beating a dead horse! The Jews have reaped the rewards of playing victims. Enough is enough," and that there were "worse people than Hitler in this world." Of course, Miss Khan is a Muslim and when she was questioned about the comments, she added: "No, I'm not a Nazi, I'm an ordinary British Muslim that has an opinion." Then there was a Neo-Nazis Planned Rally in London's Jewish Neighborhood. The group calling itself 'Liberate Stamford Hill,' says the rally is to oppose the 'Jewification' of the UK.

In fact, surveys show a spike in British anti-Semitism in more than half of the U.K. Jews fear for the future of their community. This is because polls indicate, 23% of Britons, are 'unwilling' to have a Jew in the family. Similar numbers found in Italy, Germany, and Austria, now show 45% of all Britons hold anti-Semitic views. In fact, even as far back as 2014, London suffered its worst ever month for hate crimes, 95% of which were directed against Jews.

Britain is at a tipping point: Unless anti-Semitism is met with zero tolerance, it will grow, and British Jews will increasingly question their place in their own country. Recently Jewish kids were even barred from entering a UK store outside of London telling them, 'No Jews, no Jews.' And British Chief Whip Michael Gove says, "Europe has forgotten the Holocaust" and "Far from eradicating the hatred of Jews, anti-Semitism is now considered 'chic' by some," and that, "This virus has spread across Europe." He also noted the firebombing of a synagogue in Germany, and a sign allowing dogs inside a restaurant but restricting Jews in Belgium, cautioning: "We must all remember where this leads."

UNITED NATIONS: The U.N. is set to fund a blacklist of companies which do business in Israel. It's called BDS (Boycott, Divestment and Sanctions) which means, American taxpayers can expect to find themselves funding it in the very near future. U.S. taxpayers account for 22% of the U.N.'s regular operating budget, plus billions of dollars more in voluntary contributions to the various parts of the U.N. each year.

As one person stated, "I have not seen a single mainstream news article about these UN General Assembly resolutions that were just passed." Israel's Ambassador to the UN, Danny Danon said that, "When the UN marks Jewish businesses so that they can be boycotted, it reminds us of dark times in history." The U.N. not only repeatedly condemns Israel, but won't censure Hamas, and they even put out a resolution that 'Rejects Jewish Connection to Jerusalem.'

Israeli Prime Minister Benjamin Netanyahu said in a statement regarding that, "The theater of the absurd continues at the UN. Today UNESCO adopted its second decision this year denying the Jewish people's connection to the Temple Mount, our holiest site for over three thousand years. What's next? A UNESCO decision denying the connection between peanut butter and jelly? Batman and Robin? Rock and roll?" In fact, the U.N. continues to make the most insane anti-Semitic rulings.

Stand With Us Reports: This Year's Top 10 Most Insane Anti-Israel Moments at the UN.

10. Middle East countries called out in UN after accusing Israel of "apartheid." *"Once upon a time, the Middle East was full of Jews. Algeria had 140,000 Jews. Algeria, where are your Jews? Egypt used to have 75,000 Jews. Where are your Jews? Syria, you had tens of thousands of Jews. Where are your Jews? Iraq, you*

had over 135,000 Jews. Where are your Jews? Mr. President, where is the real apartheid?"

9. The U.N. women's rights commission condemned Israel as the world's only violator of women's rights...and if that wasn't enough... The U.N. also elected Saudi Arabia to the Women's Rights Commission. *"Having obtained the necessary majority, I declare, elected from the Asia-Pacific states, Iraq, Republic of Korea, Japan, Turkmenistan, Saudi Arabia to the commission on the status of women."*

8. 16 U.N agencies signed an agreement with Palestinians to spend $18 million on legal attacks against Israel.

7. U.N. Palestine Rapporteur Michael Lynk issued a report advocating an economic boycott of Israeli companies.

6. The U.N.'s World Health Organization named Israel as the only violator in the world of mental, physical and environmental health. Then, at the behest of Syria, they deleted parts of a report on Israel in the Golan Heights because it was positive to Israel.

5. The U.N. claims domestic violence against Palestinian women is because of Israel. *"And the blockade of the Gaza Strip recognizing a clear link between prolonged occupation and gender-based violence, the gendered impact of the occupation."* Then she is asked, *"In other words what you are saying is as follows, when Palestinian men beat their wives it's Israel's fault?"*

4. The U.N. General Assembly adopted 20 resolutions against Israel and 6 resolutions on the rest of the world combined.

3. In 2017, UNESCO adopted a resolution recognizing Hebron as a Palestinian world heritage site. Hebron is the second holiest city in Judaism and home to the Tomb of the Patriarchs and Matriarchs of the Jewish religion.

2. UNRWA launched a global campaign against Israel using fake photos of Palestinian children. They were really photos of Syrian children. UNRWA used pictures purporting to be from Gaza but were actually from the civil war in Syria.

1. The U.N. blacklists companies operating in the Jewish Quarter of Jerusalem and Jewish communities over the 1949 armistice line. The blacklist is designed to inflame tensions and lead to boycott of Jewish businesses. It's time to hold the U.N. accountable and stop their double standards and blatant anti-Semitism against Israel![4]

- "Wave of anti-Israel protests sweeps countries worldwide."
- "At least 20,000 people demonstrated in London's Hyde Park calling for an end to 'Israeli aggression.'"
- "Thousands protests against Israel in South Africa."
- "Latin Americans renew their protests against Israel."
- "Melbourne protestors rage against Israeli strikes."
- "Jordanians stage massive pro-Hamas rally."
- "In New York: Hundreds protest against Israel."
- "Air France omitted Tel Aviv and Jerusalem from in-flight map displays but showed Gaza and the West Bank."
- "Israel was wiped off the map in Middle East Atlases but clearly labels the West bank."

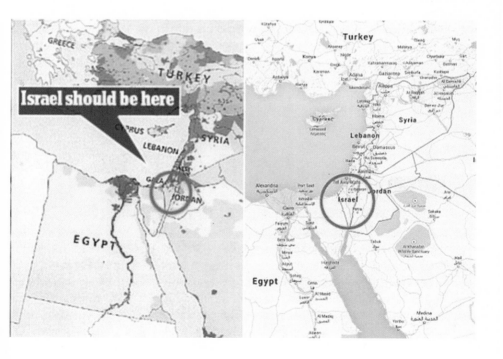

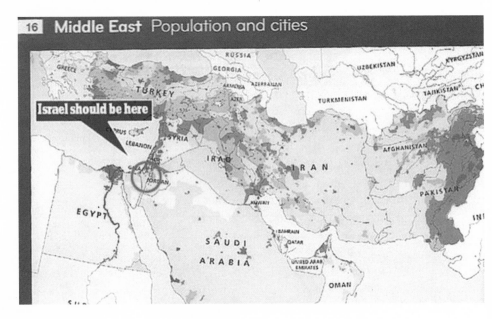

Middle East Population and cities

"Brazil Omits Israel from Passports of Jerusalem-Born Citizens."
- "The United States, Canada and France also omit Israel from passports for holders born in Jerusalem, stating only the city's name."[5]

Can you believe this? It's all happening right now! The Bible said in the Last Days, the antichrist will arise and seek to kill 2/3rds of the Jewish people, and it looks like the planet is ripe for it once again, in our lifetime, even after what Hitler did!! And you might be wondering, "How? Why? Why is this happening and why doesn't it seem to ever turn around and why is it getting worse, even on a global scale? Let me give you a few reasons why.

The **1st reason** why antisemitism is growing is because People are Being Paid to Hate the Jews.

This is yet another thing the media refuses to report on! *"Terrorists responsible for the murder of two Israeli families and two rabbis get more than 10 million shekels each from the Palestinian Authority"* Folks, that's over 3 million dollars apiece! Nineteen-year-old Omar al-Abed, was convicted in February of murdering three members of the Salomon family in their home last July and is expected to be paid a pension totaling $3,485,812. Karem Lufti Fatahi Razek, a gunman in the attack that saw Naama and Eitam Henkin shot dead in front of their children in Samaria is expected to be paid a total of $3,106,367. They're becoming millionaires to kill the Jewish People! No wonder anti-Semitism is on the rise! In fact, if the terrorist survives, he gets the money, but if he dies, his family gets the money! So, it's a guaranteed payout! In fact, one recent headline stated, *"Payments to 'martyr' families now equals half of the Palestinian Authority's foreign budgetary aid."* The new budget allocates $190,869,166 for payments to so-called "families of martyrs," up from $174,630,296 allocated the previous year. The families are defined as those with members who were "killed or wounded in the struggle against Zionism," including those killed while committing attacks against Israelis, or in any other context by an Israeli. NOW, here's where it's coming from. They get the money from donors, the U.N. and the foreign aid given to the Palestinians. And this is why President Trump recently signed a law reducing American aid to the P.A. until the body stops financially rewarding terrorists and attackers. But Mahmoud Abbas still insists repeatedly that he will not stop doing do so, *"Even if we are left with one penny, we are going to use it for paying the salaries to the Martyrs and prisoners of war,"* he declared. And the latest figure that just came out is that the Palestinian Authority is expected to pay "1.2 Billion Shekels for Terrorism in 2018" which is about $319 million in what's being called, "pay to slay" salaries. And you wonder why there's a rise in global antisemitism?[6]

The **2nd reason** why antisemitism is growing is because **People are Glamorizing Hitler Who Hated the Jews.**

This is really wild! Not to mention Dumb! 'Mein Kampf' takes off in Europe, 70 years after Hitler's death. It has now become a bestseller, while an Italian newspaper is distributing copies to readers. "Mein Kampf" is making a comeback. Adolf Hitler's notorious autobiography is gaining popularity in Europe, having become a bestseller upon the expiration of the German state copyright that was initially used to prohibit reprinting it. Jewish groups in Italy were not happy saying, *"Any interest among European readers in 'Mein Kampf' is enough to raise suspicions, as anti-Semitism on the continent has been on the rise again in recent years."* And now new copies of the book have become available online throughout the world. Hindu nationalists use it as a self-help book in India, the Greek neo-Nazi Golden Dawn party has stocked copies of it in Athens, and a comic-book edition of "Mein Kampf" is available in Japan. Now we even have this, "Hitler Clothing Store Causes Stir in Cairo."

The front of the store bears Hitler's name and even uses a swastika as its logo. Store owner Osama Farouk said, *"I adore the name and the logo, and decided to put them on the front of my shop. Why are people so angry?"*

Yet this cannot be written off as simple ignorance. *"Many Muslims joined the Nazi ranks at the behest of their Imams, and the Palestinian Arab leadership was closely allied with Hitler."* For years Hitler's autobiography, Mein Kampf, has been a best seller in the Arab world, not because local Arabs are unaware of who he was, but because the Nazi ideology speaks to the Islamist mindset. *"This is why it's no surprise that Hitler is popular in many Muslim countries and Mein Kampf is a bestseller in Turkey, Egypt, and Bangladesh, where street vendors are selling copies of Mein Kampf as well as pirated copies of The Audacity of Hope by Barack Obama. And don't forget, Mein Kampf means 'my struggle' or as they take it, 'my jihad.'"* And now you can even get a 'Holocaust' cocktail in Belarus, which is East of Poland, and 'Hitler' ice cream in India.

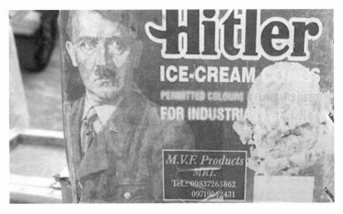

And if you can believe this, "Hitler's *Mein Kampf* is now a German bestseller, again." *"The first reprint sold 85,000 copies, topping nonfiction list and is heading for its sixth print run."* *"It has flown off the shelves since its release."* For 70 years, it was not allowed to be republished out of respect for victims of the Nazis and to prevent incitement of hatred. But now it's become a runaway bestseller again. Now, school kids in Berlin are told 'Hitler was good.' And you wonder why anti-Semitism is on the rise in the world?[7]

The **3rd reason** why antisemitism isn't stopping around the world is because **People are Being Brainwashed to Hate the Jews.**

As we saw earlier with Abbas and Netanyahu, a whole new generation of kids are being brainwashed to hate the Jews, in just about every way you can think of. But let me give you some more examples. Not only do we have footage of children being brainwashed to hate the Jews at Terror Rallies, as you can see

below, but we even have a, "How To Stab A Jew" video becoming a big hit on Palestinian social media."[8] as you can see on the next page.

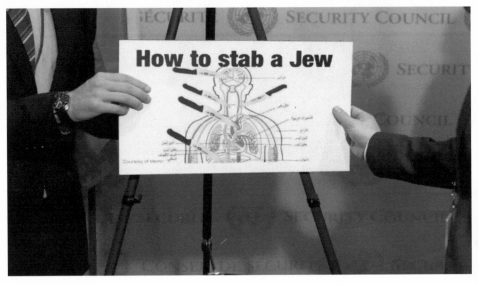

Then a video game was released called "The Liberation of Palestine," which encourages gamers to 'liberate Palestine" through any means necessary choosing armed resistance over diplomacy.' Then a Kuwaiti Muslim

Brotherhood leader said, *"Every Muslim mother must nurse her children on hatred of the sons of Zion so a new generation will erase them from the face of the earth. We yearn for death and Martyrdom."* Then another video surfaced showing a play at a preschool in the Gaza Strip where children dressed up as commandos and performed a mock hostage-taking situation and execution of an Israeli soldier. And believe it or not, *"The UK is Funding Textbooks That Teach Children to Become Jihadists."* It emerged last year that the British government gave £20 million to the effort. For instance, a science textbook intended for 12-year-olds teaches them Newton's second law of motion in the following way: *"During the first Palestinian uprising, Palestinian youths used slingshots to*

confront the soldiers of the Zionist Occupation and defend themselves from their treacherous bullets. What is the relationship between the elongation of the slingshot's rubber and the tensile strength affecting it?" And is it any surprise that, a Teacher in the UK Planned to Raise an 'Army' of Jihadi Children. *"A teacher in Islamic schools in the UK was radicalizing his students, preparing them to assist him in massive terror attacks on 30 targets across London including showing them videos of beheadings."* Speaking of which, *"A Palestinian teacher was teaching Muslim kids how to perform beheadings on their toys."*

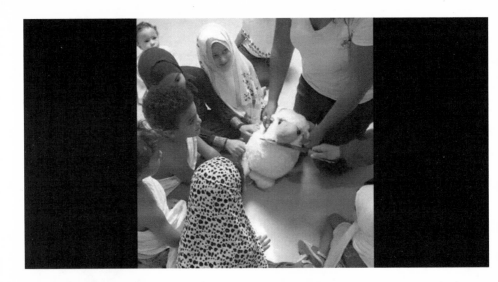

And another video showed, a child dressed as a Jihadi beheading his Teddy Bear. The pre-school aged child is seen beheading a white fluffy stuffed animal with a hunting knife while a man off camera encourages him in front of an ISIS flag. The child smiles at the camera, and appears to be encouraged by the man's words, returning to his task with renewed vigor. When the teddy bear's head is successfully removed, the child lifts his knife into the air and the man off camera calls out "Allahu Akbar!" And speaking of small kids, how would you like to have this as your child's Kindergarten graduation ceremony?

And you wonder why anti-Semitism is on the rise around the world? So, here's the point. The Bible said in the Last Days, the antichrist will arise and seek to kill 2/3^{rds} of the Jewish people, and it looks like the planet is ripe for it once again, in our lifetime, even after what Hitler did!! AND it looks like the antichrist is preparing the next generation of kids to pull the trigger with all these brainwashing techniques! In fact, if you think about it, maybe we just saw some of the actual kids who are going to grow up and become a part of the antichrist slaughter of 2/3^{rds} of the Jewish people in the 7-year Tribulation. This is why the Jewish people are saying, right now, that things are just as bad as they were in Hitler's day and *"It is time for a New Exodus from Europe!"* *"They need to start fleeing again!"*

BBC Executive: *"I've never felt so uncomfortable being a Jew in the UK as in the last 12 months,"* and another headline said, *"We are looking at the beginning of a Holocaust."* And partly because. *"A New Poll Shows Fading Memory of Holocaust, Anti-Semitism Throughout Europe."*

More than 7,000 people across Europe were interviewed, including people in Austria, France, Germany, Great Britain, Hungary, Poland and Sweden. The report maintained that a third of Europeans know just a little or nothing at all about the mass murder of six million Jews during the Holocaust and Second World War. And perhaps most striking was the young people between the ages of 18-34 – with 20% saying they have never heard of the Holocaust. The report shared how Americans don't fare any better, with 20% of American millennials also reporting they have never heard of the Holocaust. But this is why, right now, German Jews are being warned by their leaders against wearing skullcaps in Europe. And this is why, of all people, even Madonna stated, *"The atmosphere of intolerance in Europe feels like Nazi Germany and that anti-Semitism is at an all-time high."* She went on to state that France is now "completely gone."

Another article stated that, "Anti-Semitism has reached levels not seen since World War Two," and this is why Europe's leading Rabbi is saying, *"Jews Must Begin Carrying Guns. We need to recognize the warning signs of anti-Semitism, racism, and intolerance that once again threatens Europe."* In other words, it's starting all over again, just like with Hitler. Another Holocaust![9]

Who would've thought? Except the Christian! The Bible told us this would happen when you're living in the Last Days. And it's happening now! Again, here's the point. If this all happens during the 7-year Tribulation, then how much closer is the rapture of the Church which takes place prior to the 7-year tribulation? We're getting so close it's time to start doing that Rapture Practice!

This is why, out of love, God has given us this update on *The Final Countdown: Tribulation Rising* concerning the Jewish People & the Antichrist to show us that the 7-year Tribulation is near, and the Return of Jesus Christ is rapidly approaching. And that's why Jesus Himself said...

Luke 21:28 "When these things begin to take place, stand up and lift up your heads, because your redemption is drawing near."

Like it or not, we are headed for The Final Countdown. The signs of the 7-year Tribulation are Rising all around us! It's time to Wake up! If you're reading this today and you're not a Christian, then I beg you, please, heed these signs, heed these warnings, give your life to Jesus now! You don't want to be here when God pours out His Judgment upon this wicked and rebellious planet! It's the worst time in the history of mankind, so horrible that unless God shortened the time frame the entire human race would be destroyed! The only way to escape is through Jesus! Take the way out now before it's too late. Get saved today.

But, if you're reading this today and you are a Christian, then it's high time we stop goofing off and getting distracted with this world. Let's get busy working together sharing the Gospel with as many as we can! Let's be that faithful remnant, in these Last Days, exercising our privileged duty as Christians to speak up against evil, like this guy did.

He's a Jewish guy who had had enough of the Muslim call to prayer in Jerusalem, 5 times a day, as they blast it over the loudspeakers. So, every time their call went out, he has his own response. He went opposite of the Temple Mount and blasted them with his own response! The Jewish Shema, or the Jewish Call to Prayer! When it was prayer time for the Muslims and their prayers were sent out over the loud speakers, he went to the opposite side of town, facing the Dome of the Rock, with his own loud speakers and proceeded to pray to God in his Hebrew tongue.[10]

THE SHEMA

'Hear O Israel.
The Lord our God is Lord alone.
You shall love the Lord your God with all your heart and with all
your soul and with all your might.

Keep these words that I am commanding you today in your
heart.
Recite them to your children and talk about them when you are
at home and when you are away, when you lie down and when you
rise.

Bind them as a sign on your hand. Fix them as an emblem on
your forehead.
And write them on the doorposts of your house and on your
gates

Take that! That guy's got GUTS! How about us? Will we speak up? Are we speaking up? Will we be our own loudspeaker here in America against oppression, including the oppression against the Jewish People? We need to be doing two things at this time in the Last Days. One, speaking up on behalf of the Jewish People and their community remembering the words of Martin Niemoller. He was a Lutheran minister who lived in Hitler's Germany during the 1930s and

1940s and his words serves as a warning to us today:

"In Germany they came first for the Communists, and I didn't speak up because I wasn't a Communist. Then they came for the Jews, and I didn't speak up because I wasn't a Jew. Then they came for the trade unionists, and I didn't speak up because I wasn't a trade unionist. Then they came for the Catholics, and I didn't speak up because I was a Protestant. Then they came for me, and by that time no one was left to speak up." [11]

Whether you realize it or not, we too are considered the "infidel" by the Muslim terrorists. The "people of the book" are both Jews and Christians." You don't think they won't come for us? And Two, we need to tell as many people as we can about Jesus, including the Muslims or Jews so they don't have to experience another Holocaust that is coming. If they would only accept Jesus as their Lord and Savior today. That's the whole point of why we're still here and that's what we need to be doing in the meantime. Amen?

Chapter Twenty

The Jewish People & Their U.S. Antisemitism

We saw the horrible news that even after what Hitler did not that long ago, with the original Holocaust, that another one is coming to the planet upon the Jewish People, very possibly even bigger than the last one! The Bible says two-thirds of the Jewish People are going to be struck down by the Antichrist. We saw proof of that anti-Semitic mindset coming again in the international scene with the countries around the world. **People are Being Paid to Hate the Jews, People are Glamorizing Hitler Who Hated the Jews,** and **People are Being Brainwashed to Hate the Jews.** Even young pre-school aged kids are being taught to cut the heads off Jewish people and stab them because they're the supposed enemy of all! It's sick and crazy but it's the mindset that's coming back to the planet just in time for the 7-tear Tribulation Holocaust! But hey, it's a good thing we don't see any signs of this happening here in America! Yeah right! Here's your illusion! How I wish that were true! The Bible says at one point the whole world is going to come against the Jewish People! But don't take my word for it. Let's listen to God's.

Matthew 24:4-13 "Jesus answered: 'Watch out that no one deceives you. For many will come in My Name, claiming, 'I am the Christ,' and will deceive many. You will hear of wars and rumors of wars but see to it that you are not alarmed. Such things must happen, but the end is still to come. Nation will rise against nation, and kingdom against kingdom. There will be famines and earthquakes in various places. All these are the beginning of birth pains. Then you will be handed over to be persecuted and put to death, and you will be hated by all nations because of me. At that time many will turn away from the faith and will betray and hate each other, and many false prophets will appear and deceive many people. Because of the increase of wickedness, the love of most will grow cold, but he who stands firm to the end will be saved."

Why? Because God's not done with the Jewish people and He's going to sovereignly protect one-third of them via the Archangel Michael! Jesus tells them that right after they see the abomination of desolation, when the Antichrist goes up into the rebuilt Jewish Temple and declares himself to be god at the midpoint of the 7-year Tribulation, to flee to the mountains and don't even go back to your house or field. Get nothing, just run, because this is when the Antichrist goes after the Jewish people and slaughters two-thirds of them as Zechariah says. But again, God is going to sovereignly protect one-third, they're going to make it to the end via the Archangel Michael! God's not done with them. He always has a remnant!

Revelation 12:6-8 "The woman fled into the desert to a place prepared for her by God, where she might be taken care of for 1,260 days. And there was war in heaven. Michael and his angels fought against the dragon, and the dragon and his angels fought back. But he was not strong enough, and they lost their place in heaven."

In other words, Satan's a big loser and God's angels won! Including protecting the one-third remnant of the Jewish People who make it to the end of the 7-year Tribulation where He fulfills the eternal covenants to them. Now, I said all that to get to this. Notice what else Jesus said in the text. At some point, all nations will hate the Jewish people. But could that really happen here in America? Unfortunately, it's already happening!

"The U.S. State Department Says No 'Jerusalem, Israel' On US Passports." Despite the fact that President Trump recognized Jerusalem as Israel's capital and relocated the U.S. Embassy from Tel Aviv, Americans born in Jerusalem are still unable to list "Jerusalem, Israel" on U.S. passports. And of course, Pro-Israel groups are weighing in saying, "It is deeply frustrating that the State Department ignores the fact that Jerusalem is never mentioned in the Koran and that Arabs face Mecca when they pray, yet Jews face Jerusalem.

It has never been the capital of any country except Israel. In fact, it has been Jerusalem, Israel, for thousands of years according to God, U.S. law and history, but not according to the State Department." "The president has made clear that Jerusalem is the capital of Israel. So, any U.S. citizen born in Jerusalem is therefore, de facto, born in Israel, and their U.S. passport should reflect that reality." "Apparently, it is bureaucratic resistance inside the State Department." And so, the question is, "Where did they come from?" Well, apparently, it goes back to the previous administration. *"Netanyahu Fires Back at 'Obama Army' Plotting His Defeat." "Benjamin Netanyahu is demanding an injunction against the Obama U.S.-linked group trying to swing Israeli election.* (Here's your collusion and it wasn't the Russians! It was Obama against Israel!) Netanyahu stated that a U.S.-linked organization staffed with former Obama campaigners were working to defeat Netanyahu in the previous Israeli election.

"They hired 270 Strategies, a consulting firm whose senior leadership is comprised mostly of former top staffers for President Obama's 2012 re-election campaign." And they are being supported "through millions of dollars funneled from Europe, the U.S. and the New Israel Fund interested in bringing down Prime Minister Netanyahu who think 'that all means are appropriate.'"

Fox Business Network: *"Now our next guest says that the Obama Administration interfered in Israel's 2015 election and by the way got away with it. David Rubin is with us, former mayor of Shiloh, Israel and is with the Shiloh Israel Children's Fund as founder and president. I guess you know a thing or two about interfering with elections. Your charge is that the Obama team did that with the Israeli election. How did they do it? And what did they do?"*

David Rubin: *"Well this was common knowledge in Israel. There were billboards all over the country that said 'Anyone but BiBi, meaning the Prime Minister of Israel, Benjamin Netanyahu. It was wide spread. It only came out after the election that there was a far-left organization, very pro-Palestinian, hence, anti-Israel, called 'One Voice'. They were working together through another organization called V-15, meaning 'Victory in 2015'. The 'One Voice' organization received $350,000.00 from the U.S. State Department and the two organizations joined together during the Obama administration."*

Fox Business Network: *"$350,000.00? To an organization that opposed Netanyahu?"*

348

David Rubin: *"Yes, absolutely. And the election was a very intense election and the Obama administration was on board with these two organizations against Netanyahu and I might add one thing that is very important, there is a very clear link to the Obama administration because the head of the V-15 organization was none other than Jeremy Byrd who was the National Field Director for the Obama administration and the Obama campaign.*

Fox Business Network: *"And they go away with it. If that, what you're saying was interference in a foreign election, and the Obama team got away with it."[1]*

It's this kind of anti-Israel behavior from the Obama administration that led even former Senator John McCain to state, *"Israel-U.S. ties have never been worse than under Obama. While the relationship between the U.S. and Israel has not always been excellent, any observer would argue they've never been worse."* In fact, *"No other president has had such a difficult relationship with the state of Israel since it became a country. Which is a tragedy because Israel is the only functioning democracy in the entire Middle East."* And maybe that's because, Obama's brother joins Hamas and says, *'Jerusalem Is Ours; We Are Coming.'"*

It is now a well-known fact that Barack Obama's brother, Malik Obama, is in bed with terrorists, working in a terrorist state as an official of an organization created by terrorists. And one of the objectives is to spread Wahhabist Islam. Here's just one guy speaking up about it.

Fabian Calvo from AMTV reports: *"So an explosive story from Worldnet Daily, Jerome Corsi, coming out and saying that Barak Obama's brother, Malik Obama, is linked to the Muslim Brotherhood, not only linked but he is running their entire investment portfolio. According to the vice president of the Supreme Constitutional Court of Egypt the woman by the name of Tehani al-Gabali said, "to inform the American*

people that their president's brother Obama is one of the architects of the major
investments of the Muslim Brotherhood who has sympathies with the Muslim

Brotherhood in office, who's literally meeting with Muslim Brotherhood operatives at the White House."[2]

Funds contributed by the U.S. to the "cause" is going to a 501(c)3 foundation run by Malik Obama called the Barack H. Obama Foundation and was approved only one month after the application was submitted by Lois Lerner, the director of the IRS tax-exempt division, the one under congressional investigation for targeting conservatives and Christian individuals. And you wonder why Obama was so anti-Israel and why President Trump still has operatives working against him inside his own administration? Drain the swamp is right! For even more proof see our 8-hour study called, "Islam: Religion of War or Peace?" In fact, some are saying it was this anti-Israel behavior from previous administrations, including Obama's, that America faced major disasters after attempting to divide Israel. And here's the proof. There have literally been dozens of instances in recent decades when the U.S. has been hit by some sort of immediate disaster when it has made a move toward the dividing of the land of Israel. Here are 10 of the most prominent examples.

- #1 On March 22nd, 1979 the Carter administration chose not to veto UN Resolution 446 which caused Israel to give up a tremendous amount of territory. Two days later, the worst nuclear power plant disaster in U.S. history made headlines all over the globe, Three Mile Island.
- #2 On October 30th, 1991, President George H. W. Bush told Israel that "territorial compromise is essential for peace." At the exact same time, "the Perfect Storm" was brewing in the north Atlantic and traveled 1000 miles in the "wrong direction" and sent 35 foot waves slamming directly into President Bush's home in Kennebunkport, Maine.
- #3 On August 23rd, 1992, the Madrid Peace Conference moved to Washington D.C., and the very next day Hurricane Andrew made landfall in Florida causing 30 billion dollars in damage. It was the worst natural disaster up to that time in U.S. history.
- #4 On January 16th, 1994, President Clinton met with President Assad of Syria to discuss the possibility of Israel giving up the Golan Heights. Within

24 hours, the devastating Northridge earthquake hit southern California. It was the second worst natural disaster up to that time in U.S. history.

- #5 On January 21st, 1998, Israeli Prime Minister Benjamin Netanyahu arrived at the White House but received a very cold reception. In fact, President Clinton and Secretary of State Madeleine Albright actually refused to have lunch with him. That exact same day the Monica Lewinsky scandal broke, sending the Clinton presidency into a tailspin from which it would never recover.
- #6 On September 28th, 1998, Secretary of State Madeleine Albright was working on finalizing a plan which would have had Israel give up approximately 13 percent of Judea and Samaria. On that precise day, Hurricane George slammed into the Gulf Coast with wind gusts of up to 175 miles an hour.
- #7 On May 3rd, 1999, Palestinian leader Yasser Arafat was supposed to hold a press conference to declare the creation of a Palestinian state with Jerusalem as the capital. On that precise day, the most powerful tornadoes ever recorded in the U.S. ripped through Oklahoma and Kansas. At one point one of the tornadoes actually had a recorded wind speed of 316 miles an hour.
- #8 On April 30th, 2003, the "Road Map to Peace" had been developed and was been presented to Israel. Over the next seven days, the U.S. was hit by a staggering 412 tornadoes. It was the largest tornado cluster ever recorded up to that time.
- #9 In 2005, President George W. Bush (the son of George H. W. Bush) convinced Israel that it was necessary to remove all the Jewish settlers out of Gaza and turn it over entirely to the Palestinians. On that precise day, a storm that would be given the name "Katrina" started forming over the Bahamas and it ranked as the costliest natural disaster in all of U.S. history up to that time.
- #10 On May 19th, 2011, Barack Obama told Israel that there must be a return to the pre-1967 borders. Three days later on May 22nd a half-mile wide EF-5 multiple-vortex tornado ripped through Joplin, Missouri. According to Wikipedia, it was "the costliest single tornado in U.S. history."

It's almost like somebody's not reading their Bible!

Genesis 12:3 "I will bless those who bless you, and whoever curses you I will curse."

And this is also why many are saying President Trump is one of the best things to ever happen to U.S. Israeli relations in a long time!

351

Yishai Fleisher, Boomerang Reports: *"Here are four reasons why Israelis favor Trump's policies.*

1. Reversing Iran deal
The Iran deal would have allowed the Iranian Mullah regime, a world terror sponsor, whose stated goal is to eradicate Israel, to enrich uranium and build a nuclear bomb. Don't want that. Not good, not good. President Trump and his team put an end to this madness, and that took guts!

2. Fighting UN bias
The UN has been pushing an anti-Israel agenda through its various arms, and we Israelis have been living with their pernicious lies. For example, UNESCO. Now, this is the UN body in charge of world heritage sites, but absurdly, they claim that the Tomb of Rachel, the Temple Mount and Tomb of the Patriarchs in Hebron are Palestinian heritage sites."

Benjamin Netanyahu: *"That's worse than fake news, that's fake history."*

Yishai Fleisher, Boomerang Reports: *"UNRWA, it's the UN body dedicated to perpetuating Palestine refugees. Not only did they fail to settle the old refugees, they managed to create new ones by including their descendants in the same category, thus making sure that the problem will never be solved. Guess what? Under Trump the US pulled out of UNESCO, left the Human Rights Council and defunded UNWRA.*

3. 'Pay for Slay'
So, the Palestinian Authority allocates about 400 million dollars annually to pay terrorists and their families. 'Pay to Slay'. The more Jews you kill the more money you get. Finally, the US administration has decided to stop handing over US taxpayer money to these thugs. And finally...*

4. Jerusalem
For thousands of years, Jews have been praying to return to Yerushalayim, Jerusalem, and so we did. In his historic declaration, President Trump recognized this ancient fact and by moving the US embassy to Jerusalem helped make it a reality today. That's huge!

So, for these four reasons, and more, its's hard for us, here in Israel, to see Trump as anti-Jewish or anti-Israel. Remember that when American blesses Israel, it gets blessed right back."[3]

'With Jews we lose,' reads one Senate candidate's slogan in Kentucky. Campaign lawn signs with the slogan began appearing in Kentucky and Ransdell said his campaign has posted about 20 signs and plans 200 more in the weeks ahead. "Online we have had a lot of positive feedback."

"Shirley MacLaine claims Holocaust victims were paying for sins in past lives." She stated in her recently published book that the six million Jews and others who died in the Holocaust were "balancing their karma" by paying for sins in a previous life.

A California Democrat delegate calls for Israel to be 'Terminated.' This is from Hussam Ayloush who is a senior official on the Council on American-Islamic Relations (CAIR) and a representative of District 60 of California. He not only was a delegate to the 2012 Democratic National Convention, but his Twitter and Facebook pages state that *"for over 14 years, I have been a fundraiser and activist for many Democratic Party campaigns. I have also helped register thousands of new voters. I work for (CAIR-CA)."* He not only frequently refers to Israelis as "Zionazis" and said in a CAIR email, *"Indeed, the Zionazis are a bunch of nice people; just like their Nazi brethren!"* He also justified the actions of American Muslims joining ISIS.

Democrat Activist Linda Sarsour wants people to stop "humanizing Jews." She's a Women's March Leader and Democrat activist and was also arrested for civil disobedience during the Senate confirmation hearings of Judge Brett Kavanaugh. But Sarsour is a Muslim and a strong supporter of Palestine and has been known to take radical anti-Semitic positions. At the annual Islamic Society of North America (ISNA) convention in Houston, she called for the dehumanization of Israelis, and later, Alexandria Ocasio-Cortez and Sarsour both headlined the 16th Annual Universal Muslim Association of America where the two took the stage to promote women's rights and progressive values, despite the event being segregated and the women who attended almost uniformly wearing hijabs. About a week after the event, Ocasio-Cortez then took to Twitter to praise Sarsour after she got herself arrested for interrupting the Kavanaugh confirmation hearings. She said, "Our future is a shared responsibility." And this is why another report says, "Will radical Democrat freshmen turn the House against Israel?"

I24 News Reports: *"Alexandria Ocasio-Cortez, Ilhan Omar, and Rashida Tlaib, the three women who might mix the change in Congress, especially for Israel. Come January, the pro-Israel groups in Washington will need to contend with three members of Congress with their harsh views on Israel. Alexandria Ocasio-Cortez, standard bearer of the new young Democratic left who called the killing of the Palestinians on the border in May a massacre."*

Alexandria Ocasio-Cortez: *"This is a massacre. I hope my peers have the moral courage to call it such. No state or entity is absolved of mass shootings of protesters. There is no justification. Palestinian people deserve basic human dignity as anyone else. Democrats can't be silent about this anymore."*

I24 News Reports: *"Ilhan Omar, Somalian refugee, representing Minneapolis in Congress who referred to the quote."*

Ilhan Omar: *"Drawing attention to the apartheid Israeli regime is far from hating Jews. You are a hateful sad man, I pray to Allah you get the help you need and find happiness."*

I24 News Reports: *"Rashida Tlaib, set to be the first Palestinian American to have a seat on Capitol Hill, who came out in favor of a one state solution that could nullify the Jewish state. They represent a deeper trend of US politics. As support for Israel has declined among Democrats, especially says a leading Israeli expert, since 2016."*

Jonathan Rynhold, *Professor of Political Science, Bar Ilan University: "Israel is associated with Trump, so Israel is not seen favorably as it was in the past."* The pro-Israel establishment is worried the trend line. *"Sympathy for Israel has fallen. Sympathy for the Palestinians have risen among Democrats. And now there is very little difference between those two. This is unprecedented."*[4]

Opponents of Israel have something to celebrate. Rashida Tlaib became the first Palestinian-American to serve in Congress. Tlaib who represents a suburban district outside of Detroit with a large Arab population, is an avowed opponent of Israel's existence and had no problem being wrapped in a Palestinian flag at her election victory party and is well known for her support of the BDS (Boycott, Divest, Sanction) movement and other anti-Israel beliefs. She also has a kindred spirit in fellow freshman Democrat Ilhan Omar, who is the first Somali-American in Congress representing Minneapolis. At her acceptance speech, Omar greeted the audience with the Muslim greeting, "As-Salam-Alaikum" which caused many Muslims to feel this is a homecoming. Omar is also a fierce critic of Israel, who has called it an "evil" country that has "hypnotized the world," a standard anti-Semitic meme. In fact, even a Saudi Arabian News outlet noted, *"The common ground between Congresswomen Omar and Tlaib is that both are anti-Trump, especially his foreign policy on Iran and the isolation of the Muslim Brotherhood and all movements of political Islam."* Both are allied with Alexandria Ocasio-Cortez, a socialist who represents Queens, N.Y. Ocasio-Cortez said she wanted to end the "occupation of Palestine," though she didn't seem able to say whether that meant the West Bank or, as Palestinians define the term, all of Israel. This trio also allied with the Women's March whose leaders combine anti-Zionism along with anti-Semitic hate-monger Louis Farrakhan, head of the Nation of Islam. We can expect them to unite with other Democrats to undermine the U.S.-Israel alliance, such as the dozens who signed letters last year championed by figures such as Sens. Bernie Sanders (I-Vt.) and Elizabeth Warren (D-Mass.) calling for the lifting of the blockade of the terrorist Hamas regime that rules Gaza.[5]

"CNN Ditches Marc Lamont Hill in Response to His Anti-Israel Rant." Temple University professor Marc Lamont Hill is no stranger to anti-Israel vitriol with his embrace of the Nation of Islam leader Louis Farrakhan, but now he is calling for, "A Free Palestine from the River to the Sea." In a speech at the United Nations, Lamont Hill blasted Israel and later admitted on Twitter that he has never even been to Israel, even though he endorses BDS." In response to his tirade, **Alan Dershowitz**, who has debated Hill on CNN over Israel said, *"Mark Lamont Hill is a dangerous Farrakhan-loving, Israel-hating, racist propagandist who calls for Israel's destruction to be supplanted by a Hamas-Iran terror state."* And another person stated, *"He is helping to mainstream and normalize anti-Semitism."* Of course, they mean through the media. Which another headline reads, *"Media Bias Against Israel - Where To Begin?"* The media's treatment of Israel has been among the Jewish state's most worrisome challenges. It should be no mystery to reporters based in Israel that the Jewish state faces tons of enemies: Hamas in Gaza, Hezbollah, and now Iran in the north, and the Palestinian Authority that continues to glorify terrorism, pays cash to terrorists and their families, and incites the population to hate and murder Israelis and Jews. Yet that message rarely gets through. Here's just one example. When a CNN reporter who had been in Gaza for days was asked by his own anchor in Washington if he had seen the same kind of fire emanating from civilian locations, he lamely stated that he was not aware of it. Also, another example of bias carried by multiple

media organizations was the case of Layla Ghandour, the Palestinian baby said by the press to have died from tear gas inhalation during the demonstrations. It was later reported that, in fact, the baby had actually died due to a heart condition and Hamas had paid the family to lie about the circumstances. Try to find more than a few "clarifications" of this story in print or on the air. You won't. And yet, Hamas, Hezbollah, and Iran publicly call for and seek Israel's destruction. Terrorists can strike anytime at Israelis, ramming pedestrians with cars and bulldozers, stabbing people on the street, or attempting to kidnap civilians and soldiers. But many journalists don't report it that way, choosing to give those who seek to destroy Israel a free pass."[6]

Now add to this what's going on in social media. Facebook's Zuckerberg says he won't remove Holocaust denial posts. Mark Zuckerberg appeared to defend Holocaust deniers on Wednesday, suggesting that online hate speech disclaiming the *"genocide of six million Jews is misguided rather than a matter of ill-intent. Holocaust deniers on Facebook are making an honest mistake."* Facebook also came under fire after it was shown that advertisers were able to specifically target anti-Semitic or prejudiced social media users with their ads. ProPublica reported that the world's largest social network enabled advertisers to direct their pitches to the news feeds of almost 2,300 people who expressed interest in the topics of 'Jew hater,' 'How to burn Jews,' or, 'History of why Jews ruin the world.' And the ads were approved within 15 minutes. They also discovered that 3,194 Facebook users listed their employer as "German Schutzstaffel" — the German SS — and another 2,449 who said they worked for the "Nazi Party."

And then another headline reported, "Why is YouTube punishing people who translate and expose Anti-Semitism on its platform?" For years, YouTube has failed to distinguish between those who upload racist material and those who post and translate such content to raise awareness and fight against it. For instance, recently a new cartoon music video that had just been released by the terrorist group Hamas was written in Hebrew in an effort to intimidate Israelis. The animated song featured explicit exhortations to violence against Jewish civilians and included such iconic images as an ultra-Orthodox Jew having his head blown off and stuck on a spike, as well as another being shot in the head through crosshairs. So, Aslan-Levy posted the video on YouTube with English subtitles, so that non-Hebrew readers could understand Hamas's threats in it. Two days later, YouTube took down his translated video for "hate speech" and warned him that further offenses could result in the suspension of his account." This decision was all the more curious given that YouTube continues to allow many other Hamas videos, posted by their sympathizers and garnering hundreds of thousands of views, to remain on the site unmolested. Keep in mind this is not an isolated incident. For years, YouTube has been taking down videos that translate and expose anti-Semitism and punish those who post them. And then we have this report. "Twitter Being Weaponized as 4 Million anti-Semitic Tweets Posted in 2017." The Report highlights an uptick in anti-Semitic tweets when President Donald Trump announced the decision to move the U.S. Embassy in Israel to Jerusalem from at least 3 million different user accounts. Keep in mind that such tweets are being allowed, despite previous verbal assurances by the social media company that it would be tackling racist content on its platform.

And this has led to, "Google Being Sued Over Alleged Failure to Block Anti-Semitic Content." A Jewish man in Spain has filed a lawsuit against Google regarding the search engine's apparent failure to censor racist content after a takedown notice was filed by his attorney. After conducting a Google search in Spanish using the search terms "Holocaust" and "truth." The results included defamation against Jews, labeling them as "degenerate" and the "embodiment of evil." The results belong to a Nazi website with a significant following across the Spanish-speaking world — not only in Spain, but also South America. However, "No action was taken by Google."[7]

- "19 Swastikas Painted on North Virginian Jewish Community Center."
- "Anti-Semitic graffiti on Indiana synagogue."
- "Jewish cemetery in Missouri vandalized."
- "Attacks on Jewish Cemeteries Provoke Fear in Philadelphia."
- "American Jews Confront a Wave of Bomb Threats."
- "Second Orthodox Jewish man attacked in Brooklyn in 2 days."
- "New York cab driver shouting 'Allah' brutally beats man, 62, on his way to synagogue in the middle of the road in anti-Jewish hate crime."
- "Anti-Semitic Hate Crimes in New York Up 94% Over Last Year."

Elizabeth Midlarsky, Psychology Professor and Holocaust Scholar: *"I picked up the mail and saw this swastika. To put it mildly, it was extremely shocking."*

I24News Reports: *"Elizabeth Midlarsky, a professor at Columbia University is still shaken by the disturbing discovery in her office. Swastikas spray painted across her walls."*

Arielle Hixson, correspondent: *"How did it make you feel?"*

Elizabeth Midlarsky: *"You know its hard to even say. I didn't really feel or think anything, but utter shock. I started trembling. I'm still trembling"*

Arielle Hixson: *"This is just one of the many anti-Semitic attacks that lead headlines over the past month. To get a visual of the timeline over the past month alone. 11/03 Metal pipe thrown through window of Brooklyn synagogue during a Shabot service. Weeks later, two large swastikas and anti-Semitic slurs were found on the walls of the office of Ms. Midlarsky. On 11/29, two young Jewish boys were attacked in Williamsburg on the streets within 30 minutes of each other. And the most recent act of violence was on 11/30 when a Jewish man was punched in the head. The surveillance photo shows that his back was turned and never saw it coming as the man ran up behind him and punched him in the head. The Anti-defamation League claims that anti-Semitic incidents in the US rose nearly 60% in 2017 and now the spotlight is on New York. The NYPD reports that last year there were 138 anti-Semitic hate crimes in the city. This year there were 176.[8]*

- "Florida man hit with hate crime charge for threatening to 'kill all the Jews."
- "The Deadliest Anti-Semitic Attack in US History in Pittsburg."

Fox News Reports: *"The investigation is in full swing as the city and nation mourns. President Trump is in Minneapolis today to speak about the horrendous shooting."*

President Trump: *"This wicked act of mass murder is pure evil, hard to believe and frankly something that is unimaginable."*

Bob Jones, FBI Special Agent: *"This is the most horrific crime scene that I have seen in the 22 years of FBI crime scene investigations. Had it not been for the quick and heroic response, this would have been much worse."*

NBC Nightly News Reports: *"Today's violence in Pittsburg comes amid a rise in anti-Semitic attacks across the country in recent years. Jewish centers in New York. Oregon, and Massachusetts have been vandalized. Arson at a synagogue in Nevada, and just this month swastikas found in Northern Virginia."*

CNN Reports: *"In Omaha, Nebraska, a Veterans memorial is scarred with a swastika, in Indiana, a synagogue is desecrated. In Sacramento, California, a flyer targeting Jewish students on campus. It screams of the same kind of tactics* *and design that the Nazis used. This is Potters County, Pennsylvania; a country store is covered with swastikas and slurs."*

NBC News: *"It's a complete disgrace. There is no place for hate. The anti-defamation league reported nearly 2,000 incidents last year. Nearly a 57% increase.*[9]

- As one reporter stated, "The worst hasn't happened, it's coming." Before the massacre, an anti-Semitic attack had been carried out by a Muslim who was caught on video beating a Jewish man while shouting about, "Allah" and screaming at him that he hates the Jews and he would like to kill all the Jews. Such assaults are less devastating than the mass murder of eleven people, but also much more commonplace. They repeat from month to month and year to year and top the list of hate crime statistics every single year. The age of innocence is coming to an end. America is changing. The same forces that made Obama have also made Farrakhan relevant once again. Muslim migration will transform America the way that it did Europe. The cities will feel it first. But they won't be the last.[10]

Can you believe this? It's all happening right now! The Bible said in the Last Days, the Antichrist will arise and seek to kill 2/3rds of the Jewish people, and all nations will get in on it! Apparently even America will hate the Jewish People, and it looks like the planet is ripe for it once again, in our lifetime. Even after what Hitler did! Can you believe it? And you might be wondering, How? Why? Why is this happening and how could this be here in American where we've historically been a staunch supporter of Israel, except Obama, and we're supposed to be a Christian nation? Well, let me give you a couple reasons why.

The **1st reason** why anti-Semitism is growing even here in America is because **The American Schools are Promoting It.**

Just like we previously read, with the other countries around the world, this anti-Semitic attitude, this hatred of the Jewish people, is being crammed in our young people's minds even here in our own country via the secular school system! As we've seen before in other studies, our school system has been hijacked by atheists, humanists, and liberals who are pushing a whole different agenda. But they're now full of anti-Semitics!

A Pennsylvania high school history teacher named Sam Schindler, at a private school in Lancaster, PA, is not only lying to his students about Israel, but he's falsely accusing them of being, "the occupation and oppression." He then goes on to boast about his results. He notes that "the class collectively reached a universal conclusion about Israel and Palestine: The oppression of Palestinians is not sustainable, nor is it justifiable." "Wisconsin High School students give group Nazi salute in prom photo."

The photo was taken last spring and resurfaced on social media shortly after the Pittsburgh synagogue shooting.

A University of Michigan professor promised a student he would write her a reference required to take part in a semester-abroad program in Israel. But later wrote back, "*As you may know, many university departments have pledged an academic boycott against Israel in support of Palestinians living in Palestine. This includes writing letters of recommendation for students planning to study there.*" Yet this same professor endorses student visits to communist China and Cuba, or the repressive regimes in Saudi Arabia or the PLO in the West Bank. And this behavior is not a coincidence. The American Studies Association (ASA) was one of the first such academic groups to vote and endorse BDS in 2013 that has pledged to support programs designed to eradicate the Jewish state. In another article entitled, "Hating Jews at Berkeley" it stated, "*The University of California, Berkeley's graduate student labor union is voting on whether the State of Israel should continue to exist.*" One of the leaders is Lara Kiswani who has stated, "*As long as you choose to be on that side (Israel), I'm going to continue to hate you.*" Ironically, she is also the director of the Arab Resource and Organizing Center. And then in an article entitled, "*Your tax dollars at work: inciting next generation of Israel-Haters on campus,*" it states, "It's hard to believe, but state governments are funding anti-Israel incitement on college campuses across the nation." How? By sending millions of dollars to support Middle East Studies programs which are dominated by Israel-hating, anti-Semitic professors. Almost half of the programs are led by faculty who have endorsed academic boycotts of Israel and develop and lead BDS rallies and other anti-Israel activities. All of these combined efforts in the school system are nurturing and growing the anti-Israel movement in the United States, which has been going on for decades, and it has horrific long-term ramifications for Israel and the Jewish people. We are funding the academic headquarters for anti-Israel incitement. This funding has to stop. Why? Because it's leads to these kinds of people in our American Schools!

"The speaker is at the podium. A girl steps up to the microphone to make her comment. "I want to say thank you for coming here tonight and presenting your point of view. It's valuable to have two sets of views at the same time. It's very useful. I am a student here at UCSD. I was reading your literature and I found that much more interesting than your talk. I found some interesting things about the MSA (Muslim Students Association), an organization here on campus which is hosting our annual Hitler Youth week. You should come out to our events.

If you can clarify the difference between the MSA and how the jihadist terrorist works. Because the last time I checked we had to do our own fund raising and we never get help from anyone, so you need to clarify the difference or if you don't have this information or if you can clarify this difference, because it wasn't too clear in the past. Please if you could just clarify." She steps back from the microphone. He proceeds to answer her question. "Do you condemn Hamas here and now?" She replies, "Are you asking if I condemn Hamas? Are you asking if I will put myself on a cross?"

He says, "I have had this conversation many times. You didn't actually read the pamphlet. The pamphlet is chapter and verse that the main connection is that the MSA is part of the Muslim Brotherhood network that we reveal in the documents." She interrupts him, "I don't believe you understood what I meant by that. I meant that if I did say something, I'm sure that I would be arrested for reasons of Homeland Security. Please just answer my questions." He then continues, "Do you condemn Hamas? She answers, "If I support Hamas, because your question forces me to say I support Hamas, I look really bad." He then replies, "If you don't condemn Hamas, then obviously you support them. Case closed!"

Applause comes from the crowd. He then continues, "I had this experience in UC Santa Barbara where there were 50 students of the Muslims Student Association. They were sitting right in the front row. Throughout my hour talk I kept asking them 'would you condemn Hezbollah?' Then when the question period came, the president of the Muslim Students Association came up. He was the first person to ask a question. I asked him, 'before we begin, would you condemn Hezbollah?' and he answered, 'that question is too complicated.' I couldn't get a yes or no answer. So, I said, 'ok I'll put it to you this way. I'm a Jew. The head of Hezbollah has said that he hopes that we will gather in his house, so he doesn't have to hunt us down. Are you for or against it?" The girl, that is still standing at the microphone then answers, "For it!" He says, "Thank you for coming today and showing us you're wearing a terrorist neckchief."[11]

Wow! So that's what our schools are producing! Hatred for the Jews! As one person stated, "This has been going on for decades now. And, as it is no wonder that by the time students go to university, there is only one nation state in the entire world that they are eager to rally against: the State of Israel. It's time to put an end to this insanity."[12]

But they're not, so you wonder why there's a rise of Anti-Semitism in America?

The **2nd reason** why antisemitism is growing in America is because **The American Churches are Promoting It**.

Now talk about super-sad hypocritical behavior! As we saw before, this is what's going on with the lie called Replacement Theology that falsely teaches that God is done with the Jewish People and the Church has replaced them, hence the term, "Replacement Theology." And as we saw at the beginning of our study, it's completely unbiblical!

1. The Bible explicitly promises that God's covenant with the Jews would be eternal (ie. unbreakable).

2. The New Testament explicitly states that the Old Testament promises and covenants to Israel are still the possessions of Israel, even during this Church age and even while the nation is currently in a state of unbelief.
3. The Old Testament explicitly teaches the future, permanent restoration of the nation Israel.
4. The New Testament reaffirms the Old Testament expectation of a future salvation and restoration of Israel.
5. Nowhere in the entire New Testament is the term 'Israel' used for those who are not ethnic Jews. Thus, there is no biblical basis for identifying the Church as the 'new Israel.'
6. If God could break His covenant with the Jews, then we cannot trust Him to keep His promises to us Christians![13]

How many of you would say that wouldn't be a good thing! But, this is why Replacement Theology is not only unbiblical, but it attacks the very heart and character of God! And yet, as we saw before many so-called Christians are buying into it! Now, I'm going to start off with those who profess to be Christians but they're not! But, the world doesn't know any difference.

The Vatican Daily, "welcomed" the proclamation of the State of Israel on May 14, 1948 with these words: "Modern Israel is not the true heir of Biblical Israel."

The same was proclaimed during the Vatican's synod in 2010 when bishops called to abolish the concept of "Promised Land" and "Chosen People."

Egypt's Coptic Orthodox Church stated, "Modern-day Jews are not God's chosen people." "Israel's liberation of Jerusalem in 1967 was a "rape" and a "ritual crime."

The Greek Orthodox Church in Jerusalem stated that "evangelical Christians" or "Zionist Christians" do "not belong to Christianity," and that they "have no connection to the values of Christianity."

The Church of Scotland said Israel does not belong to the Jewish people. "Promises about the land of Israel were never intended to be taken literally, or as applying to a defined geographical territory."

It said, "The 'Promised Land' in the Bible is not a place, rather it's a metaphor of how things ought to be among the people of God. This 'Promised Land' can be found, or built, anywhere."

And they also radically altered and re-interpreted the concepts of "Israel," "temple," and "Jerusalem."

The Anglican Synod of New Zealand removed the words "Zion" and "Israel" from their Psalter, or book of Psalms.

The Presbyterian Church USA is considering banning the word "Israel" from its prayers.

And one person stated, *"This has happened before. In his war against the Jews, Adolf Hitler instructed Christian theologians to rewrite the Bible in a bid to remove all mention of the Jews."* Their barbaric spirit is still living on in liberal Christianity today.

"United Church of Christ Continues To Promote Anti-Israel Agenda."

The denomination's leadership voted on a number of resolutions that call on the Church officers and local churches to advocate for particular social causes that they deem important. Seventeen of those resolutions were anti-Israel. Such behavior is dishonest, but not surprising. *"This is just one of the consequences of Christian replacement theology."* Taken to its logical end, this Christian ideology suggests there is only one price the Jews can pay for being accepted by the world: Israel's elimination. They go on to say, "People were horrified by these resolutions and other mainline denominations hoped that the people in the pews would rise up and revolt against the response. This turned out to be fantasy.

And yet another headline stated, *"Evangelicals are the primary target of groups working to turn them against Israel."* Evangelical Christians are some of the biggest supporters of Israel in the United States. However, there is a movement to turn Evangelicals against Israel and it's coming from other so-called Christians. It's called Christ at the Checkpoint (CATC) For the first time in its history, it hosted a conference in the United States. The event was created by Palestinian Christian activists in Bethlehem in 2010. They gathered from around the world in Oklahoma City to condemn Christian Zionists and fight Israel's "occupation" of Palestinian land. One of those speakers, Rev. Dr.

Stephen Sizer, from the Church of England, faced backlash after supporting claims that Israel was behind the 9/11 terror attacks.

In 2014, he attended a conference in Iran dedicated to promoting holocaust denial theories, and just recently he attended a pro-Hezbollah rally in London. As one person stated, *"This attack on Christian Zionism (i.e. those who support Israel) is anti-Semitism in disguise."*

And another article stated, *"Is Replacement Theology Fueling Anti-Semitism in America?" "In the wake of the Pittsburgh atrocity on October 27, leaders have issued a stark warning about the dangers of Replacement Theology and how it is fueling an uptick in Jew-hatred."*

"It is long past time to confront the growing danger of the rise of anti-Semitism in America. We must examine how our society, including our churches and education system, are helping to make this threat worse."

"History has shown that anti-Semitism doesn't stop with just the Jewish community; this hatred will soon be directed at other people of faith as well.[14]

In other words, what we read last time with Martin Niemoller, *"They'll come for you next, Christian, the real ones!"* And lest you doubt, Robert Bowers, the man who was responsible for the Pittsburg Massacre, quoted replacement theology doctrine to legitimize his anti-Semitic beliefs as he murdered 11 members of the Jewish community. So, it really does give rise to anti-Semitism and it's rampant in the Church and you wonder why it's on the rise in America? Here's the point. The Bible said in the Last Days, the Antichrist will arise and seek to kill 2/3rds of the Jewish people, and it sure looks like, in our lifetime, right now, all nations including America are ripe for it once again, even after what Hitler did! This is why, out of love, God has given us this update on The Final Countdown: Tribulation Rising concerning the Jewish People & the Antichrist to show us that the 7-year Tribulation is near, and the Return of Jesus Christ is rapidly approaching. And that's why Jesus Himself said…

Luke 21:28 "When these things begin to take place, stand up and lift up your heads, because your redemption is drawing near."

Like it or not, we are headed for The Final Countdown. The signs of the 7-year Tribulation are Rising all around us! It's time to wake up! If you're reading this today and you're not a Christian, then I beg you, please, heed these signs, heed these warnings, give your life to Jesus now! You don't want to be here when God pours out His Judgment upon this wicked and rebellious planet! It's the worst time in the history of mankind, so horrible that unless God shortened the timeframe the entire human race would be destroyed! The only way to escape is through Jesus! Take the way out now before it's too late. GET SAVED TODAY! But if you're reading this today and you are a Christian, then it's high time we stop goofing off and getting distracted with this world. Let's get busy working together sharing the Gospel with as many as we can! Let's be that faithful remnant in these Last Days, exercising our privileged duty as Christians to speak up against anti-Semitism and evil in general, unlike this Church.

"If you say, 'But we knew nothing about this,' does not he who weighs the heart perceive it?" Proverbs 24:12

"A train is rushing down the tracks. It's dark and all you can see is the light of the train and the noise its wheels make as it gets closer and closer. There you are standing in the middle of the track as it comes closer. You seem to be frozen because you can't move, and the train is going to run over you. You put your arm up to protect your face as it hits you.

Suddenly, you sit up in bed. It was a nightmare. This dream has haunted you for decades. There are some things that time does not erase. Sometimes when going forward, it's like facing the past.

This is my story. I lived in Germany during the Nazi Holocaust. A railroad track ran behind our small church. Every Sunday at exactly the same time we heard the whistle blow in the distance and then the clacking of the wheels moving over the track. It was at the same time every Sunday. We felt the rattling of the rails of the train, the cattle cars accompanied by the screeching of metal and the echo through our church walls.

It was a Sunday in the spring that would change my life forever. The minister said, "Jesus said, do not resist an evil doer, but if anyone strikes you on the right cheek, turn the other also. Loving your enemy, this is a far better way. This is how we were called to live. To understand this unnatural virtue, we must look to Jesus Christ as our model and our guide. Uniqueness was His strength, His silence, His statement to the world. We must pray for those who persecute us. Prayer is the magnetism that reaches Heaven and moves mankind. Prayer is easy to underestimate. Prayer requires action." As the minister is preaching the train passing by was different that day. Everyone ran to the window to see what was happening. The train was stopping.

We could hear people crying and calling for help. They were on the train, in one of the cattle cars, and they couldn't get out. They were calling for help to get them out. As the people are crying the minister keeps talking, "Christ is the Prince of Peace. As we better come to know Jesus, we will learn to choose as He chooses." The noises keep on. We really aren't listening to the minister now because he can hardly be heard over the noise from the train. He proceeds, "We learn to love our enemies and allow God's peace to rule within our hearts."

The minister tries to lead us in a song to try to blot out the noise that is coming from outside. No one is singing with him. They are so concerned with what is happening outside. The crying does not stop. Finally, one of the men in the congregation stands and starts to sing with the minister, then another one, then another, then the choir leader gets the choir to stand and sing. The singing gets louder and pretty soon the noises from outside can't be heard anymore.

Instead of anyone going to the door to see if they can help, gradually each one stands and enters into song. Now it is like any other Sunday when the train passes by the little church. While the church sings louder, the people in the cattle car start listening and they seem to stop crying. The music seems to be giving them peace. I got up and went outside to see what was happening.

When I walked to the train, I saw that it was full of people. A girl was looking out at me. She asked me, "What is your name?" I didn't answer. My mother came out to get me to come back into the church. I saw that some German soldiers were coming down the track yelling to get back into the church. I was crying. There was nothing I could do.

Yes, it was in the past and no one really talks about it anymore. I still hear the train whistle in my sleep. I can still hear them crying out for help. We called ourselves Christians, but we did nothing to intervene.[15]

"Rescue those being led away to death". Proverbs 24:11

How about us? Will we speak up? Will we do something? Or will we just sit there and sing a little louder? You know, someone announces, "Hey, the Jewish People are being singled out and picked on and made to look like barbaric animals, we better do something" …. "Ah who cares! What are you, an alarmist? The game is on! Sing a little louder, will you?" "Hey, let's go witness to the Jewish People, or anybody for that matter, let's just go share the gospel" "What are you? A fanatic? I got stuff to do! I got errands to run, the house to clean. Sing a little louder, will you? I'll say it one last time. We need to be doing two things at this time in the Last Days. One, speaking up on behalf of the Jewish People and their community remembering, if we don't, we're next! And two, we need to tell as many people as we can about Jesus, so no one including the Jewish People will have to go through another Holocaust that is coming to this planet again. They need to accept Jesus as their Lord and Savior today. May our tune in these Last Days be spent singing the Gospel. Amen?

How to Receive Jesus Christ:

1. Admit your need (I am a sinner).

2. Be willing to turn from your sins (repent).

3. Believe that Jesus Christ died for you on the Cross and rose from the grave.

4. Through prayer, invite Jesus Christ to come in and control your life through the Holy Spirit. (Receive Him as Lord and Savior.)

What to pray:

Dear Lord Jesus,

I know that I am a sinner and need Your forgiveness. I believe that You died for my sins. I want to turn from my sins. I now invite You to come into my heart and life. I want to trust and follow You as Lord and Savior.

In Jesus' name. Amen.

Notes

Chapter 1 *The Jewish People & Their Eternal Covenants*

1. *Abrahamic Covenant*
https://www.gotquestions.net/Printer/Abrahamic-covenant-PF.html
https://carm.org/what-is-the-abrahamic-covenant
2. *Mosaic Covenant*
https://www.gotquestions.net/Printer/Mosaic-covenant-PF.html
3: *Davidic Covenant*
https://www.gotquestions.net/Printer/Davidic-covenant-PF.html
4. *Replacement Theology*
https://www.gotquestions.net/Printer/replacement-theology-PF.html
5. *How the church fits with Israel*
https://www.gotquestions.net/Printer/replacement-theology-PF.html
6. *McArthur*
https://www.gty.org/resources/pdf/sermons/1325

Chapter 2 *The Jewish People & Their Past Prophecies*

1. *Past Prophecies*
http://christinprophecy.org/articles/the-jews-in-prophecy/
https://www.youtube.com/watch?v=ydwxy9yqhzM

Chapter 3 *The Jewish People & Their Return to the Land*

1. *Jewish Sacrifices*
http://christinprophecy.org/articles/the-regathering-of-the-jewish-people/
2. *The Gathering*
https://www.youtube.com/watch?v=ydwxy9yqhzM
3. *Replacement Theology*
http://www.kkcj.org/teaching/article/replacement-theology

4. *The Word Palestine*
https://www.youtube.com/watch?v=BHsqVB9nxFY
5. *Israel has offered land*
https://www.youtube.com/watch?v=76NytvQAIs0
6. *Jerusalem Post*
https://en.wikiquote.org/wiki/Abba_Eban
7. *Israel Compared*   .
https://www.youtube.com/watch?v=jJG83jRI7Y4
8. *Golfer and Volcano*
https://www.golfchannel.com/article/grill-room/photo-man-golfs-face-erupting-volcano/

Chapter 4 *The Jewish People & Their Rebirth as a Nation*

1. *1948 Israel becomes a Nation*
https://www.youtube.com/watch?v=4E7GxwCUp6k
2. *Cornerstone Prophetic event*
(http://christinprophecy.org/articles/the-jews-in-prophecy/)
3. *Feast and Festivals*
https://www.gotquestions.org/Jewish-festivals.html
https://promisestoisrael.org/jewish-culture-2/jewish-holidays/rosh-hashanah-the-feast-of-trumpets/
4. *Dates for Feast of Trumpets*
http://www.jewfaq.org/holiday2.htm
5. *Celebrating 1948*
https://www.youtube.com/watch?v=3HkaqO1Br8E
6. *Watch Tower*
(https://www.jwfacts.com/watchtower/generation.php)
7. *The Lost Tribe*
(https://www.israelnationalnews.com/News/News.aspx/180927)
8. *Benei Manashe*
https://www.youtube.com/watch?v=5dVkreM6cLc
https://www.youtube.com/watch?v=fHvUcfB_B0c
https://www.youtube.com/watch?v=pCXeJHCX5lI

Chapter 5 *The Jewish People & Their Capitol Currency Language*

1. *Israel recaptures Jerusalem*
https://sareltours.com/israel-bible-prophecy/
http://christinprophecy.org/articles/the-jews-in-prophecy/
http://christinprophecy.org/articles/the-jews-in-end-time-bible-prophecy/
http://www.prophecynewswatch.com/article.cfm?recent_news_id=2315#4fWGB
Y1megFeZ7eA.99
https://www.youtube.com/watch?v=WLBcCffnnY4
2. *Importance*
http://christinprophecy.org/articles/jerusalem-3000/
3. *Shekel*
https://www.gotquestions.org/sanctuary-shekel.html
https://en.wikipedia.org/wiki/Shekel
https://en.wikipedia.org/wiki/Israeli_new_shekel
https://prophecyinthenews.com/world_news/temple-movement-issues-half-shekel-coin-with-profile-of-trump-and-cyrus/
https://www.breakingisraelnews.com/102784/sanhedrin-temple-movement-issue-silver-half-shekel-images-trump-cyrus/
http://en.hamikdash.org.il/about/we-need-your-support/the-temple-coin/
https://www.breakingisraelnews.com/105767/new-special-edition-temple-coin-minted-for-israels-70th-anniversary-the-end-of-the-exile/
http://christinprophecy.org/articles/the-jews-in-end-time-bible-prophecy/
https://www.therefinersfire.org/jews_return_to_israel.htm
4. *Temple Commercial*
https://www.youtube.com/watch?v=B6C_zfpEwUI
5. *Ben Yeheida's Plan*
http://christinprophecy.org/articles/the-jews-in-prophecy/
https://www.therefinersfire.org/jews_return_to_israel.htm
http://christinprophecy.org/articles/the-jews-in-end-time-bible-prophecy/
http://christinprophecy.org/articles/the-revival-of-the-hebrew-language/
6. *Rebirth of Hebrew*
ttps://www.youtube.com/watch?v=ydwxy9yqhzM

Chapter 6 *The Jewish People & Their Renewal of the Land*

1. *Desert Blossoming*
http://www.johnsnotes.com/Thedesertblossominglikearose.htm
2. *Visitors to Israel*
http://www.johnsnotes.com/Thedesertblossominglikearose.htm

http://christinprophecy.org/articles/jesus-is-coming-soon-2/
http://christinprophecy.org/articles/israel-as-proof-of-gods-existence/
http://christinprophecy.org/articles/the-reclamation-of-the-land/
http://firm.org.il/learn/2600-years-prophecies-coming-pass/
https://www.jewishvoice.org/read/blog/prophecies-about-israel-continue-be-fulfilled
3. *Bread Basket*
https://www.youtube.com/watch?v=oxxYmn3HpDU
4. *Deforesting*
https://www.jpost.com/Features/In-Thespotlight/This-Week-in-History-Titus-breaks-through-the-Jlem-wall
5. *Israel clean and green*
http://christinprophecy.org/articles/jesus-is-coming-soon-2/
http://christinprophecy.org/articles/israel-as-proof-of-gods-existence/
http://christinprophecy.org/articles/the-reclamation-of-the-land/
http://firm.org.il/learn/2600-years-prophecies-coming-pass/
https://www.jewishvoice.org/read/blog/prophecies-about-israel-continue-be-fulfilled
https://www.jpost.com/Features/In-Thespotlight/This-Week-in-History-Titus-breaks-through-the-Jlem-wall
https://www.youtube.com/watch?v=60L6D9rhmaw
6. *Water*
http://christinprophecy.org/articles/jesus-is-coming-soon-2/
http://christinprophecy.org/articles/israel-as-proof-of-gods-existence/
http://christinprophecy.org/articles/the-reclamation-of-the-land/
http://firm.org.il/learn/2600-years-prophecies-coming-pass/
https://www.jewishvoice.org/read/blog/prophecies-about-israel-continue-be-fulfilled
https://www.jta.org/2018/06/10/news-opinion/israel-approves-30-million-plan-counter-5-year-drought
https://www.youtube.com/watch?v=x7G9v6JdYwc
7. *Milk & Honey*
http://christinprophecy.org/articles/jesus-is-coming-soon-2/
http://christinprophecy.org/articles/israel-as-proof-of-gods-existence/
http://christinprophecy.org/articles/the-reclamation-of-the-land/
http://firm.org.il/learn/2600-years-prophecies-coming-pass/
https://www.jewishvoice.org/read/blog/prophecies-about-israel-continue-be-fulfilled

http://www.israelhayom.com/2017/05/25/israeli-cows-are-worlds-best-milk-producers-new-report-shows/
https://www.youtube.com/watch?v=vjDiISq4pGA

Chapter 7 *The Jewish People & Their Light Unto the World*

1. *8 Fulfilled Prophecies*
http://christinprophecy.org/articles/applying-the-science-of-probability-to-the-scriptures/
http://www1.cbn.com/biblestudy/biblical-prophecies-fulfilled-by-jesus
2. *Light of the Nations*
https://www.youtube.com/watch?v=w5bJkFN0jx0
3. *Rewalk*
https://www.youtube.com/watch?v=2Xd27c-pz4Y
4. *Pill cam*
https://www.youtube.com/watch?v=ytJvtoGYCbA
5. *Like a fish*
https://www.youtube.com/watch?v=6k6aP_bty68
6. *USB*
https://www.youtube.com/watch?v=0g-eyo6v5UE
7. *Mobile Eye*
https://www.youtube.com/watch?v=HXpiyLUEOOY
8. *Waze*
https://en.wikipedia.org/wiki/List_of_Israeli_inventions_and_discoveries
https://www.israel21c.org/israels-top-45-greatest-inventions-of-all-time-2/
https://theculturetrip.com/middle-east/israel/articles/11-awesome-inventions-israel-gave-to-the-world/
9. *Inventions & Discoveries*
https://en.wikipedia.org/wiki/List_of_Israeli_inventions_and_discoveries
https://www.israel21c.org/israels-top-45-greatest-inventions-of-all-time-2/
https://theculturetrip.com/middle-east/israel/articles/11-awesome-inventions-israel-gave-to-the-world/
10. *Israel Defying odds*
https://www.youtube.com/watch?v=zr-ZvYpNTuo

Chapter 8 *The Jewish People & Their Military Conflict*

1. *Israel is Threat*
https://www.youtube.com/watch?v=ydwxy9yqhzM
https://www.facebook.com/official.Ray.Comfort/videos/1106314402722365
2. *World Attention*
http://christinprophecy.org/articles/the-jews-in-prophecy/
https://sareltours.com/israel-bible-prophecy/
3. *Military Strength*
http://www.jewishpress.com/news/breaking-news/israeli-air- force-is-best-in-the-world/2014/10/28/
http://christinprophecy.org/articles/the-jews-in-prophecy/
https://sareltours.com/israel-bible-prophecy/
https://en.wikipedia.org/wiki/History_of_the_Israel_Defense_Forces
https://www.jns.org/the-growth-and-operational-capabilities-of-the-idf/
https://en.wikipedia.org/wiki/List_of_Israeli_inventions_and_discoveries
https://theculturetrip.com/middle-east/israel/articles/11-awesome-inventions-israel-gave-to-the-world/
https://www.forbes.com/sites/pascalemmanuelgobry/2014/08/25/7-steps-the-us-military-should-take-to-be-more-like-the-idf/#5db88613610d
4. *Wall Radar*
https://www.youtube.com/watch?v=Z5HibDpH84o
5. *IPC & Iron Dome*
https://www.youtube.com/watch?v=DbonwQ0YNBs
https://www.youtube.com/watch?v=b4a_ie0J0hU
6. *Military Ranking*
https://www.globalfirepower.com/countries-listing.asp
https://www.globalfirepower.com/country-military-strength-detail.asp?country_id=israel
https://www.businessinsider.com/nine-nations-have-nukes-heres-how-many-each-country-has-2014-6
https://en.wikipedia.org/wiki/Israel_and_weapons_of_mass_destruction
https://en.wikipedia.org/wiki/Arms_industry
https://www.timesofisrael.com/israel-ranked-8th-most-powerful-country-in-the-world-survey/
7. *Indiana Jones*
https://www.youtube.com/watch?v=YcR9k8o4I0w
8. *Terminator*
https://www.youtube.com/watch?v=xjatJ36cJvM
9. *Golfer*
http://fortune.com/2017/09/07/eagle-creek-oregon-golf-picture/

Chapter 9 *The Jewish People & Their Religious Conflict*

1. *Conflict*
https://www.youtube.com/watch?v=zVGlqIkpl9c
https://www.youtube.com/watch?v=zQxYWTuMAbE
https://www.youtube.com/watch?v=R6llh_fe2kY
2. *Vatican*
http://christinprophecy.org/articles/the-jews-in-prophecy/
https://sareltours.com/israel-bible-prophecy/
https://www.youtube.com/watch?v=zk-8hu97g9Y
https://www.voanews.com/a/pope-recognition-of-palestinian-state-could-prove-significant/2776427.html
3. *Hidden*
http://www.jewishpress.com/news/breaking-news/israeli-air- force-is-best-in-the-world/2014/10/28/
http://christinprophecy.org/articles/the-jews-in-prophecy/
https://sareltours.com/israel-bible-prophecy/
https://en.wikipedia.org/wiki/History_of_the_Israel_Defense_Forces
https://www.jns.org/the-growth-and-operational-capabilities-of-the-idf/
https://en.wikipedia.org/wiki/List_of_Israeli_inventions_and_discoveries
https://theculturetrip.com/middle-east/israel/articles/11-awesome-inventions-israel-gave-to-the-world/
https://www.forbes.com/sites/pascalemmanuelgobry/2014/08/25/7-steps-the-us-military-should-take-to-be-more-like-the-idf/#5db88613610d
4. *What does Catholic church want*
https://www.youtube.com/watch?v=Z5HibDpH84o
5. *Catholic control*
http://continuingcounterreformation.blogspot.com/2009/01/barry-chamishs-revelations-and.html
https://israelinewslive.org/proof-vatican-to-build-israels-third-temple/
https://israelinewslive.org/vatican-now-in-control-of-jerusalem/
http://www.worldbulletin.net/?aType=haber&ArticleID=127633
http://www.israelnationalnews.com/News/News.aspx/150757#.UvvsN2bTnIU
http://www.redmoonrising.com/chamish/vaticanagenda.htm
https://www.jewsnews.co.il/2014/08/03/vatican-representative-in-israel-declares-that-jews-no-longer-the-chosen-people.html#fref
http://www.nowtheendbegins.com/vatican-representative-in-israel-declares-that-jews-no-longer-the-chosen-people/
https://www.ynetnews.com/articles/0,7340,L-4203818,00.html

http://www.cuttingedge.org/news/n1052.html
https://encyclopedia2.thefreedictionary.com/World+Invocation+Day
http://www.victorious.org/newage.htm
http://bigthink.com/ideafeed/pope-francis-speaks-before-un-why-not-a-un-for-religions
https://www.youtube.com/watch?v=e-sFJ3QwsFk
6. *Vatican One World Commercial*
https://www.youtube.com/watch?v=-6FfTxwTX34
7. *Pope @ Ground Zero*
https://docs.google.com/viewer?a=v&q=cache:MpsGzaKLPpcJ:www.phmultifait
hsociety.ca/pdf/Chief_Rabbi.pdf+Chief+rabbi+advocates+a+un+of+religion&hl=
en&gl=us&pid=bl&srcid=ADGEESjPwjIXHQxh7snB0-r9ZIFbr3JKnH-
mC_HUtdw5BlFWFdXNFdFv_SKpP5H7XaQxSBsCsCnvVqBoXzXauhIu9H6d
mi8sf5ndGiUcuX8atXASwz-
uWMy3rpUyrYM48PPMlR4tPnLH&sig=AHIEtbRfC93TEMzOWci6lG5SpEZ
K7gXBfw
http://www.christianpost.com/news/saudi-king-abdullahs-interfaith-center-in-
vienna-to-unify-the-worlds-religions-58241/
http://www.wnd.com/2009/08/105938/
http://bigthink.com/ideafeed/pope-francis-speaks-before-un-why-not-a-un-for-
religions
https://www.youtube.com/watch?v=e-sFJ3QwsFk
8. *Let's be friends*
https://www.bibliotecapleyades.net/sociopolitica/esp_sociopol_nwo15.htm

Chapter 10 *The Jewish People & Their Relocation Conflict*

1. *Vatican Control*
(https://israelinewslive.org/vatican-now-in-control-of-jerusalem/)
2. *Relocation Conflict*
http://christinprophecy.org/articles/thank-you-mr-president/
https://www.ynetnews.com/articles/0,7340,L-5053366,00.html
https://www.christianpost.com/news/netanyahu-likens-trump-bible-king-cyrus-
evangelicals-220468/
https://thehill.com/homenews/administration/393826-trump-on-israel-embassy-
move-evangelicals-appreciate-it-more-than-the
https://www.scmp.com/news/world/middle-east/article/2123352/five-things-
know-about-jerusalem-trumps-embassy-move-angers

https://www.thegatewaypundit.com/2017/12/awful-pope-slams-president-trump-recognizing-jerusalem-capital-israel/

https://www.breakingisraelnews.com/99220/times-square-worldwide-chilling-calls-massacre-jews-trump-announcement-watch/

https://www.independent.co.uk/news/world/americas/us-politics/un-donald-trump-jerusalem-israel-capital-resolution-veto-us-nikki-haley-a8117741.html

https://freedomoutpost.com/un-gets-resolution-rescind-trumps-recognition-jerusalem-capital-israel-vetoed/

https://www.breakingisraelnews.com/99725/sanhedrin-declares-un-vote-nations-choosing-blessing-curse/

https://www.breakingisraelnews.com/100479/5-biblical-prophecies-fulfilled-2017-5-expected-2018/

http://www.israeltoday.co.il/NewsItem/tabid/178/nid/33253/Default.aspx

http://www.israeltoday.co.il/NewsItem/tabid/178/nid/33117/Default.aspx

https://www.jpost.com/Israel-News/New-Western-Wall-train-station-to-be-named-after-Trump-520135

http://www.cuttingedge.org/newsletters/120617.htm

https://www.aljazeera.com/news/2017/12/al-jazeera-readers-respond-trump-jerusalem-move-171206172055295.html

http://www.prophecynewswatch.com/article.cfm?recent_news_id=1894

https://www.independent.co.uk/voices/jerusalem-donald-trump-israel-capital-decision-reason-why-evangelical-voters-us-fear-a8099321.html

https://www.washingtonpost.com/news/politics/wp/2018/05/14/half-of-evangelicals-support-israel-because-they-believe-it-is-important-for-fulfilling-end-times-prophecy/?noredirect=on&utm_term=.7a51f794a157

3. *Trump moved Embassy*
https://www.youtube.com/watch?v=hYM8he60DwA
https://www.youtube.com/watch?v=RyuMI88Mqpw

4. *Trumps promise*
(http://christinprophecy.org/articles/thank-you-mr-president/)

5. *Trump visits the Western Wall*
https://www.youtube.com/watch?v=FkliIRUHSIA
https://www.youtube.com/watch?v=FnW88wpBV9Y

6. *Western Way train station*
(https://www.jpost.com/Israel-News/New-Western-Wall-train-station-to-be-named-after-Trump-520135)

7. *Trump & Evangelicals*
http://christinprophecy.org/articles/thank-you-mr-president/
https://www.ynetnews.com/articles/0,7340,L-5053366,00.html

https://www.christianpost.com/news/netanyahu-likens-trump-bible-king-cyrus-evangelicals-220468/
8. *Embassy right thing to do*
(http://christinprophecy.org/articles/thank-you-mr-president/)
9. *World hates the move*
https://www.youtube.com/watch?v=jIhAKLdvuBc
10. *Protestors n NYC*
https://www.facebook.com/StandWithUs/videos/nyc-anti-israel-protesters-call-for-violence-against-jews/10155276917557689/
11. *Nikki Haley*
https://www.youtube.com/watch?v=5t7VC4mHOyA
https://www.youtube.com/watch?v=JL-Jf1pciok
https://www.youtube.com/watch?v=w_auKWPfjyo
https://www.youtube.com/watch?v=KVTQefA77Ys
12. *Reason for conflict*
(http://christinprophecy.org/articles/thank-you-mr-president/)

Chapter 11 *The Jewish People & Their Resource Conflict*

1. *Location*
https://worldview.stratfor.com/article/geopolitics-israel-biblical-and-modern
https://home.snu.edu/~hculbert/bridge.htm
https://worldview.stratfor.com/article/israels-strategic-position
2. *Convergence Zone*
https://www.youtube.com/watch?v=93onRmj9guc
3. *Second Manifestation*
https://worldview.stratfor.com/article/geopolitics-israel-biblical-and-modern
https://home.snu.edu/~hculbert/bridge.htm
https://worldview.stratfor.com/article/israels-strategic-position
4. *Strategic Land Mass*
https://www.youtube.com/watch?v=93onRmj9guc
5. *Strategic Gas Field*
https://www.youtube.com/watch?v=O8fXf3VXU-M
6. *Russia wants gas*
https://www.raptureforums.com/forums/threads/red-storm-must-read.108145/
7. *Strategic Oil Field*
https://www.youtube.com/watch?v=r80kI20JrVc
8. *Putin wants Oil*

https://www.infowars.com/will-the-discovery-of-huge-amounts-of-oil-in-israel-lead-to-war-in-the-middle-east/
https://jonrappoport.wordpress.com/2015/10/15/energy-wars-massive-oil-discovery-in-israel/
https://mjaa.org/huge-oil-discovery-on-the-golan-heights/
9. *Strategic Water*
https://www.youtube.com/watch?v=pvi--Tqd5v0
10. *AHAVA*
https://www.youtube.com/watch?v=CmrPjzwCvQE
11. *Wealth of Dead Sea Minerals*
http://www.biblefragrances.com/studies/minerals1.html
12. *90 Seconds*
https://www.youtube.com/watch?v=CPcGvEPI4dM

Chapter 12 *The Jewish People & Their Rebuilt Temple Part 1*

1. *Temple Painting*
https://www.youtube.com/watch?v=0vRkEyF-DBY
2. *Increase in Visitors*
https://www.haaretz.com/israel-news/.premium-75-percent-rise-in-religious-jews-visiting-temple-mount-in-2017-1.5630216
https://www.haaretz.com/israel-news/.premium-number-of-jews-visiting-the-temple-mount-rising-fast-1.6246386
http://crownheights.info/israel/609240/israeli-court-allows-jewish-prayer-on-temple-mount/
https://unitedwithisrael.org/israel-protests-to-countries-that-supported-unesco-resolution-denying-jewish-historical-ties-to-temple-mount/
https://religionnews.com/2017/07/24/jerusalems-temple-mount-launching-pad-holy-wars/
https://www.chabad.org/library/article_cdo/aid/144575/jewish/What-Is-Tisha-BAv.htm
https://en.wikipedia.org/wiki/Jerusalem_Day
https://en.wikipedia.org/wiki/Temple_Mount_entry_restrictions
3. *Reaction to Jerusalem Day*
https://www.youtube.com/watch?v=O8fXf3VXU-M
4. *Dream*
https://www.youtube.com/watch?v=93onRmj9guc
5. *Muslims say*

https://www.youtube.com/watch?v=O8fXf3VXU-M
6. *Muslim Broadcast*
https://www.raptureforums.com/forums/threads/red-storm-must-read.108145/
7. *Jewish Wedding*
https://www.youtube.com/watch?v=r80kI20JrVc
8. *Sunday Morning Rapture*
https://www.infowars.com/will-the-discovery-of-huge-amounts-of-oil-in-israel-lead-to-war-in-the-middle-east/
https://jonrappoport.wordpress.com/2015/10/15/energy-wars-massive-oil-discovery-in-israel/
https://mjaa.org/huge-oil-discovery-on-the-golan-heights/

Chapter 13 *The Jewish People & Their Rebuilt Temple Part 2*

1. *Rabbis meet with Pope*
https://www.youtube.com/watch?v=WS4K-99_FPU
2. *Rabbis Statements*
https://blogs.timesofisrael.com/please-g-d-i-dont-want-a-3rd-temple-a-radical-prayer-from-a-humble-servant/
https://www.patheos.com/blogs/rabbigreenberg/2015/01/please-god-help-us-bring-about-your-third-temple-a-response-to-rabbi-shmuly-yanklowitz/
https://www.templeinstitute.org/true-location-5779.htm
http://www.timesofisrael.com/israel-chief-rabbi-urges-rebuilding-jerusalem-temple/
http://www.prophecynewswatch.com/article.cfm?recent_news_id=564
http://www.prophecynewswatch.com/article.cfm?recent_news_id=378
3. *Temple to bring Messiah*
http://www.israeltoday.co.il/Default.aspx?nid=33685&tabid=178
https://www.wnd.com/2017/12/trumps-jerusalem-declaration-sparks-talk-of-3rd-temple/
https://www1.cbn.com/cbnnews/israel/2017/december/is-trumps-jerusalem-declaration-an-opportunity-to-build-third-temple
https://www.breakingisraelnews.com/99002/trumps-jerusalem-declaration-next-step-third-temple/
http://www.israeltoday.co.il/NewsItem/tabid/178/nid/30506/Default.aspx
http://www.prophecynewswatch.com/article.cfm?recent_news_id=1015
https://blogs.timesofisrael.com/mr-trump-rebuild-the-third-temple/

https://www.newsweek.com/jews-trump-persian-king-babylonian-exile-third-temple-judaism-744698
http://en.hamikdash.org.il/about/we-need-your-support/the-70-years-israel-redemption-temple-coin/
https://www.gotquestions.org/sanctuary-shekel.html
https://en.wikipedia.org/wiki/Shekel
https://en.wikipedia.org/wiki/Israeli_new_shekel
https://prophecyinthenews.com/world_news/temple-movement-issues-half-shekel-coin-with-profile-of-trump-and-cyrus/
https://www.breakingisraelnews.com/102784/sanhedrin-temple-movement-issue-silver-half-shekel-images-trump-cyrus/
http://en.hamikdash.org.il/about/we-need-your-support/the-temple-coin/
https://www.breakingisraelnews.com/105767/new-special-edition-temple-coin-minted-for-israels-70th-anniversary-the-end-of-the-exile/
http://christinprophecy.org/articles/the-jews-in-end-time-bible-prophecy/
https://www.therefinersfire.org/jews_return_to_israel.htm
4. *Netanyahu Rebuild Temple*
https://www.youtube.com/watch?v=xJiBu79Bids
5. *Putin & Trump to rebuild Temple*
https://new.euro-med.dk/20161115-jewish-sanhedrin-admits-it-made-trump-president-and-asks-for-his-and-putins-help-to-build-the-3-temple-of-the-antichrist.php
https://www.wnd.com/2018/08/the-day-putin-prayed-for-rebuilding-of-temple/
6. *Putin prays for Temple*
https://www.youtube.com/watch?v=xJiBu79Bids
7. *Muslims want Temple*
https://www.wnd.com/2016/07/muslim-leader-hosts-rabbis-welcomes-3rd-temple/
http://www.israeltoday.co.il/NewsItem/tabid/178/nid/29586/Default.aspx
https://www.wnd.com/2009/08/106055/
https://www.endtime.com/articles-endtime-magazine/time-build-third-temple/
http://www.jewishpress.com/indepth/opinions/a-new-muslim-vision-rebuilding-solomons-temple-together/2013/03/12/#

Chapter 14 *The Jewish People & Their Rebuilt Temple Part 3*

1. *Temple Institute*
https://en.wikipedia.org/wiki/The_Temple_Institute

https://www.templeinstitute.org/about.htm
https://en.wikipedia.org/wiki/Temple_Mount_and_Eretz_Yisrael_Faithful_Move
ment
http://templemountfaithful.org/objectives.php
https://d2saw6je89goi1.cloudfront.net/uploads/digital_asset/file/338681/Rebuildi
ng_the_Temple_-_E_Book.pdf
https://www.middleeasteye.net/in-depth/features/what-temple-mount-movement-
1610723956
2. *Temple Commercial*
https://www.youtube.com/watch?v=5bw-lJlyuqA
3. *Shofar Challenge*
https://www.youtube.com/watch?v=-2V6qNFb8Gc
4. *Gold*
https://www.youtube.com/watch?v=GfSgPSASEhE
5. *Blueprints*
https://www.youtube.com/watch?v=G_4qBOmV6oU&t=0s&list=PLE6E8D5B8
B64F8C32&index=10
6. *Animated Blueprints*
https://www.youtube.com/watch?v=A2IkxmwkayM
7. *Red Heifer*
https://www.youtube.com/watch?v=D9nE894ORAs
8. *Discovery of Red Heifer*
https://www.youtube.com/watch?v=nHnjOiagh-g
https://www.youtube.com/watch?v=mOMH2qY6RCY
9. *Messiah and the Red Heifer*
https://www.youtube.com/watch?v=WJ4xe7HdCQw

Chapter 15 *The Jewish People & Their Rebuilt Temple Part 4*

1. *Sanhedrin Chamber*
https://www.youtube.com/watch?v=vFnckQrgO7s
https://www.gotquestions.org/Sanhedrin.html
https://en.wikipedia.org/wiki/Sanhedrin
https://en.wikipedia.org/wiki/Modern_attempts_to_revive_the_Sanhedrin
https://en.wikipedia.org/wiki/2004_attempt_to_revive_the_Sanhedrin
http://www.thesanhedrin.org/en/index.php/The_Re-
established_Jewish_Sanhedrin

https://www.breakingisraelnews.com/74772/sanhedrin-appoints-high-priest-preparation-third-temple/
https://www.breakingisraelnews.com/104480/sanhedrin-calls-on-arabs-to-take-their-role-in-third-temple-as-prophesized-by-isaiah/
https://www.breakingisraelnews.com/117830/70-nations-hanukkah-altar-third-temple/
https://www.wnd.com/2018/12/7-days-until-dedication-of-3rd-temple-altar/
https://www.breakingisraelnews.com/116619/sanhedrin-jerusalem-mayor-temple/
https://www.breakingisraelnews.com/112478/restore-the-temple-mount-to-its-biblical-intent-and-usher-in-redemption/
https://www.breakingisraelnews.com/113229/third-temple-house-god-nations/
https://www.breakingisraelnews.com/114023/temple-mount-achieves-new-heights/
https://www.timesofisrael.com/want-mideast-peace-build-the-3rd-temple/
2. *Database of Jewish Priests*
https://www.youtube.com/watch?v=PvRQv1DdgI4
3. *Priests to attend school*
https://www.youtube.com/watch?v=RT0Yw6ASnZc
https://www.youtube.com/watch?v=EICu2C02sKk
4. *Passover re-enactment*
https://www.youtube.com/watch?v=LTb2UgMEqtw
https://www.youtube.com/watch?v=iwyvgG_iwIY
5. *Location of Ark*
https://www.youtube.com/watch?v=vFnckQrgO7s

Chapter 16 *The Jewish People & Their Rebuilt Temple Part 5*

1. *Articles*
http://www.templeinstitute.org/vessels_gallery.htm
https://www.templeinstitute.org/gallery.htm
2. *Temple Oil*
https://www.youtube.com/watch?v=F95C79bqzLM
3. *Harps*
https://www.youtube.com/watch?time_continue=7&v=Ng_8nmb4o5Y
4. *Stone*
https://www.youtube.com/watch?v=PPC7Ykrk-7o
5. *Temple Altar*

386

https://www.facebook.com/22738684968/videos/2334693506764789/
6. *Temple Crown*
https://www.youtube.com/watch?v=0z3T0VioVlg
7. *Misc. Articles*
https://www.breakingisraelnews.com/116471/first-jewish-perfume-packaged-purchase/
http://www.prophecynewswatch.com/article.cfm?recent_news_id=2628
https://www.jpost.com/Israel-News/First-pure-olive-oil-produced-in-2000-years-says-Temple-Institute-385250
https://www.breakingisraelnews.com/32009/altar-jewish-holy-temple-rebuilt-jewish-world/
https://www.breakingisraelnews.com/33583/new-details-emerge-rebuilt-holy-temple-jewish-world/#STuiyeOKJWlQihqC.97
https://www.breakingisraelnews.com/118474/dedication-altar-third-temple/
https://www.haaretz.com/israel-news/.premium-jerusalem-municipality-rejects-plea-to-practice-animal-sacrifice-for-future-temple-1.6729388?utm_source=Push_Notification&utm_medium=web_push&utm_campaign=General
https://www.breakingisraelnews.com/118441/miracle-dedication-altar-third-temple/
https://www.breakingisraelnews.com/104090/third-temple-calendar-launches-this-saturday-on-the-new-year-of-kings/
https://www.wnd.com/2014/05/rebuilding-the-temple-from-the-inside-out/
https://www.timesofisrael.com/the-women-waiting-and-weaving-for-the-third-temple/
https://templemountfaithful.org/articles/letter-to-pope-francis-to-return-stolen-temple-items.php
https://www.breakingisraelnews.com/89318/bible-codes-foretell-special-role-first-israeli-born-jacobs-sheep-2000-years/
https://www.breakingisraelnews.com/112803/temple-bread-baking-biblical-israel/
https://www.breakingisraelnews.com/112628/davids-harp-heralding-third-temple/
https://www.breakingisraelnews.com/112628/davids-harp-heralding-third-temple/
https://www.breakingisraelnews.com/75645/bin-exclusive-lost-stone-high-priests-prophetic-breastplate-thought-found-incredible-journey/
https://www.breakingisraelnews.com/118491/guatemalan-ambassador-jewish-identity/?mc_cid=eb90b57501&mc_eid=8828e9248e

https://www.breakingisraelnews.com/118238/bin-exclusive-construct-messianic-golden-royal-crown/?mc_cid=f3f4b4d9e4&mc_eid=8828e9248e
https://www.causematch.com/en/projects/crown_the_king/?utm_source=breaking_israel_news&utm_medium=website_article&utm_campaign=kdc&utm_content=12_6_2018

Chapter 17 *The Jewish People & Their Spiritual State*

1. *Israel is Secular*
https://www.valleybible.net/AdultEducation/ClassNotes/WorldReligions/Lesson%202%20-%20Judaism.pdf
https://en.wikipedia.org/wiki/Jewish_religious_movements
https://www.timesofisrael.com/israels-abortion-law-now-among-worlds-most-liberal/
https://www.jta.org/2017/08/15/lifestyle/can-medical-marijuana-revive-israels-kibbutz-movement
https://www.tabletmag.com/scroll/245497/israeli-kibbutz-to-become-worldwide-medical-marijuana-hub
2. *Not knowing Jesus*
https://www.youtube.com/watch?v=F7Cui-E0DOY
3. *Snake*
https://www.youtube.com/watch?v=WPa-EOLQ4tg
https://www.youtube.com/watch?v=nGESS5zfRQI
4. *Mist*
https://www.youtube.com/watch?v=ByqMLfeYYOs
5. *Signs*
https://www.breakingisraelnews.com/111405/kabbalist-stone-falling-western-wall/
https://www.breakingisraelnews.com/116242/snake-temple/
https://www.dailymail.co.uk/news/article-6345781/Snake-appears-Israels-Western-Wall-sparking-claims-Biblical-prophecy-coming-true.html
https://www.breakingisraelnews.com/116434/sinkholes-temple-illegal-waqf/
https://www.breakingisraelnews.com/114568/strange-mist-temple-mount-war-spiritual/
6. *Gay Pride Parade*
https://www.youtube.com/watch?v=aRwpMxsSc2g
https://www.youtube.com/watch?v=Ixv0GPqulwc
7. *Witnessing*

https://www.youtube.com/watch?v=67fhPR6YtRY

Chapter 18 *The Jewish People & Their False Messiah & Treaty*

1. *Messiah in NDE*
   https://www.youtube.com/watch?v=AJynlrKfsCE
2. *Messiah in Arizona Fire*
   https://www.youtube.com/watch?v=QoJZ3cieqK4
3. *Rabbi Blesses Marijuana*
   https://www.youtube.com/watch?v=uEJjSuqcwtU
   https://www.breakingisraelnews.com/118801/days-messiah-jacob-esau-complete/
   https://www.breakingisraelnews.com/119133/did-god-decide-last-week-that-this-will-be-the-year-of-the-temple/
   https://www.breakingisraelnews.com/118765/rabbi-autistic-children-say-messiah-is-here-prepare-for-final-war/
   https://www.breakingisraelnews.com/118902/reporting-messiah-happening/
   https://www.breakingisraelnews.com/118628/religious-zionism-messiah-son-joseph/
   https://www.breakingisraelnews.com/119711/biblical-prophecies-fulfilled-2018/
   https://www.breakingisraelnews.com/118860/pacific-ring-fire-end-days/
   https://www.breakingisraelnews.com/118586/yellowstone-eruption-gog-magog/
   https://www.breakingisraelnews.com/118371/hail-pounds-saudi-desert-kills-cattle-in-swaziland/
   https://www.breakingisraelnews.com/117788/anti-semitism-part-war-gog-magog/
   https://www.breakingisraelnews.com/117733/god-assign-jews-cataclysmic-meteor/
   https://www.breakingisraelnews.com/117329/un-rejects-bible-noahide-laws-abortions/
   https://www.breakingisraelnews.com/117202/netanyahu-holding-keys-messiah/
   https://www.breakingisraelnews.com/116811/idf-special-army-preparing-gog-magog/
   https://www.breakingisraelnews.com/116730/message-from-autistic-child-in-jerusalem-messiah-is-about-to-be-revealed/
   https://www.breakingisraelnews.com/114642/astronomers-search-planet-nine-

goblin/
https://www.breakingisraelnews.com/113808/worldwide-awakening-final-redemption/
https://www.breakingisraelnews.com/113770/arch-washington-exhibit-centerpiece/
https://www.breakingisraelnews.com/113577/light-coming-redemption-blinding/
https://www.breakingisraelnews.com/111518/earthquakes-eclipses-divine-signs/
https://www.breakingisraelnews.com/111356/eclipse-blood-moon-messiah/
https://www.breakingisraelnews.com/111168/messiah-born-saturday/
https://www.breakingisraelnews.com/110994/biblical-pillars-smoke-fire-arizona/
https://www.breakingisraelnews.com/110448/recent-earthquakes-in-israel-warm-up-for-pre-gog-global-upheaval/
https://www.breakingisraelnews.com/110117/scientist-recalculates-time-til-end-of-days/
https://www.breakingisraelnews.com/110001/enormous-cow-nova-has-scientists-stumped-but-rabbis-understand/
https://www.breakingisraelnews.com/109917/tarot-cards-recent-trend-ancient-evil/
https://www.breakingisraelnews.com/109422/gems-hidden-for-messianic-era-being-discovered-in-carmel-region/
https://www.breakingisraelnews.com/108971/preempting-global-warming-before-hurricane-season-2018-rabbi/
https://www.breakingisraelnews.com/108717/did-unprecedented-leviathan-appearance-off-eilat-signal-beginning-of-post-messiah-feast-watch/
https://www.breakingisraelnews.com/108565/rabbis-the-end-of-the-left-wing-signals-the-beginnings-of-messiah/
https://www.breakingisraelnews.com/108565/rabbis-the-end-of-the-left-wing-signals-the-beginnings-of-messiah/
biblical-jonathan/
https://www.breakingisraelnews.com/107294/tel-aviv-the-holy-city-and-gateway-to-the-third-temple/
https://www.breakingisraelnews.com/107234/major-kabbalist-unseasonable-rain-in-israel-is-sign-of-messiahs-imminent-arrival/
https://www.breakingisraelnews.com/107054/lag-bomer-in-torah-codes-the-day-of-messiah/
https://www.breakingisraelnews.com/106903/did-england-just-push-the-

messiah-further-away/
https://www.breakingisraelnews.com/105129/could-passover-eve-palestinian-protests-be-crushed-by-the-hand-of-god/
https://www.breakingisraelnews.com/100703/2017-year-disasters-famed-mystics-prophesied-final-pre-messiah-warning/
https://www.breakingisraelnews.com/99784/unusual-gathering-sharks-off-israeli-coast-mark-change-messianic-processwatch/
https://www.breakingisraelnews.com/99784/unusual-gathering-sharks-off-israeli-coast-mark-change-messianic-processwatch/
https://www.breakingisraelnews.com/64082/special-torah-scroll-written-messiah-completed-photos-jewish-world/
https://www.timesofisrael.com/high-court-wont-hear-man-claiming-to-be-messiah/
https://www.breakingisraelnews.com/44534/leading-israeli-rabbi-messiah-imminent-jewish-world/
https://www.wnd.com/2017/01/israeli-police-preparing-for-messiah/
https://www.breakingisraelnews.com/72238/rabbi-kanievsky-mishkoltz-rabbi-can-done-wait-messiah/
https://www.breakingisraelnews.com/69821/rabbi-kanievsky-consoles-grieving-father-messiah-already/
https://www.breakingisraelnews.com/53387/rabbi-kanievsky-warns-friends-not-travel-because-messiah-can-come-any-moment-jewish-world/
https://www.breakingisraelnews.com/51210/spiritual-leader-rabbi-kanievsky-yell-it-from-loudspeakers-the-messiah-is-at-the-door-jewish-world/
https://www.breakingisraelnews.com/66164/rabbi-kanievsky-blesses-kosher-passover-marijuana/
https://www.breakingisraelnews.com/53767/the-time-has-come-for-god-to-reveal-the-messiah-says-jerusalems-chief-rabbi-jewish-world/
https://www.breakingisraelnews.com/65107/are-jewish-people-ready-messiah-jewish-world/
https://www.breakingisraelnews.com/55777/turkeysyria-conflict-unfolding-prominent-rabbis-hint-messiah-around-corner-jewish-world/
https://www.breakingisraelnews.com/54425/following-near-death-experience-israeli-boy-returns-quoting-end-of-days-prophecy-video-jewish-world/
4. *When will Messiah come*
https://www.youtube.com/watch?v=D8jf_PTSY_Y
5. *Failed Peace Treaty*
http://news.bbc.co.uk/2/hi/middle_east/6666393.stm

http://en.wikipedia.org/wiki/Peace_process_in_the_Israeli%E2%80%93
Palestinian_conflict
http://en.wikipedia.org/wiki/List_of_Middle_East_peace_proposals#
Peace_process_in_the_Israeli-Palestinian_conflict
6. *Prince William in Israel*
https://www.youtube.com/watch?v=jDRlmX1h2z0
7. *Peace & Security 1*
https://www.youtube.com/watch?v=xpJbAE6BmHo
8. *Peace & Security 2*
https://www.youtube.com/watch?v=IGI541ovmtY
9. *Peace & Security 3*
(SEALS DOCUMENTARY – www.getalifemedia.com)
https://y2mate.com/youtube/kvaj_D9y8bM

Chapter 19*The Jewish People & Their International Antisemitism*

1. *Who is Telling the Truth*
https://www.youtube.com/watch?v=166Uq3YV9g8
2. *TV Antisemitism*
https://www.facebook.com/memri.org/videos/egyptian-tv-host-gaber-al-
karmoty-hands-out-chocolates-to-celebrate-downing-of-
i/10156174145384717/
3. *Ireland*
https://www.youtube.com/watch?v=QRD3kUUJ98k
4. *UN Rulings*
https://www.youtube.com/watch?v=1eWJfV7-lw0
5. *World Antisemitism*
https://www.jihadwatch.org/2017/12/turkeys-erdogan-issues-veiled-threat-of-
jewish-genocide-refers-to-statement-of-muhammad-about-muslims-killing-
jews
https://stockholmcf.org/turkeys-erdogan-issues-a-veiled-threat-of-killing-
each-and-every-jew-amid-jerusalem-tension/
https://pamelageller.com/2017/11/khan-hitler-
jews.html/?utm_source=dlvr.it&utm_medium=facebook
https://www.algemeiner.com/2017/10/24/fatah-admits-its-true-goals-but-the-
media-wont-retweet/
http://www.prophecynewswatch.com/article.cfm?recent_news_id=1709
http://www.israelnationalnews.com/News/News.aspx/196299

https://www.wnd.com/2015/05/leading-islamic-voice-calls-for-reconquering-jerusalem/

http://www.israelnationalnews.com/News/News.aspx/193785

https://www.jpost.com/Middle-East/Jews-using-Holocaust-to-suck-the-blood-of-Germans-Egypt-TV-host-says-392655

http://www.israelnationalnews.com/News/News.aspx/190761

https://www.haaretz.com/jewish/surveys-show-spike-in-british-anti-semitism-1.5360160

https://dailycaller.com/2015/01/06/frances-multiculturalist-agenda-makes-jews-pack-their-bags/

http://www.israelnationalnews.com/News/News.aspx/188839#.
VJh_HV4AKA

https://www.jpost.com/International/Swedish-politician-calls-for-Jews-to-abandon-their-faith-385124

https://www.michaelsmithnews.com/2015/02/no-competent-lawyer-would-advise-ralph-blewitt-to-purchase-property-in-his-own-name-when-the-union-h.html

http://www.israelnationalnews.com/News/News.aspx/187201

https://www.ynetnews.com/articles/0,7340,L-4571937,00.html

https://www.ynetnews.com/articles/0,7340,L-4552626,00.html

https://www.haaretz.com/whdcMobileSite/jewish/uk-whip-europe-forgot-holocaust-1.5264257

https://www.jta.org/2014/08/12/global/french-deputy-mayor-defends-name-of-locality-called-death-to-the-jews-1

https://www.newsweek.com/pro-isis-demonstrators-call-death-jews-hague-262064

https://www.nydailynews.com/news/world/belgian-cafe-posts-sign-banning-jews-entering-store-article-1.1879839

https://www.theguardian.com/world/2018/may/07/polands-holocaust-law-triggers-tide-abuse-auschwitz-museum

https://www.jpost.com/International/Violent-Attacks-on-Jews-in-Berlin-and-Zurich-561964

https://www.algemeiner.com/2018/03/25/french-jewish-holocaust-survivor-found-dead-in-burned-paris-apartment-security-group-everything-suggests-it-was-antisemitic-crime/

https://www.timesofisrael.com/in-britain-poll-indicates-23-unwilling-to-have-a-jew-in-the-family/

https://www.timesofisrael.com/following-attack-barcelonas-chief-rabbi-says-his-community-is-doomed/

https://www.timesofisrael.com/swedish-parliamentary-candidate-suggests-deporting-all-jews-from-israel/
http://www.israelnationalnews.com/News/News.aspx/250424
https://www.breakingisraelnews.com/118192/ireland-legal-ban-settlements-goods/
https://www.breakingisraelnews.com/118624/selling-land-jews-palestinians-killed/
https://www.worthynews.com/17615-wave-of-world-protests-against-israel
http://www.prophecynewswatch.com/article.cfm?recent_news_id=915
http://www.prophecynewswatch.com/article.cfm?recent_news_id=859
http://www.prophecynewswatch.com/article.cfm?recent_news_id=725
http://www.prophecynewswatch.com/article.cfm?recent_news_id=1896
http://www.israeltoday.co.il/NewsItem/tabid/178/nid/34217/Default.aspx
https://www.jpost.com/Diaspora/Brazil-omits-Israel-from-passports-of-Jerusalem-born-citizens-411589
https://www.timesofisrael.com/air-france-deeply-regrets-map-snafu-omitting-israel/
https://www.jpost.com/Middle-East/Israel-wiped-off-the-map-in-Middle-East-atlases-386265
https://www.jpost.com/Arab-Israeli-Conflict/Major-publisher-HarperCollins-apologizes-for-leaving-Israel-off-maps-386472
https://www.mirror.co.uk/news/world-news/harpercollins-omits-israel-atlas-because-4900618

6. *Payments*
http://www.israelnationalnews.com/News/News.aspx/245506
https://www.timesofisrael.com/pa-payments-to-prisoners-martyr-families-now-equal-half-its-foreign-aid/
https://www.algemeiner.com/2017/08/15/israel-exposes-hamas-terrorist-payment-network-in-eastern-jerusalem/
http://www.prophecynewswatch.com/article.cfm?recent_news_id=2796
https://www.breakingisraelnews.com/118966/pa-pays-1-2-billion-shekels-terrorism/

7. *Hitler*
https://www.csmonitor.com/World/Global-News/2016/0612/Mein-Kampf-takes-off-in-Europe-70-years-after-Hitler-s-death
http://www.israeltoday.co.il/NewsItem/tabid/178/nid/28663/Default.aspx
http://encountergospelnews.blogspot.com/2016/04/hitler-clothing-store-causes-stir-in.html
https://www.theguardian.com/world/2005/mar/29/turkey.books

http://www.crethiplethi.com/mein-kampf-best-seller-in-muslim-
bangladesh/english/2009/
http://www.timesofisrael.com/hitlers-mein-kampf-is-german-bestseller-again-
publisher/?fb_comment_id=1313618915366792_1313872935341390
https://www.ynetnews.com/articles/0,7340,L-4665801,00.html
https://www.jpost.com/Arab-Israeli-Conflict/Biblical-tomb-vandalized-with-
Swastikas-in-Palestinian-village-547076
https://www.ynetnews.com/articles/0,7340,L-5061597,00.html
8. *How to Stab a Jew*
https://www.youtube.com/watch?v=dtErUuBvcRc
https://www.timesofisrael.com/watch-i-want-to-stab-a-jew-young-girl-tells-
her-teacher-father/
https://www.youtube.com/watch?v=sBtEDMsl_SM&bpctr=1548875873
9. *Beginning of Holocaust*
https://www.reuters.com/article/us-germany-antisemitism/german-jewish-
leader-warns-against-wearing-skullcaps-idUSKBN0LU1F820150226
https://www.ynetnews.com/articles/0,7340,L-4631419,00.html
https://www.jpost.com/Diaspora/Madonna-Atmosphere-of-intolerance-in-
Europe-feels-like-Nazi-German-392393
https://www.theguardian.com/society/2014/aug/07/antisemitism-rise-europe-
worst-since-nazis
https://www.jpost.com/Diaspora/As-70th-anniversary-of-Holocaust-
approaches-Jewish-groups-fret-over-hate-386705
https://freebeacon.com/national-security/europes-leading-rabbi-jews-must-
begin-carrying-guns/
https://www.breakingisraelnews.com/117754/shadow-europe-anti-semitism-
memory/
https://www.breakingisraelnews.com/118398/european-jews-considering-
escape-europe/
https://www.jpost.com/Israel-News/CBS-More-Israelis-moving-abroad-than-
are-returning-502778
https://translate.google.com/translate?hl=en&sl=da&u=https://
udfordringen.dk/2015/02/new-exodus-jews-europe/&prev=search
https://www.seattletimes.com/news/europes-jews-ponder-whether-its-time-to-
https://www.ynetnews.com/articles/0,7340,L-4619696,00.html
beginnings-of-a-Holocaust-369165
https://www.timesofisrael.com/bbc-chief-anti-semitism-makes-me-question-
jews-future-in-uk/
https://www.newsweek.com/2014/08/08/exodus-why-europes-jews-are-

fleeing-once-again-261854.html
https://www.theatlantic.com/magazine/archive/2015/04/is-it-time-for-the-jews-to-leave-europe/386279/
10. *Shema*
   https://www.youtube.com/watch?v=fUSdHB1R-
   W4&feature=youtu.be&fbclid=IwAR3XCQryAF3HDGAIAqUD
   gdz45j4oXhGjzjBEp1V5HHDDUX7h-wjXYd4H8nE
11. *Martin Niemoller*
   (hSttp://www.radioliberty.com/pca.htm)

Chapter 20 *The Jewish People & Their U.S. Antisemitism*

1. *Obamas interference*
   https://www.youtube.com/watch?v=wPRUiZaDuo4
2. *Obama's Brother*
   https://www.wnd.com/2013/08/obamas-brother-linked-to-muslim-brotherhood/
3. *Trump is good for Jewish People*
   http://prophecynewswatch.com/article.cfm?recent_news_id=2609
   https://www.wnd.com/2015/02/netanyahu-fires-back-at-ex-obama-team-plotting-his-defeat/
   https://www.haaretz.com/mccain-israel-u-s-ties-never-been-worse-1.5367958
   http://shoebat.org/2014/01/28/obamas-brother-joins-hamas-says-jerusalem-coming/
   http://prophecynewswatch.com/article.cfm?recent_news_id=906
4. *Women Democrats*
   https://www.youtube.com/watch?v=nyh31KPO9jU
5. *Democrats Anti-Semitism*
   https://www.timesofisrael.com/with-jews-we-lose-reads-one-senate-candidates-slogan-in-ky/
   https://www.breitbart.com/entertainment/2015/02/13/shirley-maclaine-claims-holocaust-victims-were-paying-for-sins-in-past-lives/
   https://prophecyinthenews.com/world_news/democrat-activist-linda-sarsour-wants-people-to-stop-humanizing-jews/
   http://www.prophecynewswatch.com/article.cfm?recent_news_id=2708
   https://www.breakingisraelnews.com/117742/democrat-delegate-israel-terminated/
   http://prophecynewswatch.com/article.cfm?recent_news_id=2734

https://clarionproject.org/hit-piece-saudi-paper-new-muslim-congresswomen/
6. *Media Anti-Semitism*
   https://www.breakingisraelnews.com/117854/cnn-ditches-marc-lamont-hill/
   http://prophecynewswatch.com/article.cfm?recent_news_id=2455
   https://www.jns.org/opinion/a-whole-country-of-marc-lamont-hills/
7. *Social Media*
   https://www.quora.com/What-are-Mark-Zuckerbergs-political-views
   https://www.timesofisrael.com/facebooks-zuckerberg-says-he-wont-remove-holocaust-denial-posts/
   https://www.tabletmag.com/scroll/266679/mark-zuckerberg-holocaust-deniers-on-facebook-are-making-an-honest-mistake
   https://www.tabletmag.com/scroll/225759/why-is-youtube-punishing-people-who-translate-and-expose-anti-semitism-on-its-platform
   https://www.haaretz.com/us-news/adl-twitter-being-weaponized-as-4-anti-semitic-tweets-posted-in-2017-1.6062674
   https://www.breakingisraelnews.com/117001/google-failure-anti-semitic-content/
8. *Hate crimes*
   https://www.youtube.com/watch?v=cz6jBpI4Tbg
9. *Pittsburg Attack*
   https://www.youtube.com/watch?v=kxX0iQIH_pQ
   https://www.youtube.com/watch?v=LsgNtxv6K3Q
   https://www.youtube.com/watch?v=TpEjrXwj4xc&t=33s
10. *Increase in Hate Crimes*
   https://prophecyinthenews.com/world_news/19-swastikas-painted-on-north-virginian-jewish-community-center/
   https://www.timesofisrael.com/mike-pence-sickened-and-appalled-by-swastikas-on-indiana-synagogue/
   https://www.theatlantic.com/politics/archive/2017/02/jewish-cemeteries-destruction/518040/
   https://forward.com/fast-forward/364708/anti-semitic-hate-crimes-in-new-york-up-94-over-last-year/
   https://www.timesofisrael.com/florida-man-hit-with-hate-crime-charge-for-threatening-to-kill-all-the-jews/
   https://prophecyinthenews.com/world_news/victims-names-released-in-deadliest-anti-semitic-attack-in-us-history/
   https://www.frontpagemag.com/fpm/271813/identity-politics-americas-anti-semitism-daniel-greenfield
   https://www.jta.org/2018/10/16/united-states/second-orthodox-jewish-man-

attacked-in-brooklyn-in-2-days
https://www.dailymail.co.uk/news/article-6276297/Livery-cab-driver-kept-shouting-Allah-beat-Brooklyn-Jewish-man-way-synagogue.html
https://www.breakingisraelnews.com/117007/anti-semitic-attacks-fuels-hate-crimes/
http://prophecynewswatch.com/article.cfm?recent_news_id=2695
11.*Muslim girl*
https://prophecyinthenews.com/world_news/19-swastikas-painted-on-north-virginian-jewish-community-center/
https://www.timesofisrael.com/mike-pence-sickened-and-appalled-by-swastikas-on-indiana-synagogue/
https://www.theatlantic.com/politics/archive/2017/02/jewish-cemeteries-destruction/518040/
https://forward.com/fast-forward/364708/anti-semitic-hate-crimes-in-new-york-up-94-over-last-year/
https://www.timesofisrael.com/florida-man-hit-with-hate-crime-charge-for-threatening-to-kill-all-the-jews/
https://prophecyinthenews.com/world_news/victims-names-released-in-deadliest-anti-semitic-attack-in-us-history/
https://www.frontpagemag.com/fpm/271813/identity-politics-americas-anti-semitism-daniel-greenfield
https://www.jta.org/2018/10/16/united-states/second-orthodox-jewish-man-attacked-in-brooklyn-in-2-days
https://www.dailymail.co.uk/news/article-6276297/Livery-cab-driver-kept-shouting-Allah-beat-Brooklyn-Jewish-man-way-synagogue.html
https://www.breakingisraelnews.com/117007/anti-semitic-attacks-fuels-hate-crimes/
http://prophecynewswatch.com/article.cfm?recent_news_id=2695
12.*Hatred of the Jews*
http://prophecynewswatch.com/article.cfm?recent_news_id=2579
https://www.algemeiner.com/2014/12/05/hating-jews-at-berkeley/
http://prophecynewswatch.com/article.cfm?recent_news_id=2206
https://www.breakingisraelnews.com/116955/wisconsin-students-nazi-salute/
http://prophecynewswatch.com/article.cfm?recent_news_id=2800
13.*Replacement Theology*
https://mysouthland.com/Resources/Theology/6%20reasons%20Replacement%20Theology%20is%20false%20-%20the%20Church%20has%20not%20replaced%20the%20nation%20of%20Israel.pdf

14.*Christ at the checkpoint*
   http://www.prophecynewswatch.com/article.cfm?recent_news_id=1119
   https://www1.cbn.com/cbnnews/us/2018/october/evangelicals-are-the-primary-target-meet-the-christian-group-working-to-turn-you-against-israel
   https://www.breakingisraelnews.com/116526/if-you-hate-jews-opinion/
   https://www.breakingisraelnews.com/116422/replacement-theology-fueling-anti-semitism-america/
   http://www.israelnationalnews.com/Articles/Article.aspx/16253#.VKqo
   T9LF_Rw
   http://prophecynewswatch.com/article.cfm?recent_news_id=2303
   http://prophecynewswatch.com/article.cfm?recent_news_id=2669
   https://pjmedia.com/homeland-security/doormat-christianity-and-the-islamic-invasion/
15. *Sing a Little Louder*
   https://www.youtube.com/watch?v=ofcs9Y7qL4s